POWER PLAYS
POWER WORKS

V

POWER PLAYS

POWER WORKS

First published by Verso 1993
© Verso 1993
All rights reserved

Verso
UK: 6 Meard Street, London W1V 3HR
USA: 29 West 35th Street, New York, NY 10001-2291

Verso is the imprint of New Left Books

ISBN 0-86091-441-0
ISBN 0-86091-616-2 (pbk)

British Library Cataloguing in Publication Data
A catalogue record for this book is available from the British Library

Library of Congress Cataloging-in-Publication Data
A catalogue record for this book is available from the Library of Congress

Typeset by Solidus (Bristol) Limited
Printed and bound in Finland by WSOY

To Lisa
my cordial inspiration, my bloodiest critic,
my vital support — and my Love.

To Matthew and Lucy,
in Australia but with me.

CONTENTS

ACKNOWLEDGEMENTS

Who knows where ideas originate? The words in this book are mine, but the ideas to whose circulation they will contribute have been picked up in bits and pieces by my listening, looking and reading; they've been mixed and matched by convivial discussion and lonely thought, honed by friendly criticism and vivified by the interest, concern and enthusiasm of many. One of the many pleasures offered by cultural studies is the originality, enthusiasm and commitment of people working in the field. So the words may be mine, this particular combination of ideas into an argument may be mine—but beyond that, who can say? Though its particular effects may be hard to specify, the formative environment of the Department of Communication Arts at the University of Wisconsin-Madison has been crucial to me. Colleagues such as Julie D'Acci, Lynn Spigel (now sadly ex-), and David Bordwell have contributed more than they probably realize. So too have my graduate students: our Thursday afternoons around the table in room 6041 and the bar in the Red Shed have been my intellectual meat and drink—of gourmet quality. My thanks go to all of you, but particularly to Steve Classen, Aniko Bodroghkozy, Kevin Glynn, Yong-Jin Won, and Robert Dawson. I can identify passages in this book that conversations with each of you have influenced directly. So, too, my graduate students at the University of Minnesota have all contributed indirectly, but Jason Loviglio, Mike Willard and Elizabeth Anderson have been specifically helpful. Lisa Parks has been much more than a research assistant, and Gloria Abernathy-Lear has helped me develop whatever sensitivity I have for African American culture. I also wish to thank Paul Gilroy and Janaki Bahkle for their insightful and productive comments. My study of *Black Liberation Radio* has been made possible by Mbanna Kantako, Mike Townsend, and Ron Sakolsky who, with Jason Loviglio, have all given me time, material and ideas with a generosity that is all too rare. To Linda Henzl, whose skill, enthusiasm and general support have turned my scribbles, over-scribbles and hieroglyphs into a publishable manuscript, and have kept me (almost) up to my deadlines, I owe much more than mere thanks. And finally, to Lisa, my wife, thank you, thank you, thank you:

readers will not recognize your contribution at all, you have some idea of it, but only I know the whole.

Do I have any regrets? Of course, many: but in particular I regret not having paid enough attention to the interface between American Indians and European American cultures: the gap is due to ignorance, not lack of concern. I hope, however, that my white readers will extend whatever they learn from my attempt to listen to African American voices to other racial and ethnic cultures, both nationally and globally. There are many pleasures in studying culture, not least of which is that the next stage in the project is always just ahead.

Some of the material in this book draws upon previously published work. An account of the culture of homeless men (Chapters 1 and 6) has appeared in *Critical Studies in Mass Communication*, and some of the material in Chapter 10 has been covered in my essay in *Cultural Studies*, edited by Lawrence Grossberg, Paula Treichler and Cary Nelson.

John Fiske
Madison, December 1992

POWER AND

CULTURAL THEORY

1

POWER PLAYS

AN INTRODUCTORY INSTANCE

It is about 2:00 a.m. on Tuesday, 7 November 1989. As nearly a decade of Reaganomic policies draws to an end, a homeless man in a small Midwestern city slips *Die Hard* into his shelter's VCR. Some fifteen or twenty other homeless men are in the same lounge, all of them white. Some are playing cards, some are reading, some talking, but most are just sitting. Tobacco smoke hangs in the air, and the supervisor sits at his desk just beyond the lounge's always-open door. From here he can observe the men's behavior in this lounge and in the non-smoking one next door.

The beginning of the movie flicks onto the screen, but the men pay little attention; most have seen it before, for it is one of the few violent, masculine movies among the "family" ones that are available to them at the local library. The couple of dollars charged at video rental stores is too much for these men, so they use the free collection at the public library and thus submit their cultural pleasures to a menu drawn up according to someone else's notion of culture-in-the-public-interest as opposed to the commercial interests that inform the selection at the rental stores. Socially similar eyes watch over both the men's behavior in the lounges and the movies on offer at the public library.

The movie, which has yet to grab their attention, is about a New York cop who goes to Los Angeles at Christmas to visit his estranged wife and daughter. She left him in order to build a career for herself and she is now a senior executive in the Nakatomi Corporation. The executives' Christmas party, on the 32nd floor of their corporate headquarters, is invaded by a gang who hold the executives hostage for the $640 million in the vaults of the skyscraper. The narrative follows the lone hero as he gradually kills off the villains one by one while the LA police vainly try to storm the building from the outside. The final victory restores not only public law and order but also the law and order of a patriarchal marriage as the hero wins back his wife.

The casual glances by which the men have monitored the screen suddenly turn to rapt attention as the villains invade the executives' party. The scene climaxes with the killing of Tagaki, the CEO. He is shot coldly and deliberately after refusing to yield the computer key to the vaults. The camera closes up on his impassive Asian-American face, which shows hardly a hint of fear as he says, "I cannot give you the code, you'll just have to kill me." "OK," responds the villain, and he pulls the trigger. At the moment of death the screen explodes in red and the homeless men erupt in loud and enthusiastic cheers.

But their cheers are based as much on what has preceded the moment as on the moment itself. The scene that climaxes in the CEO's death begins as his senior executives are rounded up by the gang. The sounds of muted corporate panic filling the room are abruptly silenced by the authoritative, teutonic voice of the leader: "Due to the Nakatomi Corporation's legacy of greed around the globe they're about to be taught a lesson of the real use of power. And you will witness it." He then passes among them, reading Tagaki's vita as he searches for him. Tagaki, the homeless men learn, emigrated from Japan in 1939, was interned during World War II, became a scholarship student at the University of California, earned a law degree from Stanford and an MBA from Harvard and then became President of Nakatomi Trading and Chairman of Nakatomi Investment Group. The details of educational success leading to corporate power and wealth are an excessive display of what the homeless men lack, but which our ideology has taught them is their right to desire, if not possess.

A later scene is also greeted with cheers and whistles. The villains have gained control of the skyscraper and watch from above as the police bring up an armored vehicle equipped with a battering ram. It is, incidentally, the one used in "real life" by the LAPD to smash into suspected crack houses. The villains fire a rocket which disables the vehicle and prepare to fire another, tactically unnecessary, one. From his hidden vantage point the hero "silently" begs them not to. But they do, and the camera lingers on the total destruction of the vehicle and the cops inside it. The homeless men's cheers drown the sounds of destruction and panic.

This is the high point of the villains' success; from here on, the hero gradually gains the upper hand, and the men's interest in the movie gradually wanes. They switch off the tape halfway through the hero's final battle with the remaining villains, and replace it with one of *Robocop*. They have no interest in watching the restoration of law and order.

The men's pleasures were not centered exclusively on the success of the villains, however, for they also enjoyed the hero's victories against the villains, particularly in the earlier parts of the movie. The movie shows a variety of forms of social power in conflict with challenges from apparently weaker opponents. In each power conflict, typically represented through spectacular violence, the homeless men sided with the weaker party and took pleasure in any tactical victories won, however temporarily. The power of the Nakatomi Corporation to accumulate enormous wealth and control the lives of people all around the world was made manifest in its huge skyscraper: in addition to the $640 million in its vaults, its topmost floors were luxuriously furnished with antiques and high art interspersed with detailed models of its global capital projects. The gang of villains, well organized and equipped though they were, were clearly weaker than the corporation, so the homeless men took great pleasure in their spectacular destruction of the symbols of corporate wealth and power. Similarly, they also sided against the villains and with the hero, for he was alone and equipped only with a handgun, his physical prowess, and his ingenuity. In the early stages of the movie at least, the men allied themselves with the hero against the villains but maintained their allegiance to the villains against the corporation and the police force. The more ground the hero won and the more closely he became aligned with the police force, the less interest they showed in either him or the movie.

And they had no interest at all in watching the hero's final victory, for that carried within it the victories of the police, of the corporation and thus of the social order which, in their view, has decisively rejected them.[1]

POWER AND THE PEOPLE

Despite its vaunted victory in the Cold War, the US in the 1990s is a deeply unsettled society. The street people in almost every city are but one symptom of this instability: the cheers of these particular homeless men are a tiny, localized instance of it. But the minuteness of the moment does not mean that it is insignificant; indeed, as I hope to show, when we understand all that is going on behind these cheers, their significance is immense.

This book begins with an account of those cheers because I see them as a specific instance of a much broader paradox: at the very moment when its leadership has pushed the US into a position of pre-eminence in a "one superpower world" the people have lost faith in that leadership and in the system that empowers them. Poll after poll shows a widespread disillusion-ment with Washington, its politicians and its policies. One of the consequences of this disenchantment with "Washington" is a widespread sense that some of the most important political arenas lie outside the party political system: so the streets of LA and Crown Heights, the doors of abortion clinics, the courts and the school curricula have joined, if not displaced, the voting booth as key sites of political action. Equally significant is the low involvement in any form of political activity, whether by ballot or by activism: this is not necessarily a sign of apathy, but may rather indicate that many of the struggles of everyday life take place in arenas that traditional politics have been slow to recognize. This oft-bemoaned "political apathy" does not mean that the US is an apathetic society—far from it. There is a surging vitality, energy and creativity that makes US society so exciting, restless and unstable: the fact that those who possess this energy often direct it to areas of their lives outside the domain of traditional politics is a problem for political analysts, but not necessarily for the people.

If some of the arenas of political struggles are changing, so too are the frameworks used to comprehend the issues within them. In particular, the frame of "left wing/right wing" appears to have lost its explanatory usefulness for many people. This loss is in step with the attempt of both Republicans and Democrats to occupy the center: the centrism of the two parties is the public equivalent of the diminishing significance of the difference between left and right in the public consciousness. The differ-ence may not have disappeared, but it has become only one of a number of frames, often not the most salient, by which social differences and therefore politics are made to make sense. A recent study by Russell Neuman and colleagues of how people "framed" current political issues found that the "left–right frame" was one of the least frequently used.[2] Two frames were clearly more common than any others: one produced the key social difference as that between "the haves" and "the have-nots," and the other divided social issues into "those where I can exert some influence" and "those where I cannot." Both these frames can be seen at work in comprehending "Washington" as a place of privilege and self-seeking that differs from the US that "ordinary people" inhabit: Wash-ington is framed as the domain of "the haves" (whether they are Republican or Democrat matters less than their difference from "the have-nots"), and what goes on there is understood as lying beyond the influence of, and therefore of no relevance to, the rest of the population.

"The haves" and "the have-nots" are not objective social categories like the "bourgeoisie" and the "proletariat" or "Blacks" and "whites."[3] They are mobile categories, formed to fit the conditions of their use and their user: in some social relations a middle-class white woman, for example, may be one of "the haves," while in others she may be a "have-not." "The haves" is a category which can only be made and used from below—it is a construction of "the have-nots" and as such is tactical rather than objective.

So, too, "issues where I can make a difference" (and where, therefore, my limited energies are best directed) is also a tactical or strategic category, constructed by the user in its conditions of use: no particular issue can, on its own terms only, be objectively included in, or excluded from, it.

This tactical mobility of ways of making social sense, together with a multiplicity of axes of social difference (of which class, gender, race, and age may be the most frequently prominent) constitute the world of highly elaborated late capitalism as poststructural rather than structural. A structural world is one that can be understood by relatively stable categories in a fixed relationship to each other: such a world can be analyzed to reveal the "deep structure" that invisibly organizes those categories and reproduces itself in all domains of social experience. Understanding this deep structure is, then, the key to understanding the social reality it produces. Arguably the three "definers" of twentieth-century thought—Saussure, Marx and Freud—were all structuralists, in that they offered explanations of language, capitalist society and the psyche in terms of deep structures that organized all the infinite variety of experiences that each can offer. "Left wing/right wing" is a product of a deeply structured binary opposition that has been used to organize most of the political thinking and action of this century. At the global level, this opposition surfaces in that between capitalism and communism, which in international relations produced the "Cold War" between the USA and its allies, and the USSR and its allies. Nationally it emerged in the "two-party system" of the right and the left, of conservatism, capital and the higher classes ranged against socialism, labor and the working classes. In the workplace, management and the bosses were set off from labor, those paid salaries calculated annually distinguished from those paid wages calculated hourly. These clear divisions in the way one earned one's money translated, in the realm of consciousness, into a sense of class identity—an awareness of where and with whom one stood in the social order whose prime determinate was economic. Under these conditions, it made sense to theorize class as the main structuring principle of consciousness, social relations and international relations. Social class was the key to both the analysis and solution of social problems because class relations were where this deep structure surfaced in its economic, material, and thus most immediately experienced form.

It can be argued that early capitalism in both Europe and the US was a more structurally determined social system than that of contemporary capitalism, and that it was thus appropriate that structural theories should have been developed to explain it. But though the structural organizers of capitalism (particularly class difference) are still with us, their determinations have become more indirect and their structural relations more contradictory and more fluid. Contemporary capitalist societies are too highly elaborated to be understood by a structural model, and, as a result, class can no longer occupy a position of theoretical centrality but must take its place alongside other axes around which social identities and social systems are organized. It is still important, but has been joined by race/ethnicity and gender as perhaps the core axes of social difference. But even this core is not certain, for other axes, such as age, marital status, religion, region, locality are all important and, in any instance, any of them may join the core, or dislodge one of the core axes from its centrality.

But while class may have lost its privileged position in social theory the problems addressed by traditional class analysis have not. Economic inequality, the center of class theory, has grown greater not less, but it is now distributed along any or all of these social axes. Children are actually the poorest social category in the US (and in the world), but Black and Latino children are poorer than white children, and children in a single-parent family poorer than those living with two. Presumably (and I have seen no statistics to support this hypothesis), Black and Latino single-parented children are poorer than whites. African Americans and Latinos in general are disproportionately poor, but their poor are poorer than white poor. Single-parented families of whatever race are poorer than dual-parented ones, and those parented by a woman are poorer than those by a man. After divorce a woman's standard of living goes down and she heads towards, and often into, poverty while that of her ex-husband rises. The sick are poorer than the healthy, and the handicapped poorer than the whole. Many of the poor (though far from the majority) are, by other standards, middle class—some of the homeless recently owned homes and businesses, many were once married to men who still do. Poverty, then, is distributed by age, race, gender, class, and marital status (at least) and while some of these axes of distribution may be in general more salient than others, in any particular case they may come together in any relative proportion. The ingredients are those of poverty in general, but the way they are mixed and cooked can vary widely and produce widely different results.

The homeless people we observed watching *Die Hard* are white and male, and these axes of race and gender configure their economic deprivation in particular ways. The way in which they are members of "the have-nots" are particular to them, and not necessarily typical of the homeless in general. Because they are white and male (normally categories of privilege) their homelessness will differ from that of some others in terms of gender and race, but be similar in terms of economics. But however multiaxial is the distribution of poverty, class still counts, but it counts differently from when it was the salient social axis.

Even in its most overt forms, class difference is always articulated with other axes. We cannot understand the large category of "the working poor" simply by referring to the fact that it takes more than one and a half full-time jobs at the minimum wage to lift a family of four up to the poverty line. The working poor are, of course, a product of class politics working overtly in setting the minimum wage at $4.35 and less visibly in ensuring constant structural unemployment. But these class relations interact with race relations, not only because minimum wage jobs are disproportionately held by non-whites, but also because the meagreness of the wage is often "justified" by reference to "third" world sweatshops, which are "our" competitors: the "third" world is thus understood as the racially dis-tinguished working class of the "first."[4] When relations between the "first" and "second" worlds were preeminent, class was central, but in those between the "first" and the "third" economic relations necessarily inter-twine race with class. So, too, the classist policies by which homelessness is organized and controlled from above have a racial and gendered dimension that will be discussed later in this chapter.

This book, then, is about culture and politics, mainly about the politics of culture, but also, necessarily, about the culture of politics. In it I hope to contribute to a poststructural political analysis which, unlike some poststructuralism, is both socially critical and directed to understanding specific struggles that have clear structural oppositions within their poststructural conditions. This form of poststructuralism can, I believe, do for the late twentieth century what critical structural analysis did for its third quartile. The theoretical core around which the arguments and analyses of this book are organized derives from three main sources: a Foucauldian theory of power and bodies in argument with structural Marxist ones of ideology, consciousness and class; a Gramscian account of struggles (inflected by the work of Vološinov, Hall, and Williams) between the power-bloc and the people; and a Bakhtinian sense of the vitality of the people and the constriction of the power-bloc.[5]

At the book's heart lie the numerous modes of opposition between the power-bloc and the people. Stuart Hall makes the point well:

> The people versus the power-bloc: this, rather than class-against-class, is the central line of contradiction around which the terrain of culture is polarized. Popular culture, especially, is organized around the contradiction: the popular forces versus the power-bloc.[6]

One form of this contradiction is that between "the haves" and "the have-nots," sometimes seen as that between "Washington" and "the rest of the

US" (or "the rest of us"), or, in its most generalized form, as that between "them" and "us." It is a poststructural opposition because its categories are not stable nor structurally set, but mobile, strategically and tactically formed and dissolved according to the perceived exigencies of the issue involved and its situating conditions. "The power-bloc" and "the people" are not social categories, but alliances of social interests formed strategically or tactically to advance the interests of those who form them. A "bloc," as Gramsci theorized it, is a welding together of different components for a specific purpose and it must not be misconstrued as a "block," or solid object. Thus, for instance, Stuart Hall illustrates power-bloc alliances by those formed in South Africa between the interests of the white ruling class and those of the white working class against Blacks in general, or between racially subaltern interests (such as those of the "colored" strata and of tribal blacks) and racially dominant interests against industrial Blacks in particular.[7] His examples show the strategic nature, the multiaxiality and the historical specificity of power-bloc alliances at work, but they hold fast for a comparatively long period (though they have dissolved since he wrote the essay) and over a comparatively wide set of issues. In many cases in the US, these alliances are more issue-centered, and thus form and reform more fluidly than in Hall's examples as different issues rise and fall on the social agenda. My use of the term "power-bloc" is, then, more poststructural than Gramsci's and Hall's, for I place greater emphasis than they on the mobility and multiaxiality of the alliances that constitute it. The opposition between the power-bloc and the people is one constantly in process, never structurally fixed; it is one between the strategy of the power-bloc and the tactics of the people, and it adapts itself chameleon-like to its immediate environment.[8]

But, whatever form it takes, the struggle between the power-bloc and the people always involves power. The homeless men's cheers at the fictional killing of a CEO can only be understood in relation to a power-bloc alliance formed around the placement of the supervisor's desk and his monitoring gaze, the well-intentioned, charitable shelter providers and the somewhat less charitable policies of Reaganomics.

The power-bloc, then, is not a social class, nor even a category of people. It is a disposition and exercise of power to which certain social formations, defined primarily by class, race, gender and ethnicity, have privileged access and which they can readily turn to their own economic and political interests. One of the characteristics of the corporate and multinational capitalism in which we live is the dissolution of any simple relationship between class, capital and power. Executives and managers, as well as workers, are subject to the power of the corporation; but the subjection is not equal—senior members gain more and give up less because of their easier access to power. Power, as Foucault has shown us, operates through a set of technologies and mechanisms rather than through a social class: it is diffused throughout society rather than imposed by one class upon another. Power, then, is a systematic set of operations upon people which works to ensure the maintenance of the social order (in our case of late capitalism) and ensure its smooth running. It is therefore in the interests of those who benefit most from this social order to co-operate with this power system and to lubricate its mechanisms. This is a key strategy of the power-bloc: a social force that can be identified better by what it *does* than what it *is*.

"The people" are those who benefit least and are disciplined most by this power system. They, too, must be seen as a set of social forces rather than as social categories. The people consist of varied and changing social allegiances whose one constant is their comparative lack of privilege, their comparative deprivation of economic and political resources. The people do not have easy access to the system of power and cannot, in general, turn it to their own advantage. They do, however, have access to their own forms of power which, though socially weaker, are far from ineffective: in theorizing and analyzing these "weak" powers at work I hope to build a significant extension onto Foucault's model. But while "the people," as a concept, cannot be defined in terms of such social categories as class, race, ethnicity and gender, it does intersect with them, sometimes very closely indeed, and can never be totally separated from them. As the fluidity of this concept cuts across social categories, so it splits the category of the individual. A blue-collar white man may, for example, form a social allegiance with Black men who share his skills and conditions of subordination at work, but may, in his leisure, ally himself with other white men in relations of racial dominance. The first allegiance would be with the social force of the people, the second with that of the power-bloc.

The "weak" powers available to the people are so different from the power to which the power-bloc enjoys privileged access as to require different names. I propose to call strong, top-down power "imperializing" and weak, bottom-up power "localizing." The aim of *imperializing power* is to extend its reach as far as possible—over physical reality, over human societies, over history, over consciousness. It strives constantly to extend the terrain over which it can exert its control extensively to outer space and the galaxy and intensively to people's most mundane thoughts and behaviors. Its systems are developed and exploited best by formations of the power-bloc because they have the most to gain and the least to yield by submitting themselves to its discipline.

In contrast to this, the power sought by subordinated social formations is the power to control their immediate social conditions. It is a *localizing power*, not concerned to dominate other social formations, not concerned with constantly expanding its terrain but interested in strengthening its control over the immediate conditions of everyday life. These conditions comprise thoughts, feelings, beliefs and actions; they include social identity and social relationships as they are made material in the places, temporalities and routines of daily life. The function of this power is to produce and hold onto a space that can, as far as possible, be controlled by the subordinate who live within it. This space has four dimensions: it is *interior*, for it is where social identities, social relations and social histories are experienced; it is *socio-political*, for it exists within a social order; it is *physical*, for it is localized in the places where people dwell and play and work; it is *temporal*, for it exists only for the time in which these who construct it inhabit it. This interior social, physical and temporal space I call a *locale*. A locale's scale may vary from the spatially and socially restricted one produced by the homeless men while watching *Die Hard* in the shelter to one encompassing much larger social and physical spaces and communal consciousness such as that which many African Americans believe to be necessary for them to achieve a self-determined way of living within a hostile white society (see Chapters 11 to 13). But whatever its scale, a locale always involves continuities between interior and exterior, between consciousness, bodies, places and times. A locale is a bottom-up product of localizing power and as such is always in a contestatory relationship with imperializing power.

Constructing a locale involves confronting, resisting or evading imperialization, for imperializing power wishes to control the members of its own society as strongly as it wishes to control the physical world. To do this, it must control the places where its people live, the behaviors by which they live and the consciousness by which they make sense of their identities and experiences. It attempts to stop people producing their own locales by providing them with *stations*.

A station is the opposite, but equivalent, of a locale. A station is both a physical place where the social order is imposed upon an individual and the social positioning (stationing) of that individual in the system of social relations. The shelter for the homeless men was a *station*. It was a physical place where top-down discipline could be applied, and it simultaneously positioned them socially. They were stationed (that is, placed according to the interests of the power-bloc as a soldier is stationed wherever military interests dictate) and this stationing worked to extend itself into their consciousness of their own identities. If they knew themselves as imperializing knowledge knew them, that is as vulnerable, insufficient objects of charity and therefore quite properly "othered," their stationing was complete.

For many of them, however, this was not the case, at least, not always. Their cheers were an instance of their localizing power working effectively to turn the lounge, the movie and their consciousness into their locale. The concepts of station and locale are similar in that they both combine into a single category elements of social experience which are frequently conceptualized as separate: these are the interior dimensions of consciousness, identity or subjectivity, the socio-political dimension of social relations and the physical dimension of bodies in space and time. The difference between them is that a locale is a product of the subordinate which is typically held defensively against the stationing power of the dominant.[9]

The culture of capitalism is irredeemably materialist; and in using the two terms "material" and "culture," I am positing a difference between them that is of analytical convenience only and which ultimately must be dissolved. Any social system (that which is material and historically specific) needs a system of meanings and values (that is, culture) to hold it in place or to help motivate it to change. There is a material experience of homelessness that is of a different order from the cultural meanings of homelessness under Reaganism, but the boundary between the two cannot be drawn sharply. Material conditions are inescapably saturated with culture and, equally, cultural conditions are inescapably experienced as material.

The term "material" can also be used more literally—the shelter was a material structure as is a school, a factory, an apartment block or a city: material (economic) resources produce material (physical) places designed to control people's bodies and behaviors. Having their behavior in a charitable shelter overseen by an employed man is part of the material conditions of these homeless and jobless men, and it is equally part of their cultural conditions. Being charitably supervised weaves certain cultural meanings into the material condition of being homeless. Material and cultural conditions constantly imbricate each other, but, for purposes of analysis and interpretation, it can be useful to focus more, but never total, attention on one than the other. The focus of this book is on the cultural but only insofar as it is materially informed.

I understand culture, then, to encompass the struggle to control and contribute to the social circulation and uses of meanings, knowledges, pleasures and values. Culture always has both sense-making and power-bearing functions. Its sense-making function contains concerns such as those of knowledge, discourse, representation, and practice; within its power-bearing functions are those of power, control, discipline, struggle, resistance, and evasion. Definitions of concepts as slippery and leaky as these can never be precise or complete, for they evolve with use, and it is

13

in their uses that we can best understand them. Preliminary definitions can only help us to get started.

I use the word "knowledge" in a poststructural sense to differentiate it from its more commonsensical meaning of a totalizing, accumulative system of all that is known to be true and whose absolute demonstrable truth is clearly distinguished both from that which is false or not known, and from other conceptual systems, such as "faith," which have quite different epistemological bases. Poststructuralists tend to use the word only with an article or in the plural (for example, *a* knowledge or knowledges). A knowledge is selective and not comprehensive: it comprises both what is known (and therefore has an exclusionary as well as an inclusive function) and a way of knowing that is coherent and systematic. It involves also the power relationship between the knower, the process of knowing and the known. It serves the interests (material and political) of the social formation which produces it and is evaluated not by reference to an objective and absolute truth but by its social and historical effectivity (which can be traced and assessed) and by its relationship to other knowledges that it struggles to repress, evade or delegitimate. According to Foucault, what knowledge produces is not truth, but power, or rather, power disguised as truth. In this view, truths, like knowledges, are seen as socially produced and therefore hierarchical, diverse and contestatory, not singular, objective, and absolute. There are, for example, different ways of knowing homelessness that are systematically and socially related to the competing (but not equally competing) knowledges of capitalism in *Die Hard*. When the men switched off the tape before the end of the movie they challenged the conventional hierarchy of the different ways of knowing multinational capitalism.

Knowledge is activated socially through discourse. Discourse circulates knowledge and carries its power into specific and particular situations. We can only trace different knowledges through the discourses by which they are put into practice and through which their power is applied. Knowledge and discourse are totally interdependent. Knowledge and discourse, then, inform all cultural systems and should not be understood as being limited to verbal and visual languages. Discourse constantly transgresses, if it doesn't actually destroy, the boundary between material and cultural conditions, because discourse, through the specificity of its practices, always has a material dimension. The hiring of a supervisor and the placement of his desk within the shelter is a discursive statement about homelessness that applies the knowledge that the homeless are characterized by inadequacy, irresponsibility, immaturity, childishness and a lack of competence, and therefore require help and supervision. It applies the power of those who know homelessness in this way to the bodies and behaviors of those who know it in quite different, but less powerful, ways. Discourse applies knowledge; discourse applies power.

Discourse also represents the world by producing a knowledge of it and thus exerting power over it. There is a physical reality outside of discourse, but discourse is the only means we have of gaining access to it. It is going too far, though only by a smidgeon, to say that reality is the product of discourse: it is more productive to say that what is accepted as reality in any social formation is the product of discourse. Discourse produces a knowledge of the real which it then presents and re-presents to us in constant circulation and usage. Events do occur, physical reality does exist, but we can know neither until they are put into discourse. The importance of never forgetting that events and objects exist outside of discourse, despite the inaccessibility of that existence on its own terms, is that they can always be put into discourse differently. No event, no piece of reality, contains its own terms of existence; equally, it cannot dictate into which discourse it should be put. Putting into discourse is one way in which the social exerts control over the real. Putting into discourse is a negotiating procedure which involves the selection of certain features of the real (and thus the repression of others), the selection of a certain way of knowing and representing (and thus the repression of others), and its circulation in the interests of some social formations (and thus the repression of others). Discourse is always a matter of contestation, and it is in the interests of the dominant social formations whose alliances comprise the power-bloc to repress or deny this contestation. Equally, therefore, it is in the interests of the variety of subordinated social formations that constitute the people to engage in it as vigorously as possible. Discourse is never neutral or objective: its work of production and repression is always politically active in specific social conditions, and it is always, then, a terrain of struggle.

Besides representing a particular knowledge of the world, discourse also represents the social relations and power relations involved in knowing the world in that way. Knowledge is social and not individual (although our dominant way of knowing attempts constantly to individuate it), and thus knowing is engaging in social relations. Paradise, an African American homeless man in Greenwich, New York (half a continent away from our homeless audience of *Die Hard*), panhandles a group of businessmen: "Look corporate criminals! Hello, Mr. Executive, how you doing? You remember how to be human don't you? Come on, give me a dollar man, I bet you make $50,000 in ten minutes." The men climb into a Lincoln Continental, and as it moves away, the driver lowers the window and gives Paradise not a dollar but a piece of advice: "Get a job, will you."[10]

The homeless men cheering the death of the CEO in *Die Hard* and Paradise panhandling the corporate executives in Manhattan share a particular knowledge of corporate capitalism. Knowing capitalism in the way that they do is an engagement in social relations, for they know that their knowledge differs from the official, and that this difference is not just one of content but of power. *Die Hard*'s official ending in which law and order are restored is discursively identical to the ending of Paradise's brief encounter with the executives. In each case the dominant way of knowing capitalism (that those who earn its rewards earn the right to keep them safe from those who have not earned them, whether robbers or beggars, or to distribute them as charity if they wish) has the last word. But neither Paradise nor the Midwestern homeless men accept the last word as the final truth.

Capitalism, which is a very real socioeconomic system with very real effects, can never be put into discourse in only one way, and any attempt to do so, however skillful and thorough, must always leave traces of its material reality that escape discursive control and thus remain as intransigent reminders that different ways of knowing and representing it are not only possible but inevitable. *Die Hard* represents not just the power and ultimate justification of the dominant knowledge of corporate capitalism, but also the repression of the knowledges by which this dominance is achieved and thus, inevitably, the social relations involved in its discursivity. The homeless men found pleasure in *Die Hard* because it contained and repressed (though not totally) a discourse of capitalism which they can and do use in their social experience and in whose use they are experienced and competent: their assertion of its validity against the attempt to repress it was both highly significant and highly pleasurable to them. In cheering the representation of the temporary victories of the subordinate (and in switching off that of the more enduring victory of the dominant) they invested more psychic energy, vitality and enthusiasm than in any other part of their daily lives. Their cheers may be difficult to interpret, but there can be little doubt that watching *Die Hard* mattered intensely to the men—it appeared to be the most significant event in their day.

Knowledge, discourse and representation are agencies of power and control. Because the knowledge of reality involves the social relations involved in knowing it in that way, the power to control ways of knowing is a power over what is accepted as reality and over those among whom that acceptance circulates. Social identities, social relations and ways of knowing are inextricably linked. The different ways of knowing capitalism in both *Die Hard* and Paradise's encounter are produced by the social identities and social relations of those involved (not as individuals but as members of social formations), and then, reciprocally, those identities and relations are reproduced by the circulation of their knowledges. The power of knowledge lies in its continuous and reciprocal flow between the social and the real, and in the way it constructs each in terms of the other. The social formation to which the executives belong (and therefore its social relations and identities) is constituted by knowing that capitalism is *really* fair because its rewards are distributed according to talent and effort; equally this reality of capitalism is produced by knowing it in this way.

Power and knowledge are two sides of the same coin; each entails the other and neither can exist without the other. Both are coherent systems of production, repression and distribution: both impose disciplined ways of thinking and behaving which offer rewards of efficiency and effectivity as compensations for their disciplinarity and repression. Control and discourse are similarly linked: control is to power as discourse is to knowledge. Control is the means by which power is applied in particular circumstances. Without its multitude of points of control, power would have no mechanisms to transform its potential into effect. Control is localized, applied power at work, just as discourse is localized, applied knowledge at work.

The supervisor at the shelter for homeless men is a point of control through which the economic and social power of the providers of charity (it is a church shelter) is applied to the recipients. Control, like discourse, is productive as well as repressive, indeed its ability to repress effectively, that is with a minimum of struggle or contestation, is directly proportional to its ability to produce what people want, or can be persuaded to want. Control produces certain ways of behaving which it then represents as in the interests of the controlled: insofar as this representation is accepted by them, its repressive apparatuses can be kept veiled and unused, but never dismantled. Power and knowledge, of course, work similarly: their production of benign effects hides their repression, and the more widely the consent to their benignity can be extended, the better hidden their repression can remain. Discipline systematically works to emphasize its effective and benign productivity while disguising its repression, so a disciplined social formation or a disciplined body is one that complies with the system which controls it because it has been persuaded that its benefits are greater than its costs, that what it includes is better than what is excluded. This persuasion often involves not recognizing that, although all social formations are subject to the same systems of discipline, they are not equally subject: some formations benefit much more and give up less, whereas others give up much to benefit comparatively little.

One point of control is the men's reading matter. Respectable magazines such as *Time*, *Life*, *Newsweek*, the local daily paper and religious tracts are provided. The tabloids are not, and the men are discouraged from reading them. Pornography is banned. This is a point of control within the same power system that directs the public library's selection of its movies. It is also systematically related to MTV's refusal to play Madonna's video *Justify my Love*, to Jessie Helms's and Lynn Cheney's control over what forms of art should be supported with National Endowment for the Humanities (NEH) money, and to the Florida court's prosecution of the rap group 2 *Live Crew* for obscenity. These are all points of control. They are where a generalized and extensive power-knowledge is applied locally and thus made real. The fact that this power-knowledge (in this case, of cultural taste and ethical value) is produced by and productive of dominant social formations is part of the knowledge that is repressed by the dominant but recovered and asserted by the subordinated. The homeless men are well aware that the shelter's attempts to control their reading matter (and, incidentally, to stop them gambling and drinking alcohol and to discourage them from smoking) involve the imposition of irrelevantly middle-class values. At times their awareness of the attempt to impose a value system across the gap between its social origin and their own conditions causes resentment, at others a wry bafflement at the importance the shelter's providers attach to it.

By disciplining their tastes and behavior to this control, the men receive the very real benefits of shelter and food. But some of them gain the benefits while evading the discipline. They read tabloids and pornography under the covers of the respectable magazines; they gamble by hiding a system of tally-keeping under a visibly respectable card game and by settling accounts (in either cigarettes or money) in secret later. The hero's "silent" plea to the villains in *Die Hard* not to fire the second rocket at the disabled police vehicle and the shelter's banning of pornography are examples of the same knowledge (of "good" ethical values) being put into discourse: so cheering the villains' rejection of the plea and reading *Hustler* under the covers of *Life* are moments of resistance to the power of that knowledge and to its application. They are the practice of a localizing power which refuses that way of knowing and evades its disciplinary system. This refusal or evasion involves an engagement in social relations because it embodies the recognition both of social inequality and that the deprived have ways of asserting their view of this inequality.

We must not take an essentialist view of this process of struggle and the weapons used to wage it: pornography or violence are not essentially tastes of socially deprived men. However, in these men's current social conditions, representations of "illegitimate" sexuality or violence provide appropriate and available discursive means of expressing their opposition to the social order whose power is used both to deprive them and to delegitimize the violence they find so pleasurable. The control that the men exert over their reading, card-playing and movie-watching is the way in which they construct their locale within and against the shelter's station. This small-scale clash over who controls what and by which means is an instance of the larger conflict between imperializing and localizing powers.

Imperializing power produces and is produced by knowledges which are equally imperialist. The physical sciences are ways of knowing nature that function to enable their possessors to control and exploit it for their own benefit. Enlightenment rationalism produces knowledges of human beings and their mental and social systems that function to increase their possessors' efficiency in controlling the social order and the mental processes of those who live within it. Imperializing culture produces great works of art whose control is exerted over the meaning of humanity itself. An imperializing religion is one of missionaries whose aim is to convert the world. An imperializing economics is more concerned to produce ever-accumulating profits than the goods needed for sustenance and pleasure. The worldwide reach of the power of post-Renaissance Europe (economic, military, political) cannot be separated from the knowledges that produced and reproduced that power and were, in their turn, produced and reproduced by it. (These ideas will be fleshed out more fully in Chapter 9.)

But there are other ways of knowing nature that enable societies to live within it, rather than over it; there are other knowledges of human experience that contradict those of rationalism, and there are cultures that aim not to define humanity itself but to make sense of everyday life, that function not to extend a great vision over the world but to produce a localized social, ethnic, communal sense of identity.

Imperializing ways of knowing tend to produce cultures of representation, ones that reproduce both a sense of the world and the power to control that sense. Localizing ways of knowing, on the other hand, tend to produce cultures of practice, ones that develop ways of living in the world and which seek to control only those ways of living rather than the world in which they live.

Reading *Hustler* within the covers of *Life*, gambling covertly, and cheering the CEO's death, are each an example of a culture of practice at work. They are ways of making do with what is available. But each is also, in its own way, rule-breaking (of the shelter or of the text) and is thus a minute point of contestation between imperializing and localizing powers, between a top-down power seeking to control the daily minutiae of others and a bottom-up power attempting to control the immediate conditions of its own life. Such contests are not ones that can be permanently won or lost. They are ongoing and no "victory" is final, for what is won in them can only be held by continuing the struggle that won it. The lounge can never *be* either a charitable station or a homeless locale, but is rather the (unlevel) playing field upon which the contest is held. The homeless man watching *Die Hard* is in neither his locale nor "their" station but is practicing the struggle for control that the difference between them entails.

FROM THE MICRO TO THE MACRO (AND VICE VERSA)

All societies need to control their physical environments, their relationships with other societies and themselves. This last terrain of control, the internal, forms the topic of this section. It is exerted along a continuum that ranges from the ordering principle of the social system itself, through its institutions, to its individual members and their thoughts and behaviors. It is this end of the continuum, the control over people, with which I am concerned here. It is helpful, I believe, to conceive of control at this level as operating over three interrelated terrains—consciousness, or what people do inside their heads; relationships, or what goes on as people interact socially; and bodies and behaviors, or what people do with their physical presence as they move through space and time. In practice, these terrains are not separate but are experienced as seamlessly integrated into "a whole way of life," to use one of Raymond Williams's definitions of culture,[11] so any analysis that focuses on one must eventually broaden its perspective to include the others, and, indeed must go further still and contextualize them all within the larger systems of power that are applied within them. To understand culture we need to understand this sense of wholeness that is the product of the interrelationships among the many discrete events, such as watching *Die Hard*, which constitute our social experience and from which the analyst selects some for detailed study.

The terrain of consciousness, relationships and bodies is where the cultural experiences that matter most to people occur. If people are generally satisfied, or can be induced to feel satisfied, with what goes on in these immediate conditions of their lives, then the social formations to which they ally themselves will be comparatively stable and unmotivated to change their stationed, structural relations to the social order at large. Conversely, dissatisfaction here is one of the most important, if not the primary, origins of the desire to change. So controlling how people experience these immediate conditions of social life is crucial for any social order and it is here that culture is particularly active and where its effects can be usefully evaluated.

Watching the death of a CEO or the destruction of a police vehicle and its inhabitants mattered intensely to the homeless men, for in these moments they engaged in the struggle to control the most immediate of all the conditions of daily life, that is their sense of their relations to the social order and therefore of their identities within that order. The vehemence of their cheers and whistles were evidence of how important it was to them to win control over this tiny but directly immediate area of social experience. In winning this they were behaving not as social subjects, but as social agents who were capable both of perceiving their own social interests and of acting to promote them. They were acting as what we might call *socially interested agents*.

The debate over whether theories of agency or of subjectivity offer the more convincing explanations of how people live within capitalist societies has been central in recent cultural theory.[12] Briefly, theories of subjectivity put greater emphasis on the working of the forces of domination, which are usually explained by ideology theory, commodity theory, or psychoanalysis, whereas theories of agency focus more on how people cope with these forces. Because these forces of domination and discipline are relatively homogeneous, subjectivity theories tend to emphasize what is common to all subjects of a particular social order, particularly their consciousness (and subconsciousness). But because the material conditions within which people actually live under these forces vary widely, theories of agency tend to stress diversity. Both agency and subjectivity theories recognize that whatever goes on in our complex societies goes on within a structure of conflicting interests. Subjectivity theories focus on the power of the dominant and, in their more extreme forms, imply that the subordinate have been deprived of any real ability to resist. Agency theories emphasize more the extent to which the subordinate make the dominant struggle constantly to maintain their domination. In their more extreme forms they stress the intransigence and indiscipline by which members of subordinated social formations oppose, subvert or evade the power of the dominant to the extent that the power can be made to appear relatively ineffective, or, at least, effective only when those it is attempting to subject consent to their subjection and comply with its discipline.

The struggle over control is where the action of a *socially interested agency* becomes most visible. Social agents, particularly subordinate ones, must never be confused with so-called free agents (if such beings exist outside the imaginations of conservatives or football coaches), because their agency is always constrained by conditions that are not of their own making, and it is exercised by using resources produced by others. Social agents are creative not so much in the production of resources as in the use to which they put those that are available to them. Agency is making do with what one has. And what the subordinate have is, in general, provided by, controlled by, or inscribed with the power of the power-bloc. Making do is an act of social relations, and the struggle for control is always involved. The power-bloc, too, exercises agency and it has far greater control over social resources, so its agency is often institutionalized, either formally in institutions such as education, the law, and the media, or less formally, in more pervasive cultural resources and social organizations such as language or the family. The agency of the power-bloc is a socially advantaged agency which exerts powerful determinations on the social conditions and resources which circumscribe the agency of the people. But while it might circumscribe the agency of the people it cannot eliminate it, and, equally importantly, its lines of circumscription are drawn in sand rather than engraved in rock: as people constantly contest them, they have to be constantly redrawn.

This agency of the people is not only social, it is also interested, for it is exerted in order to promote the interests of the agents, typically by securing or extending their terrain of control. Social interests differ because people's material conditions differ: this difference is one of inequality of material and cultural resources and of social power, so difference becomes a source and point of conflict. It is in the interests of the power-bloc to minimize the perception of social difference and to emphasize consensus because the reduction of contestation secures their own position. The interests of the people, however, are promoted by the recognition of social difference and the social contestation borne within it, so their interests are served at the most basic level by asserting a social identity that differs from that proposed for them from above. The first instance of social agency is over identity and the social relations that constrain it.

The agency of the people is motivated partly by this perception of social difference and inequality, particularly as it is experienced in the struggle to control as many of the immediate conditions of life as possible. Social deprivation and constraints are experienced materially in everyday life, but the perception of these conditions as depriving and constrained is only achieved by implicitly but constantly comparing them to the "better" conditions of the more privileged. Deprivation is always relative, never absolute. Everyone's daily life involves constantly negotiating the limits of their control, and the more subordinate one is, the more these limits close in. But the desire to control is never extinguished by the difficulty of achieving it. Agency is produced by the tension between the desire to control and social constraint, and, in its first instance, is put to work at the point of control where this tension is experienced. The choice between *Life* and *Hustler* was one such point.

Agency is also necessitated by the complex elaborations of huge late capitalist societies whose lines of power always have points of contradiction and abrasiveness, despite the efforts of the power-bloc to homogenize a well-oiled consensus around its own interests. The elaborateness of social life always presents people with alternatives for action, for ways of knowing, for social identities and social relations. Again, the interests of the power-bloc lie in controlling and reducing the alternatives available, whereas those of the people are exercised by their own use of these alternatives, by finding gaps between them where top-down control can be subverted or evaded, or by extending them beyond its reach.

The contradictions that are inevitable in societies as highly elaborated as those of late capitalism mean that the people who live in them can never be pushed or pulled coherently in one direction only, despite a general directionality of the push of power. The people have to exert a degree of agency in order to negotiate the elaborations whose forces crisscross their daily lives and fill them with the need to make decisions and choices. The constant refinement of the mechanisms of social power works to extend the latter's reach into the moments when these decisions are made, but this reach is never total and can always be contested. It is, paradoxically, the elaborateness of the social order that produces both subtly pervasive power and the popular agency to resist it.

The homeless men watching *Die Hard* acted as socially interested agents not only in attempting to control their own consciousness but also in negotiating the contradictory social forces playing upon them. They were economically subordinated: by being deprived of both jobs and families they were excluded from key social relations within which to construct identities and exercise some control, yet they were still male and white and so were touched by forces of social power (and the motivation to exploit them) that contradicted their other deprivations. The contradictions between their sense of masculinity in a patriarchy and of deprivation in a meritocracy required them to choose, even if not consciously, *how* to watch the movie. This agency was exercised not only within such large-scale social forces as economic deprivation, exclusion from family and work relations, and white masculinity, but also within a very immediate physical environment. The ways in which the men lived within the shelter are the equivalent of the ways in which they watched *Die Hard*: in both they made do with resources provided by the other to construct, as far as they could, their own locale. This involved a constant "turning," so that what was used by the allegiances of the power-bloc to station them could be redirected towards their own interests.

The shelter is a station; it is a social and physical space for living saturated with top-down meanings of homelessness that attempt to permeate the identities and social relations of the men who use it. The two lounges, for instance, are furnished with a mixture of institutional furniture and items donated by, or rather cast off from, middle-class families. Both rooms were decorated by volunteers from the church and they look like a benevolent idea of what would be pleasant and comfortable for undifferentiated, impersonalized others. The decor, the cast-off furniture and the magazines lying on it are a spatial discourse controlling the place where the men live and continuing that control from place into consciousness. The restricting of behavior restricts identities, and here the social identities of the homeless are controlled by the spatial discourse of the homeowners: identities are produced by a discursive sense of what they are *not* rather than by a local one of whom they think they are. The subtlety by which a generalized power can be applied as control is illustrated by the fact that the more comfortable furniture is in the non-smoking lounge. Throughout the 1980s smoking has become more and more a mark of difference between those with power and those without: so those subordinated by race, class and age (particularly if they are young girls) are more likely to smoke than those who are more easily allied with the power-bloc. The discouragement of smoking is, in these circumstances, an extension of control via the erasure of social difference. This control is not selfish, but benevolent, but its benevolence flows from a middle-class knowledge of the men's best interests. Not surprisingly, the men choose to watch their violent movies in the "smoker."

The shelter itself is part of a Protestant church, yet is clearly separated from it. It was built onto the back of the church and is invisible from the front and the main entrance, so the men have to approach it through a back alley out of sight of the regular churchgoers. The shelter can be reached from the church itself but the door is kept locked and the homeless do not have access to the key.

The men are acutely aware of this "back-door" access to their place, and the back-door identities it gives them. One of them, Bill, made it abundantly clear that he found this troubling. He was pleased to have a place to eat and sleep, yet, as he put it, "We can't offend the decent people who come to worship here." His sarcastic and slightly bitter tone of voice is evidence of his awareness of his subordination, and his resentment at the way it is made so obvious and unavoidable. The supervisor himself is also indignant that the comings and goings of the homeless men are confined to an alley. He talks of the shortcomings of "Christian brotherhood" with regard to the shelter, and thinks that the men should be able to enter from the front and to feel more a part of the church itself and the larger society, for "the back alley" is a social space as well as a physical place. He is a Quaker who believes his denomination to be more humanely Christian than the Protestantism of this particular church. He works here only because his church does not have the money to run its own shelter. He cares deeply for the men and fights for their interests with the church administrator. Bill looks upon him as a friend and an equal, although he is puzzled by his devout religious belief, which he interprets as evidence of naivety or ignorance of the "real" world.

The difference between this "real world," which is the one experienced by the men, and the "unreal" world of the religious supervisor is structurally similar to the gap between the origins of the furniture and their current use, or that between the middle-class reading matter provided and the tabloids and soft pornography that the men actually read. The men frequently grumbled about this repression of their own cultural tastes and were resentfully aware of the pressure on them to qualify for charity by adopting inappropriately middle-class behavior and values, and thus to cede areas of their social identities to top-down control. In this context, then, reading *Hustler* under cover of *Life* is exercising a socially interested agency within and against the domain of the dominant other.

The shelter worked to control time as well as place: two key rules governed the times during which the men were allowed to use it. Their stay in the shelter was limited to thirty consecutive nights, a rule that carried the dominant sense that homelessness is a temporary problem best solved by giving people help to get through its (comparatively) short duration. This meaning carries with it the implication that long-term homelessness is, to some degree at least, the fault of the homeless themselves. Indeed, Ronald Reagan in a speech in 1984 referred to "those who live on the streets, as it were, by choice." This privileged meaning of homelessness denies the alternative one that it is a structural result of power-bloc policies that widened the gap between the privileged and the deprived throughout the 1980s. It is a way of knowing homelessness that, like all knowledge, has power built into it. Because this is a dominant knowledge and a dominant power it can be transformed into a disciplinary mechanism which offers the men food and shelter in reward for submitting themselves to its control. This control is also applied to the organization of daily time. The men have to be out of the shelter between 8:00 a.m. and 5:00 p.m. This is the period of the "normal" working day when the "normal" man is out of the house, and the homeless men are expected to conform to these norms and to use these hours if not to go to work, at least to look for it. The men, however, make no attempt to conform to such irrelevant norms and the social discipline enshrined in them. For most of them daytime is the time of maximum discomfort and the best way to pass it is asleep. Rather than looking for work, they spend their days looking for places to sleep. The night is when they can be warm, relatively comfortable and can read, watch television, or interact with each other. They have no intention of wasting it by sleeping. When not sleeping, they spend their daytime hours panhandling. Panhandling may be the unemployed's equivalent of work, but it is certainly not the work intended by the rule; indeed it is a subversion of normal "work."

The shelter was a station where power was applied and contested in the control of time and space within it. The practices of living are those of the body moving through space and time, so spatial and temporal control is crucial to any disciplinary system—whether that of work, school or home. All of these specific disciplinary systems are part of that larger, more generalized mechanism of social power, so the temporal and spatial separation of the men from the church and its congregation was experienced by them as another means of stationing them physically and socially in the unseen, unregarded margins. Stations, such as this shelter, are where space and time are organized into the routines of disciplined living. Social power is exerted most effectively through larger social structures that bear down upon these stations and become manifest in their official disciplinary procedures. But the power of subordinated people is exercised most effectively, though not exclusively, in the practices by which they can construct their own locales within, and sometimes against, these structuring, stationing conditions.

A historically specific example of these macro-level conditions is that of "Reaganomics," which in the 1980s worked through culture and economics to station homelessness. As I write this in 1990, the total numbers of the homeless are almost impossible to assess (the absence of statistics with any claim to authority is an indicator of how little attention Reaganite policies pay to homelessness—compare, for instance, the statistical abundance granted to crime). But for 1982 I found estimates ranging from 250,000 to 1,000,000 and for 1988 from 500,000 to 3,000,000. Not surprisingly, the lower figures tended to come from government sources, the higher from organizations working in the field, such as the National Coalition for the Homeless (statistics are as important a site of political struggle as any other mode of representation). But all parties agree on the increase. Even the Department of Housing and Urban Development (HUD) in its 1989 report admits that the use of shelters for the homeless tripled between 1984 and 1988.

The increase in the numbers of the homeless has been accompanied by a decrease in government assistance. Funding for HUD shrank from $35.7 billion in 1980 to $14.2 billion in 1987 to $7 billion in 1989. The number of housing units assisted by the federal government fell from 326,000 in 1978 to 95,000 in 1987. Government tax policies under Reagan reduced tax incentives for private investment in low-income housing and curtailed public-housing authorities' ability to issue tax-exempt bonds. As a result, average metropolitan rents doubled and low-income housing decreased by 30 per cent. This loss of low-income housing accompanied a rise in the need for it. Poverty rose 36 per cent between 1978 and 1983, AFDC monthly payments were reduced from a high of $520 in 1968 to $325 in

1985 (figures in 1985 dollars), and the economy as a whole lost approximately 16,000,000 jobs, most of them at the lower end of the wage scale.

The economic is not the only axis of deprivation along which the power-bloc advances its interests in the production of homelessness: gender and race are never absent from its power plays. The shelter systematically deprived the men in it of their masculinity. Our ideology gives masculinity three main dimensions by which it may be achieved—the power to influence others more than being influenced by them; the power to be independent and self-sufficient; and the power to achieve visible goals and to receive public recognition of that achievement. By denying the men the means of achieving any of these dimensions of masculinity, the shelter emasculated them. Emasculated men pose little threat to the power-bloc (the more general assault on the African American male will be discussed in Chapter 11) so national policy allies itself with that of the shelter with the result that 78 per cent of single homeless adults are men, or, to put it another way, 64 per cent of homeless adults are single men. Because, in our form of patriarchy, femininity and childishness contain meanings of dependency, women and children can more readily be considered proper recipients of such welfare as the state offers. What is called Aid for Families with Dependent Children (AFDC) becomes, in practice, aid for women with dependent children, for families where an adult male is present can rarely qualify. Even though these restrictions have now been eased, poor men are still practically excluded, for it is almost impossible for them to gain the employment record necessary to qualify for aid. In order to qualify for food stamps for themselves and their children, therefore, poor women will have to eject poor men from their households. If they are unmarried or unpartnered they will similarly have to reject proposals even from men on the minimum wage, let alone those with only part-time or no employment, for accepting the man would mean reducing their income. Poverty denies them the choice. The welfare system cuts poor men off from even the most personal relationships (within a family or with a loved woman) within which his manliness can find expression, and, in doing so, will, in many cases, weaken the woman and the family as well.

This gendered dimension of poverty, like the economic, is suffered disproportionately by non-whites. It is hardly surprising, then, that many African Americans see the welfare system as working to weaken Black families and to humiliate Black men. Its result is to shrink even further the conditions of their lives over which they have any control. When a man loses control even over whom he loves and lives with, then his locale is no bigger than the tiger cages of Vietnam. It is no wonder, then, that to poor African Americans, welfare appears to be slavery by other means: it is slavery translated from the coercive conditions of the plantation to the discipline of a "free" market, but the grasp of white power remains untranslated: it still enslaves.[13]

Whatever the race of the man, social deprivation contradicts masculinity. In their viewing of *Die Hard*, these men's deprivation of masculinity did not show itself in hostility to women or in a desire to exert increased, compensatory power over them: there was no overt antagonism towards the hero's estranged wife, and they showed no desire to see him regain his control over her, for they switched off the tape before that was achieved. Their hostility was directed against the social order that was responsible for their deprivation. They understood their masculinity in terms of the social relations of patriarchy in general, not in its gendered relations in particular. The men appeared to experience their demasculinization more acutely in their social relations than in their gender relations, perhaps because they were deprived of relationships with women where gender power or the lack of it could be more directly experienced. In other circumstances, men who are disempowered in their general social relations may well seek oppressive compensatory power over women in their immediate gender relationships.

There was, however, some evidence of hostility towards women. At times some of the men blamed women for taking the jobs that should "rightfully" have been theirs. The combination of this blaming with a taste for pornography and for symbolic violence may serve in some men to legitimate symbolic or even actual violence against women. Power of this sort, whether symbolic or physical, is imperializing not localizing power, even though it is exerted by men who, in other social relations, are subordinated. Social formations which are subordinated along some axes of social difference can align themselves with the power-bloc along others: men subordinated by class or race, for example, can and do exert imperializing power along the axis of gender; subordinated whites can and do exert racist power. The power-bloc is not a social class but a strategic set of social interests.

Homelessness is strategic. The majority of the homeless are not personally inadequate. If the homeless population contains proportionately more of the mentally and physically dysfunctional than the population at large, this is because it is they who are the most vulnerable to systematic deprivation. The combination of this systematic deprivation with government refusal to accept responsibility caused a gap that only charity could fill. Which it did: in 1989 HUD reported with satisfaction that the effort to help the homeless was "characterized by volunteerism." Such rhetoric, like the policy it serves, makes meanings of homelessness that work against the interests of the homeless themselves and *in the* interests of the advantaged, whether hawks or doves. For volunteerism, semiotically, works to disguise the structural dimension of homelessness by recasting it as a problem for those individuals concerned. The type of charity that works only to ameliorate the immediate problems of homeless people, valuable though such efforts are, is finally complicit with the policy which has produced the condition. In saying this, I intend a sharp distinction between the ethics and politics of the volunteers and donors (which are often benign) and those of the system itself (which are not). This distinction does not indicate a difference of power, for efficient power is always both benign and repressive, but rather different positions within the power system. The politicians and the donors and recipients of charity are all cogs (although of different sizes) in the same social machine.

These homeless men are some of the flesh and blood meanings of a policy that minimizes the role of the state in social life and maximizes those of capital and the market. One of the most important functions of the state in capitalism is to preserve the institutions and individual rights of a civil society independently of party political interests on the one hand or of the unfettered market economy on the other. In that form of conservatism characterized by Reaganomics, however, food and shelter are not included in the category of "civil rights," but of "charity." The social relations, and therefore the identities, of the homeless that this categorization produces are not ones appropriate to citizens whose rights and welfare are the concern of their government, but those of social castoffs waiting for one of Bush's "thousand points of light" to wink on them.

When homelessness is semiotically deviant but economically structural, the social conflict between the privileged (the "normal") and the homeless (the "deviant") becomes explicit. These social conflicts can be traced at all levels, from the most micro (the homeless men's pleasures in *Die Hard*) to the macro level of national policy.

Riot police swept the homeless from Tompkins Square Park in Manhattan because of increasing social conflict with local residents. Local merchants organized themselves to address the problem. As their president said, "All of us are liberal people.... We want to do something to re-establish a community presence in the park—not to kick the homeless out—to try to regulate it. I'm a victim of this. What happens to all the government programs? It all filters down to the community—all of us little people who are now forced to contribute our income, our time, our energy and money to finally do something. I guess that's what Reagan wanted."[14] While deploring some of the economic effects of the policy (it made local merchants spend their time and money), she shared its way of knowing by using the word "community" to exclude the homeless. She was not alone in this. On CBS News (5 November 1987) the words "communities" and "we" worked to construct a national "us" and to station the homeless as "them," the "not us:"

> ANCHOR   We pass them every day. It is estimated that there may be as many as three million of them on the main streets and side streets of communities across the country. We call them the homeless. They call the streets their home.[15]

The same discursive "othering" occurred on ABC News the following day: "There was even a momentary snow shower, which makes *people* notice the *homeless*" (emphases added).[16] The providers of the Midwestern shelter, the Manhattan merchant and the TV news anchors, all members of similar social formations, all put into circulation similar "outcast" or "cast off" meanings of homelessness. These circulators of meaning formed a power-bloc alliance with the police (and presumably city politicians) to make their semiotic power material and to cast out of public places the bodies of those who had been outcast by public discourse. In resistance the Tompkins Park homeless organized themselves into the Tent City Posse both to defend their locale and to politicize their condition by recasting it away from the charitable provision of shelter into the structural condition of poverty.

In People's Park, Berkeley, the University of California ordered similar police action to clear out the homeless and evicted People's Cafe, a soup kitchen run by the *Catholic Worker*. It is ironically significant that People's Park and Tompkins Square, both centers of love-ins and peace rallies in the sixties, should be centers of social conflict in the eighties.

Charity and volunteerism control the homeless by helping them; so too, in a different way, does social welfare. All work to produce a dependency mentality by which the homeless consent to the station that the dominant social order wishes them to occupy. Many of the homeless refuse to sign up for welfare because of the degrading dependency mentality induced by long welfare lines and condescending officers: so for them severe material deprivation is a price worth paying to keep the last vestiges of control over their own consciousness. And in many cities the homeless are fighting back. They have formed activist groups to challenge the submission to control inherent in this dependency mentality. The homeless are struggling to gain some control over both their consciousness of their social relations and the larger structuring conditions. As a member of the National Union for the Homeless said, "[The homeless] don't want shelters, they want houses, they don't want welfare, they want jobs. That's a profound threat to people who say they want to enable, but *really want to control*." Another member of the union comments "We've got a war here, you've got the poor on one side and the rich and the movers and shakers on the other.

The shelter providers are in the middle ... they grab crumbs from the powerful *to keep us from really doing battle with the system*" (emphases mine).[17]

A Minneapolis homeless activist group called "Up and Out of Poverty" (UOP) engendered local criticism for its insistence that homelessness is a political problem in which the homeless themselves must have a voice. And much of the criticism came from the traditional service providers—the charitable organizations and welfare agencies through which control is applied. Typical is an organizer of one of them, "Community Campaign for Housing Now," who criticized UOP "for victimizing vulnerable people by encouraging them to break the law in housing squats and thus making them subject to arrest."[18] The word "vulnerable" applied to the homeless is part of the same knowledge system as volunteerism, and using it is exercising the power of that system to produce for the homeless that identity of dependency by which volunteerism and Reaganomics wish them both to be known and to know themselves.

Language is a crucial site of struggle, for of all our circulation systems it is the one with the widest terrain of operation. It works extensively across the globe and across the nation to spread its own preferred ways of thinking, and intensively to carry the same cultural work into the innermost areas of consciousness. A language is a historical product and has inscribed within it the knowledges that serve the interests of the social formations who have dominated that history. Though it is a resource available to all members of a society, it is neither neutral, nor equally available.

Because the church-goers who provide the shelter for Bill and the other homeless men have interests that are readily allied with those of the power-bloc, our language provides more words and more readily available ones to describe them as they think of themselves than it does for those who wish to see them otherwise. So when Bill comments on the back-alley entrance to the shelter, "We wouldn't want to offend the decent people who come to worship here," the most readily available word, "decent," is one from their discourse, not his. But his use of it is his and not theirs. By extricating it (partially) from their discourse he is able to speak it with his accent—one of sarcasm—and thus "turn" the word against the social class whose interests it ostensibly promotes. The word does carry their meanings into his consciousness—he knows only too well the social relations it promotes—but it does not do so totally. He wrestles some of its meaning out of their control and into his. The structure of the language may prefer certain meanings and evaluations of "decent people," but Bill's practice in using it can contest them. Structure stations, practice localizes.

Language is always multiaccentual.[19] That is, it always has the potential to be spoken with different accents that inflect its meanings towards the interests of different social formations. The imperializing use of language represses this multiaccentual potential and attempts to establish the singular accent of the power-bloc as the only, the natural, the correct one. The language of imperializing power is uniaccentual. Localizing power, on the other hand, exploits the multiaccentuality. By speaking their word "decent" in his accent Bill puts social difference into practice. The word can never be purely his, it always carries their meanings: but that is what makes Bill's practice in using it so satisfying for him and significant for us. Both "accents" are contained within it, and so, therefore, is the social gap between their different places of origin. Exploiting the word's multi-accentuality is a bottom-up tactic, repressing it is a top-down one. When an anonymous homeless man, allowed a sound bite on CBS News, said "I am not mentally ill. I happen to be what you would call (pause) economically unstable"[20] he was exploiting multiaccentuality to "turn" *their* view of him into *his* view of them. The multiaccentuality of language enables the subordinate to engage in the social struggle linguistically.

The red which covers the screen at the death of Tagaki in *Die Hard* carries the power-bloc meanings of danger and horror, but the homeless men "turned" it to mean triumph. Their cheers were simultaneously a raucous assertion of their discourse and a rejection of that of the dominant other. Discourse may carry the meanings of the power-bloc, but it also exposes them to challenge. As Foucault points out, the relationship between discourse and power is always contradictory: while discourse applies power it also makes it visible. The effectiveness of power, Foucault argues, depends largely on its ability to mask its operations, so visibility is always a potential weakening which the agency of the subordinate may choose to exploit.[21]

The agency of the power-bloc has inscribed its interests in the systems and structures of our social order—in this case the language system. Popular agency, however, works through practice. It is a weaker agency because its terrain is confined largely to that of practice, whereas that of the power-bloc encompasses both structure and practice. Practice, there-fore, is how the people engage most ordinarily in the social struggle because it is where their localizing power is most effective.

If the interests of the power-bloc are best promoted through control of *structures* at the macro level, and those of the formations of the people through controlling *practice* at the micro level, then the relationship between structure and practice becomes a microcosm of social relations in the domain of theory and analysis. Practices which are structurally held in station are formative of complicit social relations; but those which evade or resist this stationing are more confrontational. In general, then, structures are where the strategies of imperializing power are most effectively operationalized, whereas practices are the tactics by which localizing powers establish and defend their locales against them.

NOTES

1. For a fuller account of the ethnographic study from which this example is taken, see Robert Dawson, "Culture and Deprivation: Ethnography and Everyday Life," paper presented at the International Communication Association Conference, Dublin, 1990.
2. Russell Neuman, Marian Just and Ann Crigler, *Common Knowledge: News and the Construction of Political Meaning* (Chicago: University of Chicago Press, 1992).
3. In this book I follow the practice of capitalizing "Black" to identify it as a term of struggle in which much ground has been reclaimed, as in "Black Power," or "Black is Beautiful." The uncapitalized form refers to the denigratory use of the word. The word "white" has not been subject (yet) to a similar struggle and therefore remains uncapitalized. See Chapter 7, note 3.
4. The absence of agreement over the "best" terms to refer to the different "worlds" leads me to use the numerical system, but to draw attention to its use in "first" world discourse by inverted commas. I admit to falling for the convenience of homogenizing the "third" world by using a single concept.
5. Most of Michel Foucault's work deals with power, discourse, and knowledge, but the works upon which I have drawn most directly are *Discipline and Punish* (London: Allen Lane, 1979), *The History of Sexuality Part I* (Harmondsworth: Penguin, 1978), and the various essays and interviews in *Power/Knowledge* (New York: Pantheon, 1972). Gramsci's theory of hegemony lies in notes scattered throughout *The Prison Notebooks*, parts of which have been published in English by Geoffrey Nowell-Smith and Quintin Hoare (eds), *Selections from the Prison Notebooks* (New York: International Publications, 1971); Antonio Gramsci, *Political Writings, 1910–1920*, and *1921–1926* (two volumes) (New York: International Publications, 1977 and 1978); and David Forgacs and Geoffrey Nowell-Smith (eds), *Selections from Cultural Writings* (Cambridge: Harvard University Press, 1985). Raymond Williams in *Marxism and Literature* and Stuart Hall in "Gramsci's Relevance for the Study of Race and Ethnicity," *Journal of Communication Inquiry*, 1986, vol. 10, no. 2, pp. 5–27, both give useful summaries/developments of this theory. In particular, Hall and his colleagues at the Birmingham Centre for Contemporary Cultural Studies significantly developed Gramsci's notion of conjunctural struggles by combining his work with that of Valentin Vološinov's *Marxism and the Philosophy of Language* (New York: Seminar Press, 1973). The combination of hegemonic struggles with the struggle for meaning has proved most fruitful in the development of cultural studies. Mikhail Bakhtin's theory of the carnivalesque in *Rabelais and His World* (Cambridge, MA: MIT Press, 1968) develops a theory of indiscipline and disruption which complements the work of Gramsci and counterpoints that of Foucault.
6. Stuart Hall, "Notes on Deconstructing 'The Popular'"in R. Samuel (ed.) *People's History and Socialist Theory* (London: Routledge and Kegan Paul, 1981), pp. 227–40.
7. Stuart Hall, "Gramsci's Relevance for the Study of Race and Ethnicity," p. 16.
8. Here I follow de Certeau's distinction between strategy and tactics. Strategies are the plans by which the powerful deploy their forces over place and time. Tactics are the means by which the weak oppose, harass and worry strategically deployed forces. Strategies are used by colonizing armies, tactics by colonized guerrillas. Michel de Certeau, *The Practice of Everyday Life* (Berkeley: The University of California Press, 1984).

9. Bourdieu's concept of the *habitus* and Giddens's of *locale* have informed this theorization of *station* and *locale*. *Station*, *locale* (in my use) and *habitus* all collapse the distinction between interior consciousness and exterior social forces; the habitus includes simultaneously a position in the social order or a social "habitat"; the ways of living appropriate to that position, or the practices of inhabiting that habitat; and the habits of taste, thought and behavior, the habituated dispositions that make up the consciousness of that habitat. *Habitus*, *station* and *locale* also share an emphasis on social differences, each of them differs according to the socio-historical conditions of its production. *Locale* (Giddens's use) is the physical place where people practice their agency. *Station* and *locale* (my use) combine Bourdieu with Giddens by forming single concepts out of consciousness, position in the social space and physical place. They extend their sources by being set in relations of opposition and struggle to each other. Pierre Bourdieu's theory of the habitus is developed in *Notes toward a Theory of Practice* (Cambridge: Cambridge University Press, 1977) and *Distinction* (Cambridge: Harvard University Press, 1984). Anthony Giddens's theory will be found in *The Construction of Society* (Cambridge: Polity Press, 1984).

10. *The Pacific News Service*, 19 April 1990.

11. Raymond Williams, *Culture and Society* and "Culture is Ordinary" in R. Williams, *Resources of Hope* (London: Verso, 1989). In his review of *Culture and Society*, Edward Thompson suggested that the definition be modified to "a whole way of struggle"—see Tony Pinkney, "Editor's Introduction: Modernism and Cultural Theory" in Raymond Williams, *The Politics of Modernism* (London: Verso, 1989).

12. For further discussions of agency see particularly, Anthony Giddens, *Central Problems in Social Theory* (London: Macmillan, 1979), Margerie Archer, *Culture and Agency: The Place of Culture in Social Theory* (Cambridge: Cambridge University Press, 1988), and Ziegfried Bauman, *Culture as Praxis* (London: Routledge and Kegan Paul, 1973).

13. Peter Marin, "The Prejudice Against Men," The Nation, 8 July 1991, pp. 46–51.

14. *Pacific News Service*, 10 April 1990.

15. CBS News, 5 November 1987, cited in Richard Campbell and James Reeves, "Covering the Homeless, the Joyce Brown Story," *Critical Studies in Mass Communication*, 1989, vol. 6, pp. 21–42.

16. ABC News, 6 November 1987, cited in Campbell and Reeves.

17. Minneapolis *City Pages*, 1 August 1990, p. 12.

18. *City Pages*, 1990.

19. "Multiaccentuality" and "uniaccentuality" are concepts developed by Vološinov in *Marxism and the Philosophy of Language*.

20. Campbell and Reeves.

21. Foucault, *History of Sexuality*.

2

U.S. CULTURES,

EUROPEAN THEORIES

There is an oddity in US intellectual life that seems to discourage it from producing its own social or cultural theories and that encourages it to turn to Europe to fill the gap. Not only does the US like to see itself through the eyes of European travellers, from de Tocqueville to Umberto Eco and Baudrillard, but it uses European theories in the same way. The difference between the two is that the travellers did at least come to the US, if only for a short time, whereas the theories were produced and developed in European conditions that, in certain respects, differed significantly from those of the US. Not all of them have crossed the Atlantic with equal success: in particular those which emphasized structure and determinism have not settled fruitfully in their new homeland, though they did flourish briefly.

The problem that these theories were designed to address in Europe was the remarkable health of both capitalism and patriarchy. As the twentieth century passed steadily by, the revolution that Marx saw as inherent in capitalism not only failed to spread through Europe but, with the growth of fascism in the 1930s and 40s and the material prosperity and complacency of the 1950s, seemed to be receding rather than advancing; so some Marxists developed the concept of ideology to explain why, in the industrial democracies of the West, people kept voting to continue the system that exploited them; others turned to commodity theory to explain why voting didn't matter anyway, and feminists turned to psychoanalysis to offer similar explanations of why so many women appeared to consent to patriarchy. These projects produced theories of subjectivity that explained the problem through people's lack of control over what went on in their heads: their (sub)consciousness became the key site for the reproduction of domination. Such explanations are relevant to the argument of this book because they point to the role of culture in the effort to control people's consciousness. They were extremely important around the third quartile of the twentieth century, but I want to suggest both that their historical moment has passed and that their development in Europe meant that, despite their general pertinence to the analysis of US society (both Europe and the USA are, after all, run by white, patriarchal and capitalist social systems; both are members of the self-called "first world"; and both try to maintain as much military, political and economic cooperation as possible), they were not well suited to explaining the conditions by which the US differed from Europe.

For there are crucial historical differences between the ways in which capitalism developed in the two continents, particularly in the realms of class and race. The new industrial working class in Europe grew out of a socially and geographically displaced peasant class which was already politicized, however incompletely, by the social relations of agrarian capitalism and/or feudalism. European histories are deeply inscribed with the class struggles of peasants against landowners in a way that US history is not. The US proletariat developed largely from immigrants and from slavery and this difference in history has produced a quite different set of class relations. Particularly, the US history of slavery brought a very different racial component into the proletariat. With some exceptions, most of which bear the influence of Gramsci, European Marxism has tended to homogenize the proletariat and to ground political action upon a shared class consciousness. The greater diversity of the historical origins of the US workers, together with the country's far greater geographical size, has meant that the formation of a proletarian class consciousness or even a coherent sense of class interests has proved much more difficult in the US than in Europe. Mike Davis tells a similar story in much greater detail.[1] He shows how divisive were the intraclass conflicts between US-born and immigrant workers, and how these resulted in immigrants forming their own communities in which ethnicity not only counted more than class relations but contradicted them. Intertwined with ethnicity was religion. Many of the immigrant workers, particularly the Irish, were Catholics who brought their form of religion into a nation founded on militant Protestantism. The US Catholic Church that resulted produced a blue-collar clergy that, as Davis points out, served to acculturate workers into a liberal capitalism while carving out its own sphere of power within society in general and the labor movement in particular. These inter-sections between class, ethnicity and religion produced in the US a more socially diverse, and sectionalized, proletariat than its European counter-part. The comparative political ineffectiveness of the US labor movement may be traced back, among other origins, to this greater diversity and its consequential problems in achieving a politically functional class consciousness.

This lack of a working-class consciousness in US society is characterized by a reluctance to identify the class at all, which, to European ears, is strange indeed. Indeed, my undergraduate students often find it difficult to apply the term "working class" to their own social experience, but when I translate it into "blue collar" the difficulty evaporates. The "working class" is set into quite different relationships with the "middle class" when their identities and differences are expressed by the colors of their collars. Collars can be changed according to the exigencies of their context: a person may identify him or herself as a blue-collar worker in one set of social relations and as middle class in another. The class relations signified by collar color appear less deeply structured, less determining and less confrontational than ones identified by labels of class. One might also add that the color spectrum allows for more positions than a binary-structured class system. So a "pink" collar can gender "white," and one might imagine a green collar to distinguish rural from factory workers, or Oxford, buttoned down or even turtleneck collars to identify fractions of the middle classes. But, laying such speculations aside, we still note that the flexibility of social identification by collar color rather than class is a significant difference between the two sides of the Atlantic. In the US, blue- and white-collar workers both tend to identify themselves as middle class. This may be because the "third" world has become America's working class, or it may be due to the existence of huge underclasses of the unemployed, the partially employed, the homeless, the criminal, the sick, from whom the employed blue-collar workers wish to distinguish themselves. In general, this underclass is less prominent in European societies, whose welfare systems have kept it smaller and less visible: class relations differ significantly when there is a class "under" the working class. One consequence of this is that there is much less self-identification with the working class in the US than there is in Europe. This was typified for me early in my life here: I was watching the TV news of reactions to a budget decision. One of those interviewed was a white man whose job was pressing panels for refrigerators in a factory. He prefaced his reaction with "Well, for ordinary middle-class people like us ..." His counterpart in Europe would almost certainly have identified himself as working class.

Another reason for this continental difference in class identification involves race. The US underclasses are disproportionately non-white. The alliance of blue and white collars into the middle classes not only differentiates the gainfully employed from the underclasses, but also, even if less explicitly, European Americans from Latinos, African and Native

Americans. Social deprivation has always been experienced in the US through race as well as class relations in a way that has not been the case in Europe (though recent immigration patterns may be moving the European situation closer to that of the US). But though class and race are both axes of deprivation, the relations between them have been more often antagonistic than friendly. By the end of the last century, the labor movement in the north was gearing up to defend itself against a feared flooding of the labor market by southern Blacks. In the south, the Farmers Alliance did manage to forge links between Black and white tenants, but, according to Davis, the defeat of the New Orleans General Strike in 1892 wrecked interracial unity among workers and produced "a stunted, Jim Crow white unionism on the one hand, and a pariah Black subproletariat on the other."[2] Davis continues his account of the regrettable history of the labor and liberal movements' failures to form effective alliance with African Americans into the rejection of Richard Hatcher and Jesse Jackson by the Democratic Party in the 1980s.

The relationship between race and class in the US may be a sorry story, but it is a specifically American one. In Europe the relations are quite different, for there the roots lie in colonialization: in the US they lie in slavery for African Americans, in conquest to the point of near genocide for Native Americans, and in economic colonialism for most Latinos. Slavery, genocide and colonialism are all products of white imperialization: historically they have always been inextricably interdependent and have shared the same motive, but still they produced historically different structures of race relations. Being colonized is not the same as being enslaved or exterminated, even though all are equally important effects of Western capitalism's desire to control the resources of the world (including its peoples). Europe has no experience of slavery in the way that the US does, and in particular has no historical event as important as the American Civil War whose origin lies, in part, at least, in race relations. The proletariat in early European capitalism was racially homogeneous, and so European Marxist analysis had no need to address race relations in the structure of class relations in a way that any analysis of US capitalism must.

A similar problem arises in the domain of gender. The theories of Freud and Lacan, particularly when inflected by Althusserian Marxism, have served white feminism in the US as well as in Europe, which is well enough. But the African American family is quite different from the European family: in particular, historical and social racism has worked to disempower the Black male (see Chapter 11) and separate him from the family, thus requiring the Black woman to play a stronger and different family role than that of her white counterpart. The family structure produced by slavery and developed under racist social conditions is quite different from that experienced and analyzed by Freud: in particular, the Oedipus complex loses its explanatory power in the different gender–generation relations of the African American family. Equally the Lacanian account of the unconscious being structured like a language assumes that language is both monoglossic and the site for the reproduction of dominance. But African Americans have a powerful oral language which is set against the dominant white one, and which was developed expressly to resist domination and maintain racial difference. African Americans are necessarily bilingual and there are no grounds to assume that the socially dominant language is the one that structures their subconsciousness. Indeed, we must question whether a consciousness (un- or otherwise) that is worked upon by arguing and contradictory languages can be explained by a monolinguistic theory.

But white–Black race relations are not the only ones by which the US differs from Europe: Oedipus would be as much a foreigner in Native American social conditions as in African American, and would feel similarly out of place in Asian American families structured by the Confucian tradition or in the greatly extended Latino ones.

Similarly, gender roles within the family are quite different when the family is fighting for its existence under slavery. The normalization of the male slave owner's abuse of the Black woman has effects that are specifically African American. Equally, racially weakened Black masculinity has developed a form of gender oppression that is not simply an extension of its European counterpart, and although white women may use Black women's blues as a way of coping with masculine use and abuse, the oppression with which they have to cope is quite different. In particular, they do not have to deal with the problem that a woman resisting this gender oppression may appear, even to herself let alone the man, to be siding with the racial oppressor whose power has shaped the masculinity that constitutes her problem.

But if one recently influential school of European social and cultural theories is ill-equipped to handle the diversity and particularity of US conditions, American liberal pluralist theories are equally ill-equipped to understand this diversity within relations of social contestation and struggle. Traditionally, such pluralist accounts of social differences situate them within an overall harmony which is maintained by a series of checks and balances that are the socio-cultural equivalents of the "natural" regulators of a free market economy. Such pluralism organizing itself into a consensus is a characteristically American social theory. Again, the histories of the two continents can provide clues toward explaining this difference.

White America has developed as a result of immigration from many different nations and ethnicities. The key problem facing social theorists, immigrants and "old" Americans alike was building a national consensus out of such diversity. So much of the American consciousness has been concerned with the construction of consensus that it is hardly surprising that US cultural theorists in the 1960s and 70s developed pluralist models of difference within consensus. They tended to turn for their theoretical underpinnings to cultural anthropologists such as Victor Turner and to treat the US as a vast tribe whose national media and national sports acted as community-building rituals.[3] Similarly, the rich traditions of pragmatism and phenomenology set the diversity and particularity that they investigated within an overall consensus. The apparent progress towards equalizing racial and gender differences which was achieved in the late 1960s and 1970s gave such consensus theories a degree of credibility.

But Reaganism in the 1980s rewrote the script. Reaganomics widened the gaps between the rich and the poor, between whites and other races, between men and women. Reaganism made it almost impossible to believe that the US was a society built on consensus because it revealed the conflicts of interest that need to be repressed both socially and in consciousness if a consensus is to be agreed to by all. So American social and cultural theorists turned to European models for guidance. Europe has always known that its societies have been built on conflicting social interests, and that culture has always been part of the social struggle. For European humanists and elitists alike culture could defend high human values against either the proletariat or rampant materialism. For European Marxists culture was both where ideology and/or hegemony was secured and where it could be contested. Cultural struggle is a European concept whose applicability to America was highlighted by Reaganism.

These migrating theories of conflicting social interests had to settle upon land already prepared by pluralism, phenomenology and pragmatism, and in this soil those which stressed diversity and particularity flourished, whereas those emphasizing homogeneity did not. One that withered was the Marxism that homogenized the subordinate and reduced social struggle to class struggle. Its tendency to overlook what it was that the people brought to social order and the variety of struggles in which they engaged in order to make these contributions made it ill-suited to its new homestead.

One theoretical school which has flourished particularly well was the Gramscian. Gramsci's theory of hegemony has features which suit it to US conditions better than those of other European Marxists. Though class is still central in his thinking, he does inflect it regionally, and in terms of the difference between urban and rural: the industrialized north of Italy exerted its hegemony over the rural, peasant south along more axes than that of class alone. Stuart Hall identifies the key ones as "the complex relations between city and countryside, peasantry and proletariat, clientism and modernism, feudalized and industrialized social structures."[4] The flexibility of such a multiaxial model suits it particularly well for analyzing the relations between the "first" and "third" worlds, either in their contemporary economic and political forms or their recent historical ones of colonialism and conquest. Hegemony theory was also developed to account for international inequality through colonialism and conquest. Hegemony of course grants economic difference a central role in its analysis, but it does not center it as totally as does more traditional Marxist thinking and thus can more readily accommodate other axes of subordination. Finally, and most importantly, Gramsci's notions of resistance and consent are historically and socially situated: hegemony, therefore, unlike ideology, must itself take different forms according to the different conditions of its exertion. Hegemony depends on the ability of the power-bloc to win the consent of the various formations of the subordinate to the system that subordinates them. Because the material and political conditions of subordination constantly and inescapably remind the subordinate of the inequalities between them and the power-bloc, such consent is always fragile and precarious, is always subject to contestation and consequently has to be constantly won and rewon. Consent has to be achieved on multiple issues between multiple social formations, and thus, as a theoretical concept, is better suited to cope with social diversity than is the more homogenized and homogenizing concept of consensus.[5]

The consent of hegemony is thus significantly different from the consensus of liberal pluralism. Consent is what both parties believe to be the best that can be achieved in the prevailing conditions. It satisfies neither, it induces neither to give up the struggle. To achieve a point of consent, each party has to yield something: each party attempts to promote its own interests as far as possible and yield to those of the other as little as possible. Hegemony theory, then, requires a notion of popular agency, it requires an account of contestatory diversity, and it requires the consideration of social and historical differences.

Despite hegemony theory's greater ability to cope with social diversity and cultural struggle, its limits are exposed in the analysis of US Black–white relations. Gramsci had no need to theorize a social order such as slavery in which consent neither existed nor mattered, but stressed rather that hegemony always worked through a combination of consent (or leadership) and coercion (or domination). The two modes of operation will be combined differently in different circumstances, but in general coercion is the strategy of last resort to be called upon only when leadership has failed to win consent. The more normal use of coercion is persuasive, for when both parties know that the dominant have a coercive power that the subordinate lack they will "agree" to a point of consent that is closer to the dominant interests than would otherwise be the case. In slavery, however, coercion is neither a back-up strategy nor a hidden persuader but is open, naked and the only means of domination required. The relations between European and African Americans are deeply inscribed with a history of coercion rather than consent, one result of which is the readiness of the contemporary power-bloc to use coercive force in race relations. Consequently, there are many social formations of African Americans who do not consent in any way at all to the dominant social order—some ignore its laws, some opt out of its educational system and others are attempting to build separate social systems within it (see Chapters 11 to 13).

The other group of migrant theories which have crossed the Atlantic as successfully as Gramsci's is one whose members extend their analytic object from the homogeneity of the power-bloc to the diversity and agency of the people. This extension often involves emphasizing practice over structure, agency over subjectivity, speech over language, and the body over (sub)consciousness. Briefly Bourdieu and de Certeau have developed accounts of practice;[6] Bourdieu has also shown us how to draw a socio-cultural map that takes account of diversity (if not of struggle);[7] Foucault has divorced social power from class, and produced an account of power, discourse and discipline which stresses the diversity of the points of application over any deep structure; Bakhtin has opened up ways of understanding bottom-up indiscipline, vulgar vitality and bad taste;[8] and de Certeau, Bourdieu and Bakhtin all reveal a popular creativity that is at least as imaginative as that of officially recognized art. And finally, all four of these theorists emphasize the body as a key cultural site; and because our bodies are the one place where we each differ indisputably from the other, theories that emphasize bodies can more readily account for social difference than ones which emphasize subjectivity and (sub)consciousness. Bakhtin, de Certeau and Bourdieu in their different ways show that the people are social agents who contribute significantly to the social order, and Foucault's theory requires a popular resistance to top-down power even if his analysis never shows how it might work. These theorists, like Gramsci, all grant subordinate formations the ability to promote their interests in struggles against the power-bloc. For all of them diversity is produced by the subordinate and works in subordinate interests; homogeneity, on the other hand, is a product of the system of domination and works to secure the interests of the power-bloc.

When poststructuralism is inflected with theories such as these it is well suited to analyze the diversity, fluidity and contradictions of late capitalist societies. The articulation of poststructuralism with theories of popular agency and social struggle can offer convincing accounts of the failures of top-down power to homogenize its terrain and secure its interests in a relatively singular fashion. But, in other articulations, poststructuralism (and postmodernism) can all too easily be made to imply that the diversity and fluidity it theorizes offer their potential freely and equally to all. Such inflections recuperate it toward a new liberal pluralist consensus that differs from the old only in that the agreement is to be different.

In the contemporary US diversity is produced by struggle, not permitted by consensus. The struggles are paying off and diversity is gaining ground despite the efforts of the power-bloc to contain it. The gain can be both measured statistically and perceived in people's sense of their own social identities. The statistics for race are the most readily available, so that is where I focus my argument, but racial diversity should serve as a figure for all forms—diversity of gender and sexual preference, of age identities, of regionality, of religions, to mention only some of the more obvious ones.

Demographers calculate that early in the twenty-first century European Americans will cease to form the majority of the population: the US will then be a society with no racial majority, but will consist of three main groups, of roughly equal numbers, of European Americans, African Americans and Latinos, together with a mixed group of Asian, Native Americans and others which will not lag far behind. Currently European Americans comprise about 80 per cent of the population, so the change, from the European point of view, will be dramatic. It is also inevitable: the differences in the median ages of these groups today will of themselves produce it. European Americans are significantly older than other groups (they should, perhaps, be called "grey" rather than "white") or, to put it the other way, Latinos, African and other Americans have youth on their side.[9] Current patterns in birthrates and immigration are accelerating the trend. During the 1990s the racial composition of the US will be characterized by a declining European majority faced with rapidly growing "minorities" whose increase in numbers will be accompanied by demands for an increase in control. In LA, this part of our future is already here. European Americans are no longer the majority of its citizens,[10] and, before the year 2000 the same will be true of California as a whole. It is already the case that white children are no longer the majority in the California school system. But the numerical change will be faster by far than any change in the internal balance of power. The gap opened up by a rapid change in numbers and a slow change in the regime of power will produce most of the urgent and anxious problems in our immediate future.

The social order of the US that emerges in the twenty-first century will differ significantly from that of the twentieth: it will *feel* different to live in this society; people will have a different consciousness of what it means to "be American." Changes in the social order around us always involve changes inside us. What goes on in our society and what goes on inside our heads are inextricably tangled up together. Which is why culture matters so much.

The change in the social order, to put it succinctly, will be one from a society organized around a general consensus to one organized around varied points of consent. The US social order of the twentieth century was one organized around a broadly shared consensus of values and priorities that stretched across the domains of politics, economics, religion, and culture. It had been legitimated by a long and powerful history in which Greco-Roman and Judao-Christian influences combined to produce first Europe and then the US as major world powers. The consensus was therefore sure of its values, it knew that they were the only ones which could produce a powerful and fair modern society. Any problems that might result, then, tended to be ones of accommodation, not of the values themselves.

The main exceptions to this consensus lay, not surprisingly, among those who did not agree either to their own arrival or to that of the Europeans: histories of slavery and dispossession make consensus much harder to achieve than ones of voluntary immigration. These non-consensual histories are gaining ground in contemporary conditions where the growing diversity of both the US and the world's societies means that a central set of values more or less agreed to by all can no longer be an effective way of achieving social cohesion. A social order held together by a homogenized consensus organized around the values and interests of dominant formations is going to have to give way to one organized around multiple points of consent in which social differences are respected and power differences reduced. These points of consent will be negotiated and achieved locally where the interests and identities of different social groups impinge upon each other. Such a social order will appear to be less stable— the points of consent will be in constant process, for as consent is achieved at one point, another point of contestation will arise. The consent that will have to be won so constantly will only be achievable if the power-bloc learns to tolerate, respect and even encourage social differences that are produced and controlled from below. There is always a degree of conflict between the social identities and social relations that those within a particular social group wish to adopt or wish to be known by, and those which other groups, particularly more powerful ones, wish to impose upon them. Under conditions of tolerance, these differences can reach points of consent, that both parties agree are livable with for the present at least.

Under conditions of intolerance, however, these differences do not produce points of consent, but points of antagonism. In these circumstances, diversity develops into separatism, and relations of negotiated consent become replaced by ones of suspicion, hostility and conflict.

A society of consent will differ from one of consensus: it will be more fluid: the points of consent will not be fixed, but will change as the pattern of historical forces changes. Similarly, the negotiations for consent will not always be between fixed social categories (such as classes, genders or races), but more often between alliances of social interests formed around the issue on the table. They will, therefore, be better understood as engagements between changing articulations of interest that constitute the power-bloc and the people rather than between stable categories such as class or race. And if negotiations fail, the antagonisms and conflict will also be between strategic and tactical alliances rather than stable social categories.

The new social order will produce a new regime of power, and the change will cause problems and anxieties for all, but not equally. The formations of the people will adapt more readily because they have more to gain, and because they are well used to living with the difficulties of adjustment to others. Those of the power-bloc, however, have generally been shielded from such experiences, and consequently will find the changes more troublesome. They also have more to lose, for to win consent they will have to yield ground.

Yielding ground and adjusting to the needs of others will require the power-bloc to develop the ability to listen. This will not come easily, for in general the US has encouraged speaking over listening, and rewarded those skilled in influencing others rather than in being influenced by them. These skills were appropriate to a period of consensus for they were of direct use in leading others to a goal that was not in question. But the constant negotiation of multiple points of consent requires a more imaginative and receptive understanding than can be achieved by talking and leading: it requires the ability to listen and follow, to learn from subordinate social formations what their social experience means to them. In such a society, all groups will, hopefully, develop the imagination that enables them to see themselves through the eyes of others. But the power-bloc is least likely to do so, because such an imagination does not appear immediately helpful in the exercise of power, and indeed, to the socially myopic, may appear actually to hinder it. Consequently, there are many men who do not understand how their masculine power appears to women; northeasterners who are not good at seeing themselves through southern eyes, and European Americans who do not know, and some who do not wish to know, how they look and sound to Native Americans or to African

Americans. The greater diversity and equality of social groups and the multiplicity of points of consent among them requires a form of understanding in which listening is as valued as speaking, in which the knowledge that we are being looked at is as fully developed as our ability to look.

An obstacle to this imagination has been theorized, though differently, by both Foucault and Freud. To put it simply, both argue that looking is an exercise of power, and to be looked at is therefore to become the object of power. For Foucault surveillance, or, as I call it in this book, "monitoring," is the application of social power, for Freud voyeurism was its sexual and individual equivalent. In both theories the power not to be seen is the crucial condition for the power to look.

The imagination to understand how *we* look to *others* has always been better developed in subordinate social formations than in dominant ones, because it has proved necessary to their tactics of survival. For the power-bloc, however, seeing itself through the eyes of the subordinate often appears to be unnecessary and even to weaken its resolve to advance its own interests. Consequently, women understand men and how they appear to men much more accurately than vice versa, slaves understood their owners better by far than the owners understood their slaves, and workers know how they appear to the bosses much more clearly than bosses know how they appear from below.

But while the power-bloc may think that it does not need this social imagination, a society of multiple points of consent does. A benevolent imperializing power may have been appropriate to, and effective in, a democracy structured around a top-down consensus. In it, those who had histories and politics that differed from those of the consensus needed to be persuaded to rewrite their histories and reform their politics in order to adjust them to the position of the dominant others within the consensus. Those already in this position, however, had less need for adjustment to the views of others. Consequently their social imaginations are stunted, for their sight over and knowledge of the social order they dominate is from a historically unchanged high spot that gives them a powerful but singular point of view. The stability of the consensus, the singularity of the view from within it, and the restricted imagination of the power-bloc whose interests are promoted by it are visibly failing to cope with the complexities of the contemporary US. But rather than trying to develop an imaginative understanding of these conditions, the power-bloc is mobilizing its forces to resist the changes that are under way.

An example which is particularly relevant to this book because it is one in which imagination and culture play leading roles is the so-called "Political Correctness" debate. This is a power struggle in the domain of the arts and humanities over the national imagination. On the one side monoculturalism is striving to maintain the European-based values of the consensus, and on the other multiculturalism is trying to develop an imagination capable of understanding not just the diversity of US society, but also the widely different ways that this society looks from the different positions within it.

Imperializing power, monoculturalism and a top-down consensus go together. Equally, localizing powers, multiculturalism and multiple points of social consent are allies. If socially subordinate formations are able to exercise their "weak" power to extend the social terrain that they control and if the power-bloc restrains its imperializing power to enable them to do so the change in the internal balance of power will be relatively peaceful. To achieve this, the socially subordinate must not only gain control over their own sense of identity, and their own history in which it is rooted, but they must also "know" that these identities and histories are understood and respected by others. They must be able to extend their influence over the imagination of others, particularly the dominant others, and thus co-produce the national imagination.

The debate between mono- and multiculturalism is so intense because so much is at stake—the conditions within which a fundamental change in the social order will occur. Far from diversifying their imagination, the power-bloc interests in the domains of cultural politics are moving in the opposite direction and are fitting themselves with blinders to maintain a centered view of the world and to keep its margins out of consideration. The power-bloc appears to be hanging on to the simple structure by which it could know the world in the good old days of the Cold War, for then it knew its enemy and it knew where it stood. The USA organized around a consensus typically uses an external threat to pull its diversified peoples together. For most of this century the USSR has filled this role admirably, both externally and internally: the Cold War was the standoff with the external enemy, and the Reds that McCarthy saw lurking under US beds were its internal equivalent. But all that has changed. With the collapse of the "second" world, the "third" has had to be cast in the role of the external enemy, the Drug War (and the Gulf War) has taken the place of the Cold War, and multiculturalism has displaced the "Red Menace" as the internal threat. Calling the result "the 'third' world war" may be going a tad too far, but the label does identify the direction of current power-bloc strategies.

But there are problems in casting the "third" world as a political devil. In particular, it is much more diverse and difficult to define than was the "second," and consequently the differences between the "first" and the "third" worlds cannot be reduced to a binary opposition as straightforward as that between capitalism and communism. Japan and Southeast

Asia threaten the USA's domination of capitalism itself, Saddam Hussein threatened control of energy, and Noriega may have been a mastermind of the Drug War, but Japan, Saddam Hussein and Noriega are very different political villains. Even more serious a problem facing the current power-bloc is that its "enemy within" is real rather than imaginary: whatever McCarthy thought he saw under the bed, the US could never have become a communist society. It *is*, however, a multicultural one.

Its multiculturalism is not yet reflected in its distribution of power, and when it is, the new balance of power will not be reached by the defeat of one set of power-bloc interests by another, but by a more fundamental change in the "regime of power" itself. The Foucauldian notion of a change in the regime of power indicates a poststructural historiography tracing how one regime of power succeeds another not through any grand narrative of history, as with either a Darwinian (capitalist) story of evolutionary improvement and the survival of the fittest or in a Marxian one of a more just social order succeeding a less just one through revolution (armed or peaceful). Instead it proposes that regimes of power change when changes in the social conditions mean that the old regime has lost its efficiency. It also proposes that one cannot predict the form or the direction of the change in advance.

A change in regime typically entails movement from the margins to the center, so that a form of power that was marginalized in the old regime becomes central in the new, and vice versa. In its literary form, often called deconstruction, poststructuralism insists that what goes on in the margins of a text is at least as significant as what goes on at its center, and its most powerful meanings have only been able to achieve their centrality by repressing others. The same is true socially. This book will consider a number of marginalized cultures and the social formations that produce them because some of them, or some of their values, are likely to move towards the center. And we cannot tell which will do so, and which will remain on the margins. I am not suggesting that the homeless will, as a popular bloc, take over power, but rather that some of their critical imagination may well become more central in the new regime. Equally, I am not suggesting that Elvis fans (see below, Chapters 6 and 9) will become a powerful social formation, but I do believe that the communal values that they keep alive will necessarily play a greater role in the new regime of power than they have in the passing one.

Foucault argues that the last major change in the regime of power was part of the change from pre-modern to modern Europe, so we may feel, as we move to a postmodern world (if that is what is happening), that the next is historically timely. The change analyzed by Foucault was from a power based upon spectacular deterrence to one based upon surveillance.

48

Pre-modern Europe set clear limits upon acceptable behavior and belief, and dealt harshly and spectacularly, usually by public torture and execution, with those who overstepped them. Such displays of physical power over the bodies of transgressors were designed to terrify the rest of the populace into remaining within the boundaries of acceptable behavior. But within these boundaries people were comparatively free from surveillance and discipline. Such a power system, by comparison with those of modern society, knew little and cared little about the day-to-day behavior of its subjects provided they did not overstep its limits: their own affairs were their own affairs. This external, coercive power, applied by the monarchy in its civil form and the Church in its religious, could be effective only over a comparatively small population leading comparatively limited lives. Each transgressive act had to be seen and dealt with individually, and if too many transgressions escaped notice, then the fear and the power were both diminished. Equally, each deterrent punishment needed to be publicly visible in order to deter, and only limited numbers could see any one spectacle. The ratio of police to citizens and punishers to victims needs to be high in such a regime.

Of course, such a generalized diagnosis is of central power. On the margins of spectacular deterrence both religious and civil power tried to develop some internalized self-surveillance through mechanisms such as those of morality, conscience and loyalty which prefigured the regime to come. Any regime of power contains on its margins elements which will become central in the regime that succeeds it. In the same way, the new does not extinguish the old, but marginalizes it. So today, calls to allow television to broadcast executions and calls for harsh sentences to "make an example of" wrongdoers are clear continuations of the power of spectacular deterrence into the present.

The historical shift to the modern regime was characterized by the increase in population and consequently in the complexity of social organizations. During the seventeenth and eighteenth centuries in Europe everything expanded—the accessible world and the wealth to be grabbed from it, the armies and navies needed to control it, cities and towns, workplaces and schools, hospitals, asylums and prisons—the Western world and its organizations all became larger, more complex and thus less efficiently controlled by a regime of spectacular deterrence. That economy of power became unbalanced and inefficient: too much of it resided in the monarchy and its agents (police, magistrates, torturers, executioners) and too little in the people. If they escaped capture they evaded power. In a regime of surveillance, however, power is exerted evenly and thus efficiently throughout the social order: it is not concentrated at points of breakdown, and the people participate in the power machine that disciplines them. Monitoring power is thoroughly diffused, and as such, is a quite different form of power from that appropriate to a regime of spectacular deterrence.

However, traces of this premodern power remain and can be activated by the power-bloc when a modern power of self-monitoring and self-discipline fails. Many Black social formations have refused to internalize the central power system, and are instead subjected to a modified form of spectacular deterrence. The modification is that the spectacular display of power upon the body is not meant to be visible to the whole social order, but only to that recalcitrant segment of it: the power of white police departments upon Black bodies works best when seen widely and clearly by Blacks while remaining unseen and unknown by whites.

But spectacular deterrence has always been a risky form of power, for it is far more likely than surveillance to provoke direct opposition. Foucault argues that a clear sign that the pre-modern economy of power was becoming unbalanced and inefficient occurred when public executions became occasions for popular uprisings rather than spectacles of power, and when popular sentiment was aligned with the victim and not the monarch. A contemporary parallel may well be the case of Rodney King in Los Angeles (see Chapter 12). This Black man was severely beaten by police after an alleged motoring offense, and in a subsequent trial the police officers were acquitted of using excessive force to subdue him. The verdict provoked Black uprisings across the nation similar to those which, at public executions, Foucault identified as symptoms of change in the regime of power.

All the signs suggest that we may well be in a period of historical change. If we are, the change is poststructural, not structural. Structural changes have been conceptualized as revolutions, whereby one social structure is replaced by another—feudalism by capitalism, capitalism by socialism. Poststructural change involves a change in the regime of power, one form of which involves decentering and recentering, or reconfiguring the relations between the margins and the center. The politics of such a change lie in the evaluation of what moves to the center from the margins, and what remains on them. The attempt to recenter a modified form of spectacular deterrence differs politically from the argument of this book. If we are moving to a social order organized around multiple sets of social interests then such a recentering will make the intersections between those interests ones of antagonism rather than consent.

Once again, LA shows us the future that lies ahead if we fail to devise a tolerant and multiple regime of power and revert to an updated version of a strong centralized one. In *City of Quartz: Excavating the Future in Los Angeles*, Mike Davis paints a vivid, detailed and terrifying picture of a city that is making no attempt to negotiate points of consent among its many social, particularly racial and ethnic, formations.[11] Instead, its infamous police force acts in paramilitary fashion to impose a naked white power that disdains any ideological dressing upon African and Latino Los Angelinos. The reverse side of this coin is that the affluent have barricaded themselves into fortified neighborhoods protected by both high-tech and low-tech security systems. High-tech electronics are supported by the low-tech labor force of a security industry which has tripled over the last decade, and which is paid near minimum wage by its employers, highly profitable multinational conglomerates. Residential neighborhoods whose lawns and sidewalks bristle with notices threatening death to intruders, whose streets are patrolled by inadequately licensed and poorly paid armed patrolmen and dogs, and whose inhabitants hire personal escorts for outside forays are concrete evidence that one of our possible futures is already here.

"Fortress LA" is the title Davis gives the chapter in which he describes the enclaves where the power-bloc defends its interests against a social antagonism it has itself created. The scenario that is played out spatially in the geography of LA is replayed more widely in the imagination of the nation. In the realms of culture and the school curriculum power-bloc interests are fending off threats from Black and Latino culture; they are trying to keep gay and lesbian visions out of their art galleries and off their stages; and they are patrolling the high school and university curricula with a vigilance that equals that of Beverly Hills. Imperializing power always needs stockades, but the ones of today are not the forts that a confident expanding power uses temporarily until the country has been subdued, for there is a fear in them, a defensiveness concerned to protect what they have (money, property, values) against an encroachment from the margins that are refusing to stay marginalized. Rather than being the products of an ongoing process of colonization, the stockades are symptoms of its decline.

"Fortress USA," to broaden Davis's phrase, is symptomatic of a consensus that is losing its demographic base but desperately clings to its power. This demographic change will slowly but inevitably erode the power structure upholding the old consensus. The power-bloc's particular turning of democracy into a system where money counts more than votes delays the erosion of its political power by persuading millions of people that voting is not worthwhile, but in the economic realm the pressures may be more immediate. A huge and growing market of poor individuals is always worth pursuing, but to capture segments of it, economic alliances within the power-bloc have to take its interests into account. Consequently in the late 1980s and early 1990s we have heard Black voices telling us

51

their view of our society through our cinemas, televisions and stereo systems, while they have been silenced in our schools, universities and the institutions of the public cultural sphere. The power-bloc gets anxious when its economic and politico-cultural interests conflict and, in its anxiety, raises its stockades even higher. The change in regime of power that is more likely to cope relatively peacefully with the social changes that are already under way is one in which imperializing power will diminish, and localizing powers will increase, or, to put it another way, weak powers will gain strength and strong power will weaken.

We may characterize such change as one between a homogeneous system of strong power and a more diverse system of weaker powers. In the former, there was a wide difference between the strong imperializing power at the center and weak, localizing powers around the margins. In the latter, some of the weak powers will strengthen and move inwards while the strong power will weaken and allow others access to its centrality. This model of social change is not a revolutionary one in which one political and economic system replaces another, but a reconfiguration of power relations. History gives us no evidence that democratic capitalism is vulnerable to revolutionary change, but there is ample evidence of the necessity for and, finally, the inevitability of, changes in its regime of power. The old relations between the center and the periphery will not survive into the next century: the question is how peaceful or how bloody the changes will be.

This reconfiguration of power will not dislodge capitalism from its global pre-eminence, but it may democratize it. Mulgan argues that something similar is taking place in multinational corporations, as they decenter their strong power systems and devolve more, but weaker, power to more subcenters.[12] He argues that this change in the corporate regime of power gives democratic values a chance to establish themselves more centrally within the system. And there are signs of similar changes within the US itself, changes which I believe we will have to make if we are to enter the twenty-first century in relative peace and calm.

NOTES

1. Mike Davis, *Prisoners of the American Dream* (London: Verso, 1986).
2. Ibid., p. 38. The citation by Davis is from David Bennetts, "Black and White Workers: New Orleans 1880–1900," University of Illinois (Champagne-Urbana) Ph.D. Thesis, 1972.
3. The work of Newcomb, Carey and Real often exemplifies this approach.
4. Stuart Hall, "Gramsci's Relevance for the Study of Race and Ethnicity," *Journal of Communication Inquiry*, 1980, vol. 20, no. 2, pp. 5–27 (esp. p. 9).

5. The emphasis upon struggle and resistance within hegemony theory is a particularly Anglo-Saxon one: Italian scholars tend to emphasize rather its power-bearing dimension. It has been suggested to me in conversation that the reason for this difference may lie in the fact that in Italy the Communist Party has held political office and occupied positions of social power, and has turned to Gramsci and hegemony theory for advice on how to exert that power.

6. Pierre Bourdieu, *Outline of a Theory of Practice*; Michel de Certeau, *The Practice of Everyday Life* (Berkeley: University of California Press, 1984).

7. Pierre Bourdieu, *Distinction, a Social Critique of the Judgement of Taste* (Cambridge, MA: Harvard University Press, 1984).

8. Mikhail Bakhtin, *Rabelais and his World* (Cambridge, MA: MIT Press, 1968).

9. In 1988 the median ages of the main racial ethnic groups were: European Americans 31.4 years, Hispanic Americans 24 years, African Americans 25.6 years, Asian Americans and other races 27 years. By 2010 demographers estimate the differences will have increased and the median ages will be (respectively) 41.4, 29.3, 31.4, 35.6 (*American Demographics*, October 1991, p. 29).

10. The 1990 Census gave the LA population as 40 per cent Latino, 37 per cent Anglo and 23 per cent Black and Asian. 49.9 per cent of its citizens spoke a language other than English at home. *Newsweek*, 18 May 1992, p,. 46.

11. Mike Davis, *City of Quartz: Excavating the Future in Los Angeles* (London and New York: Verso, 1990).

12. Geoff Mulgan, "New Times: The Power of the Weak," *Marxism Today*, December 1988, pp. 24–31; and "The Limits of Transparent Control: Soft power and the private corporate network," paper delivered at the Conference on Technologies and Societies, Grenoble, May 1989.

PART TWO

CONTROLLING BODIES

3

BODIES OF KNOWLEDGE

Because power is thoroughly diffused throughout the whole social order, and exists not as a totalizing system but in its points of application, its local and specific technologies, the changes in a regime of power must occur at all levels, and finally, must occur at the most micro level, that of the body. This section of the book is devoted to understanding the struggle over the body, the strategies by which imperializing power attempts to control it, and the tactics by which localizing powers seek to maintain, defend and sometimes even advance their own interests. The relations between top-down and bottom-up powers cannot be predicted in advance, nor can labels such as resistance, inversion or evasion encompass them all. They need to be analyzed in their own particularities, for we can understand the interplay of powers better through an accumulation of different instances than by a systemic macro-analysis of power itself.

Social agency, both of the power-bloc and of the people, is put to work on the body, for the body is the primary site of social experience. It is where social life is turned into lived experience. To understand the body we have to know who controls it as it moves through the spaces and times of our daily routines, who shapes its sensuous experiences, its sexualities, its pleasures in eating and exercise, who controls its performance at work, its behavior at home or school and also influences most how it is dressed and made to appear in its function of presenting us to others. The body is the core of our social experience.

The body is where nature and culture meet and so it is there that we negotiate the relations of difference and similarity between the two. The body is where we make sense of being social or cultured or of being natural, and the sense that we make of one defines and is defined by the sense that we make of the other. What is natural sexuality, for instance, can only be defined by its relation to moral (that is, socially controlled) sexuality and vice versa. A key word here is "control," for establishing the difference between nature and culture always involves a struggle for control; a natural body is always seen, in some way, as a body *out* of control. Because societies depend for their strength and survival upon the extensiveness of their control, they are crucially concerned to control nature by controlling the body.

The body is not only where nature meets culture, it is where the individual meets the social. Our body is the only domain of existence that is unique to each of us: it is the only domain in which we differ from every other member of our species and from every other member of our society. Bodily difference, then, becomes an extremely powerful metaphor for individuality: the control over which differences between bodies are counted as significant is crucial to the control over our sense of individuality and identity.

The relationship between the individual body and the social body, the body politic, is not metaphorical but material. Controlling the body is a first step in the control of social relations. The presence of bodies together, in the same time and space, is where social relationships are grounded; and social relationships are the lived, material experience of those more abstract, structural social relations. The relationships within a family are where the social relations of gender and age are turned into the practices of everyday life: the relationships between supervisor and workers embody the social relations of labor.

There is a continuum, then, stretching from consciousness through identities, bodies, relationships and relations that does not just extend into the social order but is constitutive of it. The body is pivotal in this, and the struggles between top-down and bottom-up forces to control the continuum all touch the body sooner or later; and no terrain can be won or held if it does not encompass that of the body.

DISCIPLINE

Discipline is the means by which people's consciousness and behavior are adapted to the requirements of power as it is applied in a specific social organization—the family, the school, the workplace, the sports club, the military, the hospital, the tour bus, the church. But, whatever the institution, the prime site of disciplinary power is the body. School graduates are not just knowledgeable and talented, they are disciplined. Schools produce what Foucault calls "docile bodies,"[1] those who discipline themselves to routinized schedules of being in certain places at certain times, and, when in them, to equally routinized ways of behaving, thinking, and relating to others. The knowledge and skills taught by schools are rarely adequate for the workplace and almost always require modification and development: what the workplace really wants is the disciplined person, for discipline enables employees to develop and modify their knowledge and skills according to the needs of their particular job, and—this is the other side of the coin—it means they are controllable.

The body, and its extension into dress, is where discipline is exerted and accepted. The appearance of the body encodes the extent of its discipline/docility, and thus makes it assessable. So Phyllis Macklin, a consultant with an "outplacement" firm, advises clients on behavior and appearance in job interviews.[2] A blue suit and white shirt are common to all male candidates: what will, according to her, really attract the corporate interest is the details. The lower tip of the tie should come to the top or center of the belt buckle and the back of the tie should go through the label so it cannot escape control and reveal its undisciplined self to the interviewer. The belt should not only be new, but should show no sign of weight loss or gain. The body of the candidate should be totally disciplined, and should indicate that it is always controllable. Weight gain or loss are signs of a body breaking out of control and having to be redisciplined. The tie relates to the belt symmetrically, producing the body as aesthetically balanced around both vertical and horizontal axes. The aesthetics of symmetry, of the repetition and balance of forms, represents human control over nature. Nature is asymmetrical, ever changing and growing. Aesthetic form is static, completed, controlled.

Bakhtin contrasts the grotesque body with the aesthetic body and links the one with the body of the people and the other with officialdom. The aesthetic body, in sculpture or in person, is perfected and completed. It has reached the apogee of development so not only does it have no need to change, it contains its own argument against change, for any change would be for the worse. Its beauty is frozen. The grotesque body, however, is incomplete, never fixed. It is an earthly, fertile body embodying the principles of growth and change: its ugliness is that which escapes the social control of the beautiful. The aesthetic is an ordering, and therefore, disciplinary system: the grotesque, in contrast, embodies the signs of disorder, the threat of the uncontrolled. These signs, however, are also ones of fertility and growth; nature at its most fertile is at its most uncontrolled.

The body of the candidate must be the disciplined body with no trace of a tie end grotesquely out of control to mar its perfect symmetry. This body would be employable by the Walt Disney World Company, whose guidelines for male employees include the following:

Costumes: As a condition of employment with Walt Disney Attractions, you are responsible for maintaining an appropriate weight and size.

Hair: A neat, natural haircut and a clean shave are essential. Hair should be neatly cut and tapered so it does not cover any part of your ears. (Putting your hair behind your ears is not acceptable.) Hairstyles termed "natural" or "Afro" are acceptable, provided they are neatly packed.

Sideburns: Sideburns should be neatly trimmed and may be permitted to extend to the bottom of the earlobes, following their natural contour. Flares or muttonchops are not permitted.[3]

The body of the employee must literally be fitted to the costumes provided by the company. Neatness is the result of control, and so can be used as the criterion by which the degree of discipline may be evaluated. But neatness is paired with naturalness so that it is turned into a way of revealing the natural body, the neat, controlled person is "actually" the natural person! The individual produced by power is presented as a product of nature.

Employers, schools and families attempt to control the bodies of those they wish to discipline. The most rigid and detailed control over bodies, gestures and behaviors may be that of the military boot camp whose sole purpose is to impose discipline, but similar bodily discipline is at work in teaching children appropriate postures and behaviors at the meal table, and in my local supermarket's rule forbidding its employees to chew gum at the cash registers. "No shoes, no shirt, no service" disciplines shoppers' bodies throughout the nation.

Professional sport is part of the culture of leisure for spectators, but is work for those who play. The football stadium is a workplace that, like any other, disciplines the bodies and behaviors of those stationed within it. American football workers are a tightly disciplined workforce: plays and players are subjected to a finely organized game plan and the controlling body (pun intended) disciplines players and coaches who break its codes of proper, sportsmanlike behavior. A small instance of this controlling power will serve to exemplify it.[4] Moments of high achievement in the game are traditionally celebrated by spontaneous (that is, undisciplined) behavior. A crucial tackle, a spectacular reception or a firstdown will often provoke celebratory and congratulatory gestures. Touchdowns, which are the key objectives of the game, provoke the most expressive behavior of all—"the endzone dance." This is nothing new: in 1976 the *Wall Street Journal* noted the recent growth of the endzone victory dance or "fancy bugaloo, juke, dickey-doo or other showboating" and commented on the difficulty some old timers had in getting use to "such carryings on."[5] In 1984 and 1991 the NFL changed its rules to extend its control over (read repression of) "any prolonged, excessive, or premeditated celebration by individual players or groups of players." The terms "prolonged" and "excessive" police the boundaries within which "spontaneity" must be contained, and "premeditated" responds to the threat of another system of control, planned by players rather than coaches and the NFL. According to the *Chicago Tribune*, the NFL Committee considers that:

> Spontaneous expressions of exuberance such as a quick spike of the ball by the scoring player or an obviously unrehearsed leaping hand-slap by two team-mates after a good play are perfectly acceptable and well within the bounds of good sportsmanship, provided they do not carry a clear intent to embarrass or deride an opponent.
>
> On the other hand, the Committee is unanimously opposed to any prolonged, excessive or premeditated celebration by individual players or groups of players. Antics such as unrestrained dances, wild flailing of arms and legs, simulated dice games, "high-five" circles in the endzone, imitations of gun-fighters, and similar behavior are deemed to be contrived exhibitionism that has no place in the sport and should be penalized five yards for unsportsmanlike conduct.[6]

Lurking beneath the disciplinary norms of sportsmanship is racial power. Vernon Andrews studied the length of endzone dances in the play-offs of the 1991 season and found that the longest and most expressive dances were, in general, performed by African American players. He underpins this finding by a detailed account of studies of African American culture which demonstrate that Black lifestyles are organized around different norms from those of whites, and that, in particular, expressiveness in body language and verbal language is valued more highly than in white culture:

> Black style is more self-conscious, more expressive, more expansive, more colorful, more intense, more assertive, more aggressive, and more focussed on the individual than is the style of the larger society of which blacks are a part.[7]

The notion of Black expressiveness is taken further by linking it to that of improvisation, which, according to Jones,[8] is both a preferred and a necessary feature of Black style. The necessity derives from the socio-historical conditions which have always limited the economic and cultural resources available to African Americans: under these conditions, improvisation is a survival skill. Improvisation is also rooted in the present, the here and now: it is, then, a way of living in "a context of oppression in which the future [is] unreliable, unpredictable and not guaranteed to occur at all."[9] Improvisation is characteristic of a culture of practice rather than one of canonical texts, which are always written with an eye on the future (see Chapters 7 and 8), and as such is characteristic of subordinated social formations whose everyday lives involve the arts of doing the best they can

61

with what they have. Improvisation thus becomes a practice of agency which demonstrates that what people do with a determining structure is far from totally determined. Indeed, in both sport and in those musical forms originating in subordinated cultures, improvisation rather than structure typically provides the high points. The tension between improvisation and structure is a tension between bottom-up and top-down control which has become, within certain spheres, a legitimated source of pleasure in our culture. The NFL, therefore, could not recognize and risk legitimizing undesirable Black behavior as improvised, so it designated it as "premeditated" (the exact opposite) and thus discursively legitimated not the behavior but its own right to control it.

In his more detailed analysis, Andrews shows that white players who dance in the endzones are, in effect, using a foreign language, and their accent betrays them. In a white accent, for example, a spike of the ball is typically aggressive and violent and tends to continue the game's aggressiveness by other means. In a Black accent, however, a spike is stylish and controlled, it is an example of an expressiveness that is what it expresses—Black consciousness, identity and control. In these moments of triumph, Black bodies escape the discipline of the game plan and speak publicly with their own accents. This speaking body is neither undisciplined nor spontaneous, but one that has changed its language and its culture. The system that now produces its behaviors and their significance is one controlled by the subordinate power, and so, in a denial of subordinate power, the power-bloc stratgically characterizes these behaviors as "out of control" rather than "differently controlled." But the Black players know that they have momentarily moved their bodies out of the domain of white power and into their own locale. It is the assertion of localized power rather than a natural spontaneous outburst that makes the behavior so threatening, and it is this assertion that provokes the white power-bloc. The argument is not over *what* constitutes sportsmanlike conduct, but over *who* controls its constitution.

Because the issue is not one of behavior but of control, in different social conditions the same expressive behavior can be viewed by the power-bloc quite differently. In its TV commercials for the World Football League (which is the NFL's attempt to spread US football to Europe), the NFL relies largely on images of the Black expressiveness that it attempts to repress back home. Presumably it feels that in Europe's different race relations (both historically and contemporarily) the expressive Black body signals not a challenge to white control but an American exuberance, vitality and stylishness which European sport lacks. Power-bloc strategies vary according to the social terrain within which they operate: what in one set of social conditions may threaten power-bloc interests may in others be turned to their advantage.

In the US, however, the vitality of the improvising, expressive Black body always carries a threat to white power, and so any signs of it exceeding the limits of "propriety" activate the forces of discipline. The young Elvis Presley, whose pelvic wildness, as we shall see in the next chapter, contained traces of Blackness, was disciplined as strictly as any Black endzone dancer and his expressive, threatening body brought back into the norms of the socially acceptable.

Andrews's study showed too, that the shortest endzone dances were also performed by African Americans often as a display of "cool," a studied absence of expressiveness, which may well be the flip side of improvisation as a survival strategy. White players, on the other hand, tended to be moderate in their endzone dances. The statistical distribution echoes social positioning: in both, whites occupy the center and blacks the margins, whites are "normal", blacks are not. Norms, as we shall see below, are not objective accounts of social reality, but are disciplinary mechanisms, so the NFL's criteria for establishing illegal endzone behavior, other than that of premeditation, are the normalizing categories of "prolonged" and "excessive."

This imperializing control was unnecessary to the sport, if not to the interests of the power-bloc. Unseen by the NFL was an unwritten code of conduct developed by the players themselves to discipline these dances. It "ruled" that expressiveness that was appropriate at home games in front of the player's own fans should be restrained on road games played in someone else's locality. Dances that exceeded reasonable boundaries of celebration and became needlessly offensive to the other team or its fans would be dealt with, unofficially but effectively, in the next scrimmage, block or tackle. But imperializing power acts because it *can* rather than because it needs to, and it is unwilling to cede to localized powers, even though their discipline might well be the more effective in their own territory.

There is no argument against discipline in principle—no one would want to live in a totally undisciplined society, if such an oxymoron could actually exist. The conflicts, when they occur, are over the points of control where discipline is applied, not over the disciplinary system itself. Many employees, for example, feel that they have the right to have more control over their bodies than the system grants them. Ms Fischette, for example, sued Continental Airlines over her dismissal for refusing to wear make-up. She won. At an annual meeting of Safeco Corporation a retired employee pleaded for men to be allowed to wear shirts other than white: he lost.[10] Beards seem to be a particularly contested point of control between employer and employee. Imperializing power constantly attempts to exert its discipline further than is required for the efficient performance of its ostensible function: it wants more than the power to get the job done and so it needs disciplined individuals with their docile bodies to comply with it. Greedy power, extending its reach beyond what is necessary merely because it is able to, produces discipline that is perceived as excessive and thus ripe for challenge. No bodies are completely docile, and agents' own sense of the proper limits of their docility may not coincide with that of the disciplinary order.

Before discipline became as socially extensive as it has in modern societies (and the US tries particularly hard to extend discipline as far as possible throughout all its elaborations), it was fostered first by religion and then by its secular offspring, education. Both of these formal institutions work to extend their discipline into the less formal institution of the home, for discipline is vital in the raising of children to become the citizens a society desires.

"Disciples" were originally those who submitted themselves to a master (the gender is deliberate) so as to benefit from his knowledge of God and the spiritual life in order to improve their control over their own lives (both interior and social) in a disciplined way and to learn to pass on the discipline to others and thus to spread the control socially. Discipline always carries the apparently contradictory forces of submission and empowerment. A disciplined person is one who submits him- or herself to the power of a particular way of knowing/behaving in order to participate in that power, to become more effective in applying it and thus to gain the satisfaction and rewards that it offers.

Religious discipline which, in its more extreme forms, required total submission of the disciple's body and mind, was transferred into the secular domain of academia with a minimum of modification. An academic discipline bears the traces of its religious origin; not only were early schools extensions of the Church and taught by Church scholars, but they taught Church discipline—the content may have been secularized but the way of thinking, the disciplinarity, was maintained.

Social institutions, such as religion or education, are never more than relatively autonomous: they are always set within, to use the Althusserian model, overdetermined relations with each other and therefore with the social order. That which the disciplines foster within any one institution can never be totally at odds with what is fostered in the others nor, most importantly, with the needs of the larger social order. But, equally, while these institutionalized systems act in their overdetermined dimensions as ideological state apparatuses, they do have a degree of autonomy: there can be rough edges in their fit with each other and with the social order, and sometimes the friction along these rough edges produces critical rather than complicit relationships. Overdetermination is neither total nor totally seamless. But it tries to be, so any critical ways of knowing which develop along these rough edges are typically subjected to disapproval and delegitimation by those of the "proper" discipline. Such a denial of disciplinary status leaves the newer ways of knowing free to criticize and press for change, but it also denies them access to the benefits and effectiveness of the power system.

In academia, new and critical ways of thinking are often inter-disciplinary because they develop along the rough edges of the traditional disciplines and avoid (some of) the constraints and therefore the authority which they impose. Breaking a disciplinary boundary exposes the author-ity which is secure within it to challenge and thus to change. The sanctity of boundaries is crucial to discipline and power. So, in the current debate over the canon (notice the religious origin of the word) in the humanities, the traditionalists use arguments of disciplinary purity to maintain the boundary between canonized and non-canonized art, and to insist that schools teach mainly, if not exclusively, the canon. In this way, the discipline and its authority can remain unchallenged within its secure and rigorously policed boundaries. What lies outside is marginalized and denied access to the power which is the privilege of a "proper" discipline. The "multiculturalists," on the other hand, wish to invade the boundaries of the canon and thus to destroy the power of its border guards to exclude the previously uncanonized from the privileges of disciplinarity. The enlarged and diversified canon that will result will open its access to disciplinary power to a wider variety of social formations. Diversifying the canon will "Americanize" it, against the desire of the monoculturists to maintain its European homogeneity and exclusiveness.

Power works strategically to secure its boundaries and thus to exclude that which lies beyond its control from the universe of "what matters." Sharply drawn lines, in the sand, in the curriculum, in people's heads, are the product of power. The NFL was drawing its line between the bodily behaviors which should and should not be seen on its fields; Alan Bloom was drawing his between good and bad art, and George Bush was drawing his between Kuwait and Iraq, and thus between the oil that the US did and did not control.

The power-bloc is ever alert to rush its border patrols to repair any breaches in its boundaries and thus to reinscribe its power. These border skirmishes have become typical of cultural politics in the contemporary United States, and it is both fascinating and frightening to watch the power-bloc scurrying to repair breaches or hold the line, and, more worryingly, to regain ground which it had earlier lost. The abortion debate, arguments over equal-employment legislation, the exclusion of the disempowered races and classes from basic health care are material versions of the cultural struggles over the humanities curriculum and the entertainment industries. This picture of the center trying to hold its ground against numerous border incursions can be cast in terms of homogeneity against heterogeneity or, in the curriculum debate, monoculturalism against multiculturalism.

Disciplines homogenize. They limit the diversity of popular agency and direct it to the top-down agency which the discipline requires and rewards. Disciplined agents are effective and empowered, but their effectivity and power is theirs only to the extent that the discipline allows it to be. The disciplined person can access this power and effectivity only if he or she adopts the identity which the discipline requires. The ways of knowing and behaving which constitute a discipline act socially and within the sphere of consciousness, particularly consciousness of self. The disciplined individual is a social site from which undisciplined components of identity are excluded and disciplined ones produced.

THE INDIVIDUAL

The constitution of individuality is fundamental to social life, and the boundaries of that individuality are among the most fiercely contested. Disciplined individuals (or docile bodies) are essential to the smooth running of an elaborate society and so those components of individuality which can best be disciplined are the ones which the power-bloc promotes as those which matter. Those over which its control is less effective are, conversely, defined as trivial and denied, as far as possible, social effectivity.

Marxism quickly and accurately diagnosed individualism as the servant of capitalism because its emphasis promoted the competitiveness upon which capitalism thrived and prevented the development of the proletarian class consciousness upon which, in Marxist theory, social change depended. The diagnosis has much to be said for it, particularly in its analysis of individualism's service to the economic interests of capitalism and thus the class interests of the bourgeoisie. Historically one of the most common and effective defensive strategies of the power-bloc has been to prevent the growth of any sense of solidarity or community of interest among subordinated social formations. "Divide and rule" is a slogan whose effectiveness history has amply demonstrated.

But traditional Marxism made the error of conflating individuality with bourgeois individualism, and thus yielded "the individual" as a political terrain to capitalism: instead it focussed its energies on developing class consciousness as a way of opposing both capitalism and individualism.

66

The consciousness of being an individual which most people have, and *enjoy* having, was seen as a false consciousness produced by ideology, so promoting or encouraging *any* sense of individuality became a way of participating in the work of that ideology and thus playing into the hands of the enemy. The important historical struggle was defined as one between class consciousness and individual consciousness, not one over what should and should not count in constituting the individual, and over who has the power to make that determination. Marxism's failure to establish itself as a broadly popular movement in most Western capitalist nations, and in the United States in particular, may be due in some large measure to the gap between its denial of the individual as a site of authentic experience and the sense of most people that what happens to them and how they think *as individuals* are matters of crucial importance. This failure to consider the politics of individuality (and, incidentally, those of the family) as a valid political arena disconnected Marxism from people's everyday experience, and explaining the resulting gap as a product of people's false consciousness did nothing to narrow it. Our desire to control as much as possible of our consciousness and of our immediate social conditions requires the struggle over what constitutes individuality. The social relationships we form are continuous with our sense of who we are as individuals, and these social relationships are our most ordinary ways of contesting or complying with the social relations proposed for us by the dominant social order. Individuality is not, per se, opposed to class or other relations of solidarity: some forms of individuality are, but others are its prerequisite.

Foucault's notion of *individuation* as an effect of power and knowledge casts the issue in a somewhat different light.[11] Individuation is a power process which separates an individual from others for the purposes of documentation, evaluation and control. The end result of this process is stationing—the placing of the individuated person in the position required by the social order. Individuation produces an individuality that exists only in the data banks of the power-bloc. The process of producing and documenting such individuals has developed continuously since the introduction of fingerprinting and the police "ID" photograph in the nineteenth century. Now the computer has multiplied exponentially the separation and documentation of individuating data.

Individuation is top-down power at work: opposing it is a bottom-up sense of identity. Bottom-up individuality is the product of a person's history, of family ties and continuities, of relationships with friends or community groups, of choices in leisure-time activities. The history of how an individual has made use of the resources and structures of a social order is quite different from the history of that individual that is documented in the data banks of the power-bloc. Such bottom-up identities may be hard won and hard held, for imperializing power reaches into families, into communal relationships and into leisure. But they *are* won and they *are* held. Indeed, a defining characteristic of people's consciousness in disciplinary societies is the sense of difference between the individuals that *we* think we are and those whom we know *they* want us to be. The ability to masquerade or to dissemble identity is a survival tactic; it is a defensive power by which workers maintain identities against those required by management, by which women hold theirs against patriarchy, or gays and lesbians theirs against heterosexism; it is the power of children to keep secret areas of identity beyond the knowledge of teachers and parents.

I am not arguing here for the idea of an *essential* self that is the fixed site of a true identity which remains unchanged throughout our life span. Neither am I arguing for a stable nuclear identity around which our various experiences and relationships are organized. Even if we add the socio-historical dimension to these concepts, neither of them foregrounds identity as a terrain of struggle upon which an identity can be formed only in opposition to others. The identity that really matters is the one produced by bottom-up, localizing power, but though it is produced from below it is defined by its struggle against the operations of individuation. Individuation identifies the individual but cannot produce identity: indeed it is threatened by identity, so works to evacuate it from the individuality it identifies.

Identity, then, is a crucial pressure point in the consciousness of people living under a power-bloc. The tension is not that between a subjectivity ideologically produced from above and a class consciousness materially produced from below, for such a struggle, important though it may be, is confined to the terrain of collective consciousness and misses that of the individual. The struggle between individuation and a bottom-up individualized identity *precedes* that between social collectivities, whether of class, gender, race or other categories. Individuation, as we shall see later in this chapter, works to prevent "horizontal" social relationships that are under the control of those who engage in them and that form the only possible basis for internally directed collective relations. Individuation is a vertical power that separates and stations the body and thus works to control both its individuality and its social relations.

Individualized identities, however, in opposition to individuated ones, can break through this separation to form horizontal social relations, ones of *communitas*.[12] A *communitas*, in the sense I use it here, is a social formation whose main, if not only, purpose is to produce identities and relationships that are in the control of its members by means that are denied to them by the dominant social order. A *communitas* is a social formation which is neither required nor produced by the social order: as such it lies beyond the reach of imperializing power and thus threatens it, always potentially and sometimes actually. A *communitas* can be produced only by allegiances among those who control their localized identities: it is the social extension of locale and as such is necessarily opposed to individuation.

Foucault argues that the control over what the body does in space and time is the control that matters because consciousness and social relations follow from this, not, as ideology theory would have it, vice versa. Foucault, however, does not develop a concept equivalent to "station" because he has no concept of "locale" to which it is opposed. His theory of power is one that I have characterized as typically European because it focusses on its operation as a relatively homogeneous system whose stations may vary only superficially: a school desk, for instance, a place on an assembly line, a computer terminal and a waitress's set of tables, may each differ from the others, but all work identically as points of control, for they all individuate those who occupy them so that they may be rewarded or punished according to their efficiency and disciplinary compliance, or, in Foucault's word "docility." Though Foucault argues that resistance is a necessary product of power, he never theorizes or investigates it beyond defining it as that which power has to overcome. He thus provides us with no account of the diversity of forms that resistance can take, nor of the bottom-up creativity evident in them. His is a theory of imperializing power, that does not extend to consider those localizing powers (and I stress the plural) to which it is opposed. Stations are systematically produced and thus relatively homogeneous; locales are produced from outside the system, and are thus widely diverse, though always related antagonistically to stations.

A European theorist who gives far greater weight than Foucault to the diversity and creativity of forms of resistance is de Certeau.[13] While Bakhtin's paradigmatic metaphor is one of a vital life force[14] and Foucault's of a machine, de Certeau's is of guerrilla warfare. De Certeau likens power to that of an occupying army which controls place and time. Within the territory it occupies there are people who may, most of the time, comply with its rule and live a life of subjection under it. But the law-abiding, subjected peasant always has the ability to become a guerrilla fighter. The weak can and do attack the powerful as guerrilla bands attack the occupying force. These attacks are fleeting, opportunistic: they are mounted when weaknesses are spotted, when gaps in the army's deployment of force can be exploited. Armies move by strategy, guerrillas by tactics: power-bloc control is strategic and is challenged by the tactical raids of the people.

This strategic power can only be deployed over time in a physical place, whether this be the working day in a corporate headquarters or a university, or the domestic house when the family is at home. Power holds place and time. Tactical raids, however, use place and time, but they cannot hold them: they work within the place and time held by the dominant other, they make do with what is not theirs, and turn the other's resources to their own use. They exist only in their practice.

La perruque (which is French for "wig" or falsified identity, a masquerade) is, for de Certeau, an example of a tactical raid by the weak upon the strategy of power in the workplace. *La perruque* is the secretary writing her personal letter on a company typewriter in company time; it is the student playing computer games on the school's computer instead of using it for his math assignment; it is a workman using company time, tools and scrap materials to make something for himself instead of for "them."

The creativity of the people lies in the art of making do with the resources available, resources that are usually provided by the dominant other and thus inscribed with its power. The homeless men's creativity lay in how they made do with the cultural commodity of *Die Hard*; Bill's creativity lay in *his* use of *their* word "decent."

The art of making do extends into the art of making "our" space within "their" place. So renters make their space by the practices of dwelling within the landlord's place. Locales are made by "turning" the resources which, in their "straight" use, produce stations. The providers of shelter for the homeless used their ownership of the physical place to station its users, while its users attempted to construct within it locales which they could control themselves. Hidden gambling is a *perruque*, it is the space of the weak carved out of the place of the powerful, a locale made out of a station.

Guerrilla fighters are secret fighters: any power that they have depends upon being unobserved. The function of the wig is to hide what is underneath, to keep it unseen and unknown. It is here that de Certeau's metaphor of warfare reaches its limits, for an army applies its power by force, yet in industrial democracies at least, comparatively little power is applied coercively, though the threat of coercion is always there. Discipline serves power by making coercion unnecessary.

CONTROLLING KNOWLEDGE

The most powerful knowledge is disciplinary, that is, it is produced by a discipline and it disciplines (or orders, controls) its object. Non-coercive control can only be exercised over people through such knowledge. The known can be controlled, the unknown is beyond control, so power-knowledge invalidates that which lies beyond it. As we shall see in Chapter 9, scientific rationalism, probably the most effective power-knowledge discipline yet developed, constantly denies those parts of human experience (such as intuition or premonition) which lie beyond its grasp the status of being real: it relegates them to the realm of the unreal, the imaginary, the delusionary, and thus defines "reality" as that which it knows and can control. What can be known about the individual is a knowledge that simultaneously produces and controls identity. Individual actions, thoughts and pleasures which lie beyond the reach of the power systems, which are unknown and unknowable by it, are the ground which subordinate control must hold if it is to survive. One of the vital functions of popular culture is to maintain and extend those areas of social identity which the people can keep out of the reach of the power-bloc.

One strategy of power is to construct its stations in as fine detail as possible so as to minimize the gaps wherein locales can be established. In its most repressive form, an example of which is analyzed below, this strategy aims to totalize the station and exclude the locale. Most typically, this strategy is one of the workplace and the military. In subtler, less repressive forms, a degree of subordinate control can be allowed or even encouraged, but it is permitted to operate only within limits which it does not set and towards ends which it does not choose. It is a disciplined control, but it is, nonetheless, control, and workers who are permitted to exert it over their immediate workaday conditions are often more productive (an aim of the company) but also more satisfied (an aim of the worker). Good discipline is generous as well as repressive, but neither its giving nor its taking are equal: it is always the top-down power system which draws the limits, sets the objectives and monitors the effect of bottom-up control.

We have developed computers into precise machines for control. Their capacity to produce detailed knowledge about the physical or social worlds and thereby to extend our power over them is not my main concern here. I am concerned more with their power to know their users. Sharon Dannon has provided us with a revealing example of this power being applied to the individual whom it knows and therefore produces.[15] The point of control is a print-out of the day's work of one of the 350 employees, almost all of them women, in Trans World Airline's reservation center. The computer works "externally" to allocate customers to seats and "internally" to monitor its operators. In this tiny fragment of working life we can trace the macro power systems of individuation and knowledge which Foucault diagnoses as the prerequisites of a modern society. This scrap of paper is imprinted with the marks of the workers' dual supervisory systems, for the computer record of her work is scrawled over by the handwriting of her human supervisor.

The room in which she sits is a vast hundred-foot-square enclosure cut off from the outside world and separated from the rest of the airline's offices. The first operation of power is always to enclose its territory, within which to concentrate rather than dissipate its energies. Enclosure entails separation, not just the separation of the enclosure from the rest of the system (which is actually an insertion into it), but, more importantly, the separation of the individuals who have been enclosed. This enclosure is, therefore, divided into the 350 work stations which are occupied by the 350 bodies whose behaviors are controlled to produce the airline's profits. Each station is equipped with a telephone headset, a chair and a computer terminal. Here the body becomes the machine, here any differences between body, station and individuality are dissolved. In the center of the enclosure is a small glass-walled one in which the supervisor sits. She monitors the 350 bodies visually and electronically, for each telephone line is connected, not just to the outside world, but to her. She may be a slightly larger cog in the machine, through which its power passes to the 350 smaller cogs, but she is still a cog. Her movements are locked into theirs; the machine holds her in place as precisely as it does them. Her behaviors are as closely monitored as theirs.

We live in a monitored society and monitoring, or, as Foucault called it, surveillance, is the core of social discipline. Foucault's analysis of our modern regime of surveillance is centered on the institutions developed to monitor and control behavior at the social margins, especially asylums for the mentally deviant and prisons for the behaviorally deviant. But he stresses that the surveillance systems (that is, systems of knowledge and power) developed on the margins of society are interrelated with more socially central ones such as the military, the school and the workplace, and, cumulatively, with the social order itself.

Emblematic of such a regime was the prison designed in the 1780s by Jeremy Bentham called "The Panopticon." It was built like a wheel, with a supervisor's tower at the hub and 144 cells on six levels around the circumference. Each cell had a spy hole on the inside through which the supervisor could survey the behavior and body of its occupant, a window on the outside so the occupants were backlit, and unbroken walls between it and its neighbors. The interior of the supervisor's tower was dark so the prisoners could not see the watcher: They were seen but not seeing, known but not knowing.

In contrast to the overcrowded, communal dungeons of the previous regime, this new prison was humane rather than degrading. It embodied the principle of correct training rather than that of vengeful punishment. Its occupants were clean and well fed, but individuated. Each prisoner was under the constant monitoring of the supervisor who determined the rewards or sanctions appropriate to each individual. Prisoners thus individuated could be examined, rated against the norm and ranked on a scale of "good" behavior. But the gem of the system was not just that one supervisor could monitor many prisoners and thus improve enormously the ratio of police to citizens but, in theory at least, this ratio could be increased almost infinitely. Because the prisoners could not see the supervisor and could not know when they were being watched or not they would have to behave as though they were being watched all the time and thus would monitor themselves.

Bentham's Panopticon had 144 cells around the supervisor. TWA's system has 350, but the principle is the same. Originally Bentham wished to connect each cell to the supervisory tower by pipes so that the supervisor could monitor by ear as well as eye; he dropped the idea probably because of the impossibility at the time of keeping the flow of knowledge one-way—the prisoners would be able to hear the supervisor as well as vice versa. Electronics has overcome this problem, and TWA's supervisor can hear without being heard, can see without being seen.

Power is uni-directional, and the direction is always vertical. Individuation can only be maintained if the flow of knowledge, communication and relationships can be confined to the vertical dimension. TWA's workers cannot communicate with each other or the outside world, except through the supervisor; Bentham's prisoners were separated from each other by solid stone. Horizontal flows of knowledge and the relationships built upon them challenge top-down control. Prisoners housed together in a dungeon, school students working together at a table, or workers working in groups cannot be controlled as finely as when they are individuated.

Individuated control requires stations which are open to monitoring from above and closed off horizontally. Each station is designed to encourage desired behavior and discourage what is prohibited by making it visible. The more completely the body's behavior is monitored, evaluated and recorded, the finer the control over it. But behavior takes place in time as well as space. TWA's computer logs every moment of work and non-work between SIT and SOT (Sign In Time and Sign Out Time). The non-work times are categorized into the legitimate (meal breaks) and illegitimate (toilet breaks or a personal phone call) and each are computed precisely. At the end of the day, the human supervisor rates them against an unspecified norm and, in this case, has found them too high.

The time the worker spent on the job is monitored equally closely.

TNCH (Total Number of Calls Handled), TATT (Total Average Talk Time per call) and TACW (Total After Call Work, the paperwork generated by each call) were each logged and the daily totals computed. Each measure is computed to the nearest hundredth of a minute, and all of them are finally combined into a "percent utilization" which produces a rating to two decimal places of the efficiency of each worker's use of time.

But the data produced by these measures are not in themselves "knowledge"; we can only know what they mean when they are inserted into a system of norms. This worker, for instance, has a 93.55 per cent utilization; she handled seventy-nine calls in the day, spent 3.53 minutes on each and completed her after call work in 0.39 minutes (about 23 seconds). On the face of it, this might seem a pretty hard day's work, but the norms and the supervisor judged otherwise. Normal per cent utilization is 96.5, normal TNCH is 150–200, and any TACW over 0.3 of a minute is criticized as inefficient. Norms do not exist in their own terms, but only as products of a monitoring knowledge system. They are one of the most direct effects of the power of this knowledge, for without them the knowledge of any one individual can be neither evaluated nor ranked, and thus cannot be applied upon the individuated body as rewards or sanctions. The normal is a product of power.

The final handwritten evaluation reads "There is no excuse for this bad time management! You have complete control! Please make the necessary improvements immediately!" The only surprise in this comment is the word "please." The word "control" here is spoken, obviously, with the accent of management: the control it refers to is the control to make the body of the worker conform to the norms of the system. The supervisor may call the control "yours," but the "you" is the individual produced from the top down, into whom the system projects its control. This individuated worker, to the extent that she complies with the discipline, exerts "their" control over herself. The control is "hers" only in their sense of her individuation, not in any sense of her identity that she might recognize as her own.

The individuated body is merged with this computer terminal. Power exerts its control physically (that is, through space and time) over this unified entity of the body-station or stationed body. It must extend and refine its control at least as far as efficiency requires it to, but within this it may allow some limited space for subordinate control (it may allow, for instance, personal photographs on the desk or postcards on the bulletin board but not personal phone calls). But as a general principle, an efficient discipline is one which completely fills the time and space available with its required activity and which leaves no room in either for "idleness" or "indiscipline." "The devil finds work for idle hands to do" is a paradigmatic example of the power-bloc turning its discipline into commonsense.

Even the shelter for the homeless men, despite the lack of any productive activity for them, was a station which applied discipline upon them both spatially and temporally. Its disciplinary mechanism, however, was far less fine-tuned and insidious than that of TWA, with the result that the men could find more gaps within which to produce their own locales than could any TWA computer subject. TWA's reservation enclosure has, as far as we can tell, excluded completely any space for individual locales: its control is total.

Twenty-six million workers in the US are individuated and monitored electronically, and while the system described above may be as precisely engineered as any yet developed, it is not untypical. Foucault's analysis leads us to identify even more of the processes which produced this print-out than we have commented on so far. The individuated worker known in this way can now be entered into the filing cabinet or data bank and stored as documentation. Documented knowledge is used to evaluate the individual against the norms, to separate him or her from others into a hierarchical ranking and thus to enable the award of individuatedly appropriate rewards or sanctions. School records, work records, driving records, credit records, purchasing records, medical records, criminal records are all used to construct by documentation what counts as each one of us; in them we can be examined, assessed and held to account. If each of us is the smallest, final wheel in the mechanism of power, the digits of our social-security number are the cogs that ensure we turn in unison with the rest of the machine.

Disciplined individuals have to be constantly examined. Our perform-ance is examined at school and in the work place, our bodies, teeth and cars are examined annually, the IRS examines our finances, officials examine our travel to other countries, our churches examine our con-sciences, and psychotherapists examine our childhoods, our marriages and our orgasms. We have to be examined before we can drive a car, practice law, or become a citizen. The more examinations we pass the more normal we become and the further up the hierarchy we can go: examinations, like the discipline which requires them, are necessary, productive and generous but they submit us to power.

As a British national, "I" had to be examined in great detail in order to become a resident of the USA. The results of this examination, documented on my "Resident Alien" card individuate me according to "their" definition of who "I" am. On the front is a photograph showing my face and right earlobe, the print of my right thumb and my signature (all identifiers of my body and behavior). There is also my name, my birth date, my alien number, my port of entry and class of visa. On the back are seventy-one digits, which presumably encode all the knowledge deemed necessary for the system to know me. I must carry the card at all times as an identifier of who (they think) I am. A Norwegian friend examined it with a mixture of incredulity and amusement and then commented, very seriously, that no country that had been occupied by a foreign power would ever allow the centralized documentation of its citizens which is so commonplace in the US. The power over the individual which is the effect of such thoroughly documented knowledge may be used, on most people most of the time, in benign and non-repressive ways, but it is a top-down, all-monitoring power, and as such it always has the potential to be used quite differently. The paradox between the tightly disciplined nature of respectable US society and its deeply held belief in freedom is defused by the willing entry of people into its disciplinary systems. The result is that the system is experienced not as repressive, but as enabling and productive. If discipline, the belief appears to run, is "freely" entered into, it cannot limit freedom.

INDISCIPLINE

The historical work of Bakhtin and Foucault and the more theoretical de Certeau provide us with a complementary set of perspectives on the control of the body. Bakhtin focusses on the vitality of the people which is actualized in the body and repressed by officialdom. He was writing in the early years of the USSR, and could not argue explicitly that the forms of social control which stifled the vitality of the people would produce a constipated society that would eventually and inevitably die from self-constriction. But he hardly needed to: the joy he finds in the life of the people suffuses his descriptions of it, and so, conversely, does his disapproval of its repression.

Foucault, equally, analyses the systems of power and control with a critical eye. He constantly reminds himself and us that discipline is necessary and productive in modern society, yet we feel that in these reminders he is pulling back only momentarily from the position that matters most to him, the one from which disciplinary power is seen as repressive and, in a way which is deeply felt if not specifically defined, anti-human. Foucault's analytic energies are directed to the disciplinary power, Bakhtin's to the nature of the indiscipline which needs to be controlled, and de Certeau's to the popular creativity involved as it struggles with the powerful: the sympathies and politics of each lie in the same place, on the side of the people. But however deeply each is worried by the gradual and insistent stifling of this undisciplined life force, none actually analyzes or theorizes it in any detail.

For Bakhtin, it is a life principle which is part of nature. It is literally and metaphorically a bottom-up force: it grows from the earth into the body and the body of the people. Higher social formations try to distance themselves from the earth, the body and therefore from natural life. They repress it in the name of a higher order to which it is opposed; this higher order is, of course, their definition of society, so the repressing of popular forces becomes one of the ways in which society controls nature. The danger is that controlling it may kill it, and killing it may be suicidal.

De Certeau, too, locates the life of the people closer to nature than that of the power-bloc. He compares the popular art of making do, by which the people turn, as far as possible, an alien environment to their own advantage, with the power of fish and animals to adapt, to avoid the threats and exploit the benefits of their environment, to construct their locales within habitats over which they have no control.

There are strong arguments that society depends upon the imposition of order, and discipline upon nature or the disordered, the undisciplined. The conceptual categories of language and the aesthetic values of art impose order; agriculture and police forces impose order; education, families and airports impose order. Societies work because they are ordered and their orders of life are maintained through their disciplinary procedures. Teaching children the grammar of language is disciplining their conceptual processes as TWA's monitoring system disciplines its employees. Poets and advertisers fracture grammatical conventions to help us see things differently; TWA's monitoring allows no poets, it permits no difference. Difference is potential disorder, it threatens indiscipline.

We risk overextending the meaning of the word "nature" if we wish to argue that it is in the nature of humanity to impose order on nature, for that would involve using the term to encompass both a process and that to which the process is applied. There may be nothing wrong with this, and indeed, there is a powerful imaginative appeal to the idea that our desire to control nature is itself natural. But the danger of such an idea lies in its tendency to obscure the intermediate and inescapably social processes by which this desire is put into effect. It is more productive to argue that humans have become the dominant natural species because of their ability to devise a wide variety of systems whereby this desire to order can be applied as control. Control may not be a fundamental principle of humanity, but it certainly is of society.

Unlike Bakhtin and de Certeau, Foucault does not define power in opposition to something "natural" and thus avoids the danger of locating the origins of resistance in nature rather than society. For him, resistance operates in the same sphere as power, and, indeed, is not just a reaction to power but is a necessary condition for it: without resistance there could be no power, for there would be nothing for it to push against. Resistance is itself a form of power; what distinguishes one form from the other is not an essential difference between them, but a difference in their relationship to the social order. The power which Foucault calls "power" is a top-down power because it serves a hierarchical social order which grants its higher social formations better access to its power. They have this privileged access because the power system and the social order which advantages them have developed historically in tandem. The power which Foucault calls "resistance" is the bottom-up power of those low in the hierarchy. The many forms which it can take are never analyzed by him, for the great paradox of his work is that his sympathies lie with resistance but his energy is devoted to the analysis of power.

I prefer to characterize what Foucault calls resistance as the desire to control one's immediate conditions. Foucault's power is an imperializing one, ever extending its terrain outwards and deepening its reach into the minutiae of what it already holds. Its imperialism is both macro and micro in scale, its ambition is universalist and monopolist. Resisting power, however, is defensive and localist. Its terrain is no more extensive than that which it deems necessary for a relatively secure, satisfying and pleasurable existence. It can take a huge variety of forms because of the diversity of physical, social and historical conditions to which it has to adapt in order to exercise. It is tolerant rather than monopolist, for it will allow other forms of power provided they do not encroach upon its limited locality.

Such an account of localizing power can offer a more satisfying explanation of the cheers of the homeless men at the fictional death of the CEO, and of the Black bodies dancing in the endzone than either Bakhtin's or de Certeau's: locating the origin of these behaviors in nature denies their systematicity. But Foucault's account of resistance as simultaneously a precondition and a product of power is not entirely satisfactory: for explaining these behaviors as resistances produced by the power to which they are opposed denies the agency of those who resist to bring to the process anything not already produced by the power system and thus containable by it. Localizing power is never independent of imperializing power, but it is never totally encompassed by it either. The agents who exert it do bring to it something that is theirs, that is the product of *their* histories and that is applied through *their* social competencies. Black expressiveness and improvisation are not *just* products of white repression and structure (though in part they are), but are produced at the intersections between a white power and Black locales that African Americans have maintained historically outside of (and often unseen by) the power-bloc by devious, subtle and creative tactics. What matters about Black expressiveness is not just its resistance to white discipline, but its continuation of Black localizing powers over which the power-bloc has no control. It is an exercise of Black socially interested agency.

Top-down and bottom-up powers do not operate in different spheres (that of nature opposed to that of society) but are different directionalities of the same desire to control. Popular formations and those of the power-bloc are not so much differently motivated as differently situated. The desire for imperialist control is not limited to the formations of the power-bloc, nor is the desire for localist control limited to those of the people. Material social conditions mean that the formations of the power-bloc are better able to exert imperialist control, but they wish to control their immediate social conditions just as closely, and indeed are often better able to control them as well. The formations of the people have limited access to the means of imperializing power (though they may well grasp whatever opportunities they can), so through material necessity their desire to control actualizes itself more typically through localizing power. Because locales are where this form of control is most effective and its desire best satisfied, what goes on in locales matters intensely. To the formations of the power-bloc, imperializing control may well be the more satisfying and the one to which, consequently, they direct their greatest energy. To the formations of the people, however, the converse is often the case, and consequently what goes on in the locale is what matters most because it is here that the desire for control, frustrated elsewhere, is best satisfied. A locale, however, is not just a second-best empire, and the characteristics of localizing cultures are not just the inverse of those of the dominant culture. Because locales are produced by the diversity of subordinated social formations and because they can be extended into "horizontal" communities, they can provide the means from which cultures of *communitas* and difference may be formed. Such cultures threaten imperializing control because they resist or evade its homogenizing and incorporating strategies. The diversity of these cultures in the US and their increasing assertion of their rights to control more of their own local conditions threatens not only the imperializing powers within the US, but also the adequacy of European social theories to explain them.

NOTES

1. Michel Foucault, *Discipline and Punish* (London: Allen Lane, 1977).
2. "Dressing the Part," *Minneapolis Star Tribune*, 18 June 1991, p. 1E.
3. *Harpers*, June 1990, pp. 40–42.
4. Vernon Andrews, "Race, Culture, Situation and The Touchdown Dance." Paper delivered at the North American Society for the Sociology of Sport annual convention, Milwaukee, November 1991.

5. Edwin McDowell, "How Martha Graham has Influenced Football," *Wall Street Journal*, 20 January 1976, cited in Andrews.
6. Dan Pierson, "Ickey Rule is Proving to be Sticky for NFL", *Chicago Tribune*, 1991, cited in Andrews.
7. Thomas Kochman, *Black and White Styles in Conflict* (Chicago: University of Chicago Press, 1981).
8. James Jones, "Racism: A Cultural Analysis of The Problem", in John Dovidio and Samuel Gaertner (eds), *Prejudice, Discrimination and Racism* (San Diego: Academic Press, 1986), pp. 279–314.
9. *Nightline*, ABC, 3 December 1990.
10. "Dress Codes," *Minneapolis Star Tribune*, 18 June 1991, p. 1E.
11. Foucault, *Discipline and Punish*.
12. My use of the term *communitas* derives from the work of Victor Turner (particularly *The Ritual Process: Structure and Anti-Structure*, Chicago: Aldine 1969, chapters 3–5). Turner argues that there are two dimensions of culture: that of *structure*, which organizes hierarchy, social roles and that process of control which he calls civilization; and that of *communitas*, which is horizontal rather than vertical, and is where we engage in social relationships rather than social relations, and which promotes equality or similarity over hierarchy. He also, more problematically in my view, suggests that *communitas* is "natural" rather than civilized. For Turner these two dimensions work together harmoniously though not without some contradictions. I prefer to model them as conflicting domains of power in which the power-bloc has colonized *structure* and uses this structural power to control, limit or prevent the people exercising localizing power in *communitas*. The experience of *communitas* does not, in this model, serve to reposition people in *structure*, but rather offers opportunities to construct identities and relationships which contradict or evade those of structural individuation. *Communitas* opposes individuation, *structure* promotes it.
13. Michel de Certeau, *The Practice of Everyday Life* (Berkeley: University of California Press, 1984).
14. Mikhail Bakhtin, *Rabelais and his World* (Cambridge, MA: Massachusetts Institute of Technology Press, 1968).
15. Sharon Dannon, "Cracking the Electronic Whip," *Harpers*, August 1990, pp. 58–9.

4

SPORTING SPECTACLES:

THE BODY VISIBLE

Electronic surveillance is widespread in this society. Ross, for instance, estimates that 70 per cent of corporations use it to monitor workers, with in many cases the result of inhumanely high stress and stress-related illnesses.[1] The computer's ability to monitor every key stroke and record every second that the operator leaves its keyboard has proved a highly refined technology of power.

But however sophisticated the power machine, the people always try to develop ways of coping with it, ways of enlarging the space within it that they may make their own. Workers are constantly developing practices which enlarge their terrain of control within the workplace. These are not always resistant or disruptive, but may at times be complicit with the aims of the corporation, and may make its operations more efficient. Localizing power is not fixed in its relations with imperializing, top-down power: indeed, it is impossible to specify in advance what form these relations will take. The difference between the two forms of power lies in the interests they promote rather than the direction in which they are turned.

Although the relations between the two types of power may vary as widely as the points of control where they meet, there is always an element of oppositionality in them: top-down and bottom-up powers always struggle for control over the body, its behaviors and its immediate environment, and there is always a struggle to establish knowledges of the world that are appropriate to each. Power is not a sleeping dog that can be awakened to full strength when needed: power exists in its practice, and if it is not exerted it tends to wither and weaken. People keep localizing power alive and develop their skills in applying it, not only by looking for the weak spots in the power machine, but also by extending areas of social experience that lie outside it.

The people do not live the entirety of their lives stationed as cogs in a machine: their universe of experience is not encompassed *in toto* by the transmission of power upon and through them. The resistance of a cog to mechanical energy is called either inertia or friction: both inertia and friction are Foucauldian concepts of resistance, for they are that which power has to overcome within its own system. People are agents, however, which means that they bring to the disciplinary system the interests, identities and social competencies that they have developed from their own extra-disciplinary histories. The people are not inert, they are not a mass which has to be put in motion and then controlled. They may be frictive, however, but their friction is not just the result of inertia, but rather of sand which they have put into the gearbox from outside.

The ways in which the agency of the people copes with the power that tries to control or deny it are as varied as the material conditions within which that power is applied. These next chapters will look in some detail at four of them, which may be characterized as tactics of inversion, opposition, disruption and evasion. The studies—of sports fans, of Elvis fans and of popular violence—do not constitute a comprehensive account of popular coping, but are illustrative. Inverting or temporarily reversing the mechanism may be the most complicit of the three; evading it and using the space created to establish other ways of living may set up critical differences whose challenge is long-term and indirect; while disrupting or opposing it may offer more direct challenges with more directly traceable effects. Popular agency does not necessarily work to change the system that subordinates the people: often it works to enlarge popular spaces within the system, to extend the locales over which popular control can be exercised. In fact, popular agency is often directed not towards the overturning of the power system, but rather towards promoting the interests of the people within, outside or against it. Sports spectating is a case in point: it does little to challenge power-bearing surveillance, but it can reverse its gearing.

The football stadium is the panopticon turned inside out. Instead of the one in the center monitoring the bodies and behaviors of hundreds around the perimeter, the thousands around the perimeter monitor the behavior of the few in the center. One reason for the popularity of sport as a spectator activity is its ability to slip the power-knowledge mechanism of the workaday world into reverse gear.

The popular choice to invest large amounts of scarce leisure time and of psychic energy in watching sport does little to oppose the system of power and knowledge. Spectating is popular because what it changes is the position of the spectator in that system. The function of statistics is a case in point. As TWA and its computers know well, statistical power–knowledge is particularly finely tuned: statistics can engineer the perfect machine in which every numbered cog is individuated from, yet precisely related to, every other, and the laws which drive the mechanism appear as universally objective as any of Newtonian physics. Statistical knowledge individuates, examines, ranks and orders with seductive precision both *extensively*—the scope of the data it can know stretches, literally, to infinity (which it has turned from a mystical concept into a statistical one)—and *intensively* so that there is no detail of our everyday lives too small to be quantified and assessed against a norm.

Football, for instance, is played on graph paper. The grid on the astroturf and the digital clock on the scoreboard divide its world into spatial and temporal squares that enable each play and player to be precisely plotted, fed into a computer and thus comprehensively known. The stream of statistics that surround and saturate every game and every play control the way it is known as rigidly as the umpires control the way it is performed. Teams and tactics, plays and players are multiply monitored by cameras, by slow motion and freeze-frame replays and by computer data banks. And the computer that knows the game in such detail prints its own data, which is why the press can afford to disseminate such intensive knowledge so extensively. The poor football player is examined as minutely as any TWA reservation clerk: his body's behaviors in space and time are as statistically stationed as hers.

The first application of power–knowledge is enclosure. There is no sharp line between knowing and doing (what we do in our heads is continuous with what we do with our bodies), so the physical enclosure of the game in time and space is continuous with the statistical enclosure of how to know it. Statistics enclose the knowledge of players and teams and exclude what lies beyond their control: what they cannot count does not count.

Players are known statistically by the age, height and weight of their bodies. Their performance is known by the statistics of yards carried or passed, of passes completed, sacks and blocks achieved. And their numbers are always rated against those of other players and, more importantly, against norms—averages for the team, for the league, or for the universe of football, every game that has ever been played—the whole historical and geographical dispersion of football is known by statistical norms to two decimal places. These norms, of course, exist nowhere. They are never experienced by player, coach or fan: they are control mechanisms which steal the significance of the immediate performance or play and relocate it in an abstracted, imperializing knowledge system which exists only to subject the myriad experiences of football to monocular control.

The uniform works like statistics: it turns the player into a physical body knowable only by its height, weight and speed and by its position on the field. He can thus be stationed in the knowledge of fans and coaches as precisely as he is on the field. The number and name on the back serve first to individuate this body from others and then to insert it into the data bank of statistical knowledge. Here the name individuates but does not individualize. In local knowledges, names individualize by carrying personal identities and family histories, but in imperializing knowledge, such as that of the data bank, TWA's worksheet or my Resident Alien card, they individuate. The struggle over identity and its social production is one between a top-down and a bottom-up knowledge of who we are and of how we relate to the social order. Bottom-up, individualized identities have particularities which an abstract knowledge system can never know. These particularities, which can be known only by those whose locales they constitute, are where individuality differs from individuation. They exist outside the enclosures of imperializing power. In the official knowledge of sport these individualities are excluded, for what counts for them is not counted statistically. So the head that appears from under the helmet is like the face on my Resident Alien card or my driving license: it individuates and separates from others but does not identify an individual. But I know who (I think) I am underneath that face, and the sports fan knows the individualities of players with a knowledge that exceeds their statistical individuation.

But statistics still count. The fan who, in the workplace, is monitored and totally known, in sport turns the tables and becomes the monitor: sports fans have access to the knowledge that fuels the power machine. They know the players and the play as completely as, at work, they are known. The football stadium, as reversed panopticon, gives the small cogs the experience of being at the control panel, of reading the dials instead of being the data that are read on them. Televising sport extends this power to see and know: multiple cameras and slow-motion replays enhance the power of knowing. One camera, often identified as "the coach's," explicitly gives the fans access to "management" knowledge. Coaches and umpires, the equivalent of supervisors and controllers at work, are made knowable to the fans. The replay video not only gives the fans the same knowledge as the monitors, it also provides knowledge *of* them; their decision-making is revealed for examination and assessment by the fans. This technological extension of the power to know is taken to its extreme in televised baseball where even the flight of the ball between the pitcher and the bat is statistically examined: by recording its speed at various points in its trajectory each pitch can be ranked against others. In spectatorship, players, coaches and umpires all become the objects of knowledge of those whose will to know is frustrated in their workaday lives. In the inverted panopticon the statistical subjection and total visibility of the football player turns him into a bobo doll upon which the fans can punch away their frustration.

Inverting the panopticon loosens its power to individuate. Spectating involves intense horizontal relationships of community with other fans, whether on a massive scale in the stadium, or on a much smaller scale in front of the TV in the family rec room or the sports bar. Bodily expressions and experiences of this commonality are intensely pleasurable. "The Wave" is a generalized experience and expression of both community with other spectators and of participation in the spectacle of sport. Other such expressive experiences signal team identities: in the 1991 World Series the "homer hankies" waved by the Minnesota Twins and the "chop" performed by the Atlanta Braves identified both the community of the home team and the alienness of the road team. And all seven games of the series were won by the home team. The "high fives" given by TV spectators in a sports bar is a scaled-down version of this experience/ expression of *communitas*. As we will see later, this *communitas* is often experienced by fans in terms of "release," because the individuation of panoptic monitoring prevents it.

In Britain, one attempt to control football hooligans was a plan to do away with the cheap standing areas in stadia and to place each spectator in a numbered seat: individuation and separation are technologies of control. Not surprisingly, the plan met with vehement opposition from fans, and, in those stadia which implemented it, the seats were, on occasion, torn up and used in the hooliganism they were meant to control. In the US the pleasures of communal release from vertical control rarely take such a disruptive form, but they are nonetheless very real for the fans who experience them. Release is not just pleasurable in itself, it also produces spaces in which fans can construct identities and relationships that enable them to know themselves differently from the way they are known by the monitoring order.

Knowing is continuous with doing. The investment in knowledge pays its dividends in social life, otherwise knowledge would have no power. Bourdieu[2] has shown us that the links between economic capital and cultural capital are not just metaphoric but are made material in the structures of social difference which inform the institutions of capitalism. Fan knowledge is that of the "autodidact"; it is self-taught and thus differs significantly from the cultural capital legitimated by the educational and cultural institutions on the one hand and the class power of those who possess it on the other.

Because fan knowledge is not institutionalized like legitimate cultural capital it is not convertible into economic capital. The institution of education works, via official qualifications, to convert knowledge into employability and thus to formalize the mutual convertibility of economic and cultural capital. Via its continuous ranking of every performance of every body the educational system individuates students into a precise statistical hierarchy which, as its end result, legitimates economic and political inequality. The individuation, examination, ranking and documentation of the educational system is a mechanism of top-down power; it is a technology of power that works in precisely the same way as that of the economic institutions of corporate capitalism. It produces the means by which Bourdieu's two forms of capital can be so readily converted into each other. Fan knowledge, however, lacks institutional legitimation, so its capital is non-convertible: its economy is that of the black market—it shadows the official economy in everything but its legitimacy.[3]

The baseball card is an interesting commodity in this shadow economy of fandom. It is a physical sign of knowledge—the possession and collection of cards is the material evidence of acquired and accumulated knowledge: a collection is each fan's data bank, knowledge of which is controlled by the fan rather than being knowledge by which the fan is controlled. Each card individuates the player to subject him to this control. Like my Resident Alien card, it has on its front physical identifiers and on its reverse statistical identifiers.

Knowing the player by owning the card is a way of owning the player. This allows for fans to trade cards among themselves in the way that team owners trade players. The shadow economy comes close to the material economy here, so that the cards of the better players become more valuable as do the players themselves. The trading of cards becomes one way in which the capital of fan knowledge can be converted to economic capital, thus shadowing the real world. But the shadowing still inverts—for the aim of fan trading is to improve the collection and increase cultural capital and thus status within the fan community: rarely does it aim to produce economic profit. Indeed, fans who make money from their fan capital are viewed with extreme suspicion by, and often excluded from, the fan community. Those who profit financially from this shadow economy—the dealers and producers of cards—are outside the community that values their cultural capital.[4]

The power of fan knowledge is effective only within its own *communitas*, and this *communitas* is masculine. In it the fan expert will earn status, but such status is not divisive or individuating because it is produced by members of the *communitas* according to their own criteria. Fan expertise is shared and is used to perform communal membership: its circulation is one of the key definers of the *communitas*:

A. He should have lateralled the game.
B. Yeah, but that would have been risky.
A. Ever since I saw that Miami lateral...
B. Yeah...[5]

Male fans will often use their expertise to "argue" with the official experts—the commentators. For male fans sport is a field of knowledge which they can know and master, rather than one by which they are known and mastered. But it is an unofficial knowledge: it has no links with institutionally validated knowledge such as that produced by the educational system. Consequently the distinction of its experts is not convertible into economic and social advantage: unlike the distinctions of education, it cannot become part of the structural inequalities of the social order.

But many women watch sport quite differently. In their study of gender differences in the watching of televised football, Duncan and Brummett found that many women knew as much about football as men did, but they did not use this knowledge in a masculine manner.[6] Men inserted themselves into the power-knowledge system in the empowered position of knower rather than the disempowered one of known, but women used their knowledge skeptically, to distance themselves from the masculine way of knowing sport. They used their knowledge of sport to exercise their knowledge of men, so what they were watching with such enjoyable and empowering skepticism was not sport, but masculinity. For them sport's display of male bodies was a chance to mock masculinity—they laughed at awkwardnesses, commented on arrogance and stupidity. At one pile-up a woman wondered "Do we need 85 people in there" and, when a celebratory "spike" by a quarter back went wrong, "I love it when they slam the ball down and it goes f-t-t-t-t-t."

Male bodies were the source of mockery: "*Great* shot of a tushie," "That gut's got to go" or, as a player readjusted his clothing, "Looks like he's taking inventory." This particular study found little evidence of a female erotic pleasure in the display of male bodies: other studies, however, have.[7] Television close-ups and slow motion replays aestheticize the male body and turn it into an object of feminine visual pleasure and therefore power. Both the mocking of the male body and the eroticization of it reverse the normalized relations of gender power. The women's mockery of the masculinity of sport was also a mockery, even if less explicit, of male fans' reverence and seriousness. The subversive carnivalesque mocking of masculinity is not confined to sports spectatorship, but is a valuable tactic in women's strategies for coping with patriarchy in general. The women's irreverence at sport may have been a way of sharpening their skills for coping with masculine power in the more serious domains of everyday, workaday life. Their ways of knowing sport disturbed the panoptic system of knowledge-power in a way that the men's did not.

An account such as this of the pleasures of spectating locates them in their relationships of similarity and difference to the displeasures of the workaday and everyday lives of their fans. Inverting knowledge-power and becoming the knower rather than the known, and exercising this power horizontally within a *communitas* rather than vertically in a structure of individuation provide two of these pleasures.

A third is the way that sport always exposes the limits of officialdom to control both it and the way it is known. Every game has moments which demonstrate that the disciplinary system of norms cannot account for the totality of experience. The pleasure in seeing a player who has batted 150 all season bat 400 in the World Series is not just the pleasure of his performance but also the pleasure of overturning statistical normality. When the Minnesota Twins go from bottom of the American League (West) in 1990 to World Champions in 1991 they demonstrate the possibility of the abnormal, and this is intensely pleasurable to those for whom normality is an instrument of subjection. Sport's power to release the fan from normality is often experienced as "magic" or "a miracle"— words which fans use frequently in describing their fandom.

Sport's "magic," an experience beyond the normal, shows that the account of the pleasures of inverting the power-knowledge that produces the normal tells us only part of the story. The inversion and exposure of dominant ways of knowing opens up gaps in which localized, embodied experiences can insert themselves. And they seize the opportunity. Crucial to sports fandom is an intensity of feeling, a passion, and a loss of control which are produced by an embodied way of knowing that is rooted in the body's presence in the experience that it knows. It is a way of knowing anchored in the here and now of its production and thus quite different from an abstracted, statistical knowledge.

What it knows first of all is that the experience *matters*. In the intensity of the experience the bodily sensations and passions become fully engaged with the externality of the moment of the game and with the environment of the stadium, its players and fans. This full engagement, or *identification*, of the body with its environment, of the interior with the exterior, matters so intensely because it is almost impossible to achieve in the monitored conditions of everyday normality. The discipline of the workplace, the school of the family controls our bodies from the outside, it requires us to behave and thus identify ourselves by criteria that we know are *theirs*, not *ours*. It entails a separation between whom we think we are (the interior or our individualized identity) and whom we know they require us to be (the exterior or our individuated identity). We are all of us adept at negotiating this separation but the adeptness should not mask the tension involved, for the negotiation always involves our inserting ourselves into *their* system of control: self-control is actually an internalization of *their* control. The TWA operative may have been told that *she* had "complete control," but the "she" was a product of the power system, as was "her" control.

Fred Exley, a lifelong fan of the New York Giants, tells of football's ability to overcome this deadening sense of separation:

> Why did football bring me to life? I can't say precisely. Part of it was my feeling that football was an island of directness in a world of circumspection.[8]

He gives a detailed account of how his body, watching the Giants on TV in a bar, joined in the game and "took high swimming passes over my right shoulder and troddled, dipsy-doodle-like, into the end zone," an experience he likens to that of a mad man. One reason that popular culture matters so much to people is its ability to provide peaks of intense experience when the body identifies with its external conditions, and thus shakes itself free from the repressive difference between *their* control and *our* sense of our identity. This intensity is often experienced by fans as a sense of release, of loss of control. When our individualities, our bodies and our immediate environment are experienced as a unity, we feel free. We feel free because this unity is a sign that we have shaken our locale free from their control and made it, however temporarily, our own at last. The control that is lost is theirs. Fans often use metaphors of madness to describe this freedom, and madness, as Foucault has shown us, is what lies just outside the boundary of civilization and control. When the Minnesota Twins reached the play-offs a fan wrote: "This pleasurable insanity, this incurable state of being a Twins fan, rabid but happy, is now fully upon me."[9] Over two hundred fans responded to the Minneapolis *Star Tribune*'s invitation to write and share with others their pleasures of fandom. Another wrote:

> Perhaps the greatest example, though, is that, being a relatively non-demonstrative person, the Twins give me moral courage to yell "Charge," even when no one else in the section is yelling.
>
> I owe a lot to the Twins, mostly hours of pure enjoyment. Yes, I'm a good fan and I think a better person because of it.[10]

The word "nondemonstrative" speaks of her experience of the separation between her controlled body in normality and the different identity held down by it: she begins her letter "The Twins really bring out the best in me"; her fandom gives her the moral courage to bring out her interior identity, which is "the best" and thus to feel "a better person" than her individuated self is allowed to be in normal life.

Some fans, however, while recognizing this contradiction between the sports experience and the discipline of the everyday, align themselves with the everyday. After saying how much baseball meant to him in his youth, a male fan writes:

> That was then and this is now. I'm 33 years old now and find myself less enmeshed with the Twins. . . . Let us not live in denial. Many people in our society from various economic levels have significant problems in major life areas. I guess I choose to enmesh myself with the real world. I still love baseball. However those Twins perform, I just choose to put it in perspective.[11]

These peak experiences matter so intensely because they integrate identity with the body: they are ones of significance rather than signification. And their significance matters so much that they often serve as *nodal points* around which other experiences are organized in the lives and memories of the fans. In many countries, the government promotes sport in an attempt to harness its significant intensity to nationalism, and thus to construct a nationalist sentiment which can erase the differences of interest between the power-bloc and the people. This erasure of difference will, then, hopefully, deny the popular knowledge that a nation is generally constructed by and for the power-bloc and not its subjected people. Because sport is a cultural form in which the interests of the power-bloc and the people are often closely aligned, it lends itself readily to such strategic use. More frequently, however, the intense significance of sport serves local rather than national relations and identities, and works to form felt relationships either with the locality of city or region, or within the more immediate locale of family. Family relationships can often be enhanced by sharing an experience that matters so intensely. Sport commonly provides fathers and sons with an intimacy that their masculinity often prevents them expressing directly. But sport's relational terrain extends to include all members of the family, all relationships. Indeed, it can even reform ruptured family bonds:

> I began to ask myself what was missing from my life that would make a bunch of baseball games seem so important. Then one day it hit me like a line foul off Kirby's bat: I was avoiding some unfinished business.
>
> Later that year, I began the search for my missing piece. To my eternal delight I found it, and this year I went to the Twins home opener with the person who would've grown up in Minnesota if things had been different 23 years ago: my son. There was more magic that night than the Dome could hold. I knew it would last me a lifetime, and hoped it would last the Twins at least a season. So far so good.[12]

These nodal points can reconnect the past with the present. Adult fans recalling the times and places of their childhood often organize these memories around sports experiences. The contemporary experience of sport seems to do more than just remind them of a distant experience; it closes the gap and almost enables them to re-experience the past in the present.[13] It may be that many of us experience a separation between the child that we were and the adult that we are—a separation exacerbated by the social and geographic mobility required by elaborated capitalism—so that there is a real pleasure in reconnecting the past with the present, in re-establishing a sense of our own identity that is powerful enough to sustain itself through all the changes that this complicated social order puts us through.

This changing mobility is experienced geographically as well as historically. Our different life experiences often occur in different places, and the sports experience is often used to identify the meaning of place. Our social identities and social relationships are lived in places; the identities and relationships between places are as formative in our sense of who we are and how we relate to the social order as is the structure of social relations. Sport identifies place, gives it a significance that works only for those who live in it.

This experiential knowledge of sport is known in and through the body. Its affective intensity provides vital experiences around which fans can organize their sense of their personal histories and relationships, and in which it becomes possible to experience identities that are their own. Because these identities are not produced by the disciplinary process of individuation they can be extended horizontally into intimate relationships of *communitas*. Another reason for sport's popularity is its ability to reproduce but invert the power-knowledge mechanisms of workaday life. This inversion does not challenge the normal working of the system, but it does reposition the fan within it. This repositioning allows the space for a contradictory way of knowing, an embodied, experiential one, to enter the picture and to produce a body of knowledge from within rather than without, a body whose significances are particular and thus knowable only by itself. But this localized power exists only in the spaces created by inverting an imperializing power-knowledge over others. Any transformative effect it may have is confined to the immediate conditions of fans' lives by the use of the knowledge system that normally controls them and, as such, may be seen as partially complicit at least with the system of the power-bloc.

NOTES

1. Andrew Ross, *Strange Weather* (London: Verso, 1991).
2. Pierre Bourdieu, *Distinction: A social critique of the judgment of taste* (Cambridge, Mass: Harvard University Press, 1984).
3. For an elaboration of these ideas, see John Fiske, "The Cultural Economy of Fandom," in Lisa Lewis (ed.), *The Adoring Audience: Fan Culture and Popular Media* (New York: Routledge, 1992).
4. Henry Jenkins, *Textual Poachers: Television, fans and participatory culture* (New York: Routledge, 1992).
5. Margaret Duncan and Barry Brummett, "Liberal and Radical Sources of Female Empowerment in Sport Media," *Sociology of Sport Journal* (forthcoming).
6. Ibid.
7. See Margaret Morse, "Sport on Television: replay and display," in E. Ann Kaplan (ed.), *Regarding Television* (Los Angeles: American Film Institute, 1983), pp. 44–6; and Beverley Poynton and John Hartley, "Male Gazing: Australian Rules Football, Gender and Television" in Mary Ellen Brown (ed.), *Television and Women's Culture* (London: Sage, 1990), pp. 144–57.
8. Fred Exley, who turned his fan experiences into a novel, *A Fan's Notes*, quoted in the *Washinton Post* ("Passions Run Deep for Devoted Giants Fan"), 26 October 1991.
9. Letter to the Minneapolis *Star Tribune*, 6 October 1991.
10. Letter to the Minneapolis *Star Tribune*, 6 October 1991.
11. Letter to the Minneapolis *Star Tribune*, 6 October 1991.
12. Letter to the Minneapolis *Star Tribune*, 6 October 1991.
13. The following letters from the *Star Tribune*, 6 October 1991, are examples of how fans can organize their memories of time and place around sport.

> Although I live 1,000 miles away in Helena, Mont., I still follow the Twins. I grew up in Minnesota, and this season has made me reflect on my past. Even with the large salaries and egos I realize how baseball always returns us to the days of our youth. I reflect on the times listening to Halsey Hall and Herb Carneal on the radio while throwing a ball against the garage or hitting a whiffle ball, pretending to be the heroes of my youth: Killebrew, Oliva, Allison, Pascual, Kaat.
>
> I see my 9-year old son's eyes at his first major league game last year at the Dome and think of my first game at the MET. I saw his heroes reflected in his eyes—Kirby, Hrbek, Harper, Gladden—and I think of my past heroes. This season has made me reflect on my youthful days of summer, days of reaching adulthood but with baseball still being a game and reflecting on the miracle of '87 and seeing it recur in 1991.

> The Minnesota Twins represent both a link to my childhood and a source of present pleasure. Growing up in Mankato as the daughter of a devoted Twins fan, I have many memories of attending games during the Harmon Killebrew, Bob Allison and Tony Oliva years. In my father's book of "The Twins Fan Rulebook," Rule 1 was "Never go to a single game if you can go to a doubleheader instead." ... As an adult dealing with the pressures of a family and career, I find that the Twins provide me with excitement, diversion and entertainment. A co-worker recently reminded me that baseball is "a children's game played by adults." My head knows that well but my heart says, "Thanks for the fun and GO TWINS."

> Growing up as a spoiled kid in New Jersey during the '50s, I got to see Willie Mays at the Polo Grounds; Duke Snider, Gil Hodges & Co. at Ebbots Field, and all of the great Yankees teams in the Bronx.
>
> Returning from Vietnam, I was spoiled again by the Miracle Mets in 1969 and "Ya gotta believe" by Tug McGraw in 1973.
>
> Time passed, and a decade in Minnesota has given me the thrill of 1987 and finally this year. What a joy to root for this team! Hometown heroes like Kent Hrbek

and Jack Morris. A character like Dan Gladden and a rookie like Chuck Knoblauch. And a future Hall of Fame center fielder who never runs out of that boyish enthusiasm, just like Willie Mays.

There's only one other way I could ever be spoiled: if Minnesota built a ballpark.

5

ELVIS: A BODY

OF CONTROVERSY

ALIVE: THE DISRUPTIVE BODY

Elvis Presley has always formed a body of controversy. In life and in death, his body has been a constant terrain of struggle between the power-bloc and formations of the people, a point where imperializing and localizing powers face up to each other. His body was not just muscle and movement but a point of intersection for the social axes of age, gender and race, and as such a strategic point of control where power was applied and contested.

When, in 1956, the young Elvis erupted onto the US public scene, attention focussed immediately on what he did with his body and then on how he could be stopped from doing it. His nickname, Elvis the Pelvis, identifies the part of the body that caused the trouble. His performance of "Hound Dog" on the *Milton Berle Show* of 5 June 1956 was more than adult America could endure in dignified silence.[1] So it erupted in disciplinary fervor. The uproar had little to do with the song, but everything with the body of the singer. The performance of his hips was widely seen as one of offensive sexual abandon. His young body was "loose" and its physical looseness was quickly taken as a sign of moral laxity. The fluidity of his pelvis did not so much simulate the movements of sex as display a body that had loosened the strings of social control. To adult America, Elvis was out of control.

The performance, of course, was far from uncontrolled, for not only does it require physical control to make a body move as loosely as Elvis's, but his body and song were tightly choreographed together. The principles which ordered the body-song came from outside the control of the power-bloc and constructed an order which was not theirs and which they did not "know." Not knowing the order, the power-bloc saw it as disorder, but Elvis and his fans knew exactly what his body was doing and why, and that, of course, was the real problem. The body of Elvis was not a site where human "nature," particularly its sexuality, escaped social control and produced "mass hysteria," it was a site where a subordinate social formation contested the power of the dominant to order and control their lives.

The two sides of the struggle were made explicit in an exchange on the TV talk show *Hy Gardner Calling*:

GARDNER You create a sort of mass hysteria among the audience of teenagers—is your shaking and quaking a sort of involuntary response to this hysteria?

ELVIS (long, baffled pause) Will you say that again, sir?

GARDNER When you shake and you quake when you sing, is that a sort of involuntary response to the hysteria of your audience?

ELVIS (pause) Involuntary?

GARDNER Yeah.

ELVIS Well, ... I'm aware of everything that I do at all times ... it's just the way I feel.

Hy Gardner, the adult, and Elvis, the youth, both identify the body as the site of the experience being discussed, but for Gardner the bodies of the fans and/or performer are "hysterical," their actions "involuntary"—they epitomize the body out of control. For Elvis, however, his actions are well within this control; they express bodily what he feels.

Hy Gardner's word "hysteria" is part of the gender politics of the Elvis panic. Foucault has shown us that "hysteria" was produced as a concept in the nineteenth century as a way of putting women's sexuality under patriarchal control through both discourse and medical practice.[2] The TV cameras of the 1950s continue this discursive control: the rock-'n'-roll fans they show are almost exclusively teenage girls. The male performer and the hysterical female fan become the conventional way of representing rock music for adult America. The Elvis panic (like the James Dean panic) was integral to that major social anxiety of the period—the "juvenile delinquency" problem. In the public imagination this took the form of male socially delinquent behavior backed up by female "hysteria" (read "sexually delinquent behavior"). The hysterical female fan figured, literally, the body out of control, and her constant public representation "proved" that the loose individual body of Elvis "loosened" the multiple bodies of his fans until they threatened the body of society. The body of the female fan was the canvas upon which adult society could see and thus verify its own panic.

But these teenage bodies were not out of control. They may have been breaking out from a disciplinary system, but their "hysteria" was not an example of the entropic principle of disorder in nature: it was rather evidence of a bottom-up, subordinated power contesting its normal restraints. The order of Elvis's performance orchestrated the order of his fans' "disorder." The bodies of the fans and the body of Elvis participated mutually in a carnivalesque escape whose "looseness" they exploited to form a *communitas*, a social formation whose links were horizontal and thus under the control of the subordinate and beyond the disciplinary reach of vertical individuation.

Such social formations inevitably galvanize the power-bloc into action. In the case of Elvis its forces quickly allied themselves across the domains of entertainment, politics and religion. In the world of entertainment, the critics launched the first offensive: his performance of "Hound Dog" on the *Milton Berle Show* was widely taken as proof that Elvis was a "no-talent performer" who could neither sing nor dance and was merely riding the wave of a short-lived and superficial trend. The TV networks joined the critics in the drive to re-establish control over the teenage body. A petition of 18,000 signatures, and large public demonstrations by teenagers carrying banners such as "We Love Gyratin' Elvis" gave commercial alliances within the power-bloc motive enough to rebroadcast him, but to maintain the links between these and more moralistic alliances the TV industry controlled his representation as tightly as they could. His next appearance was to be on the *Steve Allen Show*: NBC kept one eye on its profits by refusing to bow to the pressure to cancel his appearance and the other on its "public" (read "power-bloc" not "popular") reputation by announcing that Elvis would not be allowed to "bump and grind." A few months later Ed Sullivan exerted a similar control: Elvis could appear on his show only if the cameras never strayed below his waist. For the *Steve Allen Show*, which, in Steve's words, was "Elvis's first come-back," Elvis was dressed in a tux and tails; the studio was set with back-lit Grecian columns and candelabra; he was provided with a soft, melodic backing by an unseen crooning chorus; and, as introduction, Steve Allen said "It gives me great pleasure to introduce the *new* Elvis Presley. ... I think your millions of fans will get a real kick out of seeing a different side of your personality."

Held in this disciplined station of setting, dress and body movement, Elvis sang the offending "Hound Dog" to a lugubrious basset hound also dressed in a tux, as a clear sign of submission to the adult order. His other song on the show was the crooning ballad "I want you, I need you, I love you." George Kline, a lifelong friend of Elvis, says that Elvis told him that this was the first time that he felt he had really "sold out." But the sell-out was not total. In both numbers Elvis's performance contained residual traces of his pelvic abandon that the discipline could not repress entirely; from them those who knew the original could reconstruct it and thus "see" what was repressed as well as its repression. Steve Allen's introduction gave Elvis a similar opportunity to refer to this particular instance of the opposition between the people and the power-bloc:

> ELVIS It's not too often that I get to wear a suit and tails, but I think I have on something that's not quite correct for evening wear...
> STEVE ALLEN Not quite formal, what's that Elvis?
> ELVIS Blue Suede Shoes.

At the reference to one of his "disruptive" hits, Elvis and Steve Allen both look down at the offensive footwear, but the camera is not allowed to carry their affront into the suburban home and they remain unseen by the viewers. Similarly, on his second, waist-up-only appearance on *The Ed Sullivan Show* Elvis still moved wildly, his audience screamed enthusiastically and he constantly looked down, so by sharing his gaze, his fans "saw" what the camera was not allowed to show them. Controlling the camera did little to control Elvis.

The fan response to Elvis was probably more multiaccentual than that of the power-bloc. The power-bloc homogenized Elvis and in their panic saw only his threat. But Elvis also carried the traces of the social order he apparently threatened. He frequently insisted that he lived "a clean, straight life"; he didn't smoke, he didn't drink, he wanted to meet the right girl, marry her and raise a family. He stressed how much his own parents, particularly his mother, meant to him. Similarly, although his first gold record was the rocking, disruptive "Heartbreak Hotel," it was quickly followed by his second—the ballad he crooned so submissively for Steve Allen "I want you, I need you, I love you." This was (almost) as sweetly inoffensive as anything that Perry Como was singing on the hit parade at the same time. Neither popular culture, nor the lives of the people, can ever be untouched by the power-bloc, but both must contain that from which they differ.

Even the offending performance of "Hound Dog" was shot through with contradictions that the offended social formations missed entirely. Its body movements were so exaggerated as to open them up to self-parody. On the sound track we can hear at least as much laughter as screams from the studio audience and the young woman who had been preselected to stand for "the hysterical female fan" (the cumbersome studio cameras of the time could not move freely about the audience but had to be prepositioned) laughed delightedly at least as much as she screamed. The self-mockery, which Bakhtin identifies as a feature of carnivalesque laughter, is heteroglossic for it carries within itself, if not a representation of that which is being offended, at least a recognition of what the offending performance might look like from the social position which it offends. The difference of Elvis fans from the mature social order was never total and was not meant to be. The traces of the social formations from which they differed were what allowed the fans to negotiate their social relations. They had no desire to emigrate but rather instead to establish their own territory within the mother country.

But moral panics and demonizations work best when the threat is straightforward and uncontradictory. The newsreels of the day have recorded for us some of the voices allied within the power-bloc to discipline this demon. An overweight politician (dark suit, white shirt, bow tie, leather chair, polished desk, emphatic voice):

> Very frankly, we're lovers of music in Jersey City, and we've gone out of our way to bring music concerts and dances to the teenage people in order to keep them entertained. We feel, based upon the experiences throughout the country, that this rock and roll rhythm has been the seat of trouble, and we want to keep trouble out of Jersey City.

The benignity of the control over teenagers exercised by "keeping them entertained" by music chosen by the controllers is fractured by the power-laden othering of the phrase "the teenage people." The politician's linking of rock-'n'-roll with civil disorder is continued and given a moral dimension by a preacher (not much older than Elvis, thin faced, tight lipped, no jacket, shirt as white as his congregation, tie precisely centered, impassioned voice and gestures):

> These men come down here from New York and Florida to find out my reason for opposing the rock and roll music, and why I preach against it. I believe with all of my heart that it is a contributing factor to our juvenile delinquency of today. I one hundred per cent believe it. Why I believe it is because I know how it *feels* when you sing it, I know what it *does* to you, I know of the *evil* feeling that you *feel* when you *sing* it, I know the *lost* position that you get into ... the *beat*. Well, you talk to the average teenager of today, and you ask them what it is about rock-'n'-roll music that they like—the first thing they'll say is "The Beat! The Beat!! The Beat!!!"

The crescendo of his voice and the gestures of his hands leave little doubt that "the beat" is that of the body in evil (that is, sexual) abandon, the body out of control. At times even the law joined the disciplinary efforts: a judge in Jacksonville, Florida, issued a restraining order banning Elvis from "offensive gyrations" during his concert there. On stage, Elvis mocked the order by moving only his little finger—and his fans still went wild.

The struggle to control Elvis was a struggle between the power-bloc and the people, or rather between alliances formed within each. These alliances are not formed by organized groups or individuals, but through a recognition of common interests. The preacher, the Jersey City politician and Ed Sullivan had never met and had not agreed on a common strategy, but their social interests overlapped, and in promoting them they formed an alliance of interests. Similarly, there was no organization of teenagers across the nation but there were "teenage interests" that underlay a common pattern of belief, taste and behavior. These alliances may be based in social categories such as class, gender, race and age, but they are not confined to them and can cross their boundaries with comparative ease depending on the issues around which they are formed and the conditions within which they operate. These alliances can also transcend the boundaries of the individual and promote struggles between different formations of the power-bloc (or the people): the TV producers formed economic alliances to profit from Elvis which contradicted the socio-ethical ones to restrain him. These alliances can split not only individuals but also class interests or those of social groups. The interests of capital were served by promoting Elvis and encouraging the teenagers to spend money on establishing their (threatening) social identity. But other interests of that class—interests of order, control and morality—were served by repressing Elvis. The power-bloc, while less heterogeneous than the people, is not a completely homogeneous formation, and its internal contra-dictions, as much as those between it and the people, mean that its power is exerted through issue-based rather than class-based alliances.

The struggle of these alliances to control the social body through the body of Elvis had both an explicit dimension and a repressed one. Explicitly the power-bloc attempted to control the new social category of the "teenager." The fifties were when US society reshaped itself after World War II. The returning male workforce pushed the women back into the household, the growing prosperity moved the household into the ranch house in the suburbs, and this reconfiguring of the urban landscape reconfigured the social relations of those who lived within it. The suburban single family house on its individuated block of land enclosed the terrain within which the nuclear family could re-establish itself and discipline its members. The new media of communication—cars, telephones, radio and, crucially, television—made the individuation of these new domestic stations possible and bearable by connecting them in a limited and controllable way to society at large, and, to a much lesser extent, to each other. Suburbs individuated the nuclear family more efficiently than city streets, and life within them could become as clipped as their lawns. Lynn Spigel has shown how hard the TV industry in the 1950s worked to cast television as a pro-family force.[3] Advertisements claimed not only that TV would educate children but, by making them want to stay home to watch it, would keep them within the family space and therefore control. When the kids are watching TV the parental purchaser of the set will know what they are up to.

Mary Beth Haralovich recounts how the suburb was produced as a disciplined homogenized place through a conjuncture of social forces.[4] The Federal Housing Authority, through zoning, loan policies and "protective" covenants, aimed to produce "harmonious, attractive neighborhoods" which excluded, according to Hayden, the single or divorced, the white working class, the elderly and racial minorities in general. The harmony of the neighborhood was the white prosperous middle-class family singing in tune with its neighbors.[5] The new house sang the same melody. Its open floor plan where living, dining, kitchen and recreational areas flowed into each other, encouraged a lifestyle of family togetherness. Haralovich shows us how two popular sit-coms of the period, *Father Knows Best* and *Leave it to Beaver*, showed this built environment working to construct ideal families in ideal suburbs.

Television played a crucial role in this, not only by showing the suburb to itself, but by enhancing the individuation and therefore discipline of each household by ensuring that its links with the outside world would be made within the place "held" by the house—the *househeld* space. The women, who were as held by this household as firmly as they participated in its hold over their children, were advised on how to rearrange their furniture and routines not just to make room for television as though it were a guest but to treat it as a family member. Seating was rearranged, new TV chairs and TV tables were purchased, and new TV dinners were devised to be eaten together around the set. The schedule of television was to be used to enhance the routines of domesticity, the return of the husband/father from work, the evening's relaxation of the family together, the bedtimes of its younger members, the more mature shows after these times. Television was to be integral in the ordering of family life, in both space and time.

So when this new agent of order invaded the family with images of pelvic disorder, parental outrage was inevitable. Under the outrage lay a deep anxiety about what was going on outside the househeld order. The social forces which individuated the suburbanized family produced also a threat to it—the teenager. Those in this new social category had a new sense that their social identity was actually theirs: that they could possess a time outside the control of school, work and the family. Besides the time, which its routines allowed teenagers to claim as theirs, the suburb provided space also. The material prosperity built into the ranch house resulted in new spaces such as individual bedrooms and basements which teenagers could lay claim to. The individuation of the house meant that parents had to go "out" to socialize and thus to leave whole houses which could become teenage territory for an evening. The prosperity also put older teens on wheels. The car, filled with rock-'n'-roll, was not only a teenage locale in itself, particularly well suited for social and sexual encounters, but was also a means of controlling other places: to cruise was to control. The teenage body-in-the-car could drive parents sleepless by driving out of their territory and into his or (more rarely) her own.

The "teenage problem" was not one of age only, but also of gender. As postwar suburbanization repositioned the woman into the household, it also repositioned her into femininity. Rosie the Riveter in her boiler suit had to be turned back into June Cleaver in her pinafore. The suburban household space was homogenized through gender difference. The kitchen was Mom's, the den Dad's: the shared family lifestyle was one in which girls grew up into women and boys into men. Men left the house-suburb to enter the masculine sphere of paid labor, whereas women worked to maintain the domesticity the men paid for. The house-suburb was thus feminized, and while the men were in it they could accept the feminine influence without threat to their masculinity, because there was a masculine sphere of work, politics and public life that was exclusively theirs. The suburb domesticated and privatized the feminine: it made the place of feminine labor into that of masculine leisure and it disciplined differences into harmony.

This renewed femininity was central to suburban respectability and to the disciplined order of the nuclear family. Teenage daughters screaming at Elvis and using bodily excess to challenge the tight-lipped respectability of the suburban feminine had to be brought back in line. Calling their bodily release from discipline "hysteria" and thus pathologizing it was a discursive disciplinary strategy which had the effect of locating both the disease and the cure in the teenager. Adult society could then view itself as the doctor and not as the environment that spawned and nourished the virus. In relation to the male rock-'n'-roller, the female fan may appear reactive and disempowered, but when the fan and performer are seen as interdependent partners in the rock-'n'-roll experience, and this experience is set against the norms of suburbia, her bodily passion may seem both an evasion of, and a challenge to, an even more disempowering sense of the feminine.

In their study of the gender politics of "Beatlemania" (which peaked in

1963, just seven years after Elvis erupted onto the cultural scene), Barbara Ehrenreich and her colleagues cast the young female fan as a key player in the social changes that were brewing around the turn of the decade and that gathered momentum as it wore on.[6] Indeed, they provocatively argue that the "hysterical" female fan was a precursor of the women's movement. The 1950s and 1960s were equally sexualized and sexist, and in this steamy atmosphere the "good" teenage girl was expected to be not only "pure" herself but to enforce purity upon others. Advice books charged her with the responsibility of ostracizing "easy" girls, and, more importantly, of regulating the advances of the overeager boy as he attempted to progress from kissing (acceptable), through necking (still OK), to light petting (doubtful) and heavy petting (*not* what nice girls did). The bodily behavior that lay beyond here was, of course, so totally unacceptable that it wasn't even articulated. Good girls did not "give in" to their own or their boys' bodies; they never "let themselves go" but "saved" themselves for their wedding night. The teenage girl's body should be held as securely in its suburban station as any TWA operative's.

It is hardly surprising, then, that in these conditions of aroused sexuality but repressed behavior, rock-'n'-roll offered the teenage girl a locale where she could shake off the docility of her disciplined body and assert her own right to its pleasures and emotions. Rather than being the site of sexist manipulation by the male rock-'n'-roll performer, her body became the locality of freedom from the gender power of the suburbs. So girl fans screamed in unison, pummeled police who tried to hold them back, peed in their pants and, in extreme cases, lost consciousness (perhaps the ultimate evasion):

> To abandon control—to scream, faint, dash about in mobs—was in form if not in conscious intent, to protest the sexual repressiveness, the rigid double standard of female teen culture. It was the first and most dramatic uprising of *women's* sexual revolution.[7]

Ehrenreich et al. underscore this point by noting how rebellious it was for girls to display their own desiring sexuality which made the male singer into the object of their desire.

> To assert an active, powerful sexuality by the tens of thousands and to do so in a way calculated to attract the maximum of attention was more than rebellious. It was, in its own unformulated, dizzy way, revolutionary.[8]

And this active sexual desire rejected marriage—the appeal of Elvis and the Beatles lay in part in their unmarriageability and their image of a life free from marital constraints. Two adult Beatle fans, recalling their youth, make the point clearly:

A. I didn't want to grow up and be a wife and it seemed to me that the Beatles had the kind of freedom I wanted: no rules, they could spend two days lying in bed; they ran around on motorbikes...

B. I liked their independence and sexuality and wanted those things for myself... Girls didn't get to be that way when I was a teenager—we got to be the limp, passive object of some guy's fleeting sexual interest. We were so stifled, and they made us meek, giggly creatures think, oh, if only *I* could act that way, and be strong, sexy and doing what you want.[9]

The erupting female fan did break from social discipline and this "break" disrupted and weakened the sexism of the fifties. It was therefore a key component of the social conditions which nourished the new women's liberation movement (Betty Friedan's book *The Feminine Mystique*, often identified as a founding moment in the movement, was published in 1963). The adult social order was quite justified in panicking at the sight of Elvis's loose hips and their ecstatic fans, for the looseness and ecstasy were real threats to its hegemonic control.

The teenage body was the heartland of the teenage territory. So fashion, hairstyles and make-up, postures, gestures, and behavior (often while listening, moving, dancing to music) were what teenagers used to embody their control over their immediate social conditions. These cultural commodities produced financial profit for the power-bloc but cultural profit for the people – economic power-bloc interests can often be allied with cultural popular ones, much to the consternation of other power-bloc formations. Rock-'n'-roll is one of the most contested and contradictory cultural commodities, for music, with its ability to fill space and time simultaneously, is a particularly effective localizing resource. The 1950s teenager, surrounded by rock-'n'-roll, could keep adult society at bay. Within these loud locales teenagers could, and many did, extend and enhance their bodies by exploiting their chemistry—hormonally via sexuality and pharmaceutically via drugs. The teenagers' control over this entity of body-locale through the infamous trio of sex, drugs and rock-'n'-roll caused deep anxiety in adult social formations.

This anxiety was not entirely groundless. Rock-'n'- roll movies, such as *Rock around the Clock* or *Blackboard Jungle*, provoked (in adult eyes at least) uncontrolled, anti-social behavior. Teenage audiences used their music to extend their control over the place of the cinema for the time that they occupied it. They left their seats and danced in the aisles; at times they even tore up rows of seats (the signs of order) to make room for their dancing (the signs of disorder).[10] Such behavior was readily knowable by adult social formations as "juvenile delinquency" and they could make their sense of it by inserting it into a continuum which linked an individual teenager's sulky rejection of family discipline through public forms of social disorder in the streets and cinemas to illegal, criminal behavior. The juvenile delinquent figured the extreme towards which rock-'n'-roll was leading the more normal teenager away from the manicured ideals of suburban lifestyles and their lawns. When not even their grass was allowed to grow wild, it is small wonder the sight of their daughters abandoning themselves to "jungle rhythms" should have driven parental America into disciplinary fervor: Jailhouse Rock was what their offspring would end up breaking if they continued to listen to it.

James Dean was, to adult eyes, as delinquent a juvenile as Elvis, and the movie *Rebel Without a Cause* caused as much moral panic as Elvis's pelvis. Elvis admired James Dean and reportedly knew by heart all his lines in the movie. The adult moral panic had social roots: there was an alliance of teenage interests that challenged those of the adult power-bloc. Putting this behavior into discourse as "juvenile delinquency," then, was a strategic way of making sense of the "problem" in general and of Elvis in particular. His pelvic thrust into the bodies and minds of the young was a threat to the future of society and so, in the interests of mature responsibility, it had to be countered as decisively as possible.

The challenge of Elvis's loose body was not confined to the axes of gender and generation alone: the pelvis may have been young, but it was also Black. The explicit anxiety over generational disorder masked an equal, if repressed one, of a racial threat. Elvis had gained his start in the recording industry because, when he walked into Sun Records in Memphis, Sam Phillips, the proprietor, had been on the lookout for a white boy who could sing black. "Race records" (as Black music was called) was becoming increasingly popular on independent radio stations, and Sam Phillips had spotted the trend. He felt that white teenagers were ready for Black music, if not Black people, for Black music had the rhythm and vitality lacking in the white crooners of the day but central to the emerging lifestyle of "the teenager." Elvis fitted the bill precisely. Elvis's "Blackness" is highly problematic. Greil Marcus claims that he had a greater ability to hear Black music and to remake it than any other white musician. His early songs such as "Heartbreak Hotel" and "Jailhouse Rock" were hits on Black radio stations, and before he made any records at all, Elvis was a regular performer in the Black clubs of Beale Street. But very quickly, his audiences became almost entirely white. His "Blackness" was translated into white language; it was not, with a few exceptions, a Blackness for Blacks.[11]

If Elvis's career began because of his links with Black culture, it may be no coincidence that the links emerge again at its end. As we shall see in the next chapter, one of the most controversial photographs "proving" that Elvis is alive after his alleged death shows him with two leading figures in contemporary African American culture, Mohammed Ali and Jesse Jackson. Before his "death" Elvis became friends with Ali, and one account of his life after "death" has him living in Ali's well-guarded estate in Michigan. To support this account there have been a number of reported "Elvis sightings" in Kalamazoo, Ali's local town.

Be that as it may (and it may well be), the Black dimension of Elvis and his music underlay much of the anxiety he caused in mature white America. His "Blackness" was more than musical, it was physical. "Hound Dog" was a Black number, but the offense of Elvis's performance lay in his body as much as the music. No white body had ever moved in public like that before. In the US of the 1950s, racial segregation was still legal, civil-rights protests were growing, Martin Luther King was emerging as a leader and there was a sense that the Black body politic was stirring and flexing its muscles. In this context, Elvis's loose body could be seen to incarnate racially disruptive forms of the American social body. The new teenage consciousness and the new Black consciousness were made flesh in the body of Elvis; its looseness, its immense energy, its unprecedented movements, all evoked the terror of the new and the sense of loss of control by the old. The music, the body, the grain of the voice, while not in themselves Black, had Black inflections and carried the threat of an oppositional Blackness into the heartland of white culture arguably for the first time. The racial relations of Blacks to whites spoke with a threatening, disruptive accent in Elvis's body music in a way that they did not in that of, say, Paul Robeson or Nat King Cole. And the threat was all the greater because it was embodied under white skin.

So, for his reappearance on television, Elvis had to be not only disciplined, but whitened. On the *Steve Allen Show* the tuxedo and the basset hound tried to erase the Blackness of "Hound Dog," and Elvis's other song, "I want you, I need you, I love you," was a white melodic ballad sung by a white crooner. Elvis's move, later in 1956, from Memphis music to Hollywood cinema, also involved whitening him. In *Love Me Tender*, his first movie, he was tamed into the all (white) American, good-hearted farm boy. The whitewashing of Elvis on the screens of America may have prefigured that of Black footballers in its endzones, but neither the taming nor the whitening were total. His success still had a Black enough tint to open the door for Black rock-'n'-roll musicians to reach significant sections of the white audience, and to insist on their right to contribute to and profit from white popular culture. The flip side of this, of course, is that Elvis also established the practice of white singers covering Black original numbers and making enormous profits from them while killing the Black original. Whites making money out of Black talent is not a new story, but Elvis certainly revivified it.

Elvis may have been a white impersonation of Black, but traces of the Blackness were essential parts of his appeal (and, incidentally, have been brought to an ironic full circle in the person of Clarence Giddens, a currently popular African American impersonator of Elvis). The meanings of Blackness for white US society have always intersected complicatedly with those of class and sexuality; meanings of subordinated races and classes are consistently associated with and expressed in the body, and the body is where the appeal and the threat of sexuality is most clearly located.

The body of the Black male in the imaginary of the white middle class carries the wild energy and strength of natural, pre-civilized masculinity whose appeal and threat depend upon the fear that the civilized white male has "lost something." (One Black account of what he has lost is given by "The Cress Theory," summarized in Chapter 11.) Preserving this ordered, but in some way emasculated, white society from the potentially dis-ordered, but highly masculine, Black society of the white imagination has often historically and viciously been performed by white men castrating and killing Black men for supposedly violating white women. A similar sexualization of racial fear and guilt lies only just below the surface of the threatening image of the "Black" Elvis and the hysterical white female fan. The fear that "Blackness" can reach areas of human nature (typified by female sexuality) which are inaccessible to the white is as deep rooted as it is disturbing to white consciousness.

In the 1950s these Black traces in the body of Elvis and in the voice of rock-'n'-roll were clearer than today: they were readily available to be taken up by white youth to perform and embody their sense of their own difference from the white mature order that dominated both them and Blacks (the domination in each case, of course, was neither equal nor similar, but it was still domination). In the explicit attempt to control its own young, the mature white order was, if less overtly, attempting to extend this control racially. The deep social anxiety over "juvenile delinquency" was fed by an even deeper anxiety that Black social formations, too, were beginning to demand greater control over their social conditions. It is not merely coincidental that the progress achieved in race relations by the Civil Rights Movement in the sixties was achieved in part by social allegiances formed between Black activists and young whites who had grown up with rock-'n'-roll. The traces of Black culture and Black identity carried by rock-'n'-roll into the white suburbs may well have been one formative component of the young white consciousness that eventually resulted in direct social action in the Civil Rights Movement. The alliance of these young whites with Black interests showed that the panic of the power-bloc over the control of its young was not groundless. The power-bloc knows well the importance of age politics, for two of the most effective of recent popular movements (the other was over the Vietnam War) have been strongly influenced by youth.

In pointing out that the decade after Elvis did bring significant disruptions to the traditional social relations of race, gender and age, I do not imply that Elvis was a cause of these disruptions, but only that his popularity was conjunctural with the social conditions within which they developed. His body and his body of fans were sites where repressed forces within the social body could be experienced as alive and kicking. They were sites where the socially general and abstract could be turned into the particularity, vitality and public visibility of actual people and actual behavior. That is why Elvis mattered so much.

DEAD: THE EVASIVE BODY

On 16 August 1977, Elvis died. As a body of bone and muscle, he may be lying beneath the tombstone inscribed with his misspelt name at Grace-land, but as a body of controversy, a body of knowledge, he is still circulating among us. His fans of today, who give material form to this body of knowledge, are very different from the teenagers of the 1950s. They are mainly older, though they include all ages; they tend to be blue collar (though not exclusively) and they are almost exclusively white. They are much less threatening and much less visible than the 1950s teenagers. The change is characterized well by Terry Teachout when he writes:

> I was raised in a small town whose only movie house showed Presley's pictures regularly, and I remember, a couple of years before the singer's death, my father making, apropos of nothing, the following remark: "I never cared much for Elvis back in the 50s. But he changed. He grew up. He started giving the people good, clean entertainment."[12]

Even for today's fans Elvis may be dead, but his body won't keep quiet. It still tells contradictory stories, it is still a terrain of struggle. The struggle has changed, the social formations have changed, but it is still a struggle to control. The struggle here is not over behavior, though it has a behavioral dimension, but over knowledge, and its power to produce truth. Producing the truth of Elvis's death is engaging in social relations. The arguments over whether or not he *is* dead, and, if he is not, over how to know the life that followed his "death," involve stand-offs between localizing, popular knowledges and the official one (these are analyzed in some detail in Chapter 9). The ways of knowing his death differently are ways of performing social difference. A knowledge of Elvis's death is also a knowledge of the social formation that produced it.

In death Elvis's body is a book which, like any other, is read differently by different social formations. Our bodies are our personal history books, they are the record of our life experiences, they are where "we" are inscribed and where society is inscribed upon us. In de Certeau's words, the social "intextuates" the body and the body "incarnates" the social.[13] The struggles between the power-bloc and the people are literally incarnated in Elvis's body and in its intextuation of his own life history and, by extension, those of his fans. In this body of knowledge, no fact is uncontested, no belief not countered. Truths multiply and argue with each other, for here no truth is factual or objective, but each is nakedly dependent on the power of those who speak it.

Elvis's dead body is a text inscribed with the struggle to control his life. Reading this text involves producing a body of knowledge that is no inert set of facts or data but a socially situated and socially active way of knowing that is always in competition with other ways. For a body of knowledge to be transformed from data and the frame that organizes them into a socially active way of knowing it needs to be believed. Knowledge that is not transformed into belief remains distant and inactive, possibly understood rationally, but not imbricated into a way of life. Belief is activated, produced and localized knowledge: it is the means by which ways of knowing inform ways of living. Locales are constructed out of knowledges which have become beliefs. Equally, therefore, not believing is a tactic by which a locale can be defended against imperializing "truth."

Official scientific knowledge is circulated among and validated by members of the power-bloc, and it "knows" that Elvis is dead. Many fans, however, "know-believe" with an equal certainty and a far superior passion that he is not. The knowledge of Elvis's body given in the autopsy report was produced and validated by scientific instrumentation and procedures, a mode of production/validation whose social accessibility is limited and which therefore serves to alienate it from other, more popular knowledges. Such official "autopsical" knowledge has proved insufficient for many fans whose knowledges contest it, not only for what it says, but also for its mode of production and validation. These fan knowledges of Elvis are produced and validated experientially in the ways in which his fans saw, heard, and felt him. Such popular ways of knowing are lived, situated and believed, and operate quite differently, both socially and epistemologically, from abstracted, generalized, objective knowledge. Such popular knowledges are multiple and because they are "weaker," both socially and instrumentally, they make no pretence to autonomy but always situate themselves, more or less explicitly, against official knowledge. They are always multiaccentual because they contain the accents of that from which they differentiate themselves.

The tabloids attempt constantly to straddle the popular and the official, veering sometimes in one direction, sometimes the other.[14] One major set of mediations extends the official knowledge of Elvis's body into popular knowledges by offering less scientific, more popular evidence to complete the gaps left by official knowledge but not to contradict it: in them Elvis remains "dead"; what remains to be known is whether he died by error or suicide. The "error" stories are closer to official knowledge, the "suicide" ones to popular knowledge.

A typical "error" story is "What Really Killed Elvis."[15] The article is based on an unpublished book, *The Death of Elvis*,[16] and begins by citing the authors' summary of the key points in the autopsy report as the most official (medical and legal) knowledge of Elvis's body:

1. An accumulation of fluid was found in the lungs.
2. There were small hemorrhages from the abdomen up to the neck.
3. There were signs of conjunctivitis around the eyes.
4. There was a cyanotic or bluish condition around the abdomen from lack of oxygen in the blood.

They then cite the autopsy directly:

It is our view that death in the case of Baptist Memorial Hospital A77-160 resulted from multiple drug ingestion (commonly known as "polypharmacy"). Of particular note is the combination of codeine, ethchlorvynol and barbiturates detected in body fluids and tissues.

Elvis's body, individuated as "Baptist Memorial Hospital A77-160," was read scientifically: such official knowledge had no need to know the history by which these signs were written on the body. The book's authors and Elvis's fans, however, do. The authors reveal that, when alive, Elvis's body was allergic to codeine. On the day of Elvis's death, his dentist had given him codeine tablets, so Elvis had asked his physician for dilaudid instead. Because the two drugs were dispensed in very similar tablets, Elvis mistakenly took the codeine instead of dilaudid. His body took charge:

While sitting on the toilet, his allergic reaction kicked in. He began to feel itchy and short of breath. He had trouble calling for help. No one was on duty in the valet's bedroom. His girlfriend, Ginger Alden, was asleep.

Suddenly, the book he was reading was heavy, an encumbrance. He threw it aside. With much effort, he stood—but stumbled as he tried to pull up his pajama bottoms. He fell forward on his chest with his head to one side. Moments later, the King of Rock was dead from polypharmacy, an accidental overdose of multiple drugs.

This reading of the body extends the official one to include the personal history written in the pharmaceutical signs, a knowledge that inflects the official knowledge of body "Baptist Memorial Hospital A77-160" with the popular knowledge of Elvis and thus mediates between what the coroner knows and what the fans know. Though this reading is addressed to the popular, it is far from popular itself: it extends the coroner's knowledge to make it continuous with that of the fan; it does not challenge the official way of knowing, but mediates it. The journalist's investigation uses the same validating criteria of objectivity and facticity as does the scientist's, but widens their boundaries, so that what a scientist might call a deductive probability can enter the journalistic category of fact. This is a minimal inflection of official knowledge which can only just qualify as a form of media populism.

The Sun mediates the same unpublished book quite differently (even to the extent of giving it a different title: *Elvis, Dead on Arrival*) but still emphasizes the bodily behaviors and desires of his death: Elvis had neither showered nor bathed for months before his death, he was incontinent and impotent, and died, sitting on the toilet, reading pornography—a more corporal moment of death is hard to imagine.[17]

"Suicide" stories, however, tend to pay more attention to popular knowledges than to the official one, and to adopt accents which are closer to those of the people, both in how they speak and in what they say. In these accounts suicide becomes the act by which Elvis reasserts control over a body that has escaped it. In this popular knowledge, Elvis's life had escaped his control, his fame and success had isolated him, cut him off from the ordinary (popular) way of living that was "really" his. This "other" way of life wrote itself upon Elvis's body by drugs, the strain of living a life controlled by "them" was inscribed in the degeneration of his bodily organs and tissues: his inability to control the weight of his body was a sign of his inability to control his life. Success took the power to control his life away from Elvis and gave it to the industry and its alliances within the power-bloc. The Elvis–industry alliance was winning over the Elvis–people alliance. The fans are caught uncomfortably here, for they are inculpated in Elvis's fame; their excessive love for him was because he was really one of them and they could form a *communitas* with him, yet this love also produced the economic success and social fame which took him away from them. This ambivalence of guilt and love produces the common fan response, "We understand why he did it" (whether the "it" was suicide or the faking of his death): they do not feel let down or deserted. In their view, Elvis controlling either the truth or the falsity of his own death was reasserting the popular Elvis against the official, degenerating one. Elvis's sickness was the inscription of his alienated lifestyle upon his own body, an inscription over which he had no control, for the loss of control was precisely what the inscription "said":

> "Elvis had three heart attacks that he didn't even know about, cancer, glaucoma, arthritis, high blood pressure, a spastic colon, a bad liver, and he still drove himself to please his fans. He was in incredible pain. The autopsy showed he had bone cancer all through his body." Elvis chose to die on his own terms.[18]

In the "error" stories, the death of the body was outside Elvis's control, as was the life that immediately preceded it. The "suicide" stories, however, show Elvis struggling to control his own body, both in life as he willed it to keep performing for his fans, and in death as his final, if desperate, act of control. His body was a site of multiaccentual struggle and the suicide stories grant the fans and their "true" Elvis a more active role in it. He would not allow his body's degeneration to dictate the meaning of Elvis, the victory of wealth over popularity, of the power-bloc over the people.

A fan, retelling the day of his death, struggles explicitly to produce her popular knowledge of Elvis's body (it was beautiful) in opposition to "theirs" (it was bloated). She writes her meaning on the body in opposition to that written by cortisone and all it stands for:

> We drove and drove all day long to get here [Memphis] and my daughter, she said, "We'll never make it to see him," you know they said they was gonna close and not let nobody in after 6:00. And she said, "I can't stand it. I think I'll die if I see him in the casket and I think I'll die if I don't see him." And you know what I told her, I said, "Well no, we've got to see him, it's the last time we'll see him." ...
>
> And Elvis, he was so beautiful. But he always had long slender fingers with pretty slender hands, and you know, he took that cortisone that swells you up. He wasn't fat. Elvis was never fat. He'd swell up in his stomach and his face and his hands, and his poor hands were swollen up. He was bloated from that cortisone. And we saw him in Birmingham in December, you know, 1976, and he looked marvelous. He looked like he weighed about 180 pounds. Two months later we saw him and his face, oh it was that cortisone. ...
>
> 'Cause Elvis was such a handsome man, beautiful eyes, long eyelashes. My daughter said, "That poor thing." You know, smiling his pretty laughing eyes and that crooked grin. But Rodonna says, "He's still beautiful to me. I don't care how he looks. He's still beautiful to me."[19]

The struggle over the aesthetics of Elvis's body (was it an incarnation of the bloated, degenerate social forces that were controlling him, or could the fans still intextuate onto it their counter-knowledge of Elvis as beautiful and sensitive?) is extended into a struggle over "knowing" the physical body. The identity of the body lay beyond the inquiry of official knowledge but is central to some fans who know that Elvis's ultimate act of control over his body and life was not the commission of suicide but the faking of it.

THE BODY "LYING" DEAD

For Elvis to fake his death, he had to make his body tell a lie, perhaps the ultimate lie. The first such lie was told privately by the body on the floor of the toilet: it was not dead. Brewer-Giorgio accounts for this lie by Elvis's ability to exert "total mind control over his body" (p. 127), which he had developed through his interest in Eastern spiritual religions: he frequently, according to her, practiced "using his body as a decoy" to fool his entourage into believing he was in a drug-induced coma.[20]

The second untruth was that of the body "lying" publicly in the casket, and it is around this that most popular knowledges circulate. Some of the fans and relatives who knew Elvis best claim that they saw through this lie as they viewed the body (see Plate 1). Most of the fans, however, have seen only a photograph, and here, too, they are not fooled by the lying body. They know that the body pretending to be Elvis is not: they know that the nose is "puggy" (read "bloated") whereas Elvis's is really "classical" (read "beautiful"). They know, too, that the hairline is wrong, as though a wig were lying on the body.

There are two popular truths of whose body was in the casket: one claims it was a wax dummy, and the other that it was the body of an English look-alike fan who had been invited to Graceland because he was dying of cancer. The first truth is supported by the fact that the casket weighed 900 lbs, most of which was accounted for by the built-in refrigeration unit needed to keep the wax from melting and by the testimony of some fans who felt a chill as they passed the casket.

But by far the more productive truth, because it resonates with a much richer and more satisfying body of knowledge, is the "look-alike" one. (It is, incidentally, significant that these truths are never opposed to each other in fan knowledge, but always to the official truth that Elvis is dead.) One sense of this knowledge is circulated in the huge culture of Elvis impersonators, who metaphorically embody him, so that the body of Elvis is multiplied into multiple bodies which are, literally, in the control of the fan-impersonators who use them to re-embody the relationship between Elvis and the rest of his fans. This multiplicity of bodies provides not just a postmodern denial of the ultimate truth of any one body but the opportunity to exploit the uncertainty as to who Elvis really was. So one account tells us that the "Elvis" who performed in the final concert tour before his "death" was a body double. His duplicity is exposed by his hairy chest (see Plate 2), for the true Elvis had a hairless one which he tried to hide from the cameras:

> He didn't like pictures taken of his bare chest... So it was only rarely that you would see him walking down the beach without a T-shirt on or a robe. ... Yet in his last concert tour "Elvis" flaunted his hairy chest to women in the audience, bawdy behavior that was totally out of character.[21]

The *National Examiner* supports the claim with two photographs, one of a young, slim, smooth-chested Elvis, and the other of the bloated hairy-chested Elvis on the final tour. The "look-alike" was bloated because it was he, and not Elvis, who was suffering from cancer and thus receiving the drugs. And all the time, the "true" Elvis was in fact not fat and bloated but, offstage, in control of his own life and body. This "knowledge" is one of probability rather than of facticity, but the probability is "factualized" because it is a deduction made from evidence by a senior LA Police Department detective (official, though off-duty) and not just the wish-fulfilling fantasy of a fan. The probability is turned into credibility by the multiplying of Elvis bodies among the impersonators, one of whom is, according to some, Elvis himself. This uncertainty of *who* any one of these Elvis bodies actually *is* is increased by the knowledge that Elvis's twin brother Jesse was not stillborn, as official knowledge would have us believe, but is very much alive and adding his body to the confusion.

There are two popular explanations for the faked death: in one it was Elvis and his entourage who executed the plan in order to free him from the prison of superstardom, and in the other it was the FBI, possibly as part of its witness protection program. The knowledge that supports the first includes the fact that Elvis was unhappy, even suicidal, because of the falseness of his life as a superstar and the fact that Colonel Tom Parker, who made him the superstar and then exploited him, was himself a fake— he was an illegal immigrant without a passport or other official identity— and thus would be as expert in constructing a new false life for Elvis as an ordinary person as he was at constructing his old life as a superstar. The most elaborate corroboration of this belief was provided in 1992 by the Reverend Sam Beatty who, in a deathbed confession (he had been diagnosed with terminal cancer), admitted to helping Elvis fake his own death. The body in the casket was a wax effigy flown in from Germany four days before, while the body of Elvis was out of sight and experiencing its wax counterpart as not entirely false:

> "Elvis was not only alive on the 18th, he watched his own funeral from a secret location and he shed a few tears in the process," said the minister. "He knew that in a way he really was dead, that he had forsaken his friends, his family and his stardom for ever."[22]

To verify his insider status, Reverend Beatty showed the *Weekly World News* dozens of photographs of himself with Elvis and a diamond-encrusted gold ring inscribed "God Bless You, Reverend—El" dated 8/18/77 (two days after Elvis's death). What Sam Beatty has to tell is what fans already know, but he can tell it in Elvis's own words: "If I don't get out now, Reverend, I'll have to kill myself. The life I'm leading is no good. I'm dying a little bit every day." The three deaths blur into each other: the public death of the wax body, the bloated "false" Elvis dying a little bit every day, and the "true" Elvis dying as he watched his own funeral. One might be forgiven for believing that, in the case of Elvis Presley, the only real death is that of objective truth.

Evidence that it was the FBI who faked the "death" comes, *inter alia*, from the six hundred pages of FBI files on Elvis and includes the official facts that in 1970 Elvis was enrolled by President Nixon as an honorary drug enforcement agent charged to work against drugs in youth culture, that a member of his band was an agent in the Drug Enforcement Agency, and that he had received many anonymous death threats, aimed at both himself and his family, some of which may well have come from drug dealers. He had also become involved in "Operation Fountain Pen," a move by the Indianapolis office of the FBI against an international crime fraternity. His final concert was in Indianapolis, FBI agents were photographed backstage during it, and his "death" occurred just before the case against the fraternity was to go to court.

Whether it actually "was" the FBI or Colonel Tom Parker who organized the faked death and undercover life is, for fan knowledge, unimportant, for both of them occupy a similar space in the popular imaginary, a space labeled by one fan (whom we shall meet later) as that of the "upper echelons"—the mysterious (and suspicious) world of wealth, fame and influence into which his superstardom took him.

The knowledge that Elvis is alive entails knowing what sort of life he is living, so the popular imagination has produced two alternate, and quite incompatible, lives for him. One is that he is living an ordinary life, if an undercover one, possibly in Kalamazoo, Michigan, possibly on a horse ranch in Arizona. The other is an extraordinary life as a missionary/healer in South America. A German priest, Father von Secker, met a white-haired, limping Elvis working with lepers in Bolivia in 1988:

> Presley told me that for the first time in his life he was doing something worthwhile. And he added: "I came to this place because it was God's Divine Will."[23]

The French anthropologist Henri Boujean found a tribe of Brazilian Indians who

> were so impressed with Elvis Presley when they met him in 1981 that they still wear homemade Elvis wigs—and dance to jungle versions of his tunes![24]

Typical evidence of his ordinary life is that provided by Terri Starnes, 40, of San Diego who was at her local convenience store:

> When I got up to the check-out I realized I was short of money and the guy behind me gave me 5 bucks. It was Elvis Presley!

More extreme, but still consistent, was the experience of Maggie Flynn, 36, of St Petersburg. She was drowning:

> Slowly I felt my life slip away. Then, the next thing I knew, my eyes opened and I felt myself gasping for air again. I was lying on blessed solid ground and the handsomest man I've ever seen was giving me the kiss of life.
> "Welcome to the land of the living, Honey," he said to me, and that voice—that "Honey"—hit me like a truck. Then I looked into that fabulous face and I KNEW IT WAS HIM—I knew it was Elvis. . . .
> I'd refused to read any of those Elvis is Alive stories, but now I knew they were true, true, true! Still, I had to ask.
> "Yes Ma'am, I'm Elvis," he told me. . .[25]

Both his extraordinary and his ordinary lives tell the same truth about Elvis—he is a caring, helpful, gentle man.

Probably more important than these "actual" lives of Elvis is the knowledge that he lives on in his fans. The large copy in an ad for an impersonator show reads "Elvis is Alive, now experience him Live in Concert. The Tom Green Show, A Tribute to Elvis." Smaller type announces "Elvis' Music will always live. You've heard him on the radio. You've seen him on TV." "Live" means simultaneously both not-recorded and not-dead, and the not-dead meaning is embodied ambiguously in the "him" who has been on radio and TV. Whether the "him" is Elvis or Tom is not at issue for "he" is ultimately a figure in the popular imaginary who combines both of them into the one body/performance.

During his show Tom Green read aloud a note handed up to him:

"Please sing "Loving You" and thank you for keeping Elvis alive." He looked up and drawled in his "Elvis" voice, "Yeah, but it doesn't work quite like that ... we Elvis impersonators ... Elvis would still be the greatest entertainer in the world ... even without us ... we love and respect him too, but it's you, everyone in this room is a fan, and it's you fans who keep Elvis alive, alive in your hearts, not us."

At the interval I sat at a table with five fans, two women I would guess to be in their fifties, two in their twenties and a teenage boy. Three of the women had brought white silk scarves which they handed to Tom Green during the performance. Reproducing an act of Elvis, he put each round his neck for a moment, wiped the sweat off his brow with it and then leant down and put it round the neck of the woman. I talked about the scarves with the two older women:

A.   I've got a drawer full, I don't know, maybe 50 or 100.
B.   No, more like 500!
A.   No.
B.   Yeah, the drawer's stuffed.
ME   Do you get one from each impersonator, or one from each performance?
A.   No, only the good ones.
B.   They've got to be good—we're very discriminating.
ME   Is this guy good?
A.   Yeah, got plenty from him.
ME   Why do you do it?
A.   Oh it's a bit of Elvis.
ME   Do you label each one, where you got it, or can you remember?
A.   No it doesn't matter where they came from ...

The scarf is not a sign conveying meaning but a "significant thing" (see Chapter 10) conveying Elvis's body (his sweat) to hers. The sweat is physical evidence of how much of himself Elvis put into his performance for his fans (souvenir stores in Memphis still sell "Authentic Elvis Sweat"). The drawer full of sweaty scarves is not stuffed with texts, but with experiences of her physical connection with the body of Elvis. Reading it, then, is not an act of decipherment which anyone could perform for it involves a credulity, a knowing become believing, which is particular to her. I suspect, too, that the accumulation of these objects of knowledge and belief speaks to their importance—the plenitude of the drawer full is a material sign of how much the knowledge-belief matters to her.

The "truth" that the sweat is Elvis's is similar to the truth that communion wine is the blood of Christ: neither is a scientific truth, but they *are* truths in different orders of knowledge. The fan knows-believes that Tom Green is not Elvis and, yet knows-believes equally well that he is; the movement along this continuum of knowledge-belief is under her control and is motivated by her sense of her own pleasures and interests. Both impersonators and fans are explicit that these performances are not reincarnations of Elvis but impersonations of him which allow fans to enter the world of the "as if"—while knowing that the impersonators are not Elvis, the fans can also know-believe-behave *as if* they were.

What is particularly characteristic of these "Elvis lives" shows is the whole-hearted, engaged *fun* that the fans experience during them. The ability to have fun, particularly in a disciplined society, depends crucially upon the ability to move at will from the world of the "is" into the world of the "as if."

The "real," the world that "is," is where the people experience most directly the order of discipline and subjection. It is a "reality" controlled by the imperializing knowledge-power which constructed it. Locales can evade the reach of this order and in them people can construct "horizontal" social relations and therefore individualities whose construction proceeds along quite different lines from that of top-down individuation. The *communitas* of Elvis is organized around the fan knowledge of him as a caring, healing, generous, spiritual person who felt deeply for the well-being of ordinary people but was prevented from living in *communitas* with them by the class-divisive effects of his success. The stories of him working for the oppressed tribes of South American Indians, or helping his white fans who are sick or in trouble, are not *unreal* or *untrue*; they tell a truth about Elvis, a truth that is not only believed but embodied in social action. His fan clubs devote much of their energy to charitable causes, not as a form of benevolent control like that of the shelter providers, but as a performance of Elvis, in which they put into practice their knowledge of his identity and the social relations appropriate to it. Knowing Elvis as they do enables them to act as they do. In performing Elvis they are contributing towards their own social identities and relationships by building them horizontally and communally in direct contradiction to the vertical, competitive ones of individuation. The group of fans who shared their table and conversation with me performed this *communitas* throughout the evening, indeed the *communitas* was the object and fulfillment of the evening. As a social formation they existed only around Elvis; they hardly knew each other except as Elvis fans and almost never met outside their Elvis *communitas*. But within it their relationships were close and pleasurable: They traveled together (for nearly two hours on this particular occasion, and often for longer), they talked together, they sang together and when they danced they would often dance together in a circle of five. During one of their dances, a thin, shy-looking girl of about fourteen approached them and they instantly enlarged their circle to include her. Her shyness was transformed into enthusiasm, almost abandon, as she danced with them. They had never met her before, but their *communitas* included her, and including her was a performance of Elvis.

The South American tribe with Elvis haircuts who have adopted his music and bodily movements into their culture are an exotic retelling of the same truth of Elvis which is told time and again in the lives of his fans and impersonators. The knowledge which informs this truth is known through the body and its behavior: it is an experiential, embodied knowledge and as such differs diametrically from the generalizing, abstracting ways of knowing of official knowledge. Collecting silk scarves is a way of experiencing a relationship with Elvis. It produces no truths which can be abstracted from their performance, generalized and then represented to others. Its truths are *the fan's*: The meaning of the collection cannot be abstracted away from her practice in it. Locales are made out of practices and things (see Chapter 10); things, in particular, can overcome the temporary nature of locales, they can bring a sense of permanence which offers localizing cultures a way of controlling time. Localizing knowledge-power works through things and practices, imperializing knowledge-power works through texts and representations, and the body is a key site of the struggle between them.

Fandom frequently involves movements when bodies escape from individuation into communal "hysteria," and from stations into locales. The sports fan screaming for the team, the homeless men cheering the death of the CEO, and the ecstatic female fan are all bodies behaving outside the norms of social discipline. A Bakhtinian sense of carnivalesque indiscipline may well be involved here: the bodies are taken over for the pleasure of those who inhabit them and who experience this pleasure as a release from external control. This pleasure connects the body of the individual to the social body in social relations that are communal rather than ones required by the hierarchical social order. The TV cameras that shoot the erupting female fan in close-up also give us wide shots of a whole screaming audience and thus make visible the threat of carnival by showing the continuity between the individual and the social body. The social formation of fandom is a form of *communitas* whose social relations are horizontal and controlled by its members, so its indiscipline (hysteria, bodily abandon) should be understood as a transference, rather than an absence, of control. In sport, this transfer is licensed and, with comparatively rare exceptions, adequately contained: no such license was granted to either the homeless men or to Elvis fans and, as a consequence, their evasion of normal discipline was socially threatening not just because of any disruptive behavior it may have occasioned but rather because of its unsanctioned transfer of control. The only control that the "hysterical" Elvis fan was out of was that of her parents.

LOCALES OF DIFFERENCE

The reality produced by localizing knowledge may be quite different from that of imperializing knowledge, but to dismiss it uncritically as "unreal," or "less real," is to participate in imperialization by refusing to recognize not the difference alone, but the validity of the difference. The experiences of sports fans and the *communitas* of Elvis are as real as the stations produced by TWA's computers. Their realities may have less power, in the sense of power to impose itself upon others, but conversely they may have more power within the consciousness of the immediate conditions of social life. A locale is not ineffective because its effects are local.

In language the conditional mood (that of the "as if") is as important as the indicative; it prevents us accepting the indicative as all that there is. It isn't. Locales which exist *as if* those who construct them are not subject to imperializing power are as real a part of social experience as is the tyranny of the indicative. Locales evade the disciplinary mechanism, they are where social experience is controlled differently. They may, at times, seem to lubricate the mechanism by enabling people to endure the docility which its smooth operation requires of them, but they can also introduce grains of sand into it which wear the cogs, loosen their fit and open up play. However lubricative a locale may be, it always has the potential to turn frictive, and to dirty the machinery. Those social formations which benefit most from the power system are constantly alert to identify locales which are potentially frictive for they are the ones to which their controlling effects must strategically be directed. Teenage locales built around the younger, rockier Elvis (Elvis the Pelvis) appeared more frictive and attracted more repressive energy than those of today's fans built around the older, croonier Elvis, the Elvis of Las Vegas in a spangled jumpsuit instead of drape jackets and drainpipes.

These fans evade the disciplinary mechanism instead of bringing friction to it, and their power to evade enables them to construct an alternative social reality where they can be more true to their view of themselves and where they can live according to more real values than those that the disciplined workplace allows. For many of them it is the world of work that is unreal, untrue. They endure its necessity by adopting the individuated identities (which they know are not truly theirs) which the top-down system requires of them, and to which it attempts to restrict them. The social reality and its range of experiences and identities which capitalism requires is narrow, restrained and mean-spirited: it sits in pale contrast to the diversity of realities, identities and experiences that are locally produced.

The evasive uncolonized locales of Elvis fans offer no directly apparent threat: the fans' agency is directed towards constructing their own identities and relationships rather than challenging top-down control. Evasive agency is as productive as resistive agency and is, in many circumstances, more appealing because it is exercised more pleasantly without that edge of antagonism. It is more fun. But its evasion is never total: what is being evaded is necessarily there both in the form that the evasion takes and on the margins of the consciousness of the evading agents. Evasive locales tend not to provoke the direct disciplinary action that more resistive ones do, not just because they are less threatening but also because they are less visible and less known. Evasive forms of localizing power serve their interests best by keeping their operations unseen by the power-bloc, for if to see is to gain power, then remaining unseen is to evade power and to create space where localizing power may be put into operation. The formations of the power-bloc do not know what is going on in the locales of Elvis fandom, but they scorn it. Their scorn may be in part a disciplinary strategy of relegation to the trivial, but it may also excuse the ignorance of those who are excluded from the knowledge of that which they scorn. However unthreatening evasive agency may appear, evasion is itself a threat. A disciplinary system whose efficiency depends upon its power to monitor is necessarily weakened by the presence of what it cannot see. The power to evade and the power to resist are continuous with each other, not mutually exclusive alternatives.

Sports fans, on the other hand, do not have to evade the disciplinary mechanism and, as a result, their fandom can remain highly visible, secure in its social acceptability. Indeed, it is more likely to be aligned with the interests of the power-bloc than not. While spectatorship may invert the panopticon, it does little to challenge the knowledge–power of panoptic seeing, but rather extends access to it. Sports fandom, consequently, can comfortably include those who participate in power over others, at work or at home, as well as those who are its object. The inverting power of sports knowledge can easily return to an alliance within the values of the power-bloc:

> The Twins use many of the same values I will teach to my daughter. It is just a game, but supporting a team, win or lose, is important. The team is made strong by each person doing their best. Take it one day at a time—just do your best today.

Or:

> The 1991 Twins are more than a baseball team, they are a lesson in life. ...
> This team proves that you can fight back from adversity to become a winner,
> and we all need that reminder in the struggles of everyday living. Baseball
> might be only a sport, but it's definitely much more than a game.[26]

The *communitas* of sports fans fits easily into the social structure
because it shadows the legitimate flow of power and knowledge within its
communal relations. Its embodied knowledges compensate for the limitations of panoptic knowledge but are not threatened by it and consequently
neither challenge nor evade it. Sports fandom propagates no alternative
ways of knowing as does the *communitas* of Elvis fans; nor does it produce
oppositional understandings equivalent to those of the homeless men. As
a consequence its bottom-up knowledges produce locales which constitute
a terrain of popular control that the power-bloc encourages because it
poses little threat and can be easily commodified. Generally speaking, the
inversion of panoptic power is a mirroring which works to compensate
rather than critique.

These highly visible locales of sports fans offer little, if any, challenge to
the social order. Any social criticism implied by the less visible, evasive
locales of Elvis fans remains potential and implicit in the social order at
large, though it is more explicit in the fan *communitas*. The homeless,
however, are both highly visible and highly threatening: consequently, their
locales are subjected to constant, repressive discipline.

The locales within which they produce their own meanings of homelessness and which they extend into their own horizontal social relations
might form a base for an actual challenge to the power-bloc. So they are
curtailed from every direction. Unlike Elvis or sports fandom, homelessness is an unignorable sign that something is wrong. Its very existence
within one of the wealthiest nations in the world is a sharp piece of social
criticism. The place of homelessness in the conceptual order of those with
homes, and the place of homeless people in the streets, bus terminals and
charitable shelters call for top-down control. The power-bloc may satisfy
itself by labeling Elvis fandom as merely silly, but the homeless men's sense
of their own condition provokes far more coercive disciplinary measures.

Repressive measures which lack an enclosure within which to focus and
totalize their power are hamstrung. One way to discipline homelessness
would be to institutionalize it—preferably benignly by an effective welfare
system. But that would cost money, and power-bloc discipline must be
cost-effective. The economic interests of the privileged that limit the
provision of welfare for the deprived also, paradoxically, limit the
discipline to which they can be subjected. The impossibility of controlling

all the physical space through which the homeless move means that control over their interior and social space must have equivalent limits. While the deprivation of the homeless may be almost total, their discipline is not.

NOTES

1. He had, of course, been performing both locally and nationally before this, but it was this performance that made him into a figure of general controversy.
2. Michel Foucault, *The History of Sexuality* Volume I (Harmondsworth: Penguin, 1978).
3. Lynn Spigel, *Make Room for TV: Television and the Family in Postwar America* (Chicago: Chicago University Press, 1992), and Lynn Spigel, "Installing the Television Set: Popular Discourses on Television and Domestic Space, 1948–1955," in Lynn Spigel and Denise Mann (eds) *Private Screenings: Television and the Female Consumer* (Minneapolis: University of Minnesota Press, 1991), pp. 3–40.
4. Mary Beth Haralovich, "Sit-coms and Suburbs: Positioning the 1950s Homemaker," in Spigel and Mann, pp. 111–42.
5. Dolores Hayden, *Redesigning the American Dream: The Future of Housing, Work and Family Life* (New York: Norton, 1984), in Haralovich.
6. Barbara Ehrenreich, Elizabeth Hess and Gloria Jacobs, "Beatlemania: Girls Just Want to Have Fun" in Lisa Lewis (ed.) *The Adoring Audience: Fan Culture and Popular Media* (London: Routledge, 1992), pp. 84–106.
7. Ehrenreich et al., p. 85.
8. Ibid., p. 90.
9. Ibid., p. 103.
10. Thomas Doherty, in *Teenagers and Teenpics: The Juvenilization of American Movies in the 1950s* (Boston: Unwin Hyman, 1988). Chapter 5 gives a good account of the "juvenile delinquency" panic and its relation to movies. He cites a *Variety* article (25 November 1953, p. 19) which illustrates clearly the clash between teenagers and official control:

   Damage runs into thousands of dollars each year. M. Idzal, managing director of the 5,900 seat Fox Theatre [in Detroit], states that most of the trouble is caused by teenagers traveling in gangs.... "Our problem is not out of control," Idzal said. "We try to screen them out, but it is a difficult job and they frequently get by us. Some sneak in through the exits and cause trouble. They are rough and tough. They descend on the theater in packs, usually on Sunday afternoons. Their ages are from 10 up."... Another exib said seat repairs is a never-ending job in his six houses. A crew is kept constantly busy repairing seats slashed by hoodlums. This theatreman stopped the sale of suckers because youngsters were throwing them through the screens.

11. Interview in *Lingua Franca*, August 1991, p. 29.
12. Terry Teachout, review of *Dead Elvis* by Greil Marcus (New York: Doubleday, 1991) in *The New York Times Book Review* (3 November 1991), p. 11.
13. Michel de Certeau, *The Practice of Everyday Life* (Berkeley: University of California Press, 1984).
14. In the tabloids we can trace the social contest over Elvis's death, for in them we can hear multiple voices, those of the fans who know, in various ways that Elvis is not "really" dead, those of anti-fans who turn their skepticism on other formations of the people, and those of the power-bloc. But the voices one hears least clearly in them are those of the fans, for the discourse of these tabloids is that of media-populism rather than of

the people. The distinction between the popular and media-populism is an important one: by "the popular" I refer to the knowledge and interests of the people in their various and multiple formations; by "media-populism" I refer to the commercial media's attempt to speak with their version of a popular voice. Media-populism is, then, a strategy of mediation and, like all mediations, is crisscrossed with the discursive traces of the social formations between which it mediates. It is not "of the people," but we can trace in it echoes of the speech of the people: populism may be a strategy of the power-bloc to exploit the popular, but the exploitation can only succeed to the extent that it offers the people some space for their own voices.

15. *The Star*, 25 December 1990, p. 43.
16. Charles Thompson II and James Cole, *The Death of Elvis* (1991).
17. *The Sun*, 19 December 1990, p. 10. This is a populism addressed to a distinctly different popular formation from that of the fan, that of the anti-fan. It takes the body away from the fan and, by emphasizing its offensive, degraded reality it implies that the fan's body of knowledge is idealized and unreal. The popular skepticism of the anti-fan is turned against another popular knowledge rather than the official knowledge which is its more normal target. Media-populism, used here to mediate between different formations of the people, appropriately turns Elvis into the inverse of a Bakhtinian carnivalesque body: in carnival bodily excess, the pleasure in bodily functions, grotesque corporeality and the reduction of experience to the plane of the body upon which all are equal, are signs of the vitality of the people; here they are signs of death. The carnivalesque is itself an inversion of the official; it is a "world upside down": by inverting the grotesque corporeality of carnival, this account returns Elvis to the official body of knowledge: the anti-body is made anti-popular.

It is significant that *The Sun* in this report is not mediating the book directly, but the *Chicago Tribune*'s version of it. And when the *Tribune* attemps to speak to some of the people rather than to the power-bloc, those it addresses will, in its own estimate, be significantly different from the popular formations of Elvis fans, and therefore a different populist accent will be adopted in order to reach them.

18. *The Globe*, 8 November 1988, pp. 8–9.
19. Hazell Brock, of Fort Payne, Alabama, taking to Susan Hacker.
20. Gail Brewer-Giorgio, *The Elvis Files* (New York: Tudor Publications, 1988), p. 127.
21. *National Examiner*, 4 November 1989, p. 20.
22. *Weekly World News*, 19 May 1992, pp. 4–5.
23. *National Examiner*, 1 May 1990, p. 17.
24. *Weekly World News* 4 April 1989, p. 47.
25. *Weekly World News*, 7 July 1991, pp. 24–5.
26. Letters to Minneapolis *Star Tribune*, 6 October 1991.

6

THE BODY OF VIOLENCE

Sports fans may, on most occasions, appear complicit with top-down power, while Elvis fans evade it. The homeless, however, enter quite different relations with the power-bloc. Traces of complicity or evasion may be found among some homeless, others may pretend complicity to gain shelter and food, but, in general, their social relations are oppositional.

Oppositionality can take many forms in many sites. This chapter will focus on the taste for violence as one form, and the locales or stations of the homeless as one site. But the taste for representations of symbolic violence and, at times, the performance of physical violence, is widespread in the contemporary US, and, in this respect, homeless men can stand for other deprived social formations. While this taste for violence may seem predictable for homeless men (and other subordinated males), it would appear much less likely to exist in women's culture. Women are some of the most frequent victims of violence in our society, and one might expect, therefore, that they would find little pleasure in its representation. But some do, however uneasily, and in particular they know that represented violence, even if unpleasurable, is *relevant*, all too relevant, to their lives. To these women and homeless men, symbolic violence is pleasurable and relevant, not least because it makes the oppressiveness of social relations highly visible and highly charged.

THE TASTE FOR VIOLENCE

Violence is social opposition at its most conflictual. It may be symbolic and make sense of contestatory social relations through images of bodies in conflict, or it may be physical and socially confrontational. Both forms are prominent in the contemporary USA, whose screens and streets are among the most violent in the world.

Violence works in diverse ways; homogenizing it into a singular concept—"the problem of violence"—does nothing to help us understand it. Violence in the lives of homeless men is not the same as wife-beating or gay-bashing, nor is it the same as racial violence in the streets of New York or gang violence in those of Washington DC, and all of these are certainly very different from violence on the football field. But, having said that, violence is violence: whatever form it may take, violence involves social bodies in conflict in specific places; it is conflictual social relations played out bodily. It is also largely, but not exclusively, masculine.

The violence in the lives of those homeless men we have been following was in general symbolic, though it had links, however indirect, with actual violence. They selected violent movies to watch, and within the movies they selected violent scenes to pay most attention to and invest most pleasure in. The popularity of represented violence has long been a major concern in US society, and has constantly produced calls to censor or control it. The desire of some social formations to enjoy symbolic violence is met by the desire of others to prevent them. The taste for violence is itself a site of conflict, and within it we can trace the social relations between the forms of symbolic violence that are popular and the social interests at work in the desire to control or repress them.

Much of the violence that is popular on television is directly related to the social relations of capitalism, particularly as they are enacted along the axes of privilege. The heroes (that is, those whose violence is narratively effective and socially conservative) embody the dominant social values: statistically, they tend to be white, male, classless (an encoding of middle class), in the prime of life and good-looking. The villains and victims (that is, those whose violence is either immediately or eventually ineffective though socially disruptive) tend to embody one or more of the social characteristics which marginalize them in the dominant value system: these include being non-white or non-American, too low (or too high) in the class scale, not male (or at least not very masculine), too old or young, and ugly. (The heroes will, incidentally, often be equipped with a non-white [or less white] sidekick or even, occasionally, a woman, to demonstrate that a socially integrated team under white male control is particularly effective.)[1] Symbolic violence is, then, an incarnation of unequal social relations: its structuring principles and motivations are social, not individual. It shows masculine bodies contesting, in the most direct way possible, their place in the social order and, after their disruptive incursions, being returned to it. Small wonder that the homeless men did not watch the end of *Die Hard*, for it involved repositioning those bodies that were still alive into their appropriately ordered places. Violence is performed through the clash of individual bodies, but in popular symbolic violence, heroes, villains and victims are incarnations of the social body, and the relations between them are consequently social.

Die Hard is statistically typical. The hero, played by Bruce Willis, fits all the disciplinary norms: he is white, middle class, good looking, in the prime of life and effective. Tagaki, the most spectacular victim, is Japanese American, past the prime of life, has risen too high on the social scale, and his features are, to US eyes, orientally impassive (read "ugly"). The villains are led by Hans with his marked German accent (read "Nazi") and the gang includes among its members many of the social characteristics which are directly opposed to the norms embodied in the hero.

The paradox within the popularity of such symbolic violence is that it uses socially unacceptable means to achieve socially legitimate ends. This contradiction can be exploited by alienated social formations to produce the pleasure of aligning themselves with its illegitimacy while standing back from its legitimacy. This is how the homeless men watched *Die Hard*.

Violent images can be used in constructing social identities, or locales within the head and, from them, antagonistic relations to the social order. The imagined locales of these homeless men were conditional upon their material social conditions and the physical place where they were stationed. The social identities that violent images helped them construct were ones *as if* they were not disempowered. Their world of the *as if* was related critically, not complicitly, to the social order: They did not produce identities for themselves *as if* they were conventionally successful, but *as if* they had the power to act against the social order that subordinated them.

Besides excluding them from social relationships over which they had any degree of control, the economic deprivation of these jobless, homeless men also deprived them of their masculinity, for masculinity is as socially produced as any other component of identity. Their cultural life offered opportunities, which their social life did not, to exert some control over their social and masculine identities. Yet top-down discipline tried to prevent their control even over what went on in their heads. Their cultural "masculinizers" of symbolic violence, gambling, and pornography were all subject to disciplinary disapproval and regulation. These cultural resources were all that the men could find from which to construct for themselves locales *as if* they had some economic, social and gendered power. Those whose social position gives them real access to these forms of power have little interest in understanding the function of bottom-up culture except as a terrain over which to extend their power even further by delegitimating, regulating or repressing it. Social formations within the power-bloc draw the power to control their own locales from their efficient complicity with the disciplinary machine: their power is socially produced and its use is socially supportive. They would watch *Die Hard* quite differently and would almost certainly not switch off before the end, for their social interests are met by the restoration of law and order.

Identities are never confined to consciousness, they are always embodied and performed in space and time. Locales of the *as if* are constructed by those who live in the here and now. There is an unbreakable continuity between consciousness, social presence and behavior and social relations: that is why consciousness matters. The continuity is two-way: our social relations produce, in part, our consciousness, just as our consciousness produces, in part, our social relations.

The popularity of symbolic violence needs to be understood from both ends of the continuum. Chapter 1 showed that the increase in homelessness was a specific instance of the more general tendency of the Reaganomic style of capitalism to widen the gaps between the privileged and the deprived.[2] The width of these gaps is where the taste for violence grows. Our capitalism is not just a classist system, it is a sexist, racist and ageist system as well and it distributes its privileges along a multitude of axes, of which these are only the most salient.

These particular men experienced their deprivation in economic and gendered terms rather than racial ones, so these axes are the most appropriate to understand how they used their taste for violence to produce frictive locales, and how the desire for violence and the desire to regulate it are part of the struggle between imperializing and localizing power. When they chose to watch violent movies, the choice was made in a social station deeply inscribed by signs of rejection and deprivation. Their taste for symbolic violence was significantly associated with their resentment towards and alienation from the society which systematically denied them access to the rewards that its dominant ideology tells them are their rights.

The origins of the taste for violence do not lie in the aggressive instincts supposedly born into every member of the human race and developed especially in the males. Studies have shown that although the taste for violence may be formed at all social levels, it is disproportionately concentrated among men from lower income groups with low levels of formal education. The disproportion is increased if the men are African American.[3] The taste for violence flourishes when economic, educational and racial axes of subordination come together in a contradictory relationship with masculinity, which is an axis of domination. The common-sense view that the appeal of violence originates in our "basic instincts" cannot explain why the taste for violent images is stronger among subordinated and repressed social formations than among dominant ones except by implying that the socially deprived are closer to "animal" nature.

Structured images of violence are widely popular, not because of a universal aggressive instinct, but because of widespread, almost universal, conditions of subordination. Young urban Aboriginals in Australia derive great pleasure from watching old Westerns on television; their pleasure peaks at the moment of the Indians' triumph, when they take the homestead or the wagon train.[4] The supervisor of the homeless men told of an almost identical cultural practice of homeless Native Americans in another shelter: they would watch Westerns on the VCR and switch off the tape at the moment of the Indians' victory, thus erasing the restoration of white colonializing "law" in the second half of the narrative. Other Australian Aboriginals found pleasure in Rambo's violence when they read it as representing the conflict between members of the "Third World" and the white officer class.[5] African Americans at the turn of the century read the violence in Buffalo Bill's touring Wild West Show as a representation of Indian genocide that paralleled their view of their own history.[6] Working-class male youths in London made Kung Fu movies from Hong Kong into their popular culture just as readily as Australian Aboriginals made Rambo movies from Hollywood into theirs.[7]

Certain representations of violence enable subordinated people to articulate symbolically their sense of hostility to the particular forms of domination that oppress them. These representations are those which contain markers of ethnic, class, age, or national difference which are portrayed not as natural essences, but as structural agents of power and disempowerment. Symbolic violence is an enactment of social inequality, and its popularity suggests that it can offer the subordinated both a representation of their own fighting ability and an articulation of their resentment towards the social order that oppresses them.

The violence in *Die Hard* is always associated with power. The terrorists deny any political agenda, they have no desire to overthrow or change capitalism; all they want is the power that capitalism itself validates, the power of money, the $640 million in the corporation's vaults. The power is made material in the Nakatomi skyscraper itself, in its art objects and antiques, its elaborate computer systems, the numerous models of the corporation's capital projects around the world—all of which are spectacularly and systematically destroyed during the course of the movie. The pleasure of spectacle is that of participation, for spectacle cannot function without complicit and participatory spectators. Here it offered the deprived the opportunity to participate in vicarious revenge against those who have exploited the system that has deprived them.

Economic power is localized in power over people in the face-to-face relationships of everyday life. The homeless men were deprived of this, too. Not surprisingly then, the *Die Hard* that they chose to watch was the one whose power struggles reversed the norms that subjected them. In *their Die Hard* the small group of villains gained power over the huge corporation and defeated the police, the isolated male gained power over the villains, and the Black cop gained power over the white chief of police. By erasing the end of the movie, when the normal reasserted itself, they made sense of the temporary victories of the weak *as if* they were permanent. In each of these relations of power, the homeless men aligned themselves with the weaker parties and gained great pleasure from their triumphs over the stronger, or from their endurance in the face of it. Violence is the way these power struggles are represented and indeed is the only way they can be enacted popularly, for if the deprived are to have their moments of victory, these moments can most spectacularly and effectively be represented through the only resources of which they cannot be deprived—their bodies, their physical strength and endurance, and their resourcefulness. The fights in the movie are spectacularly prolonged, the body's ability to inflict and endure excessive punishment is displayed in fantastic detail. Towards the end of the movie the hero is as battered, as bloody and as weakened physically as the homeless are socially. But he endures, and it is his endurance rather than his final victory which gives them most pleasure.

Both forms of power are articulated with and in masculinity. Imperializing power is shown in the maleness of the boardroom (interrupted only by the hero's wife, who, significantly, is at this point corporate, maritally separated and thus defeminized). It is challenged by its mirror image—the organized power of the invading gang. Localizing power is shown by the male body in violent action, and the hero is popular with these viewers as long as he exhibits only this sort of power.

In a patriarchy masculinity is informed by both sorts of power. Men who have comparatively limited access to imperializing power may well devote more energy to localizing power, for that is the sort they can most realistically expect to achieve. The homeless men invested their pleasure in the spectacle of male bodies in conflict for the most localized power of all, the power to win the immediate fight.

Our patriarchy expects masculinity to express itself at the localized level in self-sufficiency and independence—that is, in control of oneself and one's immediate conditions. At the imperializing level masculinity is expected to show control over others and over social relations by "leadership." Both forms of control require public performance and recognition: masculinity is not only a state that men have to achieve, they have to be seen to achieve it. When a society gives men this sense of their masculinity and then positions them in conditions which deprive them almost totally of any means of achieving it, then the taste for violence, both real and symbolic, will flourish.

Images of violence may at times work to minimize power difference, at others may work to increase it; but because symbolic violence always shows both sides of the struggle, however unequally, the role of these images in locales, behavior and relationships can never be predicted from the images themselves. Censoring violent images rarely protects the weak from the social use of the top-down power portrayed in them. More often than not, censorship works to preserve the power-bloc from challenge from below. Horror movies, for instance, are often criticized for exploiting the victimization of women to provide their thrills. Yet their images of victimization are typically contradicted within the movies themselves by ones of women fighting back: the images of victimization are necessary groundings for those of women's strength or revenge. There are many women fans of the genre, and their pleasure lies in using images of the victimization of weak women as lessons of what women should not do or be and those of strong women as positive. Listen to some of these fans:

LINN   Most of the women that are the victims, ... we've got this name for them ... when you see a character that walks into the screen and doesn't say a lot, and looks like a total yutz, we say, "Well, did you notice the big GV on his forehead, or her forehead?" It means "gratuitous victim"— they're only there to be slaughtered—that's the only reason they were written into the script. They're the ones that you're saying, "Don't go in there" and they walk in without a light, I mean they're asking for it. Anyone who's dumb enough to do that deserves to get it—as far as horror movies go. They're usually just written into the script for that.

CHRISTIE   The best example of that I ever saw was in something called *The Hills Have Eyes*. These young people are out in the house in the desert in the middle of nowhere. Half of them have been killed already. They all go off alone in different directions. And one girl decides this is a really good time to take a shower!

EDIE   That's so dumb.

LINN   Forget it, she asked for it.

CHRISTIE   Yeah, anyone who's that mindless deserves to be slashed.

Later in the conversation:

DAWN   In slasher movies ... I think one of the reasons I like them is because I look at these women like Jamie Lee Curtis who are fighting off Jason or Freddie Kruger or whoever ... I really admire them for being able to have the wit to—I mean I hate women who try to run away screaming and fall down ... and I know I wouldn't do that.

CHRISTIE   They *always* trip and fall down.

DAWN   I actually admire the women in it. They may be victims of the monster, but they have more strength than I kinda think I might have in that situation.

130

EDIE They're so resourceful.

LINN You can look at the women and kinda say, well I, yeah, I kinda like to think maybe I could do it. I don't know if I would, I'd like to think I would—because I know the justice system in this world. I know that's one thing I would think about doing ... But whether I actually would. ... I hope to God I never find myself in that situation ... we see women overcome things that we don't know we can handle ... wishing we could.[8]

Linn's conditional world of the *as if* (as if she were strong) is directly related to the indicative world that *is*: When she says "I know the justice system in this world," she has no need to include the adjective "patriarchal." Images of violence against women are not, for these fans at least, simply agents of victimization but images of both the terrain over which women have to fight and of their fighting ability. The "GVs" do not naturalize the victimization of women, but are negative images of those aspects of femininity which must be rejected. Censoring the violence would also censor images of the struggle against the patriarchal order within which the violence originates. Censoring these images in the name of protecting women might, in this case, end up by protecting patriarchy from women.

This is not to say that this is the only use of the symbolic violence of horror movies: some men in the audience may well align themselves with the rapist-monster. But even here there are contradictions: masculine power is "properly" used to protect the weak as well as to exploit them, and the monster may well arouse both uses in its male viewers.

These contradictions were played out in the responses of some of its female fans to *Twin Peaks*. The TV show self-consciously foregrounded the conventions used to represent violence, particularly gendered violence, on television. One scene, for instance, appeared to represent male violence to women as a "natural" masculine wildness (the violence in question was complicated by being incestuous). Carol, a fan, was so enraged at it that she reacted physically, she yelled at the TV and fantasized throwing a chair at it: her fantasy was so nearly realized that she claimed she could bodily feel herself going through the act of throwing. Many women's responses showed that their pleasure in the show was suffused with a deep anger at its representations of gendered violence. It is not easy to explain this pleasure of anger,[9] but it may derive from the differences between a textually produced anger (that allows some empowering reaction) and a socially situated anger at real violence to women that allows none. In real violence there are no contradictory forces that women can turn to their own advantage and thus there is no pleasure in the anger that is commonly felt by women who have suffered it.[10] But in symbolic violence there are.

The show's stylistic exaggeration allowed some women to use it to critique the more "normal" representations of violence on TV. Suzanne, however, was more conflicted: she admitted that the violence "sucked her in," and felt angry at herself as a result:

> Because you're sitting there and you're getting all riled up, but you know something is really wrong and you begin to—not hate yourself—but feel really bad and angry. You know, because you're getting your cheap thrills out of something you absolutely don't agree with. That angers me.

When watching *Twin Peaks* alone or with her boyfriend, Suzanne felt intensely the contradictions of fascination and repulsion. When rewatching a violent scene with three other men, however, her reactions to their responses were quite unambiguous: "They were just glued to it, I left the room because I couldn't be in a room with four men who were behaving obnoxiously." She went on to liken the experience to that of watching *Fatal Attraction* in a crowded movie theatre: "... you think something is really wrong here, because you hear people around you screaming 'Give it to her, kill her'."[11]

Representations of violence against the subordinated social formation of which she is a member deeply conflicted Suzanne; for the homeless men, however, the representations show the violence of the subordinate against the dominant—quite the reverse situation. Their response, therefore, can be unambiguous and unconflicted—they enjoy it wholeheartedly. The women fans of *Twin Peaks* continued to watch the show with pleasure, and did not argue that represented violence against women should be censored from the TV screens, probably because they know that it exists socially and that silencing that knowledge would do nothing to help address the problem. But even though they judged that *Twin Peaks* represented the violence "better" than conventional TV, sometimes even from the female victim's position, they still felt deeply contradictory about both their personal responses to it and the more general textual politics of its representation. Maybe that is the best one can hope for: what audiences do with internal conflict after their encounter with a text is more their responsibility than the text's. If the text sets up the contradictions which prevent complacency its politics are facing in the right direction at least. We must recognize, however, that *Twin Peaks* by itself did not prevent this complacency in Suzanne's male friends, but Suzanne did. Her walking out of the room jolted them into apologizing for their viewing behavior. Her exit activated the contradictions in the text that their watching of it did not and thus changed its politics for them at least.

Philip Schlesinger and his colleagues conducted a comprehensive study of women watching violent television and videos and found that, in general, women did not want violence against women to be censored from their screens, though they did desire some control over it, and they did demand that it be realistic and sensitive.[12] There was a widespread belief that properly represented violence "may have a positive effect upon the lives of individual viewers and social life in general."[13] To be judged realistic and sensitive, televised violence "should not be sensationalist in nature, should not trivialise the violence, should not blame the women for men's violence and should not minimise men's responsibility for their behavior."[14] Depicted in this way, represented violence might help women think through the problem of real violence, it would alert men to other men's violent behavior, and it would make society face up to the reality of gendered violence. Television violence, the study concludes, "was not defined [by the women] as 'exciting or entertaining,' but rather as 'educational' or 'relevant,' while at the same time as 'disturbing' and sometimes 'offensive.' Thus the importance attributed to what was viewed was not in terms of pleasure, escape or fantasy but in terms of relevance and social importance."[15]

Behind these general conclusions, however, there were many contradictions and differences. Some women, for instance, feared that television violence could incite rather than expose real violence, could desensitize people and upset children, and could, when race was involved, encourage racism. These differences were produced in part by the women's class and ethnicity, and by whether they had experienced violence themselves; the women did not speak with a single voice, but very few, even of those opposed to televised violence, argued for outright censorship.

Censoring speech or images has rarely helped the subordinate, whose problems are social rather than symbolic. Historically censorship has been most effective most frequently as a strategy of the power-bloc to control the ideas in social circulation. It has served less to protect the voices of the subordinate than to preserve the dominant from challenge from below. Speech which contributes to the oppression of those who are already oppressed (particularly, in our society, racist or sexist speech) calls for immediate action (such as an emphatic exit), but the most appropriate action is contradiction or argument rather than censorship. Suzanne's exit was argumentative. Politically or morally offensive speech should generate more speech, not less. Argument and a greater diversity of ways of looking at the world are progressive and equalizing forces in the realm of symbolic life. Repressing speech, reducing the diversity of voices to be heard or images to be seen generally protects the interests of the status quo.

Physical violence in social, not symbolic, life is quite different from symbolic violence and is properly dealt with by legal prohibition. The best way to reduce symbolic violence in society is to change the social conditions that produce the taste for it, not to repress the images, for the crux of the matter is not the images but the social conditions that nourish the taste for them.

Censorship may not be the solution, but it is in the interests of the power-bloc to make it appear to be. Censorship is a strategy of power and typically contributes to the oppression of the subordinate by repressing the cultural tastes and voices which they can use to control their own locales. It also represses the knowledge that the society which produces the most violent images in the world, the contemporary United States, is also one with the least developed mechanisms for equalizing wealth and for caring for its weakest and most disadvantaged citizens. By focussing on the *symbolic* order, censorship keeps the *social* order off the agenda for change. The taste for violence originates in the structural effects of the social system that privileges those who call most vehemently for its censorship. The assumption that social violence is caused by images of violence serves as a social alibi, for it enables the privileged to avoid the uncomfortable idea that their position of privilege is itself a significant feature of the social conditions which nourish both the taste for symbolic violence and the commission of physical violence.

An article from the Boston *Globe*, nationally syndicated in 1991, is symptomatic.[16] It derives from 235 academic studies of the effects of violent images: these range from the physiological arousal of the nervous system (which was certainly evident in the homeless men's watching of *Die Hard*) through sociological ones to historical ones. One study reported that "the best predictor of which male would commit a violent act by the age of 30 was the amount of violent TV watched at the age of 8." The context of the article makes it easy to infer from this that reducing TV violence will reduce social violence. What is repressed from the original research and thus from this report of it is the social situation of those males who both watch symbolic violence and commit real violence: the absence of the social dimension allows the symbolic to be related causally to the real rather than both being seen as symptoms of the social. The power of discourse to repress embarrassing knowledge is nowhere more evident than in the conclusion of one expert that those who are most vulnerable to the effects of TV violence are teens who live in communities where violence is endemic. The idea that violence is endemic within the community itself rather than in its subordinated relation to the social order situates the problem exactly where the power-bloc wishes.

When history is brought into the discussion, it too is used to hide contemporary social conditions rather than to explain them. This form of history locates the problem in the past: the US has had a violent history, the argument runs (without identifying nations which have not); from the early settlers through the expansion of the western frontier, the US has developed the sense that making war is tough but making love is soft.

In criticizing the "common-sense" view that images play a causal role in the problem of violence, we must not imply that they play *no* role. In the continuum between conscious behavior and social relations images are active and formative, but their action depends upon the specificity of the continuum within which they work. Violent images are always part of social conditions: they may, when sexist or racist, serve to exacerbate inequality; they may also, in other circumstances, work to mitigate it. The day after *The Burning Bed* was shown on TV, women's shelters reported an increase in the number of abused wives leaving their husbands. Four women also burned their husbands to death, and one man set his wife on fire. Seventy-five million Americans watched the movie and it is possible, if not probable, that many of them became more conscious of wife abuse both as a social problem and as one in their own relationships.[17] There can be no scientific proof that the movie contributed to the nation's increased awareness of domestic violence in the 1980s, for the relationship of one to the other is not causal, but mutual and organic. Equally, the movie did not "cause" the four killings, and to "blame" it, instead of the abuse the women had suffered, is a reprehensible power ploy. But these incidents, like the case of the homeless men, do demonstrate that there is a conjunctural connection between symbolic violence and actual violence. The two forms of violence need to be understood not in terms of a cause-and-effect relationship to each other but in terms that recognize the complex mix of social forces of which each is both a product and a constituent part.

Symbolic violence makes social conflict explicit: it is therefore dis-approved of by the power-bloc, whose interests are served by suppressing the awareness of social conflict, but taken readily into the culture of subordinated men and, less readily, into that of women. To whatever degree our social order may deprive men of the opportunities to exercise the power upon which their masculinity is said to depend, it can never deprive them of their bodies. The body is where an imperializing power must meet its limit: the body must always, to a degree at least, be localized.

The necessity of the body to occupy space and time means that there is a continuum of equivalence from the body to its immediate physical environ-ment. The villains' occupation and destruction of the corporate suite in *Die Hard* is symbolically equivalent to their destruction of the bodies of the executives. The hero, initially confined to the service ducts and elevator shafts of the skyscraper, gains physical territory as he kills off the villains. The power of the body is manifest not only in its violent conflict with other bodies but in its control over its immediate surroundings.

In the shelter the control of the homeless men over their bodies/ surroundings was reduced to the minimum. In the streets, however, their bodies could be disciplined less directly and the confrontations could be more explicit. In the Midwestern city in which they lived the general social relations were not tense enough for the confrontations to be violent—at least not in the normal sense of the word. In big cities with their more antagonistic social relations, violent relationships between panhandlers and passers-by, ranging from verbal abuse through to physical threats, mugging and even murder, are becoming more and more common. According to the Pacific News Service, a class war is brewing between angry indigents and disgruntled citizens forced to step out of their way.[18] But despite the lack of violence in the less stressful conditions of a small Midwestern city, violations still occurred. Like their big city fellows, the homeless men would deliberately position themselves so as to disrupt the normal walking patterns of pedestrians on the sidewalk. Jean, a respectable passer-by interviewed by the Pacific News Service, reacted antagonistically when a homeless man left his "proper station" on the edge of the sidewalk to violate her "right" to its center: "I'll give when they're just sitting there on the ground, but not when they come onto you like that."[19] The homeless will also intransigently occupy park benches, often deliberately choosing ones in the most favored spots. To control this, Los Angeles has designed benches shaped like upturned barrels, which can be rested against but not lain on. As part of the same strategy the water sprinklers in its parks are located and timed to prevent the homeless from violating public space by sleeping in it. Their small victories in the struggle to occupy public space were a source of conscious satisfaction for the men. If the only means of power that society had left them was the ability of their bodies to occupy space that was desired by the more socially central, then that was what they would use. Forcing a pedestrian to the edge of the sidewalk or making someone walk on who wanted to sit were ways of engaging in social relations; they were ways of using their bodies' occupation of physical space as an assertion of their right to a recognized position in the social space.

Occupying not a bench, but a whole park, as in Tompkins Square or People's Park, is both physically and socially more confrontational. Occupying not public, but private, property as in housing squats violates even more dearly held "rights." Physically violent clashes between the homeless and the police in housing squats in Minneapolis or in Tompkins Square in Manhattan are all part of the same continuous terrain, stretching from the consciousness of the men cheering at a CEO's fictional death through to organized protest marches at the seat of government.

Because locales exist in physical places as well as in social space, when they become too confrontational they call up discipline on both fronts: the police force disciplines them physically and the public discourse of politicians, local merchants and news anchors disciplines them semi-otically. For the police physically to evict them from a public park such as Tompkins Square, the homeless have to be discursively excluded from "the public." The park as a social station is controlled physically by the police and discursively by the merchants and media. The locale of the homeless refuses to accept this physical and semiotic positioning, so violence, both imagined and social, is the result.

The homeless men's pleasures in *Die Hard* and the TV News excluding them from "our" society; Paradise's verbal confrontation with the executives in Manhattan; and the police evicting squatters in Minneapolis or clashing with the People's Posse in Tompkins Square; Reaganomics, volunteerism and Christianity: the relationships between all these are conjunctural, not ones of cause and effect. Each is interconnected with all of the others, but the power-flows along these interconnections are neither constant nor equal. One particular audience of *Die Hard* may seem a minute and insignificant part of the whole picture, yet watching the movie was a significant part of that audience's social relations. The conflict between their locale as they watched and their stationing by the shelter is part of the conflict between the police and the People's Posse. To be effective imperializing power has to discipline people at all levels of social experience: to oppose it, then, localizing power needs, too, to establish itself in consciousness, in relationships, in places and in the social order. The two directionalities of power are unequal: that of the power-bloc is more effective in invading the immediate conditions of the people than that of the people in affecting the workings of the power-bloc. But within its own sphere of operations, the localizing power of the people is ultimately undefeatable—there is always an inner portion of the locale which can be held and defended against overwhelming odds.

BOTTOM-UP DIFFERENCE

These three chapters have looked in some detail at three different types of locale: that of the homeless men, which we might call resistive or oppositional, that of the Elvis fans which is more evasive and alternative, and the inverted panopticon of sports spectating. Because sports knowl-edge mirrors official knowledge, it produces no new ways of looking at the world, though it does relocate the viewer. But in sports fandom, in Elvis fandom and in homelessness there are ways of experiencing capitalism differently: each of them produces a different world of experience whose knowledge is conditional rather than indicative. These worlds, which I have called "worlds of the *as if*," are neither freely produced nor independent, but are related antagonistically to the world produced and controlled by the power-bloc. We have to be able to elbow the workings of the power-bloc aside to be able to produce a world as if their discipline were weaker and our spaces larger. The Elvis fans constructed an imaginary world as if the disciplinary system had lost its power to tell them what was true and what was not, as if it lacked the power to produce their identities and social relations through individuation. The conditional world of the homeless men was one as if they had the power to assert themselves and promote their own interests, not, significantly, one as if the power-bloc were benignly concerned for them, nor one as if they were successful in power-bloc terms. But the world of the *as if* is never sufficient, and indeed perhaps I should not have given it a name and thus an identity of its own. The people live in a world of very material constraints, and no purely imaginary world, however utopian, can ever provide a viable alternative in the face of this imperative materiality. The world of the *as if* is only worth imagining if it can be embodied or made material in the immediate conditions of everyday life. A purely imaginary world is not, in general, worth the effort involved in producing it. A locale is where a worthwhile *as if* can be made material, where the conditional can become indicative. It is where the differently imagined continuum between identity and social relations is performed in social behavior and relationships. It is where imagination is materialized by being given spatial and temporal dimensions, and thus turned into experience. The locale is a concept which does away with the familiar distinctions between the interior and the exterior, between imagination and reality, between the mental and the material. The locale as a concept does not allow identities and imagination to be separated out from their bodily performance in presence, behavior and relationships and from the places and times of that performance. This local production of the people is always performed against or away from the social station where the power-bloc attempts to position them.

The conventions of marriage, for example, work to station couples in the gender identities and relationships preferred by the patriarchal social order. But within such stationing individual couples or individual members may produce locales wherein they form quite different identities and marital relationships. A movie such as *The Burning Bed* may enable some women to *know* their own locales and their right to control them against the stationing of patriarchal relations in general and their own husbands in particular. Such localizing power–knowledge may enable them to leave an abusive husband or, driven to intolerable extremes, to kill him.

The *as if* world of Elvis fans may also work to construct locales which conflict with social stationing. Some Elvis fans, for example, leave their husbands because the stationing power of their actual marital relationship does not allow them to develop the locale that is achievable within their *as if* relationship with Elvis. The *as if* world can be made real by being localized. The *as if* is always a resource upon which localizing power can draw to change its immediate social conditions: the conditional may at any time become the indicative.

The tabloids frequently carry extreme examples of this in their stories of Elvis fans who have divorced their husbands because they felt that being with another man was being unfaithful to Elvis. "Wife names Elvis as lover in divorce case" runs the headline in *The Sun*'s story of Vicky Hanwell, who was told by Elvis in a dream that he is now free of his earthly burdens and ready to love her: "He didn't tell me to leave Don," she sobs, "but my conscience just won't let me be with another man besides Elvis." Her husband, Don, however, has abruptly stopped being an Elvis fan: "Now I can't stand to see his picture or hear his voice any more. He's ruined my marriage and busted up our family."[20]

In the fan video *Mondo Elvis*, Frankie Harrocks tells of how, as a newlywed, she realized she had to leave her husband "because I was in love and it wasn't with my husband." She finally left him and her children in New Jersey and moved to Memphis "to be where Elvis is." Wearing a T-shirt proclaiming "Elvis didn't die, he just moved to a better town," she tells how her husband divorced her, citing as cause "excessive devotion to Elvis Presley." She faces the camera and grins: "And I love it!"[21] While such extremes may be abnormal, their abnormality lies in magnifying, not distorting, the normal. Leaving a disempowering marriage is an extreme case of what more normal women may do within one—that is, enlarge the space over which they can exert their own power and control.

Elvis is equally embodied in the sexual relationships of the Carroll twins. They explain:

JENNY   When we bring people home, guys mainly, because we don't...

JUDY   And when we bring them home they're all set and ready to go hop in the sack...

JENNY   And we put on our Elvis Presley music...

JUDY   And if they don't like our Elvis Presley music they get thrown out on their ass, and if they say anything against God or Elvis they get thrown out on their ass again.[22]

The locale of the Carroll twins comprises a continuum between their physical space (their house and their beds), their behavior within it and their personal relationships, and their consciousness of their identities as Elvis fans and Christians. The body is pertinent at all points along the continuum, for it is the body that links them into a coherence of both identity and experience. The body-locale is where a person's own sense of his or her individuality is produced through its coherence of identity and experience. Locales take the form that they do because they are where people identify themselves.

The homeless occupying Tompkins Square Park or squatting in unoccupied houses are, by extending the physical dimension of their locales, changing their social relations into ones of collectivity: control over place enables an oppositional *communitas*. Their eviction by the police, while performed physically, also pushes them back socially. The Manhattan merchant and the TV news anchor evict them discursively from the place they wish to occupy in the social order in a precisely parallel disciplinary move. So, too, the welfare worker in Minneapolis who criticized Up and Out of Poverty for victimizing the homeless by encouraging them to break the law was evicting them from *their* sense of their social relations and identities just as "really" as the police who drove them from the empty buildings. Like the back-alley entrance to the shelter, these all work physically, socially and discursively to station the men where the power-bloc wishes.

While evasive and resistive locales both set up critical relations with the social order, the relations are different, and the difference is produced, in part, by the extent of the threat they appear to pose, that is, by how they appear from above. The teenage fans of Elvis in the 1950s produced locales that were seen to disrupt the social order physically in juvenile delinquency and crime. They were visibly embodied in undisciplined vertical relationships in the family and school, and in evasive "unordered" horizontal relationships among the teenagers themselves ("teenage gangs"); finally this disruptive indiscipline made itself visible in their embodied identities, their hairstyle, dress and body posture. The problem was not that "they didn't know their place" (or "station"), they knew it perfectly well, but rejected it. Equally, many of today's homeless refuse to occupy the stations the power-bloc has prepared for them. Disciplinary energy and repressive action are a result of a perceived immediate threat.

The evasive locales of today's Elvis fans, however, were more private. They had nothing to gain by a public display of their *communitas* and its different identities and relationships. Evasion as a cultural tactic is best practiced unseen. Dawson gives a good example of an evasive locale whose physical dimensions were continuous with the social and individual. "Tim" is a 9-year-old boy in a successful middle-class family. When his parents argue he goes to his own room upstairs. Dawson describes the scene:

On one such occasion I followed him upstairs ... I found him in the small bedroom in front of the television. He had placed a blanket over himself and the television and created a tent like structure. The antenna served the function of a tent pole. I asked if I could crawl in and see his fortress (this is what he called it) and he said okay. Inside the fortress the television was on but the reception was very poor. He was playing with some toy cars by the light of the television. He told me that he came here often when his parents fought. He had in some way created a home, a safe place, a place that he constructed and could control.

His parents had no idea of what he was doing: in the age of the insidious monitor, being *unseen* is a survival tactic that should not be undervalued because of its silence.

A low profile goes with a low level of perceived threat, and earns the space within which to move and play without the need for constant defense. What goes on "backstage" is not unimportant because it is unseen. Indeed, for the players it can often seem more important, more real, more true, than the lives they perform under the public eye. This backstage culture may be important, too, for society at large, as well as for its players. In their locales, Elvis fans assert and develop alternative social values, alternative ways of relating, identifying and behaving, which are repressed by the disciplinary machine because they are not efficient for its purposes. These alternative ways of living, ones appropriate to a *communitas* rather than an individuated social order, may well be ones which, marginalized in our regime of power, are the seeds from which a new form of power/discipline may grow. The feudal regime of power, based upon spectacular deterrence, marginalized the consciousness as a site of control. But consciousness was the *sine qua non* of the regime which succeeded it, the regime of surveillance. The consciousness of individual subjects may well not have appeared at the time to threaten the machinery of spectacular power. But history proved otherwise. A regime's own perception of what threatens its power may not, over time, prove to be accurate. The different ways of living of the Elvis *communitas* entail, as we shall see in Chapter 9, different ways of knowing. These different ways of knowing-relating-being evade rather than confront the current social order, but this on its own does not disqualify them from participating in social change over the longer term.

In the short run, however, more resistive locales, such as those of the homeless men, do seem to exert more immediate pressure for change. In such confrontational relations, the antagonism can reach a point when their conflict of interests becomes expressed in violence. Violence can pervade any or all of the dimensions of the locale: it can play its part in imagined identities, it can be realized in immediate relationships, and it can inform the public expression of social relations. Cheering at *Die Hard*, violating the space of the passer-by and clashing with the police at housing squats or protest marches exist continuously with each other in the localized terrain that the homeless "know" they have the right to control. Such violence extends their locale and thus changes their social relations. One of the main differences between these resistive (sometimes violent) locales and the evasive ones of the Elvis fans lies in their different perceptions of their social relations.

When subordination or deprivation is taken too far, its social relations become ones of exclusion. The point at which this occurs is located in the perceptions of the subordinate rather than in their objective social conditions, but it is a crucial line, for once it is crossed evasive locales become separatist and resistive ones become violent. Violating the space of the passer-by on the sidewalk or park bench lies on one side of that line, mugging on the other. Violence and separatism are often the only perceivable solutions when the subordinate feel that imperializing has gone too far in limiting their ability to exert some control over the immediate conditions of their social lives. An equally debilitating effect is despair and apathy.

Violence and separatism are also encouraged when subordinated social formations perceive that the institutions which claim to guarantee and protect their rights as citizens are used against them. In the contemporary US, the subordinate "know" that it is the money of big corporations rather than the votes of the people that decides elections, and this knowledge underwrites the graffiti "If voting made a difference it would be illegal."In the legal system, they "know" that the money to buy the lawyer determines the innocence of the defendant, as they "know" that the police are the agents of the power-bloc. Sophisticated "counter-knowledges" of the dominant social order produced by African Americans are described in Chapter 11 and should cause whites acute anxiety about the social effects of power-bloc actions. Resistance that has become violence, and evasion that has become separatism, produce no-go areas in our cities and no-go areas in the cultural lives of our citizens. Some of the legal and economic conditions which violated women's rights as a gender may have been eased, but such easements at the level of social relations have been contradicted by increased violations of their bodies in the immediate conditions of their lives. Equal employment opportunities (particularly as they exist more in the letter than the fact) may seem small solace to women who cannot walk down the street without fear and who find this same fear within the four walls of their "home." The restriction of one's locale through fear of physical violence may be the most oppressive politics of all. Dominant power may have "ruled" that women are equal to men in the workplace, but it has still built the "glass ceiling." Equally, at the local level, the sexism experienced at the secretary's desk may violate her locale more invasively than structural discrimination at the level of explicit corporate policy. The experience of being invaded at both local and structural levels is a characteristic of a social order whose overimperialization of power and intolerance of difference push resistance into violence and diversity into separatism. Violence and separatism result in apartheid, which, even if chosen from the bottom-up because it appears to offer the only viable option, is no recipe for a society in which one can live and die at peace both with oneself and one's neighbors.

NOTES

1. George Gerbner (1970), "Cultural Indicators: The Case of Violence in Television Drama," *Annals of the American Association of Political and Social Science*, 338, pp. 69–81; and John Fiske, *Introduction to Communication Studies* (London: Routledge, 1982).
2. During the 1980s the salaries of Chief Executive Officers rose by 212 per cent, whereas those of factory workers rose by 53 per cent (*Business Week*, 17 February 1991). The 1990 census shows a rapid increase in poverty during the same period, which resulted in an astonishing 13.5 per cent of the population being officially designated as "living in poverty." Of course, poverty is not equally distributed: 11 per cent of European Americans are poor, compared to 32 per cent of African Americans, 28 per cent of Hispanic Americans and 12 per cent Asian and other Americans.
3. H. Israel, W.R. Simmons, and J. Robinson, "Demographic Characteristics of Viewers of Television Violence and News Programs," in G. Comstock and E. Rubenstein (eds) *Television and Social Behavior*, Volume 4, *Television in Day-to-Day Life: Patterns of Use* (Washington DC: US Government Printing Office, 1972), pp. 87–128.
4. R. Hodge and D. Tripp, *Children and Television* (Cambridge: Polity, 1986).
5. E. Michaels, "Aboriginal Content," paper presented at the Australian Screen Studies Association Conference, Sydney, December 1986; and J. Fiske, *Understanding Popular Culture* (Boston: Unwin Hyman, 1989).
6. G. Lipsitz, *Time Passages: Collective Memory and American Popular Culture* (Minneapolis: University of Minnesota Press, 1990).
7. P. Cohen and D. Robbins, *Knuckle Sandwich* (Hamondsworth: Penguin, 1979).
8. D. Bernardi, "Masks of Pleasure: Female Fans of the Contemporary Horror Film," unpublished paper, University of Wisconsin-Madison.
9. Ellen Seiter and colleagues also found that anger provoked by male villains was pleasurable to some women soap opera fans: Ellen Seiter, Hans Borchers, Gabrielle Kreutzner, Eva-Maria Warth, "Don't Treat Us Like We're So Stupid and Naive: Towards an ethnography of soap opera viewers," in E. Seiter, H. Borchers, G. Kreutzner, E-M. Warth (eds), *Remote Control: Television, Audiences and Cultural Power* (London: Routledge, 1989), pp. 223–47.
10. Philip Schlesinger, Emerson Dobash, Russell Dobash and Kay Weaver, *Women Viewing Violence* (London: British Film Institute, 1992), pp. 14, 15.
11. E. Anderson, "Blue Balls: Pleasure and Resistance in *Twin Peaks* Watching," unpublished paper, University of Minnesota, Minneapolis.
12. Schlesinger, et al., *Women Viewing Violence*.
13. Ibid., p. 168.

14. Ibid.
15. Ibid.
16. Reprinted in St Paul *Pioneer Press*, 11 August 1991, "The Violence We Crave is Killing Our Sensibilities and Scarring Our Children."
17. Elayne Rapping, "The Uses of Violence," *The Progressive*, August 1991, pp. 36–8.
18. Pacific News Service, 16 April 1990, cited in *Utne Reader 41*, September/October 1990, pp. 50–55.
19. Pacific News Service, *op. cit.*
20. *The Sun*, 21 February 1989, p. 23.
21. *Mondo Elvis.*
22. *Mondo Elvis.*

PART THREE

REPRESENTING

AND KNOWING

7

ACT GLOBALLY,

THINK LOCALLY

A culture of power is a culture of representation. The intellectual, ethical, religious discourses of power may well tend towards high art (great representations), and their more economic, pragmatic ones towards industrialized art (mass representations), but both rely on their ability to produce representations of the world and, more importantly if less explicitly, of themselves in the world. These next two chapters focus on knowledges which work through representation to render the world and the nation knowable and controllable, the next three on knowledges which seek to control not the world but one's immediate conditions within it. The former are appropriate to an imperializing power, the latter to a localizing one.

Imperializing power is often put to work on the world through representational texts, but localizing power is more likely to operate through localizing texts, significant things and practices. A localizing text is one which confines itself to a specific social formation, and functions to identify the communal identity of that formation for its own members. It is a "local representation" and its power, which may be considerable, works to establish control over its own social terrain, to defend its boundaries, sometimes vigorously, against outside forces, but not to take over other social formations and their territory. If at times it is an aggressive power, its aggression is limited to extending its boundaries to encompass that which it knows it has a right to control. Social formations organized around sexual preference often produce such localizing texts whose power to know is exerted only within their own *communitas*: these texts and their representational power need to be clearly distinguished from the "great representations" that form the main topic of this chapter. Some Black, defensive rather than imperializing, representations of the white world are considered in Part Four of this book.

Significant things work, like localizing texts, only within their own locales. But their sphere of operation tends to be more limited still, usually to a household or family. Things are not texts, for they indicate rather than represent, and indication works through particularities rather than the commonalities of representation. Significant things circulate locally, their significance is confined to the community of origin and does not seek to extend that significance and therefore the reach of that community to and over others. An example may make the difference clearer. I have a photograph of my late-Victorian grandfather. It is still in its original walnut frame, carved and inlaid with brass. For me, this photograph is one of my *things* and hanging it on my wall is a practice of localizing. The photo indicates my grandfather, the frame the place (he thought) he had achieved socially—it was, like his stern sepia expression, part of the unique identity he wished to present to the world and to continue in his family history. Hanging that photograph is one way in which I construct my locale within a house built by another and lived in by many others before me: it is a practice by which I give my history-identity a presence; it is not a text that represents it. But this photograph can only be one of my things in my locale. Were it to be sold as an antique and hung on someone else's wall it would become a representation of Victorian bourgeois individualism and masculinity. The frame would represent the ability of sophisticated modern machinery to reproduce and commodify the old-fashioned labor of the craftsman. As a representation, the photograph would refer not to my grandfather but to the Victorian bourgeoisie. Removing it from its original locale denies the particularities that make it a significant thing and transforms it into a representational text for others. A similar transformation from thing into representation occurs when an object (particularly one that European discourse would call "ethnographic" or "native") is transported from one culture into another: relocated it represents not the native, but the relations between the native and the colonial; finally, therefore it represents the power that transports it. A Navajo pot on a white-middle-class bookshelf is not the pot it once was. Now it represents not just a "native" culture to a white, colonizing one, but also, through the ability of the white to incorporate the native it represents white meanings of race relations, ones of authenticity, of white ability to appreciate the "finer" (that is, universal, depoliticized) points of those it has colonized-destroyed. Though made by Navajo hands, the pot has been remade into a white text that re-presents *us* in *it*. The pot has almost certainly been made intentionally for this white use: for the Navajo it is an economic commodity to be exchanged for material necessities; it is a means of transferring some white money into the reservation. But the economic power of the white consumer to buy the commodity and remove it physically entails the power to remove it culturally and turn it into a (white) text—it was bought for the display shelf, not the kitchen. Now it can represent the same white meaning of racial difference that produced the reservation upon which it was made. If it were an older, more "authentic" (and hence *much* more expensive/exclusive) pot made by Navajos for Navajo use, the power of the colonizing white to use it to represent himself (gender deliberate) would be even greater.

Cross-cultural communication which is initiated and directed by the more powerful of the two cultures (for power difference is always part of cultural difference) always runs the risk of reducing the weaker to the canvas upon which the stronger represents itself and its power. This risk increases in proportion to the power difference between the two cultures. To point this out is not to propose that cultures should isolate themselves from each other, for intercultural communication is becoming more, not less, necessary for a peaceful planet, but rather to warn that the weaker of the two cultures must always exert a satisfactory (to it) degree of control over the communicative relationship. It must be able to say what it wants to with reasonable confidence that it will be listened to: it must, in other words, be able to represent itself rather than be the object of representation. This entails a distinction, which is necessary but often difficult to draw, between one culture listening to another, and one exoticizing the other. In the first case, cultural difference can produce genuine diversity in the imagination of the listeners, but in the second it serves only to reinscribe existing power relations and to constrain and constrict imagination. Any attempt to hear and learn from what another culture wishes to say works towards equalizing power relations, particularly when what is said may not be what the listener wishes to hear. Listening is the opposite of representation, which is why the first act of the power-bloc on rising in the morning is to insert its ear plugs.

A culture of representation, therefore, is not limited to what is often thought of as representational art. Abstract art, for instance, can represent the ability to impose an external order upon even those parts of nature (subjective feelings) which appear to be most disordered, most entropic: it can give a public form to the most private of experiences. Its ability to extend control into those realms of experience which once seemed to be well beyond its reach may be one reason why it is the style of art most collected by multinational corporations to hang in their foyers and boardrooms:[1] multinational capitalism represents itself in the abstracted, insidious ordering of what is not non-representational art. But, despite the

Navajo pot on the white bookshelves and the Jackson Pollock in the boardroom, the workings of representation can best be traced in what is most commonly meant by the term "realistic reproductions" and it is on these that this chapter focuses.

Representations are representative in three ways. In the first the sampled miniaturization of reality (which is what a text is) is taken as representative of the whole. The Navajo pot is representative of "Navajoness"—the ugliness of the word appropriately represents the process of giving a colonizer's meaning to the colonized. Similarly, the Victorian capitalist in his machine-made frame (no longer my grandfather) is representative of his era or he could not re-present it. In the second a representative is one who speaks for us, one who promotes our interests in the wider world and is thus instrumental in extending our power beyond our immediate conditions. The business representative on the road or the politician in the House of Representatives are power-extenders. In the third, a *re*presentation presents again selected features of an absent "reality" or referent. By presenting us with a particular experience or knowledge of the real a representation actually produces that reality, for our experience/knowledge of it becomes reality-for-us. Reality is always represented, we cannot access it raw: it never exists in its own terms, but is always "reality-for-someone."

One of the key representational strategies is "othering." The "other" is always a product of representation and, as such, whatever form it may be given, always applies the discursive and material power of the representing social order upon that part of the world it has made into its other. Edward Said and Frantz Fanon,[2] for example, show how European and US imperializations have worked consistently throughout history to other the Middle East, Africa, Asia and Latin America. This othering works in two ways. First it imposes upon the so-called (or othered) "third" world meanings that bear, as their unspoken obverse, the superiority of the "first" (representing the "third" world as "third" is a fine example of this process), and second it represents the "third" world as the terrain where the power of the "first" is quite properly exercised. Similarly, feminist scholars have shown how the power to other the feminine works both to settle meanings of inferiority upon it and to naturalize it as the object of patriarchal power. Representing the other is representing "our" power in it, and is not just a semantic sleight of hand but is a material exercise of power. Representation is *really*, not symbolically, powerful.

TV news *represents* the world, in all three uses of the word. A story, broadcast by CBS on 17 April 1991, is representative of the news's work of representation:

ANCHOR   On the Turkish side of the Iraqi border, US troops and Western volunteers are just starting to get a handle on the refugee crisis, Allen Pizzey is on the scene.

REPORTER   Thousands of refugees are finally being taken off the mountain-sides where they were starving and without clean water. Their new home is a camp on a flat plain where it should be easier to help them, but so far the Turkish government hasn't supplied enough food and the refugees complain there still isn't adequate medical help for sick children.

Back in the mountains it's still a hell hole, but there's a new "can-do" spirit in the air and US special forces hit town today. They came up the road in a truck and were greeted with smiles and waves. The first thing they did was make friends with the kids, the way soldiers always do, they handed out smiles and candy.

NAT SOUND   (soldiers talking) All right men let's do it.

REPORTER   Then they linked up with the other "can-do" people of the camp, the Dutch branch of Doctors Without Borders set up the doctors' operation here without Turkish permission, because the refugees needed it. While Turkish soldiers were beating refugees away from food supplies, the Dutch doctors have had people lining up to the only medical care in the camp.

NAT SOUND   (doctor holding a baby) She's had no food and she has diarrhea.

REPORTER   Ground is already being cleared for a field hospital. George Bellas, an American Fulbright scholar teaching in Turkey decided this was the place to spend his spring break.

GEORGE   I mean people die up here and they shouldn't die. There's no reason for people to die.

REPORTER   They still do die, but there is a palpable improvement in the camp's atmosphere. The military men say the camp is full of talented people who want to help themselves.

SOLDIER   We've done a leaflet drop asking these people that when we come in to come up and identify themselves, and they're coming up to us in droves and offering assistance.

REPORTER   There are US army men all over the camp trying to figure out what to do where.

NAT SOUND   (radio voice) All right Roger-wilco and out.

REPORTER   That meant persuading refugees to move their tents from the proposed landing zones so they wouldn't be blown away. The refugees still stuck here seem to know that it's not going to be as bad as they feared or even as bad as it was.

The problems of this camp were so massive that no one group could hope to solve them alone, but it looks like the right people are finally getting together to do the job many of them say the Turks should have at least started weeks ago.

The CBS images of refugees or of sick and starving children are like the

Navajo pot in the white living room: they represent the "third" world to and for the "first". They represent US power in it, not just mimetically by showing US soldiers benevolently at work but more insidiously by presenting the "third" world as the proper field for US power, a field that is only knowable by this power, for without it, it is unformed and useless (see Plate 3). The "third" world is not and cannot be represented in its own terms, for in "first" world imperializing knowledge there are no such things: its mode of representation is a "first" world product which reproduces the "first" world in all that it represents. Within such representation of the "first-in-the-third" world, US soldiers can move easily from bombing Iraq to setting up field hospitals for Iraqi Kurds, because bombing Iraq was "really" setting up a field hospital for Kuwait. The "new can-do spirit in the air" represents (the) US (of A) in them, for it is the spirit that put *us* into the driving seat of the "developed" world and which the "developing" world is now discovering in itself: for it is "full of talented people who want to help themselves" but who are represented as incapable of doing so without US aid:

> We've done a leaflet drop asking these people that when we come in to come up and identify themselves, and they're coming up to us in droves and offering assistance.

This is a miniature representation of US foreign policy in general: the economics and politics of its distribution of international aid are a product of its discursive representation of the relationships between the "first" and "third" worlds, and their realities circle back into the discourse to guarantee its representation and "prove" its accuracy. It is significant that the phrase "these people" is used here as a benignly disempowering representation in precisely the same way as the Jersey City politician used it to refer to American teenagers (see p. 98).

What is represented in the second paragraph of the reporter's introduction and the visuals that accompany it is representative of this imperializing discourse. The "third" world is a "hell hole" of inadequacy: The US provides both the spirit and the means to "develop" it.

This representation continues down to the smallest detail of the story. The phrase "to get a handle on" is accented by US vernacular speech; it sounds like the "authentic" America breaking through the official language of public events. But the word accented by this vernacular authenticity is "handle," an instrument of control. Similarly, the vernacular "trying to figure out" authenticates the Americanness of scientific rationalism which has turned the "can-do spirit" via technology into material achievement. The American national identity represents itself in its representations of "the refugee crisis." The power to represent the world in this way is the power to behave in the world in this way. The US military and US television represent US similarly, and the presence of the TV crew in the "third" world is, in the operation of power, identical to the presence of the soldiers.

Over half a century earlier, for a different colonizing nation and a different form of colonization, E.M. Forster's novel *A Passage to India* represented the Indian city of Chandrapore for English readers. The time and place may be different, but the power to represent remains the same:

> Except for the Malabar Caves—and they are twenty miles off—the city of Chandrapore presents nothing extraordinary. Edged rather than washed by the river Ganges, it trails for a couple of miles along the bank, scarcely distinguishable from the rubbish it deposits so freely. There are no bathing-steps on the river-front, as the Ganges happens not to be holy here; indeed there is no river-front, and bazaars shut out the wide and shifting panorama of the stream. The streets are mean, the temples ineffective, and though a few fine houses exist they are hidden away in gardens or down alleys whose filth deters all but the invited guest. Chandrapore was never large or beautiful, but two hundred years ago it lay on the road between Upper India, then imperial, and the sea, and the fine houses date from that period. The zest for decoration stopped in the eighteenth century, nor was it ever democratic. There is no painting and scarcely any carving in the bazaars. The very wood seems made of mud, the inhabitants of mud moving. So abased, so monotonous is everything that meets the eye, that when the Ganges comes down it might be expected to wash the excrescence back into the soil. Houses do fall, people are drowned and left rotting, but the general outline of the town persists, swelling here, shrinking there, like some low but indestructible form of life.[3]

There are disturbingly close equivalences between this passage and the CBS news item, though this may be the more blatant in its imperializing. The equivalent of the hell-hole in the mountains is the dirty muddy monotony of the town and its people (the "first" world always brings cleanliness and hygiene). The "can-do spirit" which the US has but the Kurds do not is aestheticized here. So Chandrapore's few fine houses do not display themselves publicly and imposingly as would European ones, and such art as there is is confined to these upper classes. Similarly, the (Indian) river is not aestheticized into a spectacle, there is no (European) river-front, and its "shifting panorama" is rendered invisible by the bazaars whose aesthetic underdevelopment is evidenced by their lack (to white eyes) of paintings and carvings. They do, however, we presume, sell what the local inhabitants need to buy. The temples are "ineffective" only in their inability to please the cultivated developed eye. As temples they are, presumably, perfectly effective for those who worship in them, but this local knowledge is subordinated to their failure to provide aesthetic satisfaction for the European. This aesthetic failure represents the same "third"-world-for-the-"first" as does the Turks' failure to provide medicine and food for the refugees. The English colonial power, for which Chandrapore is represented as the proper field, is no less imperializing for working aesthetically. The "third" world's undeveloped sensibilities represent, in the sphere of aesthetics, the advanced development of the English just as, in the more material sphere, the Kurds' helplessness and the Turks' ineptitude represent US expertise.

The news and the novel share more than the meaning of their names: both represent the familiar, old "us" in terms of the exotic, new "other." The novel's representation of Chandrapore—"Houses do fall, people are drowned and left rotting, but the general outline of the town persists"—is representative of TV news's images of the "third" world as a place which indestructibly persists despite the decay and death that characterize it.

The "third" world also exists within US cities. And suddenly, early in 1991, a representation in which it spoke, or rather screamed, for itself was widely circulated by the media. On 3 March, LA cops stopped an African American driver, Rodney King, for a motoring offense, pulled him out of his car and beat him so severely that the fillings were knocked out of his teeth. He survived. This was not an unusual occurrence, but what was unusual about it was, first, that a nearby resident videotaped the event, and second that local and then national TV played and replayed the videotape so that it became one of the most widely heard Black statements of the year. This was one of the rare occasions when a text can be shown to have direct social and political consequences. It provoked a passionate nation-wide debate over the ways in which the social relations between the police and minorities were embodied and enacted, as opposed to institutionally represented. What the video represented was not the "third" world as the proper field of power, but the "first" world as the improper exercise of that power.

The police officers involved were charged, a new hotline for civilian complaints was set up and averaged thirty calls a day over the next six months, and a civilian commission of inquiry reported virtually unchecked racism throughout the LAPD's 8,300 members. In the midst of all the other repercussions, Daryl Gates, the long-time, hard-nosed chief of police, agreed to take "early retirement." Most significantly of all, Amnesty International announced that it would investigate the LAPD to see if brutality, racism and a disregard for human rights were systematic in the department. Amnesty International's usual sphere of operations is the "second" and "third" worlds—a fact that was not lost on an LA Police Commissioner who complained on CBS News that "They're treating us like a third world country."[4] When the report was released, in July 1992, Police Chief Gates, on his last day in office, replied to its charges of brutality occasionally amounting to torture, by denouncing Amnesty International as "a bunch of knucklehead liberals" who "attack everything that is good in the country ... and good in the world."[5]

Tom Bradley, the Mayor of Los Angeles, himself an African American and a former cop, admitted that he had long known of such racism and brutality within the LAPD but, without a way of representing that knowledge to the public and thus of making it powerful, he was hamstrung. When it was his own, personal knowledge it was localized and restricted: while he might have been able to use it in his own locale as an African American citizen he could not, apparently even as Mayor, translate that knowledge into an anti-imperializing one that was "strong" enough to challenge white imperialist power in its own sphere.[6] Only when that knowledge was made representational (in all senses of the word) could it gain the power to "imperialize"—that is, to extend its power far beyond the immediate conditions of those who know it experientially rather than representationally. African American and other racial minorities "knew" policing in this way from their localized experience of it, but while the European Americans may have known *about* it, such knowledge was distanced and marginalized in their consciousness. The power to represent reality makes its representations real; it is a real power and police racism became known as reality. The (counter-)imperializing power of representational knowledge, in this case at least, had greater effectivity than the power of the police batons upon the body of Rodney King.[7]

The important point made by this example is that there is no essential correlation between subordinate social formations and localizing power/knowledge on the one hand, and dominant ones and imperializing power/knowledge on the other. The power to represent is not a class-specific power in itself. But, like all other forms of power and discipline, both access and subjection to its operation are unequal, and these inequalities can, historically, be described in terms of specific social differences—in this case, of race. Indeed, when it is in the interests of subordinate formations to contest the power of the dominant in particular circumstances they may need to exercise their agency through the same technologies of power to which the dominant have historically privileged access. The power-bloc serves its own interests by restricting popular access to the machinery of power.

The novel, the news and the video are all "realistic." Realism, as a mode of representation, is particularly characteristic of Western cultures and, therefore, in the modern world, of capitalism. It is as powerful and attractive as it is because it grounds our cultural identity in external reality:

by making "us" seem real it turns who we think we are into who we "really" are. To achieve this, it must "know" reality in the way that science "knows" it, as an objective universal whose existence and truth are independent of culture.

Realism and scientific rationalism go hand in hand, and both grew in parallel to become the dominant ways of knowing of post-Renaissance Europe. The secular humanism which is common to both taught that man (sic) could, through reason, control his own destiny by using that reason to understand, represent and control the reality within which that destiny would evolve. Similarly, the new capitalism taught that man could control his own economic destiny. The historical conjuncture of humanism, scientific rationalism, representationalism and capitalism launched European societies on their voyage to dominate the world. These are the -isms of power which worked as effectively for the West in the modern world as they did for Greece and Rome in the classical.

The power to represent the world in the way that both CBS and E.M. Forster did is a power to map the world in a particular way. Maps are crucial to imperial power, for we cannot control what we do not know, and we cannot know a territory until we can map it. In general, non-imperializing societies do not produce maps, but instead give their members directions for travel. Directions for travelling through a territory differ significantly from a map of it, and the differences are produced by different power/knowledge relations between a society and its physical environment. Maps are powerful discourse, for they bring together science and representation to function as explicit instruments of control.

The TV news of the Gulf War constantly represented it to us in the form of maps. The maps gave us the objective, all-seeing, all-powerful truth of the world. Equally importantly, of course, they gave the US military the all-seeing eye that Iraq lacked. In maps representation and scientific technology become one. The scientific way of knowing, coupled with its will to know, produced the ability to build the satellite which reproduced its own way of knowing in the form of maps. These representations were as instrumental as the bombs and tanks. American power was the power of knowledge as well as of heavy armor and high explosive. The war was represented to us-US, in part at least, as being one between smart technology and blind faith. The Iraqi army was blind because they could not see Saddam Hussein any more clearly than they could see US troop movements. Being able to see or know is not just a prerequisite for control, it is part of that control. The mapping disparity was as great and as influential as the hardware disparity.

This is not news, for it has always been so. Europeans mapped the world as they explored, exploited and colonized it. The maps produced by

Mercator's projection, his scientific way of representing a globe on a flat surface, have become part of Western common sense because they represent, not just the world, but Western power in and over it. To flatten the curvature of the earth, Mercator made the meridians parallel and so progressively widened the distance between them as they travelled northwards. To compensate for this, he enlarged the distances between the parallels proportionately. The result was a map that empowered Europe in two ways. Instrumentally it was an efficient navigational tool because it allowed a straight line on its surface to be sailed by a straight compass bearing on the surface of the earth: it distorted the distance but held the bearing. When time and distance were less crucial than direction, the map was a superb technology for capitalism for it allowed the merchants and the military of Europe to find their way to any part of the known world and bring back to Europe the resources and the glory of their power to see and to sail. Representationally, the projection enlarged Europe. Flattening the curve of the earth entailed enlarging the northern land masses which "happened" to be the ones occupied by Europeans. But this was not Mercator's only representational technique. Because most of his customers needed to know about and sail about the northern hemisphere, he dropped the equator to almost two thirds of the way *down* his map. He also standardized the idea that the north should be on top—in the position of discursive as well as political and economic power. Europe became the enlarged center of the world (see Plate 4).

Eurocentricity is literally represented in the position of the Greenwich meridian, the imaginary line through London on which one has to stand to divide East from West. Technically, all meridians are numbered in the two categories East or West from Greenwich, but the power of the categories is at least as effective representationally as it is instrumentally. There are as many places on the earth from where the US is East and Asia West as vice versa. Australia is one of them, and Australian versions of Mercator's map put Australia in the bottom center with the US on the right (East) and Asia on the left (West). Yet while Australians travel east to the US and west to Asia, they categorize them as "West" and "East" respectively: Such is the power of the representational world over the physical, of history over geography.

This Eurocentric representation of the world was part of Eurocentric action in the world, for knowing and doing are continuous. European-derived societies have retained it as one of their commonest maps, if not the normal one, because we are still engaged in much the same global enterprise as the seventeenth-century helmsmen.

Mercator's birth name was Gerhard Kremer. By Latinizing it he allied himself discursively with the classically educated class; and, to extend his alliance to include the emerging bourgeoisie, he chose a Latin name meaning "merchant." His name and his map similarly represent the power-bloc of preindustrial capitalist Europe: they are part of the same way of knowing, they are both instruments in imperializing. CBS shows us the Kurds and the Turks and E.M. Forster shows us Chandrapore by Mercator's projection. The world map that forms the backdrop to CBS's news studio is, predictably, Mercator's (see Plate 5).

The news of the world and the maps of the world both constitute the world as a sphere of knowledge and therefore action for those whose power enables them to know it as they do. The connections between news and maps as ways of knowing are close. The maps and atlases of the sixteenth and seventeenth century were consistently entitled "new" or "newly described," and Pieter van der Keere, a printer and engraver who worked with Mercator in the production of his atlas, also produced the first English-language newspaper: in 1620 he printed the single sheet *coranto* (the name means "current" or "new"), which has come to be regarded as London's first newspaper.

The other period of energetic European imperialization was in the nineteenth century: its representational arm of power this time worked less through maps than through news. At least three major factors motivated the nineteenth-century development of the news industry. Imperialization produced the need to know the world more efficiently: the spread of literacy produced a larger public for that knowledge and the rising standard of living made that public a source of profit. And finally technology made possible the mass production and distribution of newspapers: the telegraphic cable system enabled news to be collected, the steam and then rotary press accelerated printing from 150 copies per hour in 1814 to 12,000 by 1848, and the new railways enabled the overnight distribution of the papers themselves. International news agencies grew rapidly to provide the required knowledge. In 1869 the imperially named Agency Alliance Treaty did away with unprofitable competition between the three major agencies, and divided the world up so that each could have its own colony of knowledge. Reuters of London controlled the knowledge of the British Empire and the Far East, Wolff of Berlin that of Northern Europe and Russia, and Havas of Paris that of France, Spain, Portugal, Italy and their respective empires. Subsequent reorganization brought US players into the game (Associated Press and United Press International) so that now the news of the world is controlled by five agencies: AP, UPI, Reuters, AFP (Agence France-Presse, the successor to Havas), and Tass. These are all under the control of European-derived, imperialist powers. So, too, is the technology by which their power is applied: the satellites which distribute the information (and incidentally produce both our modern maps and that specialized news called military intelligence) are, inevitably, part of the same societies as the agencies.

As the development of cartography in early modern Europe had a strong commercial dimension, so did the development of news. Not only was news itself commodified, but newspapers distributed commercial knowledge (called "advertisements") inseparably from, and uncontradictorily with, their imperializing knowledge (called "news"). News and advertising travel on each other's backs. Imperializing knowledge always has multiple dimensions—political, military, economic, representational.

The power of imperializing knowledge works in the texts discussed in this chapter by both oppression and repression. It oppresses first by "othering" or exoticizing its object of knowledge, and thus producing it as the terrain for imperialization. The imperializing agency may be abstracted from this terrain, as are the invisible but nosy Englishmen in Forster's Chandrapore, the US TV crew in Turkey, and the greedy European navigator in Mercator's world, or it may be embodied in visible representatives such as the benign GIs on the Turkish border. But whether we see the agency or not, it is always part of the process of representation.

Powerful knowledge exerts its control not only over what it chooses to represent as real, but also in its repression of what it chooses to exclude. But the power to repress is rarely total, so traces of the repressed remain obstinately present in the representation. The US "representatives" in the Middle East wear military uniform, and no representation of their benignity can obliterate the knowledge that soldiers kill and have killed. So, too, the pictures of Kurdish families and the information about their wide range of talents contain traces of social identities and a social order which is theirs and which can, and should, be known quite differently from their US representation. Similarly, the Chandrapore houses that turn their backs on the English gaze "other" the intruder as he "others" Chandrapore. The bazaars which look on themselves rather than the river, and the streets whose meanness is not that of their users, indicate a local Chandrapore which can be known quite differently. "The Ganges happens not to be holy here" not only exoticizes the religion of the other, but also, in the word "happens," exposes the inability of imperializing power to comprehend a system of sacredness and mundaneness which lies outside its own knowledge.

Mercator's map, the most scientific and hence instrumentally powerful of all the representations, represses other ways of knowing more efficiently than do the others. But they are possible and they do exist. Mercator's projection exists competitively with others, even if the knowledge of that competition is repressed. In 1974, Arno Peters, for example, produced a projection which represented the size of all countries in the world with proportionate accuracy (see Plate 6).[8] It is still a "scientific" map, indeed, its supporters claim that it exemplifies better science than Mercator's. To the white world, in whom Mercator has been normalized, the effect was shocking. North America, Europe and the USSR appear to be squeezed and misshapen. Africa, South America and the south appear elongated. Not surprisingly Peters's projection has been enthusiastically promoted by members of the "third" world and by organizations such as the UN or international churches. Those who believe that the best way of knowing the world as we move towards the twenty-first century is one that respects its diversity and minimizes power difference between nations find that this map represents their knowledge more realistically (accurately) than does Mercator's. Equally unsurprisingly, the Peters projection has been rejected or ignored by most of the agencies of the power-bloc in the West—school boards, the major map and atlas publishers, the TV news networks and the federal government. CBS news could hardly backdrop its account of the US military in the Gulf or in the Kurdish refugee camp with Peters's way of representing the world.

People live in places. The power to control place is always the power to control people. Power is never exerted only through technological control, but always through discursive control as well: the power to do and the power to know are inseparable. George Bush's line drawn in the sands of Saudi Arabia and the US tanks that enforced it were part of Mercator's projection of the world, not Peters's. Science and rationalism produce knowledge about the physical and social worlds which enable those who possess it to dominate and exploit those worlds for their own ends. It is not surprising, then, that those nations whose power-blocs have promoted scientific and rationalistic ways of knowing have come to dominate and exploit the world, just as, within those nations, those same power-blocs have used those same ways of knowing to dominate and exploit other social formations within their own nation. Such an instrumentally power-ful way of knowing disguises its political instrumentality with the rhetoric of objectivity. This displaces its truths and locates them in external nature or reality rather than in the power of those who produce and use them, and in so far as it is effective in this (and in general terms its effectiveness is almost total), it naturalizes this power by casting it not as the effect of a history of domination but as the effect of being able to know the truth. The physical and political instrumentalities of this knowledge are mutually endorsing and interdependent: they are two sides of the same coin.

Representation is control. The power to represent the world is the power to re-present us in it or it in us, for the final stage of representing merges the representor and the represented into one. Imperializing cultures produce great works of art (great representations) which can be put to work discursively as armies and trading houses work militarily and economically. Shakespeare, Jane Austen and maps were as important to English Imperial power as was the East India Company, the British army and the churches of England. It is no coincidence that modern Europe, the Europe of colonization, was also the Europe of "great art," and no coincidence either that it was the Europe of great map makers, for unless we can control the world discursively by maps we cannot control it militarily or economically. Mercator, Molière, Columbus and Captain Cook imperialized in different ways, but they all imperialized, and ultimately the effectivity of one depended upon and supported the effectivity of all the others. Similarly the US form of contemporary colonization, which involves occupying economies and political parties rather than physical territories, is accompanied by the power of both Hollywood and the satellite to represent the world to and for the US.

NOTES

1. Roseanne Mantovella, *Corporate Art* (New Brunswick, NJ: Rutgers University Press), 1990.
2. Edward Said, *Orientalism* (New York: Random House, 1978); and Frantz Fanon, *Black Skin, White Masks* (New York: Grove, 1967).
3. Richard Hoggart gives a slightly more charitable reading of the colonial tone of his passage, in "A Question of Time: Problems in Autobiographical Writing," in Richard Hoggart, *Speaking to Each Other*, Volume 2, *About Literature* (Harmondsworth: Penguin, 1970): pp. 166–88.
4. CBS News, 23 September 1991.
5. Jack Miles, "Blacks vs. Browns," *The Atlantic Monthly*, October 1992, p. 64.
6. The *Star Tribune*, 28 July 1991, p. 19A reports him as saying:

   > Without something of a dramatic fashion to hit the people squarely between the eyes, there was no way that you could convince the majority of the people in the city that these kinds of (abuses) happen. . . . I have seen evidence of it from time to time and knew that there was much more of this racism and excessive use of force present in that department. . . . Had that tape not been there, these officers no doubt would have denied that it took place and we would have had the same kind of situation: charges, allegations, denial, matter dismissed. That videotape, I think, has shaken not only law enforcement in this city, but across the nation.

7. The officers' acquittal, in May 1992, provoked uprisings in LA and other cities. Gates' "early retirement" had still not taken effect. Some comments on the white power evidenced in the trial and its after effects are made in Chapter 12.
8. Ward L. Kaiser, *A New View of the World, a Handbook to the World Map: Peters Projection* (New York: Friendship Press, 1987).

8

GUNFIGHT AT THE

P.C. CORRAL

THE WEST AS AMERICA

The nineteenth-century imperializing movements which produced the categories of "first" and "third" worlds were not confined to European nations: in the "New World" ("new" only to Europeans) the settlement and development of the West was the US equivalent. In the spring of 1991 the Smithsonian Institution mounted an exhibition in the National Museum of American Art called *The West as America, Reinterpreting Images of the Frontier, 1820–1920*. Its aim was to reveal the political labor involved in the great representations of the West, particularly in the way they rendered it knowable to the patrons of the Eastern states whose money underwrote (and multiplied itself in) the colonization.[1]

The exhibition showed that the material power of the military and the farmers, of mining, railroad and telegraph engineers was accompanied by the representational power of painters, photographers and sculptors. By making explicit the power of great works of art to represent the political, economic and ideological interests of the power-bloc, it provoked a minor but significant skirmish over the cultural control of America and the American control of culture. Most critics and visitors agreed that the collection of representations was just fine; what caused the uproar was the "political correctness"[2] of the "wall texts," slabs of prose accompanying each art work or group of works that cumulatively reinterpreted the development of the West, not as the flowering of the US frontier spirit, but as capitalist exploitation, sexism and genocide. My brief discussion of this exhibition and its contestation for US history will focus primarily on the

162

racial or genocidal dimension of the controversy it aroused; nevertheless, economic motivations lie just beneath the skin of racism.

One family may stand as a figure of the controversy. The Graysons emigrated overland to California in 1846 where Andrew, the father/ husband, prospered rapidly through business ventures and land specula- tion. In 1850 he commissioned the artist William Jewett to record the historical moment when he and his family reached the summit of the Sierra Nevada and saw, for the first time, the Sacramento Valley. The resulting picture, *The Promised Land—the Grayson Family*, is an amalgam of the discourses of imperializing power (see Plate 7).[3]

The Christian discourse of its title and its compositional references to traditional representations of the holy family frame discourses of the Western frontier and Western civilization, embodied in the representation of Grayson himself. He wears buckskins and carries a long rifle with which he has, presumably, just killed the deer whose carcass lies directly behind him. This frontier discourse speaks not of a return to nature, but of the frontiers of civilization, for his (well-tailored) buckskins are worn over a white shirt and tie that, like the clothes of his wife and son, are signs of polite, urban society. The aesthetic discourse of the painting itself circulates in the same parlors and salons as does the family's fashionable dress and represents a similar civilizing process. It forges intertextual links with eighteenth-century European pictures of members of the aristocracy surveying their estates. Grayson may not hold legal title to the land he overlooks, but the painting offers up the virgin territory of California (the metaphor is appropriate, for its sexism approximates that of the painting) for his visual possession, just as the body and life of the deer have become his through the ultimate act of power. Indeed, the body of the deer is so painted into the landscape as to become almost indistinguishable from it: the deer and the landscape are equally his prey. The spectator of the painting is invited to align himself (gender deliberate) with Grayson's proprietorial gaze.

"Westward the course of Empire takes its way" was the first line of a poem written over a century earlier by George Berkeley, an Anglican churchman. The poem's title was "Verses on the Prospect of Planting Arts and Learning in America" and, like the painting of the Graysons, it combined religion, colonization and civilization into a single work of art. The cumbersome title resonated little, but, according to Patricia Hills, its opening phrase became the unofficial motto of the expansionist spirit. It became, for example, the title of a huge mural painted by Emanuel Leutze in 1861, which was commissioned by Congress to grace the enlarged Capitol at the time when western acquisition was enlarging the United States. Four of the pictures in the exhibit catalog had titles reproducing the phrase more or less precisely. One was a drawing by Robert Weir of Leutze at work on his mural, and the other three were all of the railroad. (Part of the exhibit's revisionism was to tell how railroad money sponsored many of the artists and how railroad technology whisked them out to the West on flying visits and back to their Eastern studios.) Hills cites as another example an article of 1859 which, under the headline "Westward the Star of Empire," trumpeted:

> The westward movement of the Caucasian brand of the human family from the high plains of Asia, first over Europe, and thence, with swelling tide, pouring its multitudes into the New World, is the greatest phenomenon of history. What American can contemplate its results, as displayed before him, and as promised in the proximate future, without an emotion of pride and exultation?[4]

California was, of course, the final Promised Land of the Caucasians, for if they continued their "westward movement" any further they would end up in the East (California is, by this measure, the only place in the world from which one cannot go west!).

A contemporary account of "The Grayson Family" placed it within the same discursive frame. Hills writes:

> The painting was justly famous in its own time. When exhibited at the First Industrial Exhibition of the Mechanics' Institute in 1857 in San Francisco, it was described as a subject "particularly interesting to Californians. ... The early pioneer has survived the perils of his arduous journey, and, feeling that his family is safe and his object attained, calmly and joyfully surveys the scene. The composition representing the high idea of the progress of civilization westward will render this picture of ever-increasing value in the history of the arts in California.[5]

The Smithsonian wall text, however, took a different tone. It pointed out: "Ignored were the less honorable aspects of California history—the profiteering, revolts against Mexican authority, and Indian massacres." (1846 was the year in which US pioneers, led by John Charles Fremont, rebelled against Mexican authorities, and in 1850 the Sacramento Valley was opened up for prospecting and mining.) Its rhetoric may have been somewhat didactic, but the wall text does foreground the struggle over the meanings of California: was the state "better" represented as virgin land or as an occupied territory whose indigenous peoples had already been colonized by a foreign power? It makes explicit, too, the idea that the promotion of any one way of knowing involves the repression of others: painting the dead deer *into* the landscape and painting the Native Americans *out* of it are equivalent strategies of representational power.

The juxtaposition of the contradictory knowledges in the wall text and the painting disrupts the security of a singular truth and faces the spectator with the uncomfortable recognition that evaluating knowledges involves not so much assessing their accuracy to an objective truth as exercising political judgement.

Actually, the wall text may be working a little too hard, and consequently risks overemphasizing the uniaccentuality of the painting itself (as well as coming perilously close to replacing one uniaccentual "truth" with another). To my less than sympathetic eye, for instance, the ludicrous inappropriateness of the Grayson family's dress to the wilderness (how on earth did they get there in those clothes?) demystifies the power that the painting otherwise naturalizes. Equally, their stiff postures disconnect them from each other and question the meanings of the family that otherwise they represent. I can almost see the urban studio in which the Graysons must have posed showing through the painted scenery that is meant to hide it. Such discursive contradictions within the painting do not, admittedly, fill in the absences of which the wall text quite properly reminds us, but they do fracture the seamless monosemy implied by the wall text.

Howard Lamar, in the exhibition catalog, traces the origin of The West to three commercial motives: securing the fur trade for the US, seeking fertile new lands for Jefferson's farmers, and opening up a "passage to India" and the lucrative trade with the Far East.[6] The links between E.M. Forster's invisible Englishman in Chandrapore and Jewett's all too visible European American in California lies less in the specificity of the "passage to India" than in India as a motivational image of imperial imagination— a land of exotic riches ripe for commercial and political exploitation. These three objectives—fur, farming and the Far East—motivated Jefferson to send the military officers Lewis and Clark with their "semisecret Corps of Discovery"[7] on the first transcontinental march by European Americans (their title makes explicit the links between a military body [Corps] and a body of knowledge [Discovery]). They achieved all three objectives (though not without problems[8]), and their triumph included, predictably, according to the argument of the previous chapter, the production of the first map of the upper trans-Mississippi West. Lewis and Clarke were simultaneously figures of military, commercial and representational power.

Lamar also makes clear that these three objectives did not fit together as neatly as their shared commercial motivation might suggest. The development of the fur trade depended upon both a substantial population of friendly Native American hunters and a wilderness for them to hunt in, but developing agriculture meant both dispossessing and antagonizing the same peoples and destroying their wilderness; and finally, the development of commerce threatened the status of both Native Americans and farmers.[9]

In its review of the controversy over the Smithsonian exhibition, *The Nation* points out that "The West's development was not simple heroic progress: American History contains many Wests, all more or less invented":

> At the Constitutional Convention, Madison argued that the West could save America from Old World class conflict. Half a century later Horace Greeley saw it as a safety valve for oppressed Eastern workers. The doctrine of Manifest Destiny held that the West would fulfill America's divinely ordained role as savior of the world. Economic writers often viewed the West as a passage to India, a route by which America could dominate trade with the Far East. Today, it seems, the New World Order requires a West free of exploitation, racism and other inconvenient realities of American life.[10]

The painting of the Grayson family preferred one of these Wests, the wall text another: I assume that it was the discomfort of being faced with the choice and its interrogation of the singularity of historical "truth" that provoked Charles Krauthammer, in *The Washington Post*, to react splenetically: "Yes. And the Mona Lisa ignored the syphilis epidemic sweeping Italy at the time."[11]

The exhibit's "guest books" were filled with visitors' comments which ran the whole gamut of responses.[12] Many were infuriated by the disruption of the dominant knowledge of the West, others welcomed its replacement with a new (but equally singular) "truth," and yet others welcomed the struggle between truths. Krauthammer's outrage was echoed in comments such as:

> Good grief! What should be celebrated here are the great achievements and collective glory that spurred the settlements of the West. The paintings tell this story. The commentary is forced and has no relation to the paintings. Merely a polemical tool for those who wish to stir dissension and hate. American art should never be a handmaiden to political propaganda.[13]

Other visitors welcomed the substitution of the old truth with a new and "better" one, but still employed a discourse that neatly distinguished between truth and falsity:

> Those who do not learn from the past are doomed to repeat it. The narratives tell the truth. The pictures without them are a lie.[14]

But for others the "arguments" between the artworks and the wall texts exhibited the actual process of producing truth:

Not always certain where ideology divides between one generation and another—standing here, what of our times do we bring to it, what of ourselves. I loved this exhibit. I think the approach, the stimulation to thinking, the challenge of easy assumptions, are like the fresh wind blowing. I may not always agree—for me, many of Catlin's images reveal humanity and dignity, not capture—but I'm continuously made to ask myself the questions. Beyond all that, I love the selection of pictures/images and the way they are presented. Bravo and congratulations.[15]

The sense of liberation from an oppressive truth contained in the simile of "the fresh wind blowing" occurred in a number of the more sympathetic comments:

I want to record my appreciation of the courage behind this exhibit. It is, as a view of Western expansion, only disillusioning to those who have come to depend on illusions—and a number of those folks have recorded their dependence on these pages. The West cannot be the theme park of the Anglo-American imagination any longer, and I thank you for your help in liberating us from that peculiar captivity.[16]

Many visitors, too, considered the controversy in the guest books to be as healthy and stimulating as the exhibition. But the comment that had most immediate effect was one signed by Daniel Boorstin, a former Librarian of Congress, who wrote "A perverse, historically inaccurate, destructive exhibit. No credit to the Smithsonian."[17]

Ironically, Boorstin described his 1961 book, *The Image: A Guide to Pseudo-events in America*, as being "about our arts of self-deception, how we hide reality from ourselves."[18] While he and the Smithsonian may differ on which history is "reality" and which is "self-deception," Boorstin has obviously not lost his ability to distinguish between the two. His truth is confidently promoted in another of his books where he writes of the ranchers of the West that "their great opportunity was to use apparently useless land that belonged to nobody." While citing Boorstin's comment on this exhibit, *The Humanist* reminded its readers that he once excused lies about the Vietnam War as "patriotic necessities," and in 1953 named five of his former colleagues to the House Un-American Activities Committee.[19] His comment in the guest book, together with his standing within the power-bloc, alerted Ted Stevens, the Republican Senator from Alaska, to the controversy. In the Senate he proclaimed: "In the exhibit, history was distorted to depict American paintings of the West as something they were not."[20] As a member of the Senate Appropriations Committee that controls the Smithsonian's federal funding, he was able to express his outrage in a direct challenge to Robert McC. Adams, the Smithsonian Institution secretary: "You're in for a battle ... I'm going to get other people to help me make you make sense," he said, in a memorable phrase whose few words refer to both power-bloc alliances and the struggle over meaning. He continued: "To see that exhibit, I'll tell you that really set me off. Why should people come to your institution and see a history that's so perverted?" Presumably to preserve himself against such perversion, Stevens had not actually been to the exhibit.[21]

Rather than being perverted, history was being repeated. Stevens introduced into the Congressional Record an editorial by James Cooper from *American Arts Quarterly* which argued:

> If concerned Americans truly want to have an impact on the culture, they must become sponsors instead of passive consumers. It is not enough to criticize; we must select experts who will sponsor art that relates to the American experience. Culture must be approached as responsibly as family, religion and the environment. Those who control the culture determine how Americans perceive themselves and how they set the course for the future.[22]

This 1991 recognition of the need to control culture is remarkably similar to a piece written in 1845, and reprinted in the exhibition catalog:

> Someone has said, give me the writing of the *songs* of a country, and you may make its laws. I had almost said, give me the control of the *art* of a country, and you may have the management of its administrations. There can be no greater folly than that committed by our statesmen, when they treat art and literature as something quite aside from great national interests. . . . Art is too often looked upon as an abstract thing, designed only for men of taste and leisure. . . . Every great national painting of a battle-field, or great composition, illustrating some event in our history—every engraving, lithograph and wood cut appealing to national feeling and rousing national sentiment—is the work of art; and who can calculate the effect of all these on the minds of our youth.[23]

To its contemporaries, *The Grayson Family* painting represented not only the "high idea of the progress of civilization westward," but explicitly conjoined, within this idea of civilization, aesthetics and entrepreneurial capitalism. The California represented by the Grayson–Jewett alliance was:

> the promised land lying in its still beauty like the sleeping Princess of the story, waiting but the kiss of Enterprise to spring into energetic life. There below [the family] is not only the field for industry and enterprise, but a panorama of natural charms destined to inspire poets, to glow on the canvas of painters, and to take on the magic of human association and tradition.[24]

The image of California as a sleeping beauty awaiting Prince Capitalism to awaken her adds an economic dimension to the ageism and racism of the "virgin territory" metaphor. In 1991 the discursive association between aesthetics and capitalist development may be less explicit, but it is still there. Ted Stevens, speaking for the Congressional record through Cooper's editorial, concludes:

> A civilization that rejects not only beauty but also the moral and spiritual foundations of the nation, risks an internal crisis of monumental proportions. Free societies require virtuous citizens. To restore transcendent values, and courage, honor, integrity, self-discipline and humility, we must first embrace them through our culture. To those art administrators who have abandoned absolute values for trendy political causes, "It should be made clear that the arts belong not solely to those who receive its grants but to all the people of the United States.[25]

The commercial rhetoric here is as silenced by aesthetic notions of beauty, spirit and transcendent, absolute values as are the voices of the Mexicans and Native Americans in Grayson's California, but it can still be heard in the figure of Ted Stevens himself. Stevens is a vocal supporter of oil and mineral development in Alaska, and had earlier criticized the Smithsonian for screening the documentary *Black Tide* about Exxon's role in the Alaskan oil spill because it "depicted the darkest days of the oil spill and it did not have any balance at all."[26]

The way that Ted Stevens represents Alaskan (and white American) interests has further similarities with those of the "California" represented by Grayson/Jewett, for Stevens also works to repress the voices of Mexican or Native Americans. While attacking the Smithsonian for staging *The West as America*, he was also chastising it for supporting Carlos Fuentes's proposed TV mini-series "The Buried Mirror: Reflections on Spain and the New World," whose representation of America (like that of the videotape of Rodney King's beating) showed the "first" world through the eyes of the "third," and included, according to the *New York Times*, an account of "the founding of America that is reported to accuse the United States of genocide against the Indians."[27] Stevens justified his strategy by labelling Fuentes as "a Marxist Mexican" and a "noncitizen."[28]

A cynic might think that the power-bloc would find it hard to come up with three better reasons for not listening to Fuentes. But the issue is broader than that: by protecting its own interests in this way, the power-bloc is also constraining the US imagination. The contemporary US is one of the most monoglossic cultures in the world: because the nation is such a powerful exporter of culture, it imports very little, and consequently, US citizens are comparatively deprived of hearing other voices, of seeing the world (and themselves) from other points of view. And that power-bloc alliance which represents the "public interest" (and therefore public money) via the voice of Ted Stevens, seems determined that this state of affairs should continue. In this case, of course, the "imported" culture crosses not national frontiers but social ones. Stevens's cultural protectionism and the monoculture it serves is reflected in the demographics of Smithsonian visitors, less than 10 per cent of whom are of the so-called racial minorities.[29] Monoculturalism has no more interest in admitting a diversity of bodies into its institutions than of voices into its representations. Individuals within the Smithsonian, even powerful ones such as Adams and Truettner, may well wish to diversify its public, but their efforts are contradicted structurally by its architecture, and geographically by its location in the Washington Mall, that heartland of government and culture where white power plays with uncontradicted self-assurance.

A contingent strategy of Stevens's cultural protectionism, then, is to deny subordinated cultures access to the means of representation, and thus to confine their voices to their own localities. If the "first" and "third" worlds are to consent to live peacefully together (whether within the US or internationally), then the "first" will have to modify its behavior in order to win the consent of some, at least, of the "third" world communities. Such modification will never be motivated, let alone sensitively directed, if we do not learn to listen to "third" world voices and to see ourselves through their eyes. What we learn may not always be what we wish to learn, and the power-bloc alliance represented by Ted Stevens is doing its best to save us the embarrassment.

In defending his Institution's support of the Fuentes mini-series, Robert Adams admitted that "he was unaware of a rumor that it had been turned down by the National Endowment of the Arts or the National Endowment for the Humanities."[30] It is worth noting that the chairperson of the NEH was Lynne Cheney, whose husband, Dick, was Secretary for Defense during the Gulf War. George Will, that columnar voice of the power-bloc, dubbed by *Lingua Franca* "the wealthiest and most famous pundit in America,"[31] opined that

> In this low visibility, high intensity war, Lynne Cheney is secretary of domestic defense. The foreign adversaries that her husband, Dick, must keep at bay are less dangerous, in the long run, than the domestic forces with which she must deal.[32]

Fuentes's rumored rejection by the NEH and Ted Stevens's attack on him provide a clear example of power-bloc alliances at work: they result less from individuals conspiring together than from the independent and mutual recognition of shared social interests. The interests linked by these alliances do not necessarily coincide with those of empirically defined

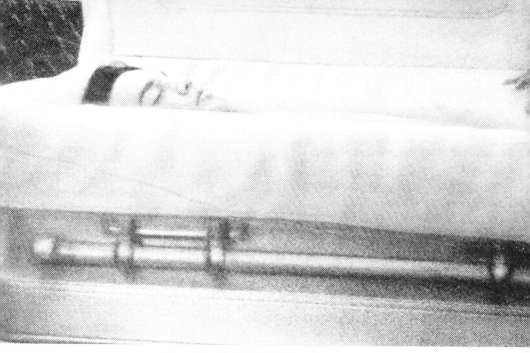

PLATE 1   Elvis "Lying" Dead

ELVIS PRESLEY substituted a doomed double before his reported death and is posing as an impersonator of himself — in England!

That's the intriguing theory of a top cop investigating The King's mysterious "death."

Detective Monte Wayne Nicholson tells the EXAMIN-ER. "It's conceivable that Elvis could have faked his death by substituting a double."

He adds: "Several thousand people disappear from the U.S. every year that are never heard from again. Many of these people do this themselves. Now once you break down the Elvis mystique and everything else the idea of him hiding is pretty simple and well within the bounds of possibility."

In the course of writing a book on Elvis 11 years ago, Nicholson says confidential sources told him Elvis had

• CASHED in several insurance policies just weeks before his "death" to avoid

IS THIS THE double who died for Elvis?

any fraud charges against his family in the event he was found out

• SUBSTITUTED look-alikes to perform for him.

Says the decorated Vietnam veteran, who has served 16 years in law enforcement in Southern California. "I didn't follow up on this because I didn't need to. I was writing a

YOUNG ELVIS was bare-chested.

Elvis arranges for a double to take his place, freeing him from the confines of superstardom.

But the look-alike, who is suffering from cancer, dies at Graceland while Elvis' daughter, Lisa Marie, is visiting. Elvis is forced to vanish.

"The theory that I came up with in my book was that Elvis really wasn't getting fat, his double was, because the double was taking medication for his cancer and getting bloated," says Nicholson.

Surgery

Later in the book, Elvis undergoes plastic surgery to make him look like one of his impersonators. He then hides in England.

Nicholson says while researching his novel, one of Elvis' bodyguards showed him a picture of two FBI agents standing by the side of a stage while The King was giving one of his last concerts.

The detective claims when he tracked down the bodyguard recently and inquired about the picture and the FBI connection the man denied either had ever existed.

It is conceivable that The King, his looks altered by plastic surgery, could be posing as an Elvis impersonator in England with the help of the British government and the FBI, Nicholson says.

"Elvis was quite a prac-tical joker," the detective

Too much hair on imposter's chest

PROOF THAT Elvis Presley sub-stituted a double before his re- hold up his hand and turn away from the camera. He didn't like pictures taken of

PLATE 2   Elvis Alive (But Which?)

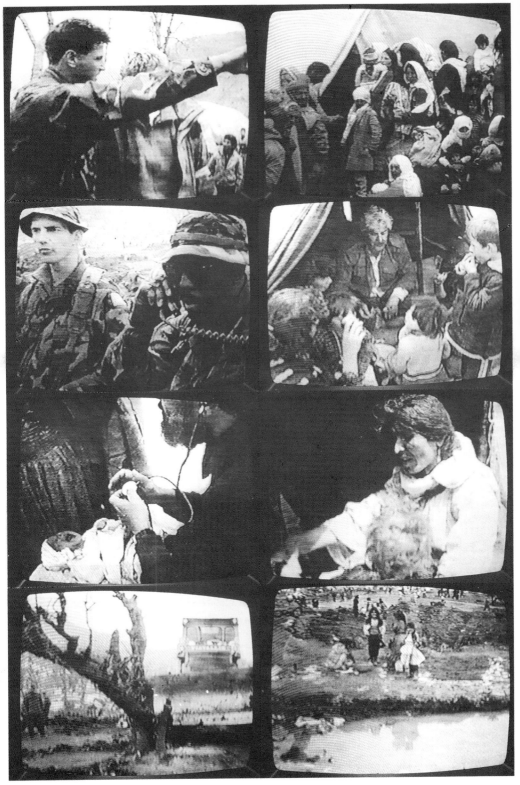

PLATE 3　The News of the World

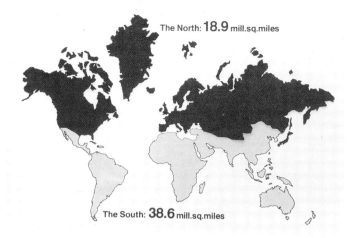

The North: **18.9** mill.sq.miles

The South: **38.6** mill.sq.miles

PLATE 4   Mercator's World

PLATE 5   CBS's World

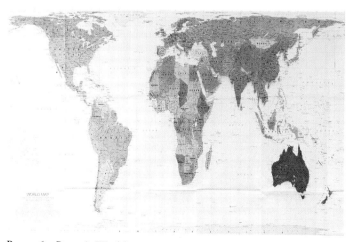

PLATE 6   Peters's World

PLATE 7   William Jewitt, *The Promised Land, the Grayson Family*

ELVIS of ARABIA

The King appears to our troops and vows to protect them

ELVIS PRESLEY has promised to protect our fighting heroes in Saudi Arabia!

That's the comforting news coming out of the Middle East war zone.

A military spokesman has told The EXAMINER that four Marines stationed in a remote compound near the Saudi border with Kuwait have reported being visited by Elvis while standing guard duty.

"They said he looked fit and trim and wore the robes of an Arab sheik — like Lawrence of Arabia," said the spokesman.

According to the spokesman, the man who looked like Elvis told them in his characteristic drawl: "Don't worry, I'll be watching over you and all your fellow servicemen. I'll act as your guardian angel and be alongside you during the battles to come."

The spokesman said witnesses tried to talk to Presley, but he simply vanished. Shortly after, they reported the incident to their superiors.

The Marine Corps refused to take an official stand on the reported sighting, but longtime Presley fans say they aren't surprised by The King's concern for the troops.

"Elvis felt a strong kinship with all military men after his stint in the Army," said Elvis expert John Jenks of Nashville, Tennessee.

"His time in Germany affected him deeply. I'm not surprised at all that he's playing guardian angel to our boys in Saudi Arabia. That's just the kind of man he was — always thinking of others."

Sighting

The Marine spokesman said officials are currently investigating the sighting.

"We're skeptical, but we're not ruling out that it took place," he said.

"The men who reported the occurrence are good soldiers and we have no reason to doubt them at this time."

But not all military officials were quick to approve the soldiers' claim.

"I'm more inclined to believe they boys were suffering hallucinations from heat and dehydration," said one senior Army doctor stationed at the Pentagon.

"Most Americans aren't used to the brutal temperatures in that region of the world.

"The average man must drink six GALLONS of water a day to keep from dehydrating, and even then the searing sun can take its toll. I'm not saying those Marines are lying.

"But in that heat the mind can play tricks on you."

— WAYNE DIAZ

SOLDIERS SAID Elvis looked just like Lawrence of Arabia.

ELVIS HAS felt a kinship toward all military men since his service in the Army from 1958 to 1960.

WOMEN'S WORK IS MURDER

WOMEN MAY well think their jobs are killing them.

"Homicide accounts for 42 percent of women's fatal injuries at work," says Catherine Bell, author of a five-year federal study.

Other causes are vehicle and machinery accidents, electrocutions, falls and suicide.

The study shows the most dangerous jobs for women are

Color of your car may warrant more tickets

THE COLOR of your car could determine if you'll receive a speeding ticket, reports the St. Petersburg, Florida, Times.

An analysis of more than 1,000 tickets handed out for speeding showed the greatest number of citations was given to drivers of white, red, gray, black, brown, maroon and green cars.

Significantly fewer tickets were given to the drivers of cars painted gold, orange, blue or silver.

But a spokesman for the Florida Highway Patrol says car color has nothing to do with it. "If you're caught speeding, you'll get a ticket regardless," he warns.

PLATE 8   Elvis of Arabia

PLATE 9   Aged Elvis

PLATE 10   Elvis, Life After Death

PLATE 11 Turner, *Slavers Throwing Overboard the Dead and Dying: Typhon Coming On*

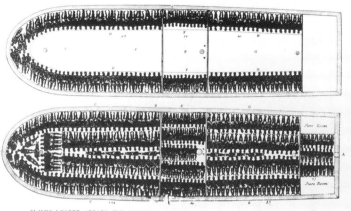

SLAVES LOADED ABOARD THE SCHOONER BROOKES, A TYPICAL ARRANGEMENT
General Research Collections of The New York Public
Library Astor, Lenox and Tilden Foundations

ANOTHER WAY OF ARRANGING SLAVES IN THE HOLD OF A SHIP
Courtesy of New Haven Colony Historical Society

PLATE 12   The "Order" of the Slave Ship

social groups or individuals, and this commonality of interests is often perceived rather than rationally articulated. The social interests represented by Ted Stevens are closely aligned with those that, in the debate over the humanities' curriculum, propound the importance of a monocultural canon and, in doing so, employ the discourse of aesthetics to justify their argument. The social institution of a political party provides one framework where individual people and social interest groups can devise concrete strategies to promote their interests, but it is only one of many and the alliances promoted within it do not constitute all the alliances of the power-bloc, but only a set of instances of them. Indeed, many of the most effective alliances are formed across institutional boundaries and thus tie social institutions into less formalized social experience, and many others are formed outside any institutionalized social structure whatever and organize themselves around momentary issues in the fluidity of everyday life. The alliance of interests is the point at issue, not the individualities or relationships of those involved. It is no contradiction, then, that Ronald Reagan may have had middle- or low-brow tastes, while his Secretary of State for Education, William Bennett, proposed a high-brow humanities canon. Ted Stevens's repression of minority voices in the Smithsonian, William Bennett's exclusion of similar voices from the curriculum, Daniel Boorstin's location of "truth" in the paintings rather than the wall texts, and Stevens's defence of Exxon's role in the Alaskan oil spill form a power-bloc alliance that is quite independent of a direct relationship among those who, on specific occasions, promote its interests. Social interests are operationalized by being embodied in individuals and social groups, but a social interest and a social category (such as a group or an individual) are not coterminous. Similarly, alliances of social interests are often embodied in relationships between groups and individuals but they, too, are not coterminous. In the Senate other Republicans allied themselves with Stevens in a strategic relationship embodying the social interests at stake in this particular issue. Slade Gordon (Washington) considered the exhibition to be a terribly distorted, negative and untrue statement about the settlement of the West,[33] and Alan Simpson (Wyoming) called the wall texts "symbolic nonsense."[34] All three Senators allied their Western voices in questioning the public funding of the exhibition. By making explicit the Western accents of the alliance, Stevens widened it to include social interests which exceeded those of the individuals actually present. He allied the Senators' West with Grayson's by casting both as victims of the Smithsonian: "We in the West live here in the East under attack all the time," he complained.[35] This West is produced by an allied set of knowledges of the "true" America which are set in epistemological opposition to the East where the falsehoods of the enemy within find sustenance and succor. The eastern edge of Europe may no longer be the stronghold from which communism can threaten the West, but the intellectualism of the Eastern fringe of the United States continues its hostility to the West that Stevens reinvents and defends so vigorously.

THE CULTURAL PUBLIC SPHERE

What is at stake in these struggles is national identity, and as a nation is, in Benedict Anderson's famous phrase, "an imagined community," the work of culture upon the national imagination puts it at the center of the battleground. The closing years of the twentieth century are witnessing a global rewriting and reassertion of national identities. The new nationalism which underlay the dissolution of the Soviet Union involved both a reinscription of national geographic boundaries and of the identities of those who lived within them. The unification of Europe and the Europe-wide footprint of the TV satellite appears to many to reverse the process, and to threaten to erase boundaries and differences. In the cultural sphere the fear is that the satellite will saturate Europe with US commercial culture ("wall-to-wall *Dallas*") and thus weaken both European identity and the national identities within it. As a result the overt cultural politics of Europe are played out in the so-called sphere of the "lowbrow" or mass culture, and the threat to national identity is perceived as a mass-mediated one from outside. (It is worth noting in passing that the transnational flow of highbrow culture is rarely seen to threaten national identity.)

In the US, however, quite the reverse is the case. With its national identity "protected" by a reluctance to import culture, the power-bloc mobilizes its forces against an internal, not external, threat and directs these forces to where its control is most effective, that is, the "cultural public sphere." This sphere is concerned with "highbrow" rather than "lowbrow" culture because the economic capital of the power-bloc is readily reconvertible with the cultural capital of the highbrow: while Ted Stevens may be a cultural philistine, he can use Cooper's high-brow aesthetic discourse with no sign of discomfort. In the curriculum debate, this same discourse can be used, in ways of which Stevens would undoubtedly approve, to disqualify minority voices as of "lesser quality" or "not true art." The terrain over which this discourse can apply its power most effectively is that of the cultural public sphere so that it is where it fights its battles. As a consequence, the prime battlegrounds are not (as in Europe) the TV screen, but the humanities curriculum in schools and universities, the exhibition policies of the Smithsonian and other galleries, the grant-awarding criteria of the NEA and the NEH, and university policies aimed at reducing sexism and racism on their campuses. Within this cultural public sphere the aesthetic discourse is all too readily joined by one of populist ethics which is unhesitatingly confident of its ability to identify obscenity, blasphemy or falsehood in art: the art thus identified is both bad art and bad for us, and so repressing it is acting in the public interest. The "people" included in such a populism and such a "public" arena, of course, are those whose interests coincide with those of the power-bloc. Aesthetics and ethics are used to homogenize US society to merge "the people" into the power-bloc (and thus to deny any conflict of interest) and to repress the diversity of US society by excluding most it from its "public."

The closing paragraph of the editorial that Stevens inserted into the Congressional record (see above p. 169) is a remarkable piece of aesthetic political discourse. Its seamless intermingling of aesthetic and moral concepts categorized as "transcendent" and "absolute" in opposition to the "trendy" and "political" culminates in a reminder that the economic power to dispense grants to the arts is also the power to control the national imagination.[36] As is typical of power-bloc discourse, this Stevens–Cooper alliance ascribes "political causes" only to those with whom it disagrees; it universalizes its own interests as those of "all the people of the United States" which, through their "transcendent" and "absolute" values, become universalized even further into those of humanity in general. The power-bloc's ability to define "the people" in its own interests and then to recruit those so defined to serve the interests that defined them is a typical discursive strategy. A clue to the definition of "the people" operating in this case is provided by the Washington Post's review of The West as America as "the most cynical exhibit ever presented under the aegis of your tax dollars and mine."[37] Conflating "the people" with "taxpayers" not only excludes the poor, the homeless and the unemployed, but also confines popular interests only to those economic ones which Stevens and his allies can control. They are careful to fight only on their own ground.

The people are often hard pressed to oppose such well-focussed strategies: for popular power to be effective its alliances often have to link different social formations and in so doing to bridge the major social differences of race, gender and class. The power-bloc has it much easier, for its greater homogeneity means that its interests rarely have to bridge major social differences. The radical media can, as in this case, monitor and make known the doings of the power-bloc; but though they may demonstrate the need for counter-alliances, they cannot, on their own, constitute them. Their limited effectiveness is a product of their limited readership, much of which is drawn from the same social categories (of class, race and gender) that the power-bloc recruits so readily into its alliances: the radical press is not the popular press, despite its promotion of popular interests. Consequently, in this particular case, there was no popular alliance formed to counter that of the power-bloc, and the interests of Stevens–Grayson–Boorstin had their way.

The cultural public sphere is often more vulnerable to direct power-bloc control than is commercial culture. The market place has never been a straightforward site of economic (and therefore ideological domination) but has always been one of contestation between popular and power-bloc interests. People's bargaining power is not confined to the circulation of money but includes the circulation of culture. In the market place, the cash register and the TV channel switch are vehicles for a form of public "speech" that economic alliances within the power-bloc are particularly eager to "hear." In the public domain, paradoxically, popular speech is less insistent: while the Smithsonian's guest books carried a wide variety of progressive voices, none had the insistence of "cash register speech." Consequently, it was all too easy for the power-bloc to listen only to those who were saying what it wanted to hear and to ignore the others. And that is what it did.

But in the commercial sphere the struggle between the power-bloc and the people is often less unequal than in the public—certainly in the way that the contemporary US power-bloc has turned the public sphere into its own tightly controlled territory. This territory is defined largely by which knowledges of the US are admitted into it and which excluded. Because the power-bloc has colonized the government of the US for its own interests, it has arrogated to itself the right to restrict federal (that is, public) money to the promotion of those interests as part of its unsleeping strategy to define "public" as "of the power-bloc" rather than "of the people." Ted Stevens may allow the history of the West to be rethought, but such rethinking is not appropriate for the "public" sphere: "That's okay if it's a private institution," he said, "but I think of the Smithsonian as a place where we really demonstrate the truth."[38] Commercial culture may actually be more open to multicultural voices than is his conservatively restricted cultural public sphere. At the time that the power-bloc was fighting for monoculturalism on all fronts, the commercial public sphere was making movies such as *Dances with Wolves* or *Boyz 'N the Hood* into box-office hits. While the revisionist representation of American Indians and the white Western expansion in *Dances with Wolves* did not go far enough to satisfy most American Indian communities (who found its accents too white), it did ask white audiences to reconsider traditional Hollywood representations of Native Americans in ways that paralleled the revisionist aims of the Smithsonian. But *Dances with Wolves* ran free of any attempt to censor its revisionism, for commercial culture is often protected by its cash-register speech from the likes of Ted Stevens or Jesse Helms in a way that the cultural public sphere with its reliance on government grants or corporate sponsorship is not. He who pays the piper calls the tune. Even *Boyz 'N the Hood*, whose screenings were associated with social violence, continued to play in cinemas with no power-bloc interference.

We might speculate, therefore, that if advertisers had used the Smithsonian to reach the dollar bills in the pockets of the minorities who never visit it and whose voices are excluded from it by the likes of Ted Stevens, those such as Adams and Truettner who wish to diversify both the museum's offerings and its audiences, might have been able to form a stronger alliance by which to resist the pressure applied to them. But any validity in speculating that commercializing public culture might diversify it should not lead us towards endorsing the *principle* of commercial over public culture, but rather to an indictment of the contemporary use of political power to monoculturalize public culture. It is our public culture that is so wrong, not commercial culture.

The cultural public sphere is where piper payers such as Ted Stevens can best influence the music, and this public sphere has no more room for the voices and rights of the homeless than of racial diversity. The moralistic alliances of the power-bloc who elect themselves as guardians of the "public" interest are often worse enemies of the people than are its economic alliances. The struggles within the cultural public sphere do not take place on a level field, for the power-bloc alliance has dug itself well in on the high ground, and it becomes a matter of deep concern that the people (or some formations of them) can argue more effectively with power-bloc alliances in commercial than in public culture.

The West as America had its planned visits to Denver and St Louis canceled,[39] and some of its wall texts were revised, so as to make them, in Robert Adams's words, "less strident in their condemnation of Western expansion."[40] Typical of the texts subjected to "modification" was one which argued that the predominant representations of Indians as either helpless primitives or as violent savages was a manifestation of Indian hating.[41] Both the curators and those who canceled the exhibit's tour claim that the changes were not occasioned by political pressure, but the fact remains that political pressure was exerted, and changes did occur. This was not as clear cut a victory for the power-bloc as it might seem at first sight, for the controversy tripled the predicted attendance at the exhibit and made the voices that the power-bloc was trying to silence more widely and clearly audible. When the terrain is as rocky as that of culture victories are rarely total and the winners often hard to identify.

The loser, however, is quite clear. What is lost is a credible and viable cultural public sphere with a guaranteed, institutionalized independence from direct political and economic influence. Of all the "first" world nations, the US would appear most to need such an independent public sphere, but far from showing any signs of developing one, its power-bloc is rather developing techniques whereby it can increase its power over and effect upon its national cultures: funding without strings is unthinkable in its conceptual repertoire. Any devolution of cultural patronage from Federal funding to corporate sponsorship merely exchanges one alliance within the power-bloc for another and does nothing to loosen the strings that prevent the "public" sphere being "for the people." Seven-figure corporate sponsorship is categorically different from the millions of single dollar bills that "talk" in the "cash register speech" of the commercial cultural sphere. As a result, the cultural public sphere, which ought to work to promote public (of the people) interests becomes tied by its economic strings to power-bloc interests. In a society as diverse as that of the US there are multitudinous voices and points of view which will never be circulated commercially because they are not profitable. When publicly supported culture represses these same voices, as well as those popular ones which can be turned into profit, the narrowing of the cultural repertoire equates all too precisely with the narrowing of the definition of "the public" in power-bloc discourse. The "public" which funds the PACs and whose voice is listened to most eagerly by the elected representatives who control the funds for public culture is a far narrower one than the public which flicks the channel switch and exchanges its dollar bills for the products of the culture industries.

While not applauding the motives that push commercial culture into giving social circulation to *some* minority voices and tasks, we must recognize that, sometimes, it does. The early 1990s, for instance, brought a noticeable increase in the representations of African American culture on network TV. No sense of public interest prompted this change, the networks were not working with the principle that the American public, of all races and ethnicities, would benefit if some of its social diversity crept into its systems of representation. The motivation was purely commercial: the higher socioeconomic groups, particularly their males, were shifting to cable TV, which better served their tastes for news, current affairs, sport, documentary and movies where sex is more explicit and violence more graphic. The loss of this preferred audience prompted the networks to look downscale, and the limited diversification of their repertoire was the result. Concluding that greed is the TV industry's Achilles heel, Gloria Abernathy-Lear sums up the market research lying behind this change:

(1) African Americans view more television than the general audience, (2) African Americans watch programs with African Americans in leading roles, (3) African Americans are a viable market, and (4) African Americans watch more daytime serials than the general audience.[42]

The one or two ratings points that decide a program's success or failure are often produced by such minority audiences, whose power to be heard is thus amplified by the power of the bottom line. The representations that resulted were not, of course, "authentically" African American but were, at best, inflections of the economic interests of the power-bloc: no popular speech is ever free of power-bloc accents; equally it is never adequately representative of social diversity. So the economic alliance of networks–advertisers–producers may have been willing to listen to African-American cash registers, but Latinos, Asian and Native Americans remained unheard and unrepresented (with very few exceptions). The comparative lack of buying power of Native Americans would predictably rule them out of commercial culture (which makes their being painted out of the Smithsonian exhibition even more regrettable), but Latinos are almost as numerous as African Americans, and their economic clout may not be much less. Similarly, Asian Americans, while numerically fewer, are economically often more successful. The almost total exclusion of Asian and Latino Americans from the commercial system of representation must have more causes than economic ones alone, and the search for them leads us to question the cultural industry's perception of Asian and Latino Americans' acceptability (compared to that of African Americans) to white audiences. If the Drug War has replaced the Cold War and the enemy within is no longer communism but the "third" world, the part of the "third" world that threatens is the Latino–Asian rather than the African. Additionally, European Americans are more familiar with a significant African American contribution to their entertainment—in sport, music, television and film—whereas that of Latinos and Asian Americans is more recent and far more limited. Of course, television's Black representations that resulted from this mix of economic desirability with limited socio-cultural acceptability, were no more pure or authentic than the representation of American Indians in *Dances with Wolves*. The white commercial system dares not alienate its white audiences, so its "black" representations might more accurately be labeled "mulatto." But, nonetheless, they did carry traces of African American voices speaking with their own accents, particularly in shows such as *Roc*, *In Living Color* or *The Arsenio Hall Show*.

The voices, viewpoints and topics in commercial culture are still far too narrow for the diversity of US society, but at least its reasons for excluding those which it does not represent are generally consistent with its known and accepted function of making a profit. Public culture on the other hand, which ought to extend our cultural repertoire beyond that which is deemed to be commercially viable, is much more hypocritical in its criteria for repression. Far from extending the repertoire so that it approximates the diversity of US society, public culture as it is currently controlled works to narrow it down, to homogenize it, and to organize it around the interests of the power-bloc. The result is that there is in effect no public culture in the US. There is power-bloc culture, there is commercialized culture (its economic, lowbrow offshoot) and there is a variety of popular cultures made by the people as best they can out of the offerings of commercial culture. The exclusion of so many voices from this repertoire is a severe restriction of our national imagination.

NOTES

1. The exhibition *The West as America: Reinterpreting Images of the Frontier, 1820–1920* ran from 15 March to 7 July 1991, at the National Museum of Art, Smithsonian Institution. A book was published to accompany the exhibition: William H. Truettner (ed.) *The West as America: Reinterpreting Images of the Frontier, 1820–1920* (Washington and London: Smithsonian Institute Press, 1991).
2. What became known as the "Political Correctness" debate was a cultural war between the mono- and multiculturalists in both racial and sexual domains that characterized most of the Reagan and Bush administrations and their educational and cultural policies. In this war, the monoculturalists disparagingly labeled the multiculturalists "the Politically Correct" or "PC." Whatever the intent of the Smithsonian, the press and the politicians immediately interpreted this exhibition as an intervention in that debate.
3. William S. Jewett, *The Promised Lane—The Grayson Family, 1850*, oil on canvas, 50⅞ × 65 inches, Berry–Hill Galleries, New York, reproduced and critically analyzed in Patricia Hills, "Picturing Progress in the Era of Westward Expansion," in Truettner, pp. 97–102.
4. Jessup Scott, the Whig editor of the Toledo *Blade*, in *DeBows Review*, 27 (August 1859), pp. 125–36, cited by Hills, p. 102.
5. Hills, p. 98. The quotation is cited by Hills from Elliot Evans, "Promised Land," *Society of California Pioneers*, November 1957, pp. 1–11.
6. Howard Lamar, "An Overview of Westward Expansion," in Truettner, pp. 1–26.
7. Lamar, p. 3.
8. Lamar writes that Lewis and Clark's report was not entirely optimistic "for they had to tell Jefferson that incredible mountain barriers precluded any easy passage across the continent and that vast stretches of dry plains, even deserts existed where they had hoped to find well-watered, arable soils." Lamar, p. 3.
9. Lamar, p. 3.
10. Eric Foner and Jon Wiener, "Fighting for the West," *The Nation*, 29 July/5 August 1991, pp. 163–6.
11. Charles Krauthammer, "Westward Hokum, Political Correctness comes to the Smithsonian," The *Washington Post*, 5 May 1991.

12. The Editorial commentary of *American Art* says that the exhibition generated 735 comments, of which 509 were positive about some aspect of the show. 199 visitors specifically praised the wall texts, and 177 criticized them. "Showdown at 'The West as America' Exhibition," *American Art*, vol. 5, no. 3, Summer 1991, pp. 2–11. *American Art* is published by The National Museum of American Art.

13. Cited by Alexander Cockburn in his syndicated column *Ashes and Diamonds*, "The Smithsonian Goes PC!", *Isthmus* (Madison, WI) 7 June 1991, pp. 10–11.

14. Cited in *American Art*, p. 5.

15. Cited in *American Art*, p. 11.

16. Cited in *American Art*, p. 5.

17. Boorstin's guest book comment was cited widely in the press: *The Nation*, *Washington Post*, *Newsweek* (27 May 1991, p. 70), *The Humanist* (Sept/Oct 1991, p. 26).

18. Daniel Boorstin, *The Image. A Guide to Pseudo-events in America* (New York: Harper and Row, 1964), p. iii.

19. Daniel Boorstin, *The Americans: The Democratic Experience*, cited by Alexander Cockburn, *The Nation*, 24 June 1991, p. 838.

20. *Congressional Record—Senate*, 24 October 1991, S 15156.

21. This comment, or selections rom it, was cited in *Newsweek*, *The Nation*, *Ashes and Diamonds*, and by Michael Kimmelman: "Old West, New Twist at the Smithsonian," *New York Times*, 26 May, Sect. 2, pp. 1 and 27. Both *Newsweek* and *Ashes and Diamonds* pointed out that Stevens had not seen the exhibition.

22. James F. Cooper: "A Season in Hell—The Inquisition of Political Correctness," *American Arts Quarterly*, Summer 1991, entered in *Congressional Record—Senate*, 24 October 1991, S 15156.

23. J.T. Headley in Transactions of the American Art-Union for the year 1845, p. 14, cited by Hills, p. 102.

24. Benjamin P. Avery, "Art Beginnings on the Pacific," *Overland Monthly* 1 (July 1868), pp. 30–31, cited by Nancy K. Anderson, "'The Kiss of Enterprise,' The Western Landscape as Symbol and Resource," p. 263, in Truettner, pp. 237–83.

25. *Congressional Record—Senate*.

26. *Newsweek*, *Isthmus*, *New York Times*.

27. *New York Times*. Adams, the Smithsonian Secretary, said, "I am sure we will not agree with everything Fuentes wants to say, and Fuentes probably will find himself saying things because of this dialogue with the [scholarly review] panel that he doesn't fully agree with," *Washington Times*.

28. *The Humanist*, *Newsweek*.

29. *Washington Times*, 6 June 1991.

30. *Washington Times*.

31. Eric Alterman, "So You Want to be a Pundit: Five Easy Steps to Fame, Fortune and Fatuousness," *Lingua Franca*, April/May 1992, cover and pp. 20–25. The article preserves Will's supreme piece of punditry: "liberalization is a ploy," he declared of East Germany, "the wall will remain"—and on that very day the demolition of the Berlin Wall began.

32. George Will, "Literary Politics," *Newsweek*, 22 April 1991, p. 72.

33. Robin Cembalist, "Tempest in a Peephole," *ArtNews* 90(7), September 1991, p. 32.

34. J. Hoberman, "How the Western was Lost," *The Village Voice*, vol. 36, no. 35, 27 August 1991, p. 53.

35. Kim Masters, "Senators Blast Smithsonian for 'Political Agenda'," *Washington Post*, 16 May 1991, D1.

36. Ironically, the $500,000 cost of *The West as America* was covered by private, not federal, money. *New York Times*.

37. Cited in *The Nation*.

38. Robin Cembalist, "Tempest in a Peephole," p. 32.

39. *The Nation*. See also Patrick Novotny, "Where Never is Heard a Discouraging Word: Collective Memory and Historical Forgetting in 'The West as America: Reinterpreting Images of the Frontier, 1820–1920'," presented at the American Political Science

Association convention, Chicago, August 1992.

40. Kim Masters, "They Went Thataway."

41. Alan McCongasha, "Smithsonian Chief Admits Exhibit Error," *Washington Times*, 6 June 1991.

42. Gloria Abernathy-Lear, "African American's Relationship to Day Time Serials," Dissertation, University of Wisconsin-Madison, 1992.

9

LOCAL KNOWLEDGE

POPULAR WAYS OF KNOWING

Scientific rationalism does not provide the only way of knowing and representing the world, although it claims to. Despite these monopolist ambitions it has to recognize, however reluctantly, that other knowledges exist and contradict it, so part of its strategy of control is to define the realities known by those other knowledges as "unreal" and therefore not worth knowing.[1] This leaves a large terrain of experience epistemologically uncolonized which is available for other, less instrumentally effective, less imperializing, knowledges to claim as theirs. What science dismisses as superstition, as coincidence or as self-delusion can, when viewed differently, appear as alternative knowledges whose power is localizing rather than imperializing. Scientific rational knowledge works constantly to preserve the boundary between the reality it controls and knows as true, and the realities of those "weaker" knowledges against which it defines its own superiority. But "weaker" though they may be, these knowledges do have a power and validity which should not be dismissed because its circulation is confined largely to the "weaker" social formations.

These social formations are ones of the people, and they use these different ways of knowing in part to establish their difference from the power-bloc, and in part in recognition that the world of scientific rationalism is *exceeded* by the world in which they live: much of the experiential world of the people lies outside the explanatory reach of science and abstract reason. The ways in which Elvis fans still experience him as a real part of their lives even though he died sixteen years ago can provide us with exemplary instances of popular knowledges working differently from official, scientific knowledge.

I use the singular form of "knowledge" to refer to that of scientific rationalism because the discourse of domination works through uni-accentuality. It does not serve its interests by accommodating subordinate knowledges, but by repressing them. It thus leaves itself as the sole producer of truth. Subordinate knowledges, however, do not have this luxury. They are multiaccentual for they cannot escape the knowledge which attempts to repress and invalidate them: they can exist only in relationship to it and can never exist in autonomous independence of it.

Similarly, the lives and experiences of the people can never be autono-mously or independently *theirs*, but must always be suffused with the touch and taste of the power-bloc. In hierarchically differentiated societies, the lives of subordinated social formations are always muddied with crosscurrents of contradictory forces. Purity of knowledge and homoge-neity of lifestyle are luxuries beyond their reach. While official knowledge may be able to dismiss all others as untrue, popular knowledges cannot dismiss official knowledge because its power to impose its truth, however incompletely, is part and parcel of the social experience of the people.

The popular knowledge, for example, that people have "real" experi-ences of Elvis after his death can never be free of the official knowledge that these experiences are "unreal". Accounts of the sick healed by visions of Elvis are typically set against a medical knowledge which is used to confirm (a) that these healings did actually (that is, according to science) occur and (b) that paradoxically, but crucially, they lie outside scientific reality.

The Sun's story "Elvis makes phone calls from heaven ... to cure the sick!"[2] carries the arguing voices of the power-bloc and the people, whether fans or anti-fans. Dr Hansel Rietzel, speaking with official accents, declares "These particular cases seem to be of a copycat nature, perhaps some form of hysteria." These fans of today, like those of the young Elvis, are subjected to the discursive control of the concept of "hysteria." Behavior which exceeds or contradicts the disciplined normal-ity known by scientific rationalism is brought back under its control by being designated "hysterical." But the doctor opens a gap in the power of this official medical knowledge by admitting that "miraculous" cures which physicians cannot explain do occur—whether through the power of God or of the human mind—and concludes "But if patients feel comforted by believing Elvis is helping them, who are we to argue." The invitation to exploit this hesitation in the official knowledge of the power-bloc is accepted by the direct testimony of fans who have been cured by Elvis. So Velda Ralphs, 52, of Liverpool, England, declared after her stomach tumor vanished, "They say it was a miracle, I say it was Elvis."

These opposing knowledges clash even more explicitly in the case of Bill Green, a 56-year-old Cleveland plumber. Elvis cured the gout that had "made his life a living hell for 26 excruciating years."

> Green's doctor confirms that his patient's gout has vanished. "There are cases of spontaneous healings in the medical literature but I seriously doubt that Mr. Presley had anything to do with it.
>
> It's probably one of those medical mysteries that we'll never be able to explain."

Green himself couldn't disagree more. He says The King "cured my gout and if the medical profession doesn't want to recognize that, it's their loss, not mine."[3]

The multiaccentuality of popular knowledge is exploited by the tabloids to allow the anti-fan as well as the power-bloc to mock the fan's belief in Elvis's miraculous powers. In the headline "Elvis makes phone calls from heaven" the contradiction between the mundane experience of the telephone and the psychic experience of a voice from the dead allows rational and superstitious knowledges to "argue" with each other multi-accentually. Which "wins" is determined not by the text, but by the social allegiance of the reader. The dots and exclamation point in "... to cure the sick!" similarly accent the statement of belief skeptically.

When Elvis appeared to some US marines on duty in Saudi Arabia, this experience was validated by the popular knowledge of Elvis (that he cared deeply for ordinary people):

> The man who looked like Elvis told them in his characteristic drawl, "Don't worry, I'll be watching over you and all your fellow servicemen. I'll act as your guardian angel and be alongside you during the battles to come." ...
>
> "Elvis felt a strong kinship with all military men after his stint in the Army," said Elvis expert John Jenks of Nashville, Tennessee.
>
> "His time in Germany affected him deeply. I'm not surprised at all that he's playing guardian angel to our boys in Saudi Arabia. That's just the kind of man he was—always thinking of others."[4]

Such fan knowledge was, once again, opposed in the same story by the scientific explanation that the marines were hallucinating due to heat exhaustion. This official knowledge does not invalidate popular knowledge for the people in the way that it does for the power-bloc: rather, the opposition between the two ways of knowing represents the social relations within which popular knowledges are formed. The story is headlined "Elvis of Arabia," and is illustrated with two "photographs," one official, "real" one, of Elvis as a soldier whose uniform is clearly tagged over his right breast "Presley" and over his left "US Army," and the other popular and "unreal" which shows Elvis's head superimposed (obviously) upon a body in Arab costume which is not that of a real Arab, nor that of the real Lawrence of Arabia, but rather of Peter O'Toole acting Lawrence masquerading as an Arab (see Plate 8). The *as if* is a multi-layered world, where notions of reality or truth are known to involve reproduction and belief.

REPRESENTING THE AS-IF

The tabloids frequently represent the conditional world of the *as if* through a genre of explicitly manipulated photography which they have established as characteristically theirs. In official discourse a photograph brings with it the objective, singular truth of the indicative. But such uniaccentuality is inadequate for popular experience, so the tabloids manipulate photographs to enhance their multiaccentuality. The name often given to these manipulated photos—"composographs"—is a sign of their multiaccentuality for it identifies them as composites of different "pieces of reality" combined to represent the *as if* and, consequently, to set the social accent that controls "reality" into counterpoint with those controlled by it. Composographs always carry references to the "truth" which the *as if* questions and distinguishes itself from. They reproduce the social relations within which multiaccentuality gets to work but which uniaccentuality represses. Multiaccentual struggles are two-way: the "photograph" of Elvis of Arabia not only represents a popular skepticism towards official knowledge but also the dismissal of the popular by the official. Anti-fans of Elvis may use it to distinguish themselves from fans. Though both may come from subordinated social classes, the anti-fans may tactically and temporally use power-bloc knowledge (and thus align themselves with interests which in other domains of their lives would conflict with their own) to establish horizontal identities of difference rather than of *communitas*. Popular skepticism may be inherent in multiaccentuality but its uses are not—they depend upon the social formation that takes it up. This "photograph" is not only skeptical of the power-bloc representation of the US presence in the Gulf but it extends its gentle mockery, through Lawrence of Arabia, to the white colonization of the region in general. It dissociates the skeptical from those who know the (imperialist) truth.

When the *Weekly World News*[5] shows us an artist's retouching of a "real" photograph of Elvis, the composograph represents the conditional world of the "as if," its truth is the truth *as if* Elvis were alive today (see Plate 9). The knowledge of the "as if" is a knowledge which can exist only by destroying that official boundary between the true and the not true, the real and the unreal. The artist's fictionalization of the factual photograph erases the boundary so the final representation is neither factual nor fictional, neither true nor untrue.

Another reason for the centrality of photographs in this media populism is their affinity with the body. Photographs reproduce the particularity of the here and now, which is where the body lives and moves. While they can be called into the service of an abstracted, representational way of knowing, they can equally be used to promote an embodied, particular way of knowing. Fan photographs of Elvis preserve his body as his recordings preserve his voice and the silk scarves preserve the physical contact between him and his fans. But fan photographs are "real" ones of the "real" Elvis: they are significant things in fan locales and work like the sweaty scarves, which embody a continuity between Elvis and fan—a continuity which is even stronger if Elvis's hand has actually signed the photograph. They work, in this case, as do family photos which embody family continuity in their very presence. They do not represent it, for they are part of the continuity which they display.

These manipulated, multiaccentual photographs, however, are a textualization of popular knowledge, and run the risk, by giving it public circulation, of exposing it to the disciplinary scorn which it knows is its public fate. Belittlement is part of the social reality of the formations among which popular knowledges circulate: it is that from which, in their evasive forms, they attempt to hide.

These photographs of the "as if" are, whatever else they may be, fun, and as such connect accentually with the "as if" world of the Elvis impersonator and the fun of entering it. They are also skeptical, and their play of belief–disbelief is always mobilized by one popular knowledge against another. Whatever truths these new photographs produce, the accent in which they produce them is one of hedonistic skepticism, a tone of voice which, whatever it says, conveys the injunction to have fun but not to believe a word that "they" tell you.

THE EXTRAORDINARY

Popular knowledge always has built into it a mode of disbelief: its ways of knowing have developed only in relations of difference from scientific rationalism and they always recognize the power of that from which they differ. When a picture of Elvis weeps real tears, the challenge is both to science, which labels the event as impossible and therefore unreal, and to official religion, which claims that if such an event were possible it could only happen to *its* saints on *its* territory. And even this claim is made reluctantly, as a response to traces of popular religions existing within its domain but beyond its control. Saints and icons that weep, bleed and perform miracles are usually experienced directly by the people outside the control of the Church and its priesthood. The imperialist success of Christianity results in part from its ability to incorporate popular elements of the pre-Christian religions which it overcame on the official level but could not extinguish in the belief of the people.

When people have such miraculous experiences, the Catholic Church moves quickly to bring them within its ambit of knowledge, and thus control. In particular, it sets up a powerful apparatus to determine which of these experiences are "truly" miraculous, and which are not. The true ones are then adopted into the Church's official body of knowledge. So, of the approximately 20,000 sightings of the Virgin Mary by ordinary people, the Catholic Church has designated three as "worthy of human faith," which is as close as it can come to calling them "true." However, official truth and popular truth remain at odds, so the people still flock to the sites of such visions at (to give two of the most popular examples) San Damiano and Garabandal, despite the Church's official ruling that the visions occurring there were not "worthy of human faith." The Church's attempt to control the understanding of these visions begins at square one. Often the people who have them are unable to understand what they have experienced, and turn to their local priest for help. It is typically he who first identifies the vision as one of the Virgin Mary and thus brings it within the Church's ambit of control.[6]

There is no official Church to take control of the visions of Elvis, so they all, together with the 2,000 recorded sightings of his physical presence, remain the truth of those who experienced them.[7] The so-called "Churches" of Elvis which exist in New York, Bonn and other cities do not have a vertical institutional power which is opposed to the horizontal *communitas* of their ordinary members, so they have neither the desire nor the ability to control how people know or experience Elvis.

But even without any explicit designation as "Church," the *communitas* of Elvis fans shares many features with organized religion. Graceland is like a site of pilgrimage where the anniversary of Elvis's death is celebrated by fans processing with lighted candles. Impersonators re-present Elvis's body in their shows much as priests do in their masses. One of them, Artie Mentz, makes this explicit when he claims to be "like a priest in church giving that live performance—God is not there in body, we cannot see him, as Elvis is not here in body, we cannot see him."[8] The places which people dedicate to Elvis in their homes, often rooms or walls filled with memorabilia, are equivalent to home shrines in that they provide a physical everyday presence of what is absent. There are also reports of Elvis's reincarnation. Rita and Chuck Clerkswell of Liverpool, England, reported that their son was born with a two-inch-wide tattoo of Elvis on his arm and began humming a melody which sounded like "Don't be Cruel" the moment his head emerged from his mother's womb. "He is the king, we have been used as instruments to carry him back into the world" Rita exclaimed to *The Sun*.[9] Her son, however, was a late reincarnation, for, according to the *Weekly World News*, Elvis had already been reincarnated four years earlier in the body of Bruno Hernandez in Honolulu.[10]

There is a consistent pattern of experiences of Elvis which, however we may explain them, are extraordinary. Popular knowledges are fascinated with what lies outside the realm of the ordinary, for that is the already controlled realm of the readily explicable. Science's claim to be able to explain everything rests upon the assumption that the world *is* explicable, that the ordinary *is* reasonable. Scientific rationalism makes the extraordinary ordinary by explaining it. What remains extraordinary is what lies beyond official explanation, beyond the control of official knowledge. The extraordinary is a terrain upon which popular knowledge can establish its difference.

The extraordinary is a continuum, rather than a category, that stretches from way beyond scientific rationalism's reality to within the margins of scientific knowledge itself. It interrogates the boundary between the real and the unreal by refusing to recognize when it crosses over. Monsters are a case in point. Yetis and Big Foots (Big Feet?) are constantly being seen both by "ordinary" people and by "scientists." Fertile dinosaur eggs are found in New Guinea, sharks and crocodiles of monstrous proportions attack people, a locust four feet long is killed (and photographed) in South America. Human beings are born with animal features—the wolf-man is a common motif—and scientists in genetic laboratories create a human baby with the face of an ape or make the centaur "real" by producing a horse with a human head,[11] which, after the outcry raised by the story, is adopted by a farm couple in Kentucky.[12] Human babies are raised by animals (wolves and chimpanzees in particular) and continue to behave like them even when brought back into society and studied by scientists. There is a continuum from the created monsters of the "secret" sciences of genetic engineering, through "natural" monsters who live (just) beyond scientific verification, to folk monsters that live in fiction and legend. The continuum does not recognize categorical differences between its "truths," particularly between fact, fiction and legend. The people's experience of seeing Elvis's picture weep is no more or less true than the fur trapper meeting Big Foot in the mountains or the horse with a human head. Whatever the status of their objective truth, there is always a social truth in these beliefs: the truth that "their" knowledge, scientific knowledge, has its limits and that even within them it can "go wrong."

The monstrous is part of popular knowledge. It connects with Bakhtin's notion of the grotesque as the embodiment of the vital processes of nature constantly producing new forms that contradict the final completion, and therefore controllability, of the aesthetically beautiful. Science and aesthetics both claim access to the final truth and the power to represent it (indeed scientific reasoning is often assessed by aesthetic criteria such as "elegance"). Monstrosities are not elegant, aesthetic or scientific, but they are popular.

The monstrous is a world that science "ought" to be able to control, but cannot. The paranormal, however, is a world that lies outside the reality that science has enclosed as its field of knowledge. The reality of the paranormal and the ways in which it is known offers a quite different challenge to scientific rationalism from that of the monstrous. Norms are disciplinary cogs, so scientific rationalism both produces them and uses them to justify itself: normality is a powerful product. What lies beyond the control of science is, then, by its own definition, the paranormal, and insofar as normality is the product of power, the paranormal is a weak product. Or, to put it another way, the power of the paranormal is localized. Popular knowledges often deal with the paranormal, not because the people are essentially "superstitious" (to use the term by which scientific rationalism delegitimates such knowledges) but because the relationship of superstition to science, of paranormality to normality, reproduces that of the people to the power-bloc. Paranormality and the locales of the people both lie outside the enclosure which is the first act of imperializing power. The popular knowledge, then, that Elvis heals the sick and protects the marines is part of the social knowledge that the power-bloc doesn't know it all and can't explain it all. Yet while so-called superstitious knowledge "explains" a reality that official knowledge dismisses as "unreal," it often does so by means which resemble those of science.

Numerology and astrology, for instance, dress themselves as "sciences" to gain some of the status from which they are officially excluded. They use "scientific" modes of observation and reasoning, and offer an alternative, but, in their own terms, rational way of relating events to each other. The relationships that they present as evidence of a coherent structure are dismissed by scientific rationalism as "coincidence," that is, random, and therefore non-signifying. For Elvis fans numerology, at least, is further justified because it was a way of knowing and controlling experience which was used by Elvis himself. Numerology proves that Elvis planned the day of his own death (or the faking of it) by positing a significant relationship between the fact that the numbers of the date of his death (8/16/1977) add up to 2001 and the fact that the theme music from the movie *2001* was adopted by him as his signature in his later concerts. The Elvis impersonator Artie Mentz calls this "a miracle that we won't understand in our lifetime," and Jenny Carroll, a fan, comments "you can figure out using your common sense that Elvis isn't dead."[13] As ways of validating a popular truth, a "miracle" and "common sense" do not contradict each other because they occupy the same space in relation to scientific truth.

Numerology is an anti-math. Mathematics works to understand, and therefore control, chance and randomness; by its common association of number with luck, numerology opposes math—a "lucky number" is mathematically inconceivable. Many popular pastimes involve this anti-mathematics: dice, the deck of cards and the lottery balls all make numbers work within a system of chance which is the direct opposite of the system of math. In poker, one plus one plus one does not equal three; it equals a million dollars.

The most important mathematics of everyday life is that of the pay check and the grocery bill. Money is numbers: the logic of capitalism is a mathematical logic, and economics as a science tries as hard as does mathematics to eliminate chance and minimize the random. Except at its extreme margins, the power of mathematics to predict outcomes is perfect, for the reality of mathematics is a perfectly abstracted system which it has produced itself and over which its control is total. The reality of economics is different altogether: social forces like politics and crime, emotive forces like greed and pleasure, and the unpredictabilities of history all ensure that no economics can ever approach the purity of pure math.

But the official use of economics attempts to give its logic a mathematical precision and objectivity: talent plus effort equals reward. Such essentialist logic serves the interests of the dominant classes in a meritocracy for it proves, mathematically, that their rewards are naturally, properly, theirs. Disproportionate wealth and power are thus the inevitable, natural, outcomes of their own disproportionate talent and effort.

But the people "know" that the rewards of capitalism are not distributed by such objective mathematics. Gambling is a way of explicitly introducing luck into the system and thus of disabling its central explanatory power. Knowing that luck is part of the explanation for financial and social success is part of the same popular knowledge that knows that the truth of economic deprivation does not lie in the lack of talent and effort of those who suffer it. Correlatively, it knows equally well that the truth that social and financial success depend upon individual talent and effort is a truth of power. Part of the pleasure of games of chance, particularly when money is attached to their outcomes, is the recognition that capitalist logic is partial and socially situated. Gambling redistributes money, and obviously the desire to get more than the official economy gives is a major part of the motivation of the gambler. But gambling's system of redistribution is based upon a way of knowing that differs not only from that of capitalist economics specifically, but of scientific rationalism in general.

An anonymous African American quoted in a collection of Black folklore makes explicit the inversions in this popular relationship of gambling to work, and finds in the inversion more control: "I plays lottery like you goes to your office. It's my whole life, man, I wouldn't give it up for nothing. If I had to choose between work and lottery, I sure would take lottery, cause I feels I can make money and still have all my time to myself."[14] In both work and gambling the subordinate lose: in work they always lose control over their time and labor; in gambling all they lose, sometimes, is their money. The official way of knowing the difference between work and gambling is quite different from the subordinate way exemplified by this speaker. Economic deprivation and social powerlessness, which are unfairly distributed by class, race and gender, underlie in part this desire to understand better and exploit the workings of chance. Scientific rationalism may be able to paint the big picture, but down among the details of everyday life it often fails to provide explanations that are of any help in guiding behavior or that offer any hope of improving one's lot. And superstitions flourish when people feel unable to exert reasonably effective control over their lives: in these conditions, the non-scientific makes more sense.

In many social formations, those who know "the numbers" are important sources of advice on immediate behavior. Knowing the numbers may apply most directly to the financial system because money is so explicitly quantified. But time is numbered also, so birth dates mean that people can be numbered; events, too, through their timing, can be known by their numbers. "The numbers" are a knowledge system which offers people ways to control their immediate conditions of life, particularly their relationships with others (the most important of which are usually romantic) and the timing of key events.

From the scientific point of view, the control promised is illusionary and unreal: the promise is false. But such a dismissal is too easy. Numerology has a long and persistent history, and scientific rationalism, for all its power, has failed to impose its knowledge that numerology is false upon the popular formations that use it as part of their way of knowing. Numerology is a localizing knowledge, for it is used not to establish general truths about universal structures as is mathematics, but rather to understand and control the relationships and events with which the user is personally and immediately involved. Because history never allows us to know its alternatives, the "control" promised by numerology can never be scientifically proved or disproved.

There may be no better "proof" that "the numbers" can improve one's marriage than the fact that psychiatry can: there is only a different system of connecting a causal event (getting the numbers right, rethinking one's childhood on the couch) and outcome (a better marriage). Psychiatry's connections are made via an abstracted, rational, scientific account of the human psyche; those of numerology are made in terms of immediate experience—"try it and you'll see." The difference between them is ultimately that between the different social formations that use them: it is difficult to argue that the control offered to formations of the power-bloc by the psychiatrist is any more or less of an "illusion" than that offered by the numerologist to the formations of the people. If people act upon so-called illusions *as if* they were true, they can become true in their effects: sick marriages *are* cured by psychotherapy and by numerology, as sick fans *are* cured by Elvis, whether coincidentally or causally. The difference between the two ways of knowing/controlling is to be sought in their different social circulations: because psychiatry circulates officially, it must lay a claim to a scientific rationalism; equally, numerology must be anti-scientific.

Mathematics and computing insert people into a system of numbers, but they number people in order to individuate, rank and discipline them. In their system, our numbers individuate us from the top down, they determine our position in the disciplinary machine and how we interact with others: my social-security and resident-alien numbers are mathematical, not numerological. Mathematics is the perfect system: every number in it is distinguished from every other, yet related to it by rigid and rational laws.

Numerology numbers people not to subject them to an external control system, but to offer those whom it numbers a knowledge of themselves that they can use in their immediate lives. It is not a knowledge of an all-powerful system which anyone can know and be known by, but a knowledge which can be used only by those who possess it and only in their immediate conditions. It offers no explanation of, or control over, the world in general, but only of particular experiences within it. It is a localizing knowledge. Numerology does not individuate, but produces a sense of individuality which is locale-based rather than imperialistically stationed.

Astrology has a wider social circulation and a higher degree of acceptability than numerology, though it is difficult to see why. On the face of it the two are very similar. The manifest content of what is known by them does not necessarily contribute towards an oppositional ideology, but often, apparently at least, the reverse. Both are used to promote love, luck (often financial) and a well-being within, rather than against, the dominant system. But that, after all, is where the people live. Most of the people, most of the time do not wish to change the social system radically, or, even if they may wish to, they do not choose to direct such everyday power as they have towards such a distant goal: increasing their control over the conditions of their everyday life is a much more achievable goal and therefore a more efficient use of their energy. Their desire to control is often directed less toward the structural determinants of everyday life than to their local applications.

It is not what is known so much as the way of knowing that is the issue here. The opposition of the popular to the power-bloc can take many forms and be negotiated along multiple axes, one of which is gender: popular ways of knowing are often "feminized." Astrology and numerology are, like intuition, associated with the feminine. In noting this, we must be careful not to imply that women are essentially more superstitious or intuitive than men, for they are not: what we have noted is yet another case where the ways of the power-bloc and the ways of masculinity have aligned themselves. Men, therefore, are less likely than women to admit even in private, let alone in public, that superstition or intuition can play significant roles in their lives. When they do, they masculinize the knowledge by concepts such as "gut-feeling," for a man's guts are where his masculinity is naturalized into his body.

The growth of science throughout the nineteenth century had a gendered dimension. Science's power to produce imperializing knowledge and capital was, "naturally," a masculine power. This power reached not only extensively over the physical universe and the public sphere, but intensively into the minutiae of everyday life. In particular, the growth of medicine and psychiatry as sciences masculinized what had traditionally been women's spheres of knowledge. The doctor interfered with the passage of traditional medicine from mother to daughter: the male doctor displaced the female midwife from even the most female of all processes: sexology and psychiatry gave men knowledge of and control over the world of women's bodies and emotions that previously women had known for themselves. Hysteria, as discussed above, is an exemplary instance.

The masculinization of science and reason and the feminization of superstition and intuition were accompanied by the association of masculinity with the public world and femininity with the domestic. It is consistent, then, that localizing ways of knowing should have become feminized, for these were most appropriate to the domestic sphere, which was where most women could most effectively exert such limited control as they could acquire.

All of this lies just below the surface in the controversy over Nancy Reagan's use of astrology to give her some control over certain areas of her husband's life as President. On 30 March 1981, President Reagan was shot as he left the Washington Hilton Hotel. The logically planned, technologically equipped, public, masculine power of the White House security apparatus had failed to protect her husband. In the private sphere of their lives Nancy, ideologically "good" wife that she was, felt that she should have the power to nurture, protect and care for her husband in his immediate, intimate life (and, what could be more immediate or intimate than his own body). Her husband's lung penetrated by Hinckley's bullet was a clear sign that when he stepped out of private life into public, he stepped into another sort of protection—masculine, rational—that was not as effective as hers. Her reaction on learning that the astrologer, Joan Quigley, had read from her husband's chart that 30 March would be a bad day for him was "I could have stopped it." Astrology, then, became a way in which she could control the timing of his public appearances to ensure his safety and success. As she says, with plangent incontrovertibility:

> While I was never certain that Joan's astrological advice was helping to protect Ronnie, the fact is that nothing like March 30th happened again. Was astrology one of the reasons? I don't *really* believe it was, but I don't *really* believe it wasn't.[15]

Nancy Reagan may be a little more circumspect than Bill Green (the plumber whose gout was cured by Elvis) but both their knowledges are grounded in particular experience. As Bill says "A lot of people think I'm just another crazy Elvis fanatic, but nothing could be further from the truth. I believe in Elvis and you would too if this happened to you."[16] Similarly, an Elvis fan told me that she did not believe that Elvis would reappear on the fifteenth anniversary of his death—but that nothing would stop her being at Graceland then, just in case!

Like the tabloid readers, Nancy Reagan swings easily between belief and disbelief. Popular knowledge is never pure, but is always contaminated by the official knowledge that it contradicts. There is always evidence in people's experience that popular knowledge is true: equally, however, the people know, with the knowledge of the power-bloc, that what their own knowledge tells them is not true.

As the case of Nancy Reagan shows, superstitious knowledge is not confined to subordinate social formations, but can be called upon in any sphere of life where outcomes are not readily predictable by the logical process of cause and effect. One such world is that of show business (another, as we shall see in a moment, is that of big business). The links between the Presidency and show business are much more extensive than the personal histories of Nancy and Ronald Reagan, but Nancy does use her background in Hollywood as one explanation for her use of astrology.

As she says: "I don't think actors and performers literally *believed* these [superstitions], but you went along with them as a way of hedging your bets."[17] Behaving *as if* the truths of popular knowledge were true can make them true, for truth is a measure of the effectiveness of knowledge. When the knowledge is knowledge of self, its truth-effect can be totally convincing: Nancy ends her astrological account of people born under her sign, Cancer, with the truth "That's me, all right."

Similarly she says that astrology was one of her means of coping with the fear she felt when her husband almost died. She attributes her ability to hold herself together to the power that astrology gave her: its effects were real in her experience. This truth-effect can also be seen in events: her husband was not shot again, the Reykjavik and Geneva summits were both (presented as) successful, and his departure for each was scheduled at an astrologically propitious time.

Popular knowledges are as widespread and as historically persistent as they are, not because people are deluded fools, but because, in the lives of the people, there is always some evidence that in some cases they work, and even if they know that they really don't, there is no harm in hedging their bets by acting as if they do. The world of the *as if* is always *as if* the power-bloc did not have the power to produce and control the world that *is*. But the world of the *as if* is not just what the world of *what is* is not: it is conditional, that is it produces a sense of what might be. What might be is always realistic to a degree and thus, under certain conditions, realizable. People can and do live their lives as though scientific rationalism were not the only effective way of knowing.

In saying this, it is important to remember that the popular is not confined to or located in a particular social category, but in relations of power to the power-bloc. As the First Lady, Nancy Reagan aligned most of her ways of living with those of the power-bloc; as a wife nurturing her husband, however, she could, contradictorily, align herself with other ways of living and knowing.

The conflict between Nancy Reagan and Donald Regan, the White House Chief of Staff, may have been personal, but the personal, in this case, became explicitly political. After his dismissal/resignation as White House Chief of Staff, Regan published a book which made Nancy's astrology public.[18] His job involved organizing the President's schedule, and his exasperation with having to accommodate his rational, logistical planning to some "occult prognostications" informs much of the book. One sentence says it all: "Only a very stubborn man could have believed that reason would prevail in a case such as this one."[19] The words "man" and "reason" carry the equation "scientific rationalism + masculinity = proper power." The words "stubborn" and "would prevail" show the conflict between (in *his* view) the proper use of power and the improper feminine one; what galls him particularly is that, in this case, the "improper" triumphed.

Elsewhere he writes of "Mrs. Reagan's dependence on the occult."[20] This sentence is the perfect reverse of the previous one. The term "Mrs." situates Nancy socially as "wife" and thus positions her as inferior to the "man" in the previous sentence. Similarly, "dependence on the occult" is the precise opposite to the masculine "reason," which, of course, is neither dependent nor superstitious.

The terms of the struggle between Nancy-woman and Regan-man are clearly identified in the titles of their books. His, *For the Record*, bespeaks masculine, objective, public knowledge; hers, *My Turn*, is reactive, situated, personalized, feminine. Hers implicitly recognizes the power difference, his exerts power by ignoring it.

Even male members of the power-bloc will turn to superstitious ways of knowing when scientific ones fail them. The world of high finance, like that of the entertainment industry, does not work as logically and predictably as reason would dictate. Cornelius Vanderbilt hired mediums to bring him investment advice from dead financiers, many top executives grab lucky numbers for their office doors or phones, and avoid unlucky ones like the plague. Fashion designer Arnold Scaasi consults a numerologist to choose the dates for his shows, and very few business meetings are scheduled on Friday the 13th. Indeed, according to the *New York Times*, "brokers and traders say it's no small coincidence that 1987, the year of the stock market crash, contained three Fridays the 13th—the most that can occur. (It won't happen again until 1998)."[21]

Even in academia, surely the most rational, logical sphere of all, superstitious ways of knowing persist. A chain letter reached me recently, claiming to have been around the world twenty times, bringing good luck within four days to all who passed it on and bad luck to those who did not. Attached to the letter were the names of some seventy-five well-known academics, and some of the letters covering its transition among them:

> Don't laugh. This is the second time this same letter came across my desk. The last time I received it and sent out copies, I received a grant from the Guggenheim Foundation *four days* after I mailed the letter. Best of luck to all my friends.

> When you're untenured and coming up for review, a little more luck couldn't hurt, now could it?

> After I received this chain letter I set it aside, nearly breaking the chain. However last night I attended a lecture by X. This morning I found this while cleaning my desk. What are the chances that a chain letter linking X with me

would be in my possession on an evening that I heard him speak? And the next morning I stumble on a letter that I had forgotten. Pretty slim, that's for sure. ... Don't get me wrong, I'm not superstitious. I'm a rational person who has the dibs on the date for Saturday's lotto.

Another example of human folly and fear of the irrational. Instructions are on the last page.

I invite you to join the list of the distinguished and illustrious scholars who have joined the appeal to the traditional and superstitious, forsaking contemporary, rational, causal modeling.

Coincidence, which is how science would explain the timing of the Guggenheim award or the lecture by X, is highly significant in popular ways of knowing. Coincidence posits a meaningful relationship between events which reason says are not related: it structures reality differently. Academics are not alone in (occasionally) recognizing a reality other than that of reason; Elvis fans, like other popular formations, know such realities well. The truth that Elvis has been reincarnated in the body of 4-year-old Bruno Hernandez was "proved" by "a mind-numbing string of coincidences."[22] So, too, fans Jenny and Judy Carroll know that they are really Elvis's daughters because of coincidences: like him, they are twins; "we have his eyes and his little cut-off lips";[23] and they and he were both laughed at and put down at school.

For many Elvis fans, coincidence is not an adequate explanation of the fact that his name is an anagram of "lives"; similarly, a Black knowledge of America finds it deeply meaningful and not coincidental that the country's chosen name is an anagram of "I am Race."[24]

There is a whole range of phenomena which scientific rationalism dismisses but which intransigently occurs in popular experience. The results of a Gallup poll, published in 1991, shows how widespread these experiences are:

One in ten Americans claims to have had a conversation with Satan.
One in four Americans believes in ghosts.
One in ten Americans claims to have been haunted.
One in four Americans believes that he or she has had a telepathic experience.
One in six claims to have carried on a conversation with a deceased person.
One in seven has personally seen a UFO.[25]

Similar knowledge circulated in advertisements for Wrigley's Chewing Gum tells us "On an average day ten people report seeing a UFO, one person reports seeing Elvis." Other information tells us that since World

War II there have been 60,000 unexplained sightings of UFOs in the US—and these are the ones that remain after science has explained away the 80–90 per cent that it can.[26] In her study of tabloids and their readers, Elizabeth Bird found that all sixteen of the readers with whom she had in-depth interviews believed in at least one type of paranormal experience, and she cites a number of studies that show how widespread belief in paranormality is—indeed, one reveals that up to 90 per cent of Americans believe in some form of ESP.[27] Bird shows, too, that this belief is selective: for instance, one of her respondents was an avid astrologer but scoffed at those who believed in UFOs, whereas another who believed deeply in psychic powers because of her personal experience of them and had also experienced a UFO sighting and believed that "we, as people, were probably placed on this earth from outer space people years ago when they were experimenting, and so they're still checking up on us to see how we're doing," yet scoffed at astrology and stories of babies with two heads.

Conversations with Satan and with the dead, encounters with Elvis, ghosts or UFOs are all very different sorts of experience; what they share is their ready categorization by official knowledge as superstition or delusions. The knowledges by which they are known are popular only because they are excluded from that of the power-bloc.

EXCORPORATION

Popular knowledges and their modes of validation are never "pure" but are muddied by their inevitable contact with official knowledge. Sometimes, as in its superstitious modes, popular knowledge distances itself as far as possible from official knowledge; in other instances it blurs the boundary between them. So, in the popular knowledge that Elvis is still alive, "hard" evidence can be subjected to the same scientific testing as official knowledge.

A tape of a post-1977 phone conversation with Elvis was proved to be his voice by the methods which proved that the voice on the Watergate tapes was Nixon's.[28] A photograph taken in 1984 of Elvis with Mohammed Ali and Jesse Jackson has been proved by "police computer scientists" to be of Elvis himself[29] (see Plate 10), and the handwriting on his death certificate has been proved by scientific graphology to be Elvis's own.[30]

Bird found plenty of evidence of this contradictory attitude to science and scientists among tabloid readers.[31] On the one hand, scientists were figures of authority and expertise, but on the other, they were allied with politicians, big business and the military into "them" or "the upper echelons"—the faceless people who run the country. (This is a popular, and accurate, perception of the strategic alliances that constitute the power-bloc.) These upper echelons live in a world the people cannot identify with and dismiss experiences that are, in the world of the people, important and real. A real experience by an ordinary person can outweigh scientific truth:

> There is a lot of fictitious stuff going on out there, but when it comes to something as real as UFOs and for people to sight those things. . . . I believe it when they say they've had an experience, I truly believe that, and for a person to say, I've seen a UFO, I don't believe any further research is needed. No amount of LSD or drugs can make a person trip out so bad—if they see a UFO they know what they've seen, because believe me it'll make your hair stand up on end and it'll sober you up, that's so true. . . . These things are reality and people need to deal more with reality.[32]

The reality experienced by the popular body (literally hair raising) is distinguished from that known by science—"research"—and from the illusions of drugs and alcohol: it is a true reality which no pointy-head scientist can gainsay nor governmental official cover up.

As paranormality is selectively believed in, so too is science. Scientific ways of knowing are excorporated into the popular when they can be used tactically to increase control over people's immediate conditions of life. They can also be used to empower popular knowledge when it attempts to challenge official knowledge in the public arena whose "rules of debate" have already been established officially: so scientists can prove that Elvis is alive. But similar strategies of excorporation are also used in popular knowledge which avoids the public arena and circulates primarily among fans. The principle of "expertise" which is so fundamental to official knowledge is often excorporated into popular knowledge, both by the constant labeling of people who speak within it as "top scientist" or "expert" and by the extension of expertise into popular knowledge, so that "top" fans can be designated "Elvis experts."

A popular knowledge is, then, never essential or self-sufficient, but can exist only in relation to official knowledge. This relationship may range from one of accommodation or excorporation to one of as great a difference or distance as possible. The tactical decision of which relationship to the official to adopt at which time for which purposes is a popular one and is part of the way in which various formations of the people can control their own knowledge systems.

SKEPTICAL FLUIDITY

Typical of popular knowledges in general is a skeptical fluidity constantly on the move between belief and disbelief. Skepticism is a way of coping with the inescapable contradictions between top-down and bottom-up power and the ways of understanding social experience which each produces. Popular knowledge is always "in between" (which de Certeau argues is the social position of "the people").

Fans may well find this one of the most pleasurable aspects of their culture. If they feel firmly held in station in their everyday lives by economic and social constraints, then this skeptical fluidity may well offer the pleasures of mobility, of being able to duck out of the side door of their station when no one is looking. Disbelief in the singularity of official truth entails a refusal of the power of the power-bloc to impose it. The core of the pleasure, I would suggest, is not to be found in the body of knowledge which is produced, but in the skepticism at the point of interface between the different knowledges. This is the culture of the interface where the people practice the arts of being in between.

At one Elvis impersonator show I attended, a woman fan engaged surreptitiously in the silk scarf ritual: she asked another women to take it to the impersonator and return it to her, and she avoided the public display of having him put it around her neck. On receiving the scarf, she immediately tucked it out of sight in her purse. This was a practice of the art of being in between, for she performed both the fan meaning of the scarf (it's a little bit of Elvis) and the anti-fan and/or dominant meaning (it's silly, and so are the people who engage in it). In conversation with me afterwards she vehemently rejected the belief that Elvis was alive; she preferred to talk technically about Elvis's musicianship, the innovation of his stress on the downbeat, the influence of his style upon other musicians—she even dropped Shostakovich's name into the conversation. There were strong traces of dominant accents in her discourse, her in-betweenness had moved closer to the dominant than the popular, yet she still showed both the crisscrossing of forces that marks the culture of the in-between and the ability to move fluidly within them when she chose to. When I brought the conversation back to Elvis's death, she shifted her position slightly, maybe because she felt she had established her "official" credentials with me, or maybe because she had realized that I was not critical or dismissive of fan knowledge:

> ME I've seen some of the evidence about Elvis's death, and I'm not convinced that all the questions are properly answered. ... There are a lot of things about his death that don't add up.... I don't know what to think about it all, I'm very undecided myself....

FAN   Yes, the upper echelons, like the Kennedys, they'd cover up anything if they thought they needed to.

ME   You don't trust the upper echelons.

FAN   Not me, if they don't want us to know what they're doing...

ME   Yeah.

FAN   I'm skeptical, really skeptical about all of them, you know, the upper echelons.... I remember even when I was young my Mom would try to keep things from me, and now it's the same with them.... The Kennedys...

ME   Do you think they did fake Elvis's death?

FAN   If they wanted to they could've done, but I don't think he's alive.

She uses the term "upper echelons" to represent the power-bloc from the point of view of the people. The upper echelons are a social formation of those who have power and who use it in part to be believed. The upper echelons move in a mysterious and suspicious world within which Colonel Tom Parker, the moguls of the music industry, the FBI, the Kennedys, the President, and one side of popular stars like Elvis and Marilyn Monroe can intermingle metaphorically, socially and sexually. This "reality" of the upper echelons is one produced by popular knowledge, and although it may appear to exist only in the popular imaginary, it *does* exist because it is a real part of their social relations and a real part of their social experience. Its reality is attested to by the precise analogy to her Mom who also, in the eyes of a child, occupied a mysterious, half-glimpsed world of power: a world that was not entirely to be trusted because it used its power to hide, to evade the eyes from below. The power not to be seen is the correlative of the power to see, for monitoring is by definition unequal. The world of the upper echelons is, when viewed from below, the world of the cover-up. One of the pleasures of popular knowledge, often trivialized as gossip, is opening a crack in the curtains and seeing what the upper echelons wish to keep hidden.

THE COVER-UP

The people live in the world of the cover-up. As Elizabeth Bird puts it, "Distrust of and alienation from the establishment were also very apparent in the political attitudes of [tabloid] readers. ... Many of those who discussed politics expressed a strong belief that the government, media, big business and scientists are hiding information from the American people."[33] Fluid skepticism is a tactically appropriate stance towards the condition: people loved Reagan the more that he was revealed to be covering up his involvement in Irangate; JFK appears to be loved even more as we learn of his covered-up sex life with, especially but not exclusively, Marilyn Monroe and Grace Kelly. This fluid skepticism both admires and mistrusts the cover-up, both loves and hates those involved in it. The exposure of the covered-up behavior of a member of the upper echelons produces in the people a sense of both pleasure and admiration because that member, be it Reagan, Kennedy or Elvis, is seen to be doing what the people know the upper echelons really do, in contradiction to what official knowledge tells us of their doings. And what they really do is cover up.

The specificities of characters and actions in this game of cover-up and exposure are unimportant. When the fan used the term "the Kennedys," she was referring to them as a figure of the upper echelons rather than as a specific family: the "they" in the final exchange in our conversation quoted above does not refer specifically to the Kennedys despite its syntactical reference to them; we both knew that we were talking about a figure in the popular imagination, and in no way believed that the Kennedys were themselves involved in any cover-up of Elvis's death.

The tabloids thrive on exposing the cover-up. Their exposures produce, over time, a complex web of interconnections among the people and actions covered and uncovered. Covered-up deaths are common; ones which have been faked include, besides Elvis's, those of J. F. Kennedy, Marilyn Monroe, John Lennon, and Hitler. John Kennedy and Bobby Kennedy covered up their affairs with Marilyn Monroe; Marilyn Monroe and Elvis are alive and in love and living in Hawaii; Elvis had direct personal contacts with the Presidency (not JFK, but with both Carter and Nixon). JFK had connections with the Mafia, who killed Marilyn Monroe and threatened to kill Elvis. The coincidences cohere into a web of knowledge in which the only constant is that *they* are covering up from *us*.

In popular knowledge, the Kennedys are the maestros of the cover-up. They are "known" to have covered up the extra-marital affairs of John, Bobby, Joe, and Ted, the deaths of Mary Jo Kopechne at Chappaquiddick and of Marilyn Monroe, and, as I write this in the summer of 1991, are engaged in covering up an alleged rape in the grounds of their Florida mansion. The publicity around this incident has, according to the *Weekly World News*,[34] provoked JFK to emerge from his covered-up death to lambast his brother for dragging the family name through the mud. The *National Enquirer*[35] explicitly links the alleged rape in Florida with the murder of Martha Moxley in Connecticut in 1975, for which a member of a branch of the Kennedy clan is, in the words of the State Attorney, "a prime suspect." "In both instances, the Kennedy family took steps to throw a veil of secrecy over the case," the *Enquirer* writes, and goes on to cite a source close to the Kennedys: "the way the family handled the murder was a page right out of the Kennedy handbook. It's just like the way the Kennedys are handling the Palm Beach rape case."

The mother of the murdered girl makes explicit the power difference between the upper echelons and the people. "It makes me angry! This family and the ones connected to it—like the Kennedys—seem to think they're above the law." The *Enquirer* gives comments from two "ordinary people" on the rape case: "Yes, I think he did it, but I also think he's probably going to get off scot-free. [She was right: he did.] If you have enough money, you can take care of anything," and "The Kennedys have been getting away with murder and it needs to stop."

Such upper echelon cover-ups of the misuse of gender power are readily associated, via the Presidency, with covering up the abuse of political power as in Watergate and Irangate. Elvis was connected with both Nixon and the CIA: manipulated photographs show what Elvis, JFK and Hitler really do look like now; and real photographs of Elvis and JFK give glimpses of them through the windows of Graceland and the White House.

Whatever official facts may or may not be involved in the cover-up, there is frequently a social truth asserted in its exposure: those who cover up are white upper-class men; what is often covered up is their exploitative relationships with women (in the case of the Kennedys) or the non-white world (Irangate), and those from whom it is covered up are the "lower echelons" of the people. Covering up and exposing are ways that power is applied in the social struggle. It is not surprising, then, that the woman fan chose the chauvinist Kennedys as the figure of those who cover up, for she was doubly disempowered by them, both as a woman and as one of the lower echelons.

KNOWING DIFFERENCE

The relationship between the knower and the known always has a social and therefore political dimension. Different ways of knowing have different politics, different social relations. These differences have deepened as our societies have become more elaborated and thus the power differentials within them are set to work along more diverse axes. In early modern Europe, different ways of knowing could coexist simultaneously and could support rather than contradict each other. So Sebastian Munster's mid-sixteenth-century maps of Arabia, India and the Middle East combine "scientific" representations of rivers, seas, and land masses with other knowledges. They show Noah's ark, for example, floating in the Caspian sea with an annotation that it eventually came to rest in the

202

Armenian mountains. Such sanctified, if not scientific, knowledge is extended on a neighboring map by representations of the natives which include a cannibal couple preparing a meal; headless men with faces in their chests; dog-headed men who "barked for speech;" a one-footed man and a gryphon. Turning further pages in his "Geographia," we come to a map of Taprobana (Sri Lanka, one of the lands lying at the end of the "Passage to India") that is embellished by a realistic representation of an elephant and an annotation that the island contains pepper in "astonishing abundance" which is whiter, hotter and "less heavy" than that currently common in Europe: the scientific knowledge of the island and the elephant sit easily alongside the commercial knowledge of the better commodity and its higher profitability because of lower freight costs.

A century later, John Speed's "Newe Mape of Tartary" exhibits even more starkly the complementarity of knowledges which today would seem contradictory. Scientifically, he tells us that "The middle meridian is 120: into which the rest are blended according to the proportion of 40 and 70 Parallels." With equal aplomb he gives us a fact which is guaranteed by the authority who produced it and is simultaneously doubted (a move that accurately prefigures today's tabloids): "Pliny placeth the Perosites here whom hee saith to be so narrow mouthed that they live only by the smell of rost meat believe it or not." Information which is potentially both commercial and technological ("In this country is a hil out of which they dig earth called by Pliny terra asbestos, having fine veines like grasse which being spun and weaved yield cloth that will not burn in the fire") unsurprisingly accompanies knowledge for military exploitation ("Batloa-zan Castle, whither in time of warre the Moscovite bringeth his treasure to be kept") and the knowledge that the exotic is dangerous because there the paranormal is normal ("In the wilderness ... they say are heard terrible noises and seen marveilous apparitions of evil spirits whereby many are misled"). The link between colonization by representation and coloniza-tion by possession is made explicit in the little word "for" in another of his annotations: "Nova Zemla, which began to be discovered for the estates of Netherlands ... in the years 1594, 95, 96." His map is surrounded with drawings of Tatars and Russians in exotic (to Western European eyes) dress, together with bird's-eye views of their main cities. This one text, or great representation, is multi-modal in its power—the realism of the drawings, the science of the map, the military, historical, commercial and exoticizing knowledges of the annotations all constitute Tartary as an object of European knowledge and thus as a proper field for European power. The knowledges are simultaneously those of the news magazine, the tabloid, and the reference library. The map not only records what is known but informs us of what is new. Knowledge today may have become more specialized and disciplined, its modalities may have been differentiated and hierarchically ranked according to their instrumentality, but the links between knowledge, representation and power are as strong as ever.

The only change, and it is a major one, lies in the means by which power–knowledge makes the world knowable from a single point of view. Early modern Europe tended to *include* all useful knowledges. Now, with our more elaborated and conflictual societies, the most powerful knowledges have to work more explicitly to exclude and repress other knowledges in order to preserve the exclusive alliances upon which their power depends. Effective power is homogeneous.

NOTES

1. Andrew Ross in *Strange Weather* (London: Verso, 1991) gives a good account of the New Age challenge to scientific rationalism, and of the work of the Committee for the Scientific Investigation of Claims of the Paranormal in policing its boundaries.
2. *The Sun*, 1 August 1989, p. 23.
3. *Weekly World News*, 8 October 1991, p. 3.
4. *National Examiner*, 18 September 1990, p. 27.
5. 26 March 1991.
6. S. L. Zimdars Swartz, *Encountering Mary* (Princeton, NJ: Princeton University Press, 1991).
7. Recorded by William Stern, *Weekly World News*, 23 July 1991, p. 22.
8. *Mondo Elvis* (videotape) Monticello Productions, Rhino Video, 1984.
9. *The Sun*, 9 May 1989, p. 27.
10. *Weekly World News*, 12 June 1990.
11. *Weekly World News*, 6 April 1991.
12. *Weekly World News*, 15 October 1991.
13. *Mondo Elvis*.
14. Langston Hughes and Anna Bontemps (eds), *The Book of Negro Folklore* (New York: Dodd, Mead and Co.), 1958, p. 206.
15. Nancy Reagan, *My Turn* (New York: Random House, 1989).
16. *Weekly World News*, 8 October 1991, p. 3.
17. Reagan, pp. 50–51.
18. Donald Regan, *For the Record: From Wall Street to Washington* (Orlando: Harcourt Brace Jovanovich, 1988).
19. Ibid., p. 359.
20. Ibid., p. 74.
21. Quoted in the *Minneapolis Star Tribune*, 10 June 1991, p. 8E.
22. *Weekly World News*, 12 June 1990.
23. *Mondo Elvis*.
24. Frances Cress Welsing, *The Isis Papers: The keys to the colors* (Chicago: Third World Press, 1991).
25. *The Globe*, 4 April 1991, p. 63.
26. *Isthmus*, 24 January 1992, pp. 1 and 8–9, reprinted from the *Seattle Weekly*.
27. Elisabeth Bird, *For Enquiring Minds: A Cultural Study of Supermarket Tabloids* (Knoxville: University of Tennessee Press, 1992).
28. *The Elvis Files* (videotape), Herar Communications, Fox Hill Video, 1990.

29. The *Examiner*, 24 October 1989.
30. *The Elvis Files*.
31. Bird, *Enquiring Minds*, ch. 4.
32. Tabloid reader cited in Bird, *Enquiring Minds*, pp. 126–7.
33. Bird, *Enquiring Minds*, pp. 128–9.
34. 21 May 1991.
35. 7 May 1991.

10

THINGS AND PRACTICES

Popular knowledges are localizing ones: they are used in the attempt to gain control over some of the immediate conditions of life. They are also used to make sense of social experience from a subordinate viewpoint and are thus put to work within the construction of identities and social relations. They are, then, formative in the non-material dimensions of locales. Such "weak" knowledges do not represent their producers' interests extensively, but are confined; they do not reach beyond their immediate conditions, but are used to build and control locales. Their particularity ties them to the body, for a practice is what the body does as it moves through space and time using resources that are not always its own, and things are what bodies use to extend their occupation of space and time and it is this use that makes them significant. Bodies, practices and things are the particularities by which a bottom-up individuality is produced, for they are where the unique and therefore most personal elements of our social histories and identities are expressed. In order to achieve this degree of control over identity, we have to extricate some at least of the means of producing it from the social order, and defend it against an imperializing power/knowledge.

Things are significant, but their significance is unlike that of a text, for it is not representational and it does not work in the public domain. Significant things are indexical and particular: as indexes, they form physical links between their referents and their users.[1] The silk scarf dampened with Elvis's sweat does not represent Elvis but connects the fan with him; the photograph of my grandfather makes the continuity between him and me material. But the scarf and the photograph are significant only in their particular locales. Significant things indicate but do not represent: their particularity not only confines their significance to their locales, but, more importantly, establishes the uniqueness of each locale and the identity which it helps to constitute. Our significant things are what nobody else has and can never have—they are powerful cultural agents in those dimensions of our identity which we wish to see as uniquely ours, and whose construction we wish to control. Things may originate in the social order and can always be returned to it, but when they are made significantly ours they are extracted from the social and made personal, their generality is particularized.

Objects, texts and commodities differ from significant things because they circulate in generally accessible systems in the social order. Objects exist in a system that is not recognized as relevantly significant. For some tourists, for instance, a rock may be an inert, unsignifying object lying on a mountainside. For others, perhaps on their honeymoon, who pick it up and take it home, that rock may be transformed into one of "their things." The couple then fill it with particular meanings and histories which it does not generally represent but uniquely indicates. The more intensely significant the personal history stored in it, the greater is the importance of the thing in its locale. Things are part of a culture of significance rather than one of representation. Commodities and texts, too, can be transformed and localized into things. A vase in a store window is a commodity, but as a gift from a close friend it can become one of our things. A gift circulates affection and indicates its givers; a commodity circulates money and represents capitalism. The difference between the two lies not in the object but in its circulation and use. Similarly a book, a picture or a piece of music may be a representational text in its public life, but when particularized and packed with our histories and our meanings it can become one of our things. Localizing commodities or texts takes them out of their economic or representational systems, particularizes them and brings them within *our* control. Conversely, significant things that are sold (such as the photograph of a Victorian forebear) can be turned into commodities or texts for others; thrown away in the garbage, they can even become mere objects.

Things work in the material dimension of locales. A locale is not only the site of identity and consciousness, it must also have a presence in time and space. Things last through time and make our occupation of space visible and real. In the Smithsonian collection of American Family Folklore are personal accounts of everyday culture, such as that of Nancy Smith:

> I have this kitchen set still. It's funny the things you grow up with . . . This set was in every house I've ever lived in. I have it in my kitchen. They're ugly chairs but they're sitting there. I keep thinking that I ought to get rid of them, BUT I CAN'T GET RID OF THOSE CHAIRS! I've seen them white, I've seen them brown, I've seen them green—they're my chairs and somehow they go with me.[2]

Things stay with us in time and move with us through space. They are what makes a new apartment or house *ours*. Richard Snyder, also on record in the Smithsonian, says:

> There was one thing which we recognized very early as being very important in a travelling life. That was to bring along with you as many objects which you can with which you have an emotional attachment: the pictures on your wall, the family albums, the things that mean home to you no matter where you are. Furniture is nothing. You know you can buy or borrow it, but the things which mean home to you are extremely important.[3]

Furniture for Richard Snyder may be a commodity, whereas Nancy Smith's kitchen chairs were very much significant things, but both attest to the importance of things in constructing an identity and a place where that identity can be established. The identity expressed by things is one developed by personal history and personal relationships, and is quite different from that produced by the individuation of the monitoring system or the competitive individualism of capitalist ideology.

In her book *Generations: Grandmothers, Mothers and Daughters* Diane Bell records her detailed and sensitive study of the culture of things among Australian women.[4] She shows how significant things passing from generation to generation carried with them family histories in ways that were highly important to women, but that men often overlooked or failed to comprehend. In a chapter resonantly titled "Daryl got the farm and Mum got the pearls," women tell her of their sense of the difference between commodities whose value is established in the economic domain (which is also masculine), and significant things whose value is private, personal and localized.

> I've tried to make it understood to my children that the things that are given to me by my parents and grandparents have special significance because of the people rather than the monetary value. Because we never had an abundance of material wealth, everything we did was done because it was important, and it didn't matter whether a gift was very small or very large or how much it cost. The point was that the people who gave it wanted you to have it.[5]

For these women the difference between public and private, between commodities and things, is explicitly gendered. Men's interests are invested in the former, women's in the latter:

> In a sense, so much went to the male cousins, and my mother was very resentful of that. The male cousins have done bugger all and don't appreciate things. She stepped in. They've got things like my grandmother's old fridge and electrical things. I prefer the china, books and rugs.[6]

Things become metonyms for the people who hold and use them. Bodies and the things they apprehend through their senses become one, so things can link bodies across space and time and thus embody relationships. I think I can hear in this next woman's voice a bodily re-experiencing of her grandmother's locale in which her grandmother, the china, the kitchen, the everyday practices of living within it, and her own childhood are all continuous:

> In Nar's kitchen the teapot sat on the table most of the day and, when there was time, you could prop the book against the teapot and read, mainly magazines; it was a relaxation. It was possible to deal with an article, not a book. They'd cycle through the family and friends.
>
> There was some white china with a little pattern around the edge. They were Johnson and Johnson's, I think. It's an English china, not a good china. It was just everyday things that you used. The egg cup, you could feel the texture around the edge. There was something else in that dresser that had a texture; it wasn't all smooth china, it was ridged. All the things had a special feel about them. You could feel the tension on the little handle, and inside the dresser there were the egg cups with the ridges on them. They all stood together, all those things, and seemed to go together: the sewing machine, the dresser, the china, and even that blue cake plate that Edna, my sister, has....[7]
>
> ...I can remember the way Nar's kitchen smelt. Every now and again I'll go somewhere, and the smell is there. Sometimes in the old house down in Arabana Street, in Canberra, I could smell that in my own kitchen. I always felt good when I could smell Nar's kitchen in my kitchen ... It was not so much happy as belonging. There is an emotional attachment. Smells attached as clean, wholesome and nourishing, and the attachment is part of identity; it's warmth not really happiness. I wonder about Nar. I suppose she was content.[8]

Bell argues that understanding the significance of things can get us to the core of women's culture. Though things are passed between women within a system of patrilineal descent, the ways in which they are passed form a feminine system whose rules and values subvert those of patriarchal property. Similarly, women's cultural values of identity and family relationships comprise a value system which subverts that of (masculine) economics because it asserts critically different principles that govern the social circulation of goods.

All societies depend upon a circulation of goods, not just for their economic base, but also because goods are always active in the formation of social relations, social relationships and social identities. Any one object may be a commodity, a gift, or an heirloom, the difference lies in its system of circulation and each system sets up different social relations among those involved in it. Capitalist societies give high priority to the economic circulation of commodities, which, in both production and consumption, produces social relations of class. Commodities establish hierarchical differences between those who produce and those who consume, between those who sell and those who buy, between those who have more and those who have less. Gifts, however, establish relationships of reciprocity between giver and receiver, they carry values of social rights and obligations. Heirlooms work generationally within families in the way that gifts do contemporaneously in broader social relationships, but both gifts and heirlooms emphasize relationships whereas commodities emphasize social relations; gifts and heirlooms are of the *communitas* whereas commodities are structural. Because the rules which govern the circulation of heirlooms as significant things derive from the needs of a family and its horizontal relationships, they are appropriate to a localizing culture, whereas those which govern the circulation of commodities are ones of hierarchical relations and so are appropriate to an imperializing culture. In the circulation of commodities someone always profits: in that of significant things, no-one (or everyone) does.

The difference between heirlooms and inheritance is a difference between the personal and the social, the domestic and the public, the feminine and the masculine. Bell argues that heirlooms constitute a matrilineal line of descent which is quite different from and can be subversive of the public patrilineal one. Each system constructs a different sense of family history and a different sense of family identity, and the women Bell worked with were quite confident that theirs was the more important, the more "true." These feminine histories asserted values other than those of name and wealth, they were counterhistories to those which focussed on the public and the noteworthy. In them women refused the masculine division between the private and domestic on the one hand and political importance on the other. This division not only makes women's labor invisible, but also denies that the identities "forged in the little worlds of home also give form to our cultural understandings of the socio-economic structures of the big world."[9] The women may have known the importance of what they were doing, but, in general, their men did not. If they were aware at all of this feminine culture, many men dismissed it as trivial or as none of their business. Some did show an interest, and even offered genealogies of things in all-male households, but others expressed their (very masculine) interest only in checking the accuracy of what their wives and mothers had said.

Things are not unique in the way they can be extracted from a general system of circulation and particularized into locale-builders: language can, too. In many families, particularized sayings or expressions function in precisely the same way as do significant things. They become verbal heirlooms. Like significant things, expressions can become encrusted with the particular identities and histories of their users and these meanings have little to do with those of the language as a social system. For 87-year-old Blanche Botto, for example, her grandmother's saying "Down to the rag" carries not only her family identity, but also a particular way of coping with the conflict between relative poverty and the ideological requirement not to allow that poverty a social face:

> My grandmother was born in 1832. A neighbor of hers was inviting the minister to dinner, so she invited my grandmother too. Well, in those days, sugar was very expensive, so she didn't have very much at hand. It seems that in those days, the sugar bowls were quite large. So she took a piece of green muslin and put it down in the bottom of the sugar bowl and then put some sugar on top. Well, it was passed around, and when it got around to a little boy at the table, he looked in, and he said, "Ma, down to the rag." So that's been an expression in our family. If anything's down low, we say, "Down to the rag."[10]

Language used indexically like this takes on the attributes of both a thing and a practice. Indeed, the expression, the rag and the particular practice of using it are one and the same cultural process. However materially deprived or politically and socially repressed a family or large social formation may be, the one area of social life of which they can never be deprived and which they can always control is that of practice. Practice is what people do with systems and resources that, in their structural dimensions, are not theirs but are of the dominant other. Practices are the tactics of everyday life, they are the means by which commodities are transformed into significant things, they are the ways in which people can produce from the language system their own sayings. These particular expressions evade the power of language to "speak" its subjects and are instances of people's ability to speak for and of themselves. It is tempting to suggest that the most materially deprived social formations, who materially possess fewest things to make significant, will accord proportionately greater significance to linguistic practice and creativity, for language is always available to everyone.

It is not, of course, equally available. While all human beings have the ability to speak (what Saussure called *langage*), this human universal is given socially and historically specific form in a language (*langue* in Saussure's account). The language that a society develops is always inscribed with the interests of that society's power-bloc, so *langue* is the site where a human universal is colonized for the social interests of historically specific dominant formations. *Parole*, or the practice of language, is where the structural power of the dominant can be evaded or contested. *Parole* is where *langue* can be particularized and localized. Oral language, which is the only fully localized form of *parole*, is often ungrammatical, and often uses words in ways that are sanctioned in no dictionary, for grammar books and dictionaries are instruments of control over the structure of language, particularly of written language. As de Certeau argues, dominant culture is *scriptural*, for scripture is where the power to represent is most effective, and popular culture is *oral*, for orality is the means by which subordinate histories and identities are maintained and circulated.[11] Orality participates in ways of knowing that are different from those of literacy. Dennis Folly, in his account of the importance of oral sayings in African American culture, makes this clear:

> Many times my great-grandmother used [wise sayings] as a way of letting us know that in spite of our formal education or our familiarity with the modern and mechanized world, there is another level of knowing that we need to pay attention to.[12]

He relates this orality (with its implied difference from European American literacy) to the "Africanness" of his family and of all African Americans. His great-grandmother remembered slavery, emancipation and the hard times that followed it, and Folly attributes the perseverance of African Americans in part to the wisdom, the humor and the courage of their oral culture. He identifies as characteristically African the high social status given to the elegant, poetic speaker, and though he does not refer directly to the importance of signifying or of rapping in contemporary African American culture, these may well be continuations of that tradition.

Folly recognizes that his education and competence in the "modern" (read "white") world is at odds with his family history, and that he has lost some of its oral, localized competence: his use of family sayings is at times awkward, not quite that of the native speaker, and he recounts how his great-grandmother would tease him for this incompetence. But despite this comparative incompetence, the practice of these sayings is important to him. He gives a detailed account of one of them, "getting the butter from the duck":

> FOLLY   I first remember my great-grandmother saying this when several of us were splitting wood to take in and keep the next few days' fires going. When my mother had just finished splitting a particularly difficult piece and breathed a deep "whew!", my great-grandmother, who was sitting nearby said, "Boy, that done got all the butter from the duck now!"
>
> JEAN [his mother]   You have to realize that a lot of these sayings are interchangeable things. They happen to mean something different to any given situation. I first heard it I think when people were cutting wood, and

you come upon a tree that was really hard to get down. You know when he was able to get it down, or whatever the job accomplished, he would say, "I tell you that thing really got the butter from the duck!"

See the fat on the inside of the duck doesn't come away easy. You can't pull the fat from the duck like you can from a chicken, or the other fowl. I think the older people associated their everyday activities with these animals and what not. It's between the skin and the meat, see? And sometimes you even rip the skin trying to get the fat out of there. But it's so rich and fat it's just like butter. You can use it in cakes and all those kind of things, just like you would use butter.

GRANNY   Yes, Lord, my momma used to use that one. 'Cause she used to go in the woods and cut wood. And sometimes when she'd get through cuttin' she'd be sweatin' and going on. And she'd have to set down, and she'd say, "Ah Lord, y'all go ahead chillun, that thing done got all the butter from me."[13]

Folly values this saying for many reasons: because of its poetry (it is a resonant metaphor for the hard, everyday labor of getting the necessities of life, which can be all the richer for their undervaluation by others, and I think there is a sense of pride in this family art of making do, in the turning of necessity into creativity); because of its remembered use in a moment of family warmth that is a highly significant one for him; because of the uniqueness of the family history embedded in it; and because of his childhood experiences when ducks were part of his daily life.

I have reproduced his account at length because it shows so well how much significant and particular history can be packed into such a saying when language is used as a significant thing. As Jean explains, the meaning of a saying is dependent upon its context; it is within the control of those who live in that context, rather than being a product of the linguistic system, and is specifically oral, not literate (for literacy always detaches language from its immediate context and extends its applicability). Sayings, significant things and practice are key means by which the particularity of a locale is established.

Practice can also give generally representational texts a particularity which enables them to work locally. Cho and Cho, for example, studied Korean women in the US watching a Korean soap opera on their VCRs.[14] The soap opera represented Korean women struggling with the gender politics of the traditional Confucian family structure in contemporary life. The husband's taking a mistress was easily accommodated within the tradition: the conflict centered around the wife's refusal to accept the situation and her eventual decision to divorce him. One woman viewer localized this mass-produced representation by using it to argue with her husband that she would not accept the traditional wifely role on their return to Korea, and if he wished to maintain their marriage he would have to allow her to develop her own career. Another localized the representation of the husband spending money on luxuries for his mistress, but not his wife: She went out and spent as much money on luxuries for herself as her husband had on fishing gear for his own pleasure. Practices localize texts into people's immediate conditions of life; practices turn objects into things with particular significance.

Brett Williams gives a detailed and insightful study of an African American culture of practices and things in a downscale neighborhood in Washington DC.[15] She shows how lack of money constrains and restricts the lives of people there, but how they fill these constrained conditions with a densely textured culture of practices and things. Lucy and Robert and their two children are African American residents of the neighborhood. Their poverty means that they have to rent, rather than own, the place within which to construct their locale. It also constrains the amount of space they can control. But the constraining narrowness of their physical place is contradicted by the richness of the locale they construct within it. Williams uses the term "texture" to describe a culture of practices and things all densely interwoven into an everyday life which is materially constrained but culturally rich. Lucy and Robert's apartment is full of significant things. To middle-class tastes it would seem unbearably cluttered, yet Robert talks of how he needs to fill what to him appears to be a glaringly empty space. This density of things is particular to this family—they have textured it with things that connect them to their own history and establish their own identities.

Like most of their neighbors, Lucy and Robert have the television on most of the time: its color, sound, and movement are woven with the things of their apartment to add density to the texture of everyday life. Television frames and provokes conversations, it fills gaps and silences, it fills time as things fill space. But besides making the texture even denser, it can also be used to escape it. By concentrating on television, people with no physical privacy can construct their own private spaces while still remaining part of the domestic group.

The wealthier have more control over more space and are likely to own rather than rent it. Contemporary upper-middle-class taste prefers fewer, more "artistic" things with a lot of space between them: the space is as significant as the things. This display of space as a possession is a luxury far beyond the reach of Lucy and Robert. The same sense of class difference nudges the upper-class things separated by this space towards becoming texts or art objects: they begin to have a representational, public function as well as a localized, particular one. Lucy and Robert's apartment is too small for them to entertain in it: their things are significant for themselves and immediate family only. The more spacious rooms of wealthier households always have some public function, however infrequently called upon, which gives them a textuality as well as a texture. Things, in this culture, lose some of their particularity and gain some of the generality of texts. Television is also used differently in this different culture: specific programs are watched as texts and the set is then turned off. The silence between TV texts is like the space between textualized things in the room. It is luxurious: it is what Robert and Lucy cannot afford.

Wealthier, more upscale people have moved into Lucy and Robert's neighborhood, buying and gentrifying what used to be working-class housing. In Robert's eyes, the difference between renting and owning produces important differences in the control that people have over their immediate physical conditions and thus in the labor involved in constructing their own locales within them. Here the renters watch the owners across the street inscribing their identities and control upon their physical surroundings by painting, gardening and generally "improving" their homes. To these renters, such assertive displays of ownership performed by optional labor are clear markers of class difference. The labor they put into their smaller apartments is defensive not assertive, necessary not optional. When many people live in limited space, that space has to have many uses that differ successively during the routines of the day. Change of use always involves labor: clearing up after supper is an experience of constraint when it is necessitated because two people have to sleep in the dining area. Constantly having to return shoes to their place under the coffee table is a labor of necessity, an experience of the deprivation of space. Lucy and Robert's two toddlers wreak havoc in the small apartment during the day. In the evening, before Lucy and Robert can reclaim the room as theirs to relax in, she has to clean it. Limited, intensively used space necessitates constant labor to keep it clean (and thus to keep roaches, mice and smells at bay) and to cope with its multiple uses: such labor is defensive, continuous and not perceived as optional.

The social difference of spatial difference extends outside the home as well. Renters see owners controlling a buffer zone between indoors and outdoors, private and public, that they lack. Sitting on porches, playing in front yards, or shovelling snow from sidewalks are displays of the extended control that comes with the possession of space. Robert and Lucy's children are not allowed to play on the grass in front of their building: apartments have no porches. The hallways that are their transitional space between public and private are not under the renters' control. They are shared and often places of social conflict that, rather than acting as buffer zones, bring the danger of "outside" to the very door of the living room.

Renters have no control over whether the elevators are working or whether they will have to climb the stairs. And the lack of control hurts.

Public space is also unequally experienced. Affluent homeowners can drive anywhere in Washington to shop or engage in leisure and social activities. The carless renters, however, are confined to their neighborhood and its Main Street. They cope with this constrained space just as they do with that of their apartments—they fill it with a dense texture. When Robert runs an errand in Main Street he 'entextures' it with numerous encounters and conversations, with memories of events that occurred at certain spots, with sights and sounds whose significance is their familiarity to him. The drive to the supermarket or mall for the house owner is a quite different experience.

The lack of space, whether inside the home or in the buffer zone between it and the outside world, results in a lack of privacy. This lack of privacy is intensely felt by the poor. Even inside their own apartments, renters can hear the conversations and quarrels of others and know that theirs are also heard. Smells, sounds and even substances leak through the walls and ceilings between one apartment and the next, between one locale and others. Being unable to control one's boundaries is constantly and deeply painful, for the defence of one's boundary is the most basic and necessary form of control.

The desire for privacy is not merely a product of the ideology of individuation, but in a crowded and monitored society is a defensive necessity. Privacy involves the control of both social and physical space in which we can be ourselves. Without physical space, social space is amorphous and difficult to control at the level of daily life. Social historians are beginning to trace how capitalism and urbanization in the nineteenth century changed people's perceptions of the three intimately related concepts of privacy, identity and place.[16] Kant wrote that "Man's identity is thus residential, and that is why the revolutionary, who has neither hearth nor home, hence neither faith nor law, epitomizes the anguish of errancy.... The man without a home is a potential criminal."[17] A home not only produced identity, it situated that identity physically and socially. Providing blue-collar housing thus became a key strategy in employers' attempts to control the social relations of workers, and therefore their behavior and attitudes in the workplace. In nineteenth-century US and Europe, architects exercised great imagination and ingenuity in making the bricks and mortar of low-cost housing embody the social relations that the new bourgeoisie wished the workers to adopt. But middle-class priorities did not always match working-class ones. In both Britain and France, for example (and we have no reason to believe that the US was different), the providers of housing emphasized hygiene whereas those who lived in it preferred privacy. In particular, what workers wanted was a private room where they could sleep, have sex and be separate from their children.[18] Sexual intimacy and the identities and relationships involved are experienced bodily, and bodies need places, indeed bodies become places. Hygiene and health, however, loomed larger in middle-class priorities because the cleanliness and health of the individual body was, to them, the incarnation of the cleanliness and health of the social body. Hygiene was part of the disciplinary apparatus, whereas private sex escaped it. Hygiene inscribed the social on the individual: privacy protected the individual from the social gaze. Plumbing or privacy was a political preference.

The renters in Lucy and Robert's apartment building protect their privacy as best they can. Many do not own cars and have to haul their purchases home in what Williams calls "the multipurpose pull-along wire cart that is the center-piece of low-income urban life."[19] Renters hauling their purchases, laundry and children along in public feel embarrassingly visible. They often line their carts with plastic garbage bags in order to retain a vestige of privacy. Their visibility is keenly felt for it constantly reminds the poor of their lack of control over their presentation of their own social identities. Privacy is a localized operation of the power not to be seen.

Opposite Lucy and Robert's building is a house now owned by Mark, a lawyer, and Susan, a business woman. Mark complains that the apartment building blocks the sun from their house, and comments on what he considers to be the astonishing amount of foot traffic and sidewalk hauling that it seems to generate. The tone of resentment may well result from the way that the building and its occupants signal the limits of Mark and Susan's control as they sit on their porch entertaining friends while watching their children play on the lawn. Lucy and Robert are aware of Mark and Susan's eyes upon them, and as they look back across the street they are aware too of how much more control house owners have over their lives: easy and safe access to their front doors, choice of labor and companions, privacy, possessed place and the power to write identity upon it—they exert visible and extensive control. As Robert said, tellingly, "When you have your own house, you have *privacy* and *say-so*."[20]

The lack of "privacy and say-so" is as telling in the lives of the poor as the lack of material goods, but the eyes of the advantaged do not always see these lacks equally clearly. To them, poverty is defined almost exclusively by economic lack, and, as in the case of the homeless men, the charity that works to ameliorate economic deprivation will often deprive its recipients still further of "privacy and say-so." While it may well be the case that shortage of the basic stuff of life makes material necessity loom large in one's consciousness, this heightened awareness of one set of needs does not extinguish other, more social ones—particularly the desire to control one's locale. Indeed, the view that the poor suffer only materially, that they live with a subsistence mentality, is remarkably similar to the white anthropologists' view of so-called primitive cultures that Lévi-Strauss castigated so severely.[21] The need to provide for the non-material things of life is not hierarchically superior to economic needs: it does not kick in only when they have been satisfied, and it is certainly not a marker of difference between developed and "primitive" societies, or between the privileged and deprived within a society. The belief that non-material life is important only to the powerful and successful is an imperialist knowledge of both themselves and the colonized.

Under their conditions of social and economic constraint, the things by which Lucy and Robert identify their differences from others and by which they construct their private locales are so significant because they indicate not only identity, but control. In being particular to their places, significant things control those places. Leal, in a study of newly urbanized peasants in Brazil, has shown similar cultural processes at work.[22] She analyzed in detail how a collection of objects or commodities have been turned into one particular family's significant things. On or around the TV set were plastic flowers, a religious picture, a false gold vase, family photographs, a broken laboratory glass and an old broken radio. Williams finds the culture in the density itself, but Leal interprets this texture. Her analysis shows how these things serve to construct a locale for people positioned within the contradictions between the city and the country, urban sophistication and rural peasantry, science and magic, the future and the past. In the suburbs they are placed on the spatial boundary between the city and the country; as first-generation migrants, they are on the equivalent historical boundary between the past and the future.

Their use of photographs was an instance of this cultural process. On the TV set were large pictures of dead or absent family members, typically ones left behind in the country, and stuck into their frames were small I.D. pictures of those who had moved to the city: the I.D. photos were not only indexes of their family, but also indexes of modern, urban life. The composite image of the I.D. pictures and the portrait photograph in the same frame is an index of the family's social mobility: it indicates their transition from the rural past to the urban future. So, too, the plastic flowers were considered more beautiful than natural ones because they indicated the urban, the manufactured, the new; and also because they cost money. They were validated by their origins in the "better" life the people hoped to find by their move to the city. Natural flowers, on the other hand, were from the life they were fleeing. Leal also shows how class-specific these meanings are: in upper-class homes, for instance, there was a reversal of values so that peasant artifacts would be displayed as representations of handcrafted, peasant authenticity to demonstrate not only their new owners' ability to transcend the commodification of urban life, but also their power to transport these objects across social boundaries and thus to transform them from things into representations. In these upper-class homes, of course, plastic flowers would never raise their cheap, manufactured, urbanized heads. Leal's study describes a culture of practice and things by which people live within the larger social order not in a reactive, but in a proactive way. The entourage of objects around the TV set comprises

> a symbolic system, including an ethos of modernity, that is itself part of a larger symbolic universe that has as its principal focus of significance the city and industry. This system of meanings seeks to "conquer" the urban power space (that of capitalistic relations), while insistently trying to differentiate and delimit urban cultural space from the rural space that is still very close to the actors, by manipulating signs that are shared by their group as indicators of social prestige.[23]

Studies such as Leal's and Williams' show how the material, densely lived culture of everyday life is a contradictory mixture of creativity and constraint that provides ways of embodying and living the contradictory relations between the dominant social order and the variety of subaltern formations within it. Williams comments somewhat sardonically that "A passion for texture is not always rewarded in American society, and more middle class strategies for urban living aim at breadth instead."[24]

The social order constrains and oppresses the people, but at the same time offers them resources to fight against those constraints. The constraints are, in the first instance, material, economic ones which determine in an oppressive, disempowering way the limits of the social experience of the poor. Oppression is always economic. Yet the everyday culture of the oppressed can take the signs of that which oppresses them and use them for its own purposes. Commodities can be extracted from the economic system of the dominant and made into the things of the people. The plastic flowers are for Leal's newly suburbanized peasants deeply contradictory: their capitalist meanings of commodification, of exploitation and economic subjection, are reaccented by their users when they are combined with the sense of escape from peasantry. The meanings, finally, are not ones of the plastic flowers per se, but of the social relations of the family whose locale they help to establish.

So, too, the accumulation of things in Lucy and Robert's apartment is not a sign of their being dupes of the commodity system. It is rather their way of filling their constrained lives with a richness of meaning and variety of sensation that the more affluent can achieve by their greater mobility through physical and social space.

Of course the desire for the expectation of variety and richness of experience may well be a product of capitalism, and certainly serves to maintain the system—for such variety, whether of objects or experiences, must usually be bought and paid for. But producing that variety, richness, density is also the work of popular creativity; it is the people's art of making do with what they have, and what they have is almost exclusively what the social order that oppresses them offers.

Many of Williams's subjects were African Americans who had moved from rural North Carolina to Washington and thus shared important social determinants with Leal's. It is not surprising, then, that both Williams and Leal find traces of the rural folk culture of previous generations within the urban popular culture of contemporary capitalism. Our thinking about such a rural or folk culture should not be nostalgically romantic: it was itself a culture of deprivation, oppression or slavery, which is why its popular creativities of making do with limited resources transfer so readily to contemporary urban conditions. The argument that some of those resources, at least, came from nature rather than the oppressor is hardly convincing, for in both agrarian capitalism and feudalism nature was transformed into land owned by the elite, its resources had to be "poached"—a constant cultural and material activity of the oppressed which de Certeau uses as a metaphor for popular practices in general. The material and cultural resources were limited, they were the resources of the other, and they always worked, in part at least, to constrain or oppress. The "continuing interplay of constraint and creativity"[25] which Williams identifies as characteristic of popular culture is a condition of oppression, and thus transfers readily from rural to urban, from a slave- or serf-based rural capitalism to its urban industrial equivalent.

Williams describes how this creativity works in, for instance, the culture of collard greens—the fertilizing, nurturing and harvesting of them in urban back yards, and the multitude of ways of chopping, cooking, seasoning and serving them. Collard greens are used to negotiate the differences and similarities between Carolina and Washington, and also between individual creativities within a common set of constraints. Barbecue sauce is another, equally important, opportunity for popular creativity. Because the ingredients for the sauce, as the conditions for growing the greens, were different in Washington from Carolina, both greens and sauce were consciously used to make comparative sense of the difference, but the difference lay in the constraints, in the resources available, not in the creativity of their use. Neighbors constantly exchange praise, warnings and advice about their collards and their barbecue sauces and through them maintain these dual dimensions of identities that are under their control: on the one hand, there are the communal identities produced and recognized by the horizontal relations of *communitas*, but on the other, there are identities of difference within this *communitas*. All neighbors know, for instance, that their style of barbecue is the best, and different from that, say, of Texas, but each will have particular ingredients (often secret) which identify his or hers and him or her as different. Popular creativity produces and controls identity.

This creativity and control is localized: it does not produce the great representations valued by the culture of the power-bloc. It is a creativity which produces a culture of things, such as quilts, diaries or souvenirs, and of the practices of daily life. This sort of culture is often invisible to outsiders not only because of its localized existence, but also because of what Levine calls "sacred inarticulateness,"[26] by which he refers to people's reluctance to put their particular cultural experiences into a generalized, objective discourse. Instead they resort to responses like "It's hard to explain this one, but if you were one of us and did it, then you would understand."[27] *Dallas* viewers "explained" their experience of the program to Williams by remarks like "if you watch it, you'll see."

This localized culture of things and practices has its equivalent in other ways of knowing. Jean Lave, for instance, has shown that even mathematical calculation works quite differently when used to localize than when used in its generalized and scientific mode.[28] She gives numerous examples of how people can perform accurate and rapid calculations in their own contexts or locales, while being apparently unable to achieve the same results in the classroom or "station." A young scorer for a local bowling team performed complex, rapid, error-free calculations in practice, but when asked to perform what the researchers thought were the same cognitive operations out of context (that is, in the classroom under test conditions) he was utterly unable to. Similarly, women in supermarkets never made a mistake when comparing the values of cans of different prices and sizes that they physically held in their hands, but were far less accurate when asked to perform the same calculations abstractly and out of their social context. The argument in this book would explain the differences by pointing out that in the classroom mathematical calculations could be used to examine, rank and individuate people: they were ways of stationing people and subjecting them to discipline. In their own locales, however, calculation enabled people to exert control as opposed to being subjected to it.

Lave cites an example of this localized math. A woman shopper was faced with the problem of how many apples to buy. She picked up the apples one at a time and put them into her cart as she verbalized her math processes to the researcher:

> There's only about three or four [apples] at home, and I have four kids, so you figure at least two apiece in the next three days. These are the kind of things I have to resupply. I only have a certain amount of storage space in the refrigerator, so I can't load it up totally. ... Now that I'm home in the summertime, this is a good snack food. And I like an apple sometimes at lunchtime when I come home.[29]

Lave comments that there are a number of acceptable solutions; 9, 13, 21. It also seems significant that the calculations are performed through the actions of picking up apples, the matching of the actions to the idea of her children eating them, and, I assume, a visualization of the amount of space in her fridge at that time, not as an abstract capacity but as a concrete particularity. Lave observes that this woman is not interested in a generalizable answer that relates to the problem in terms of a universalized criterion of right–wrong, but that problem and answer shape each other in action in a specific setting. In this material setting the shopper's cognitive processes are part of her physical relationship with the goods on display. The supermarket is a densely woven texture of commodity information and display, but through her routine practices the experienced shopper transforms information overload into an information-specific setting. As she selects the commodities she wants, so she selects the information she wants. Her selections from *their* repertoire constitute her setting which is both produced by her cognitive processes and plays a part in producing them. The "setting" is a coming together of the material specificity of the context and the mental processes by which that context is lived.

Lave's concept of the setting has certain similarities with a locale. Settings are constructed within the larger arenas which are the products of the social order. The supermarket is an arena full of the commodities of capitalism, but within it shoppers construct for the period and purposes of shopping their own settings. A setting is, in Lave's definition, "a repeatedly experienced, personally ordered and edited version of the arena."[30]

A setting is generated out of the practice of grocery shopping, but at the same time generates that practice:

> [A setting's] articulatory nature is to be stressed; a setting is not simply a mental map in the mind of the shopper. Instead it has simultaneously an independent, physical character and a potential for realization only in relation to shoppers' activity.[31]

The setting–arena relationship also relates to the difference between place and space as theorized by de Certeau.[32] For him, place is an ordered structure provided by the dominant order through which its power to organize and control is exerted. It is often physical. So cities are places built to organize and control the lives and movements of their "city subjects" in the interests of the dominant. So, too, supermarkets, apartment blocks, offices, and universities are places. But within and against them, the various formations of the people construct their spaces by the practices of living. So renters make the apartment, the place of the landlord, into their space by the practices of living, the textures of things, relationships and behaviors with which they occupy and possess it for the period of their renting. De Certeau stresses the political conflict involved, the confrontation of opposing social interests that is central to the construction of space out of place. Lave focusses more on the functional creativity of the activities involved in constructing a setting out of an arena. But for both, space or setting is where the weak exert their control.

In a regime of power where a system of strong power reproduces its operations across all the institutions that organize social life, the importance of weak powers is underestimated by many. While weak powers are clearly important to those who use them defensively to secure and enlarge the boundaries between what they can and cannot control, they also have a value that far exceeds the particularities of their applications. Weak powers maintain social differences that are not produced or sanctioned by strong power, they diversify control and enable social formations with restricted or no access to the strong power system to practice the exertion of power, albeit of a different sort. These weak powers are social resources that the current power-bloc misunderstands: they are like weeds with unrecognized medicinal properties. When a regime of power changes, the form that the new takes will depend upon the marginalized or unrecognized resources of the old. Keeping alive forms of power and control that are benign, non-threatening and appropriate to a society where diversity is produced by consent rather than struggle may not in itself secure a peaceful and ethical future, but it certainly improves the odds of our being able to achieve one.

NOTES

1. I use the word "index" in Peirce's sense: a sign that is "really and in its individual existence connected with the individual object." C. S. Peirce, *Collected Papers (1939–58)* (Cambridge, MA: Harvard University Press, 1958), p. 531.
2. Steven Zeitlin, Amy Kotkin and Holly Cutting Baker, *A Celebration of American*

Family Folklore: Tales and Traditions from the Smithsonian Collection (New York: Pantheon, 1982), p. 202.
3. Ibid., p. 200.
4. Diane Bell, *Generations: Grandmothers, Mothers and Daughters*, with photographs by Ponch Hawkes (Fitzroy and Ringwood: McPhee Gribble/Penguin, 1987).
5. Ibid., pp. 146–7.
6. Ibid., p. 147.
7. Ibid., pp. 148–9.
8. Ibid., p. 46.
9. Ibid., p. 260.
10. Zeitlin et al., p. 153.
11. Michel de Certeau, *The Practice of Everyday Life* (Berkeley: University of California Press, 1984).
12. Dennis Folly, "Getting Butter from the Duck: Proverbs and Proverbial Expressions in an Afro-American Family," in Zeitlin et al., pp. 232–41, this citation p. 233.
13. Folly, p. 236.
14. Minou Cho and Chung Cho, "Women Watching Together: An Ethnographic Study of Korean Soap Opera Fans in the US," *Cultural Studies* vol. 4, no. 1, pp. 30–44.
15. Brett Williams, *Upscaling Downtown: Stalled Gentrification in Washington, DC* (Ithaca and London: Cornell University Press, 1988).
16. See, for example, Michelle Perrot (ed.), *A History of Private Life*, Volume IV, *From the Fires of Revolution to the Great War* (Cambridge, MA: Belknap Press, 1990).
17. In Bernard Edelman, *La Maison du Kant* (Paris: Payot, 1984), pp. 25–6, cited in Perrot, p. 342.
18. Alain Corbin, "Backstage" in Perrot, pp. 451–668. Corbin traces the rise of individual identity in nineteenth-century France through the spread of things such as mirrors, photographs and personal journals, and through increasing spatial privacy. A middle-class girl's bedroom became her private identifying space, bathrooms were fitted with locks c. 1900; so, too, were parental bedrooms according to Michelle Perrot, "Roles and Characters," in Perrot, pp. 167–260.
19. Williams, p. 57.
20. Ibid., p. 61.
21. Claude Lévi-Strauss, *Myths and Meaning* (New York: Schocken, 1979).
22. Ondina Leal, "Popular Taste and Erudite Repertoire: The Place and Space of Television in Brazil," *Cultural Studies*, vol. 4, no. 1, 1990, pp. 19–29.
23. Ibid., p. 25.
24. Williams, p. 48.
25. Ibid., p. 47.
26. Levine, "Art, Values, Institutions and Culture," *American Quarterly*, vol. 24, no. 2, pp. 131–65, in Williams, p. 104.
27. Levine, in Williams, p. 104.
28. Jean Lave, *Cognition in Practice* (Cambridge, UK: Cambridge University Press, 1988).
29. Ibid., p. 2.
30. Ibid., p. 151.
31. Ibid., pp. 152-3.
32. De Certeau, 1984.

PART FOUR

WHITE POWER,

BLACK POWER

11

BLACKENED WHITE

POLICING THE BLACK BODY[1]

He was being beaten on the legs and buttocks by two policemen. One of them broke his nightstick. There were other policemen standing around. They kept telling him to put his hands behind his back.

Really hard? As hard as the King beating?

Yes, definitely, because I could hear the thud of the wand on the body, and it made me sick to my stomach. This was before he was cuffed. He was lying on his face with his hands up by his head. They were solid blows. It's a sickening sound when you hear something hitting flesh and blood that hard. If you hung up a piece of meat and hit it with a baseball bat, that's the kind of sound it would have.[2]

He was about seven minutes on the bank. The best description I can give is that it was like the same picture you see on TV when you see King's beating. Actually it was a little bit worse. I saw two batons broken on him. He wasn't fighting at all. He was mainly covering his body. The beating was so strong I saw the skin get pierced up by his right shoulder. Then they handcuffed him feet and hands down on the sidewalk and ran a rope from his feet to his hands. To me it's mainly the reason he died. He could have survived the beating if he'd just been handcuffed, but he could not breathe.[3]

So ran two eyewitness accounts of the death of Tracy Mayberry, a 33-year-old African American man, from police batons in Los Angeles on 3 November 1990, just four months before Rodney King was beaten by police from the same Department.[4] The incidents differ in that King survived his beating while Mayberry did not, and that King's was videotaped and shown to the nation, whereas Mayberry's was invisible, (almost) unreported and known only within the community who knew well that such incidents embody, literally, their social relations in a white, racist society. They know, equally well, that it is that same racism which represses their representation and thus excludes them from official social knowledge.

Imperializing power that invades the body reduces to a minimum the locale over which the subordinate can exert any control. When localizing power has no place of application its difference from and potential challenge to imperializing power can be (almost) eliminated: limiting the locale limits the power. Bodies are at the core of locales, and as the individual body is continuous with the social body, the power applied to it extends into the body politic. The Black body, then, is the object of both the physical power of white batons and the discursive power of white knowledge. It is, therefore, an appropriate starting point for a chapter that offers glimpses into Black struggles to strengthen their localizing, defensive powers in the contemporary US.

The body of Tracy Mayberry, no less than that of Elvis Presley, is known differently by those sharing his locality and by officialdom. The autopsy report on Mayberry tells his death quite differently from the eyewitnesses:

> A 33-year-old Black male, probably under the influence of drugs, was reportedly chasing a child and was combative when subdued by police with restraints. As noted he suddenly became unresponsive and could not be resuscitated at the hospital. He was pronounced dead 7 minutes afterward.[5]

The toxicologist found a potentially lethal level of cocaine in the body, but the autopsy omitted any mention of the effects of a beating upon a drugged body. Mayberry was a victim of racism. Mayberry was a victim of drugs. The official truth and the local truth differ, and, in the knowledge of those who suffer, the difference is a product of the same system as the beatings.

The white baton on the Black body is where the abstract social relations of race become material: bruised flesh is the physical point where a diffuse and generalized power system exerts its control. A caller on *The Gary Byrd Show* on 23 December 1991 likened today's police to the whipmasters on the slave plantations. Witnesses to Mayberry's death saw it re-presented in the video of King's beating, and a Latino neighbor of Mayberry said "Just like Tracy, I guess a lot of Latinos, Mexicans, a lot of people have been in the same situation. I relate King's name to Martin Luther King. We're getting freedom from some kind of slavery."[6]

His optimism is remarkable. Stacey Koon, the officer in charge of Rodney King's beating, wrote in his memoir of how he dealt with a Latino whom he suspected (like Mayberry and King) of being drugged:

> My boot came from the area of lower California and connected with the suspect's scrotum about lower Missouri. My boot stopped about Ohio, but the

suspect's testicles continued into upper Maine. The suspect was literally lifted off the ground. The suspect tried to speak, but it appeared he had something in his throat, probably his balls.[7]

Like the Rodney King beating, this one too was videotaped, but instead of exposing police brutality the tape continued it, for it was used as a training aid for young officers. In Koon's words "the tape was to become a legend in its own time."

Koon's imperializing metaphor of the non-white body as the nation turns both into equivalent terrains of white power in a way that the curators of the Smithsonian exhibit *The West as America* would recognize as symptomatic of what they were opposing. His evident pride in his white power echoes many of the offended comments in the exhibit's guest books, and casts him as a present-day, willing re-enactor of the historical role of slave breaker.

The histories of slavery and racism which continue seamlessly from the past, through the present and into the future are experienced by their victims in the thud of the baton and the boot upon today's Black body, and, equally, that thud makes sense only to those who have experienced these histories from below. The continuities between the macro level of social history and social structure on the one hand and the micro particularity of a single incident in everyday life do not need theorizing because they are lived and understood through embodied, localized knowledge.

The bruises on the body make power material: they are the site of its instrumentality, but the site of application is not necessarily, in the tactics of local power, the best site of contestation. In a society that officially knows itself as democratic, racist power can only work effectively when it is invisible. Knowing, seeing and doing are continuous with each other, and it is on the terrains of knowledge and visibility that the action of the batons can be best contested; on the terrain of the body they must be endured.

On 18 October 1990, two reporters from Chicago were discussing police brutality on *Black Liberation Radio*, a rebel radio station in Springfield, Illinois.[8] As they left the station (actually a room in Kantako's apartment in a housing project), two police officers were waiting for them. They were ordered to spread their legs and place their hands against the wall. For twenty minutes the police tried to provoke the reporters into "doing something stupid." But then, suddenly, neighborhood residents appeared on the streets, gathered round the incident and just *looked*. This inverted "neighborhood watch," which saw the police as the threatening intruder, was effective; the police stopped their harassment and allowed the reporters to leave. The "watch" had been produced by the radio. Kantako had broadcast an account of the incident as it was relayed to him by his wife from her vantage point on the porch.[9] A crucial part of the power of the power-bloc is the power to control its own visibility, to determine for itself which of its operations and alliances should be made visible, and which should not. Making visible (or in this case audible) is a form of counter-power, and the knowledge it produces and circulates works to construct and validate a counter-reality.

Black Liberation Radio is a one-watt station using $600 worth of equipment in Kantako's apartment in the John Hay Homes, a 500-unit housing project where 80 per cent of the adults are unemployed.[10] Because Springfield is so segregated, Kantako estimates that his station's one and a half mile range reaches 75 per cent of Springfield's African American residents (who make up 15 per cent of the city's 100,000 population). He trains local youth in radio skills to ensure local control over at least one medium of cultural production and distribution. The station plays Black music, tapes from other rebel stations and tapes of books borrowed from blind readers' services. (Kantako himself is blind as a consequence of a police beating when a teenager. He recalls that beating, and his belief that he was going to die under it, in terms that associate it directly with those of Tracy Mayberry and Rodney King.) Kantako interviews local people, particularly on their encounters with the police but also with other power structures, both Black and white, and he circulates news, opinions and voices that are not to be heard on other, licensed media. *Black Liberation Radio*'s programming is limited by only three rules, which are rigorously applied: no advocating of drug use, no celebration of material values, and no sexism. The station has almost no budget, and survives on local donations of records and tapes, office equipment, the occasional dollar bill and even food. It started in 1986, by 1990 was on the air seven nights a week from 8:00 p.m. to 8:00 a.m., and now broadcasts continuously.

Kantako also monitors police radio and by relaying its information to his listeners he diverts this instrumentally powerful knowledge into the defense of those against whom it was originally directed. At the acquittal of the police officers accused of using excessive force in the Rodney King beating, there were uprisings in Black neighborhoods all across the country. The John Hay Homes were no exception, and through monitoring police radio Kantako was able to relay police plans and positions so that the protesters could organize their actions more effectively. He also broadcast live phone reports from Black people in Los Angeles giving insider views that the mainstream media could not. Like the Rodney King video, Kantako's radio exposed the power that works best unseen. The station's newsletter claims that "some observers have called the "micro-rebellion" at Springfield the most sophisticated in the nation. "Scores of young people outflanked the cops in two nights of skirmishes and destroyed the police substation and the housing security office. Amazingly, no one was injured and no occupied apartments were attacked."[11] Through long practice, Kantako has learned "police language" and is skilled not only in decoding the terms dispatchers and cops use to communicate with each other but also in filling in the gaps and making what is unsaid clearly heard. What to an inexpert ear sounds like curt grunts emerging through static, Kantako decodes as "He just told that pig to give him a call, they were on their way to the hospital—they were taking someone to jail but had to take him to the hospital first—so those two, numbers 86 and 58 they must have done something to that person and somebody must have called the station about it." Sometimes his monitoring is playful and he will taunt the police who he knows are monitoring him monitoring them. Occasionally one will rise to the bait and answer him on air, much to Kantako's delight. Power is deadly serious about its operations, so mocking laughter is offensive to it (in both senses of the word), and one of the characteristics of *Black Liberation Radio* is the amount of laughter it carries. Analyzing and countering white power is serious political work, but one may as well have fun while doing it. Bakhtin would recognize both the gaiety and the seriousness of the laughter. Rebel radio versus Police radio is a short-wave skirmish in the long-term struggles over knowledge and power.

But economic restraints are not the only ones that Kantako has had to resist in order to survive. In 1989 the station devoted much of its attention to police mistreatment of Black citizens with the result that the local police chief reported Kantako to the FCC (whom he refers to as "The Thought Police"). An FCC official accompanied by five policemen arrived soon afterwards, closed down the station and fined him $750, which he has never paid. At both his hearing at the US Marshal's office and at his subsequent court hearings, Kantako was not allowed a court-appointed attorney. Realizing that complying with the system was pointless, he went back on the air in an attempt to get himself arrested in order to make his situation more visible and more widely known. He was not re-arrested. At stake, he claims, was "A First Amendment right to free speech and a representational voice in the media for blacks who live in a state of conditional genocide."[12] He points out that only 2 per cent of the licensed radio stations in the US are owned by non-whites, and of the 4,000 unlicensed ones, most are used for commercial purposes. *Black Liberation Radio* was singled out for closure because it dared to give voice to the Black experience of the police and because, in Kantako's words, "we are showing people that they do have *some control over their own lives*, and that nothing is hopeless" (emphasis added).[13]

FCC regulations allow only FM stations of 100 watts or more to be licensed; such equipment is expensive, and the capital required to qualify for a license means that micro-watt community stations such as *Black Liberation Radio* can never be legal in the US. The law which claims to operate in the interests of all by preventing clutter on the airwaves in practice restricts broadcast speech to those who can raise adequate capital (the ability to raise capital is, of course, not equally distributed around the social order). The lesson is clear, free speech requires capital.

It is not just FCC regulations that work to stifle any public form of popular or, in this case, Black speech. As Mike Townsend, a guest on *Black Liberation Radio*, points out in a discussion with Kantako:

TOWNSEND   I get a big kick out of your little radio station, you know. I don't know if people know that it's illegal here in the United States to order the little equipment that you have to run the radio station with it assembled ... it has to be sent to you in pieces so you have to try and find some kind of an electronic whiz that can put it together for you, but the same company, here in the United States, can sell that same transmitter completely put together in any other country, but not to our own people here in this country. Now what does that tell you?

KANTAKO   It's confusing ... I mean ...

TOWNSEND   They don't want the people here to be able to communicate with one another!

KANTAKO   But you can buy an Uzi assembled.

TOWNSEND   Yeah!

The power-bloc interests that are promoted by repressing illegal (read Black) speech do not confine their operations to the regulatory realm of the FCC, the courts and the legislature. The *Black Liberation Radio* newsletter of 10 June 1991 reports that Kantako's 9-year-old son "was recently arrested, booked and photographed for a police mug shot for being involved in a shoving match during a soccer game at his elementary school."[14]

Not far away from Springfield is the Illinois city of Decatur. Here Napoleon Williams broadcasts *Liberation Radio* from his home, another rebel radio station, and the only Black radio in town. Since he began broadcasting in August 1990 Williams has been charged with sexual assault, later reduced to battery (which Williams denies); he has faced police allegations of working with drug dealers, soliciting for murder and threatening witnesses. None of the charges stuck, but Williams believes they were part of a police campaign to make him out to be a pariah whom nobody would want to listen to.[15]

Rebel radio is locale based and locale forming: it is defensive of its boundaries with white society but constructive of Black unity and *communitas* within them. And it is spreading. Kantako has produced an instructional video on setting up a micro radio station, and has received requests for copies from over thirty different states and four different countries. As Black communities (and others) realize its effectiveness, its cheapness and the difficulty of enforcing the law that outlaws it, they are adopting it as an important instrument of localizing knowledge and power.

Larger Black communities can support stations that can afford more expensive equipment and that can set up a formal broadcasting organization, and thus meet the FCC regulations. The fact that they are licensed gives them a security and independence that rebel radio lacks; but though their reach is wider, their local links are just as strong. *WLIB* in Harlem, New York, is a good example. Superficially, this station may sound like professional mainstream radio—it has high production values, its talk and music are interrupted with breaks for commercials, weather forecasts and news—but these features have done nothing to "whiten" it. The news, local, national and international, is of Black interests, the commercials are for Black businesses and, as we shall see later, set up quite different economic relations than do those for White capitalist products, and there is an explicit commonality of interest across its ingredients of talk, music, commercials and news. The news that the Bush Administration has withdrawn its offer to airlift supplies donated by African Americans to the Black Haitian refugees held in a tent city at the US Guantonamo air base in Cuba could hardly be called a "break" in a discussion of how white courts and white police worked against the interests of Black neighborhoods. There is a connectedness in the Black experience of white racism which links many centuries of history with the bruises on a particular Black body, and these bruises with the Bush administration's treatment of the Haitian refugees. The connectedness draws together both the multitudinous particular experiences of racism and the African Americans who suffer them, and can, when effectively mobilized within Black communities, produce a sense of *umoja* (the Kiswahili word for unity, see below) of social experience and of Black people. Key voices within the Black community are working hard to recover and circulate this *umoja* as a basis for a new Black social order within but distinct from white society. Black media, particularly radio and press and books, are active in this recovery and circulation of Black ways of knowing white power.

It is widely known by African Americans that there is a white conspiracy against them: Black papers such as the *New York Amsterdam News*, and Black radio such as *WLIB*, matter-of-factly use the discourse of war, assault, attack, holocaust and conspiracy to describe the white practice of race relations in the contemporary US. The white power-bloc gives little sign of being aware of how its actions appear to those whom they oppress, and no sign of concern that these actions are certainly socially divisive and possibly socially explosive. The evidence within the Black experience of a white conspiracy against them and of a well-planned, multifrontal assault upon them is widespread, clear and largely ignored by whites. Dovetailing neatly into the discourse of war and conspiracy is that of slavery. A caller on WLIB's Gary Byrd Show, for instance, called the police "The head whippers" and argued that "Our people are being misled by the state because the state is sophisticated and very intelligent about how to take African people off our true course towards liberation, towards empowerment."[16]

In the course of a long and passionate discussion on the show about whether Blacks should ever be policemen, both the passion and the majority of voices were on the side of the nay vote. The live audience applauded the opinion that Black police were collaborators and traitors, and to be true to their people should resign and fight on the streets against the police "who shot Eleanor Bumpurs because she didn't pay the rent."

The story of Eleanor Bumpurs has become emblematic among African Americans of contemporary race relations and the way the police embody them in law enforcement. Patricia Williams, an African American professor of law, describes the incident thus:

> On October 29, 1984, Eleanor Bumpurs, a 170-pound, arthritic sixty-seven-year-old woman, was shot to death while resisting eviction from her apartment in the Bronx. She was $96.85, or one month, behind in her rent. Mayor Ed Koch and Police Commissioner Benjamin Ward described the struggle that preceded her demise as involving two officers with large plastic shields, one with a restraining hook, one with a shotgun, and at least one other who was supervising. All of these officers also carried service revolvers. During the course of the attempted eviction, Mrs. Bumpurs wielded a knife that Commissioner Ward says was "bent" on one of the plastic shields and escaped the constraint of the restraining hook twice. At some point, Stephen Sullivan, the officer positioned farthest away from her and the one with the shotgun, took aim and fired at her. He missed (mostly—it is alleged that this blast removed half of the hand that held the knife and, according to the Bronx district attorney's office, "it was anatomically impossible for her to hold the knife"), pumped his gun, and shot again, making his mark the second time around.[17]

And on the other coast, only the geography is different: Mike Davis recounts the slaying of "Betty Jean Aborn, a homeless middle-aged Black woman with a history of mental illness. Confronted by seven burly sheriffs after stealing an ice cream from a convenience store, she supposedly brandished a butcher's knife. The response was an incredible volley of twenty-eight rounds, eighteen of which perforated her body."[18]

Patricia Williams also tells of the answers given by public officials and law enforcement officers to questions about Eleanor Bumpurs's death by Gil Noble on the TV show *Like It Is*:

> −*Don't you think this officer was motivated by racism?* "She was psychotic; she said that she saw Reagan coming through her walls."
> −*Wasn't the discharge of the shotgun illegal?* "She waved a knife."
> −*Wasn't shooting her unnecessary?* "She made the officers fear for their lives."
> −*Couldn't the officers have used tear gas?* "Couldn't her children have paid her rent and taken care of her?" (The hypothesized failure of Mrs. Bumpurs' children to look after her actually became a major point in Officer Sullivan's defense attorney's opening and closing statements. Ironically, "a former employee of the Housing Authority said that, three weeks before Mrs. Bumpurs' death ... her relatives tried to make a payment of about ... half of the rent she owed. ... But the former Authority employee, Joan Alfredson ... who was a bookkeeper, said she turned down the payment because she was forbidden to accept partial payment without the written consent of a supervisor.")[19]

Williams shows how these answers are part of the common strategy known as "blaming the victim," used here to cast Eleanor Bumpurs as the proper object of power. (Observers with the benefit of hindsight and distance might well wonder which was the delusion—that Mrs Bumpurs threatened the lives of five armed police officers or that President Reagan was coming at her through the walls.)

"Blaming the victim" as a discursive power play was also used in the defense of the police accused of unnecessary violence in the arrest of Rodney King: they too claimed to be frightened that he would assault and disarm them if they desisted from beating him. To millions of TV viewers, King appeared totally helpless as his body was pulped on the pavement, but the trained police eye was able to detect signs that his submission was not complete enough for the ring of cops to feel safe. He brought it on himself. The defense was successful and the officers were acquitted, but in order to win this short-term victory, the Los Angeles Police Department had to announce to the world that this beating was not excessive, but lay within the norms of trained police behavior.

On the *Gary Byrd Show*, the discussion containing the reference to Eleanor Bumpurs had been started by a participant telling of how he had seen a Black off-duty cop beaten up in a bar by some of his white colleagues. As he ran down an alley to escape them, he was met by white traffic police who continued the beating. Among them was a Latino officer who was called a "Spic" and told to keep away. Other stories followed, of Black men and women cops meeting racism, sexism, and oppression in the New York Police Department. An ex-cop told of his mother's advice on his joining the force that if he could not reconcile wearing the badge with the interests of his people he should resign. He recalled being taught that a cop's duty was to protect people and property, but found in practice that property was protected far more enthusiastically than people. As property is disproportionately owned by whites, a policy that may have seemed fair in its rhetoric was racist in its execution. He resigned, but only after years of attempting to police a Black community as a Black had demonstrated that the whiteness of the system made it impossible for him to do so. The majority view in the discussion was summed up by an audience member who reminded listeners that POLICE was an acronym for Protectors Of Laws Instituted for Caucasian Empire (or Empowerment—my radio reception of the word was unclear).

James Traub, a white reporter for *Harpers*, was in the live audience for a similar discussion on the show some months earlier.[20] Incredulous of a story about two cops breaking the arm of Shareema, a young Black girl who had asked them to recover her stolen radio (apparently because her request was insulting in its triviality), he asked two girls sitting near him if they believed the story. In reply, one told of how her boyfriend had been kicked around by cops and the other said that only a few days earlier she had been stopped by police for going through the non-paying gate in the subway even though she had shown her student card. The Shareema story confirmed their experience, and they knew when the Reverend Al Sharpton proclaimed on air "They declared war on us" that he was telling *their* truth which was *the* truth.

In LA, fifteen young Black men have been strangled while in police custody. The police were employing an official restraint (now prohibited) called "the carotid chokehold;" Chief Gates defended his officers and the chokehold by blaming the deaths upon the inferior anatomy of Black bodies: "We may be finding," he said, "that in some Blacks when it is applied, the veins or arteries do not open up as fast as they do on normal people."[21] A double discursive strategy was at work here, for besides blaming the victim, Gates established norms that kept Blacks outside them. The physical power to kill Black men legally and the discursive power to define them as not normal people are one and the same power in different applications.

While racial power is applied by individual cops upon individual Blacks, the African American way of knowing it understands it not as a series of individual incidents but as a power-bloc strategy in the war against them: each incident is thus part of a much larger picture. The African Americans who wince with the pain of batons on their bodies see through the particular blows to the white social order that is delivering them. The police are the visible arm of the courts, and both are known to work against Blacks.

The Black knowledge of the Jeffrey Dahmer case in Milwaukee exemplifies this. Fifteen of his seventeen known victims were African American, but the local Black community know that there were many more, with some estimating the total at seventy-five to one hundred. Michael McGee, a Black Alderman in Milwaukee, blamed police indifference and the court system for allowing Dahmer to commit the murders. "It was," he said, "like the police were working with Dahmer, bringing the victims to him to be slaughtered." Sonny Carson commented "There's a conspiracy afoot and the Dahmer murders are but one aspect of it. I think the Black communities around the country need to be vigilant and check on the various missing persons. We certainly should be doing it in New York City where there are thousands of missing persons."[22] And on *Black Liberation Radio*, Kantako concludes an account of the atrocities of the slave trade by citing Dahmer as evidence that the white assault upon Black bodies continued unabated.

Black American knowledge understands well that the past "is always present, for Black history is rewritten in each experience of everyday life. This knowledge sees clearly that the white interests promoted by the police and the law courts are continuations of those which organized the slave ship and the plantation. And, now as then, the mainstream media serve as the discursive arm of white power. The *New York Amsterdam News*[23] makes this clear in an editorial comparison of the "Central Park Jogger" case with the "St. Johns" case. In the first, five Black youths were convicted of raping and brutalizing a white woman; in the second, three white men were acquitted of sodomizing and abusing a Black girl. The editorial argues in detail that the evidence in each case was comparable, and yet in only one was it deemed sufficient to convict. It shows, too, how the white media were part of the prosecution in the one case but were almost silent in the other. "Such is the tale of justice in this city," it concludes. "Dialogue (between Blacks and whites) has all but broken down." The Black way of knowing the workings of white society, the Black experience that the civic institutions exclude them from the *civilitas* of the US, is grounded upon material evidence.

WHITE POWER, BLACK KNOWLEDGE

This Black knowledge is not paranoid, but is based upon the hard data of lived experience, and these data, inserted into a Black way of knowing, produce a Black reality which counters white reality and its imperializing power. Some Black readers of *Harpers* thought that Traub's report on the *Gary Byrd Show* allowed this counter-knowledge of a counter-reality to be too easily dismissed as delusory. And one can see why. While being sympathetic towards the reasons for a Black counter-reality, Traub implied that the (white) reality was grounded in empirical truth, while the counter-reality was not. He gave no credence to the possibility that the reality produced by white knowledge was looking after its producer's interests as strategically as was the Black knowledge and that both knowledges were grounded in truths that were products of equivalent mixes of material experience, and socio-political interests. Far from showing that the "greater" truth of white reality was a function of the power-bloc's ability to institutionalize and operationalize it, he implied that it was, in itself, "truer." And some readers, at least, took his implication. Even one of the more sympathetic letters responding to his article referred to "the paranoid rhetoric of participants on the *Gary Byrd Show*".[24] This subtle whitewashing of Black knowledge was well exposed in the final letter published in the correspondence (I quote it at some length, but not in full):

> But of graver consequence is Traub's characterization of American blacks' concern for their present and future in this country as conspiracy-theory paranoia. I guess the motorist Rodney King whose beating by a group of Los Angeles police officers was recorded on videotape and broadcast internationally, is a figment of our collective imaginations. Harlemites were soundly upbraided for their skepticism of official handling of the Central Park jogger and Tawana Brawley affairs. The youths involved in the former incident were routinely described as "animals" and "beasts" in the media and by such notables as Ed Koch and Donald Trump. Yet no such epithets were hurled at the white youths involved in the Howard Beach incident, the white youths who killed Yusuf Hawkins, or the white youths who recently battered a young black high school student into a coma in Atlantic Beach—all of which took place in metropolitan New York.
>
> For these reasons, any black person in America today, poor or middle-class, educated or not, who is not concerned about his or her survival in an increasingly hostile environment is deluded. Traub doesn't acknowledge the mountainous evidence that blacks are at risk: the differential between blacks and whites in the rates of incarceration, completion of high school, life expectancy, AIDS infection, proximity to toxic-waste sites, etc. Without such recognition, Traub's report is only intolerant, shallow, narcissistic, and uninformed. He took an opportunity and turned it into a sham. Too bad,

because the rap from Harlem is sweet music to my ears. It demonstrates that people still have the power to control their own minds and that they have finally realized "history is a lie agreed upon."[25]

This letter details a strategic, multifrontal assault upon Black life which Black knowledge knows well, but white knowledge tends, conveniently, to overlook. Multifrontal though this assault might be, many hold that its prime strategic target is the young Black male, and through him, the Black family.

Jawanza Kunjufu has written three books under the title of *Countering the Conspiracy to Destroy Black Boys, Volumes I, II and III.*[26] In them, he presents evidence demonstrating that, in the early stages of life, Black children develop physically and mentally more rapidly than white children,[27] but that the white social order and its schools in particular, through its assault on Black families and on Black students, quickly reverses the phenomenon and turns Black children into inferior performers.

The report of the 21st Century Commission on African American males sums up the statistical evidence of this assault:

Black males have the lowest life expectancy of any group in the United States. Their unemployment rate is more than twice that of white males; even Black men with college degrees are three times more likely to be unemployed than their white counterparts. About one in four Black men between the ages of twenty and twenty-nine is behind bars. Blacks receive longer prison sentences than whites who have committed the same crimes.

Suicide is the third leading cause of death for young Black males. Since 1960, suicide rates for young Black males have nearly tripled, and doubled for Black females. While suicide among whites increases with age, it is a peculiarly youthful phenomenon among Blacks.

Many Black males die prematurely from twelve major preventable diseases.

Nearly one-third of all Black families in America live below the poverty line. Half of all Black children are born in poverty and will spend all of their youth growing up in poor families.[28]

We have seen already how African Americans know that the AFDC system is designed to split Black men off from their families and their women, and they know equally well that the military will station them in ranks and units with the highest probability of death. Even still, the Black male is safer in the military than at home, for he is the commonest murder victim in the US. The white social order puts more Blacks into jail than into college and locks them up at four times the rate even of South Africa.

Kunjufu argues persuasively that the white refusal to allow Black men the means of achieving a self-satisfactory sense of their masculinity has a historically cumulative effect in that each generation of Black boys is progressively denied immediate role models of empowered Black men. Instead they are left either with a void, or with disempowered and disempowering images of Black masculinity. There are a few nationally visible successful Black men, mainly in the domains of sport and entertainment, and also increasingly in local and state, though not national, politics. But even these can be victims of the white assault. When the boxer Mike Tyson was convicted of raping a Black woman, many Black men saw this as a white assault upon a Black role model, and pointed to the acquittal of William Kennedy Smith on a similar charge with similar evidence. The only visible difference between the two cases was the race of the defendant. Similarly, the trial and conviction of Washington Mayor Marion Barry on drug charges was seen as a strategy of the white power-bloc to remove a powerful Black from the public arena. But the comparative lack of successful Black male role models that Kunjufu bemoans is at the level of the neighborhood and the family rather than the nation, and it is this lack that he sees as racially debilitating, for it demonstrates to each generation that the norm for Black masculinity is social disempowerment—and we must not forget here Foucault's insistence that establishing norms is a key strategy of power.

Carol Freeman tells Studs Terkel of how these norms work in her own family history and her own perceptions:

> It's easier for a black woman to get a white man than it is for her to get a black man. The black man doesn't feel as though he's worthy. Take me, for instance. When I get involved with a black man, the first thing he finds out is that my son is in medical school. He notices that I'm living in this home. I have my own car. He analyzes: what do I need him for? With a white man, it's altogether different. He doesn't have to analyze. He commends me and wants to know how I was able to do it. I said, "Just like other parents do." I did without so he could go to school.
>
> The black male appears to me to be the one who's having the roughest time. That's why I was so determined for my son not to get a job but get a profession. I told him, "By the time you're ready, there won't be any jobs." [She points toward the south.] Right over here, the steel mills are all closed.
>
> You're looking at generations of black males that have been raised by women. We have not had the men to raise men. We have been doing the best we can, but sometimes we've made a mess of it. The black men have so often been put down in this society; they just disappear.[29]

Twenty-five years earlier her mother had told Terkel much the same, only she was more explicit in identifying the white power at work:

> This is something that happened when we had this business of not allowing the Negro male to make a living. See? That's why I say that Negro women have

not been able to raise men. The white man thought of that.[30]

William Grier and Price Cobbs are psychotherapists, which gives them a slightly different point of view from Kunjufu's, but they tell a very similar story.[31] When slaves were robbed of their African identities and cultures they were robbed of any firm base from which to resist the white invasion of their consciousness with identities of inferiority and failure. In some African American males this colonization is so complete that they undercut themselves when on the brink of "success" or "empowerment" so as to conform to their enslaved identities. These extreme cases which come forward for therapy are exaggerated instances of the normalized Black male consciousness in a white supremacist society. The therapy offered by Grier and Cobbs is Black and radical, for unlike most white therapists they do not attempt to help the individual to adjust to social conditions, but to come to terms with the fact that the cause of any feelings of inadequacy or maladjustment lies in the white supremacist society, not in the African American individual. The ensuing therapeutic knowledge is a Black knowledge for it contradicts the white consciousness of both Black identity and the white social order, and re-empowers the individual so that he or she can resist this colonization certainly at the level of individual identity and possibly by extension at the more public level of race relations.

An analysis such as this of the assault upon Black men runs the risk of reinforcing by neglect the double oppression of Black women. Barbara Ransby identifies its implicit masculinization of race when she writes:

> The proposition that black men are being targeted for special oppression because of their gender carries with it the implicit notion that African American women, conversely, have earned some type of gender privilege that exempts us from such special abuses. It is currently popular and acceptable to minimize the plight of black women either through glaring omission or by emphasizing black male oppression so heavily that black women's suffering is rendered invisible, just as Anita Hill's racial identity and her victimization as a black woman were rendered invisible during the public debate surrounding the Thomas hearings. While our brothers are clearly under siege from a racist society, and the alarming statistics about black male suffering should not be taken lightly, we nevertheless cannot regress in our political thinking to a point not so long ago when black women were told that it was our duty to assume subordinate roles so that brothers could redeem their manhood.[32]

It is important to remember that not only is the assault upon Black men also an assault upon Black women but that in some cases its effects upon women are intensified by its passage through the masculine sphere. The strength of "the strong Black woman" must be understood in the context of double oppression and not as a consequence of her avoiding the special targeting of the Black male.

Dr Cress Welsing, in what has become known as "The Cress Theory," takes a global perspective in order to offer Blacks a comprehensive explanation for whites' relentless and pitiless drive toward supremacy.[33] The Cress Theory proposes that human life began in Africa and that the original humans were Black. But by a process similar to albinism, some were born lacking melanin and the resulting pigment deficiency meant that these people were vulnerable to the African sun and thus had to move northwards to a more temperate climate. This melanin deficiency meant that white people were both numerically in the minority and genetically inferior, for white skin is not only abnormal, but is carried by a recessive gene. The white minority can only survive by promoting genetic purity through prohibiting interracial breeding particularly by its females, for otherwise the laws of genetics would mean that its distinctive whiteness would soon disappear and the race would die. In albinism, pigment deficiency goes along with a reduction in both sexual energy and performance, and in the physical characteristics that make the male body larger and more muscular than the female. The male albino is a "feminized" male, and, by extension, the white male is a feminized black male.

According to the Cress Theory the global white supremacist movement is driven by these three interrelated factors: white genetic inferiority, the reduced masculinity of their males, and their global minority status. The drive to dominate other races originates in the need to overcompensate for these deficiencies. This theory can explain why, for instance, the gun is a white invention that not only has enabled whites to conquer and colonize numerically superior races, but is also a phallic symbol: it compensates for white numerical and sexual inferiority simultaneously. The theory explains, too, why white supremacy has focussed its assault on Black males, for the male carrying a dominant gene is a greater genetic threat than a female; consequently lynchings were almost always of Black males, often involved castration and were usually occasioned by an alleged sexual threat to a white female. Consequently, too, the victim of today's police brutality is typically a Black man, and many of the police batons land on Black testicles.[34]

The Cress Theory, at a more detailed level, gives an exemplary Black reading of the white supremacy encoded in the National Monument in Washington: the monument is of white stone, it is phallic in shape, by law no nearby building may exceed it in height, and it bears a strong visual resemblance to the hood of the Ku Klux Klan. She concludes: "It is not without significance that the Washington monument, as a phallic symbol, towers over a predominantly Black population in the capital city of the most powerful government in the global white supremacy system."[35] Jawanza Kunjufu reminds us that the obelisk is an African form that originated in Egypt.[36] The glaring whiteness of the one in Washington may thus stand as a concrete metaphor for the whitewashing of Black achievement.

Dr Cress Welsing argues that Blacks must understand that white supremacy is fueled by a deep subconscious drive originating at the very core of the white psyche because it is a consequence of the defining conditions of the race—a *natural* genetic inferiority coupled with the *social* status of being a minority in global humanity. The political, military, cultural and economic structures that whites have established to operationalize their supremacy are where white imperialization is effectively transformed into instrumental power and control, but they are not where it originates. Blacks must understand the white psyche just as well as they must understand white structures. Correlatively, they must understand the difference between a black consciousness that is a historical product of white supremacy and a Black consciousness that is true to a larger Black history and to a Black nature that, because it predates white supremacy, is truer to the nature of humanity in general.

Blacks must also understand that because white supremacy rests on such insecure foundations, it has to work ceaselessly and tirelessly to maintain its survival. It cannot rest content with what it has, for what it has is never secure: it must always be developing ways to strengthen and extend its grasp. Consequently it mounts a continuous assault upon other races, for its survival can be ensured only by constant aggression.

This white assault upon Black culture and society takes place simultaneously on all levels of experience, from those of consciousness and the body, through family relationships and the broader social conditions of African Americans in the contemporary US, to the broadest level of global race relations throughout human history. It also takes place on many fronts: the enforcement of white law and order in Black communities, the representation of Black life in white media, the whitening of Black history and the strategic impoverishment of Blacks in a white economy.

The economic assault on Blacks means that currently average Black income is 60 per cent that of whites, that the net worth of an African American (that is, assets less liabilities) is one tenth of that of a white, and that not only is the poverty rate of Blacks three times that of whites but poor Blacks are poorer than poor whites.[37] Nearly half of Black children (45 per cent) live below the poverty line, whereas only 16 per cent of white children do. The pattern continues even among college-educated Blacks whose salaries are about three-quarters of their white counterparts, and only a few dollars above those of whites whose education stopped at high school. In times of both boom and recession, the unemployment rate of Blacks is double that of whites.[38] A typical white strategy to continue the economic subjugation of Blacks is that of taking such money as Blacks have out of Black pockets and adding it to white profits. Individually, African Americans may be poor, but cumulatively their wealth is an attractive target for white marketing. In 1988 *Dollars and Sense Magazine* estimated that, with a purchasing power of $210 billion, Black America was the twenty-seventh largest economy in the world.[39] As Darrell Gatlin says, "We are considered equal as long as we remain in our communities and spend our economic wealth in their domain."[40]

African Americans know well, for example, that Nike makes much of its profit by selling its highly priced sports footwear to them; yet, in one recent case, Nike refused to grant a franchise to a Black-owned store in an African American neighborhood of Philadelphia. In reporting this refusal the Amsterdam News commented: "All their advertising is geared to black folks and they're making millions of dollars, but they don't want us in the game," and "It's okay for these companies to sell to African Americans, to use Black athletes to promote their products, but not okay for African American businessmen to share in the process." The report concluded with the information that, of the 68,000 franchised Nike outlets, only about 100 are minority owned.[41]

This knowledge has not yet proved an effective defense against Nike's, but sometimes such Black counter-knowledge can. In 1985, for instance, a New York-based, Korean and Jewish owned company marketed a brand of sports shoes to inner-city Black and Latino men.[42] The brand name was "Troop." Rapidly a rumor spread that it was owned by the Ku Klux Klan and that it was a strategy to use Black dollars to fund the Klan's operations against them. In the rumor, Troop was interpreted as an acronym for To Rule Over Oppressed People, and it was believed that the words "Thank you nigger for making us rich" were hidden under the tread. The substance of the rumor was "untrue" in the objective sense, but the knowledge of an invasive economics was a true part of the Black experience. It was certainly true enough in its effects for the marketing director to go to a store in Montgomery, Alabama, and cut open five pairs to disprove it. Despite his efforts, the targeted market rejected the shoes, and the company folded.[43]

In a discussion on the *Gary Byrd Show* about the 1991 Kwanzaa, many expressed concern about whites profiting from the Black festival. There was unanimous horror at Hallmark's plans to market Kwanzaa cards in 1992, but there was more disagreement over locating some key events of Kwanzaa in the white Museum of Natural History, and of allowing the white *Daily News* to publish a Kwanzaa supplement and thus profit from

Black advertising while, admittedly, informing its Black readers (who comprise 60 per cent of its readership) and helping the career of the Black editor responsible for producing it. The defense of these decisions was cultural or informational—both the museum and the supplement improved Kwanzaa's accessibility—and the attack on them was economic: they diverted yet more money from Black pockets into white capital.

Even the lottery is seen by many Blacks as part of this white economic strategy. The Black knowledge of how Lotto works contradicts the official (white, scientific, statistical) account. Blacks know that all the really big money prizes go to white suburbs or rural townships far from the Black inner city areas where a disproportionately large number of the tickets are sold. So Harlem residents buy in mid-town Manhattan or even up-state New York. Charles Owens who lives in the Chicago suburb of Hazelcrest will drive up to three hundred miles to buy tickets in Peoria, Rockford, Lake Geneva—almost anywhere except Chicago's Black neighborhoods.[44] *Ebony* reports that this perception of racism in the lottery reached a peak early in 1991 when Black Chicagoans tried to win a near-record $61.5 million pot, only to see the winning tickets end up in the small and predominantly white suburbs of Cahokia, Waukegan and Zion. This was the last straw for Zeb Smith, a part-time carpenter and frequent lottery player, who has heard all the explanations about computers, mathematical odds and little bitty balls. "I've heard all that stuff," he says. "But somebody's got to explain to me why the numbers always seem to leap over Black areas and land in white areas."

It is not just the lottery winnings which are seen to go disproportionately to whites, it is also their profits. Despite the fact that Blacks spend more money on the game than whites, Black communities are not getting a fair allocation of the profits. Howard Brookins introduced a bill into the Illinois legislature that would have linked the distribution of revenues to the number of tickets sold in each community, thus ensuring that African American communities would get a fair return on their members' money. His bill was killed.

These two ways of knowing the racial inequality of the lottery (in its distribution of prizes or of profits) may not be equivalent in their relationship to those empirical data which form the truth base of scientific rationalism, but they are equivalent in the social truth of contemporary racism. A similar argument between empirical truth and socially specific truth can be seen in the case of the cheap cola. In the late 1980s, a white businessman produced a cola that tasted as good as Pepsi or Coke but cost half as much. Logically he thought its best sales would be in poor neighborhoods—thus in Black ones. Rumors spread rapidly in the neighborhoods that the cola was a secret product of the Ku Klux Klan and that it was laced with a substance that would produce impotence. An identical rumor about Church's Fried Chicken (its Klan ownership and sterilizing properties) was also widely circulated.[45] The capitalist explanation of the rumors, the one predictably held by the producer, was that they had been started by his competitors in order to ensure his product's failure and thus guard their profits. Systematically coherent with this knowledge of market competition was the knowledge that the Blacks who boycotted the product were duped, and they were thus shown to be inferior to the (white) rumor planters. Set in the Black knowledge of white economic exploitation of them, however, the rumors are understood quite differently. A white commodity which appears to minimize the amount of money it takes from the Black community cannot be properly understood in economic terms alone: this single instance must be understood in terms of the wider truth that whites exploit and subjugate Blacks. Belief in the rumor was defensive, localized knowledge whose (possible) inaccuracy in empirical scientific knowledge was of little interest and effectiveness in its immediate conditions of circulation. So, too, the perception of racist bias in the distribution of lottery prize money has a defensive, local truth which supports the more empirically based truth of racism in its distribution of profits. The base of each truth may be different, but each met the same fate in the hands of the white power-bloc—denial and rejection. It is hardly surprising that any empirical difference between these truths pales into insignificance in the light of their identical outcomes in racial politics.

So, too, white capital and Black neighborhoods understand the placement and content of billboards according to their quite different knowledge systems. In Englewood, a Black neighborhood on Chicago's South Side, there are one hundred and fifty billboards; in Wrightwood, a neighboring white community some ten blocks larger, there are nine.[46] Fifty of the Englewood billboards advertise alcohol and tobacco, one of the Wrightwood ones does. In the Black neighborhoods of Baltimore, 76 per cent of the billboards advertise alcohol or tobacco.[47] The Chicago billboard companies admitted these billboards were deliberately targeted at minorities. The Rev. Michael Pfleger, a pastor in Englewood, calls alcohol the number one problem in Black neighborhoods, and tobacco the leading killer drug in the US. These billboards are seen by many as yet other raids within the white assault: not only do they siphon off Black money into white profits, but, more importantly, they contribute to the lower life expectancy and higher infant-mortality rates and exacerbate the social and family problems which help keep Blacks down.

The same structural assault upon the health and strength of the Black body (both individual and communal) is continued in what African Americans call "environmental racism."[48] Environmental racism consists of dumping the toxic waste from white-owned industries into Black

246

neighborhoods, so that whites get rich and Blacks get sick. Three out of five African Americans and Latinos live in communities with *uncontrolled* toxic waste sites, and so do nearly half of Native and Pacific Islander Americans. A 1987 study found that race was the single most significant variable in determining the location of toxic dumps (socioeconomic status was second on the list).[49] Internationally, US industry is turning Mexico into its toxic garbage can, and in Bhopal over 3,000 Indians died from a leak in the white chemical plant owned by Union Carbide.

Closer to home, the West Harlem Environmental Action group points out that five of the six Manhattan bus depots are in or around Harlem, and are directly associated with "a high incidence of respiratory ailments, asthma and tuberculosis among young [Black] children."[50] The writer of the letter to *Harpers*, quoted above, in her list of white threats to Black survival includes environmental racism alongside AIDS infection, incarceration rates, graduation rates and life expectancy.

When Black communities, with their disproportionately inadequate health care, see themselves invaded from outside by toxic waste, by AIDS, by alcohol and tobacco billboards, they quite properly view "the drug war" as another piece in the same jigsaw. As Dr Cress Welsing, along with many others, points out, neither drugs nor guns are manufactured by Blacks anywhere in the world, yet the lethal effects of both are disproportionately experienced in African American neighborhoods. The war against drugs is seen as a white justification to intensify the assault on Black men. The war has done little to decrease the flow of drugs into Black communities, but it has had wide success in increasing the flow of Black men out of these communities and into white prisons. Military war works complementarily: while the drug war transfers the "worst" of Black men into one white institution (prison), military war transfers the cream, both men and women, into another (the military). Both wars weaken the Black community and strengthen the white, and provide solid ground for the belief, which extends well beyond Black communities, that the CIA covertly promotes the flow of drugs into Black neighborhoods as part of a strategy which has been in operation since the 1968 riots in Watts, Detroit and Newark, to induce a drugged Black quiescence.[51] The belief is consistent with the Black knowledge of the strategies of tobacco and alcohol advertising and of toxic waste disposal. As Patricia Williams says, "drugs bring pleasure to the biological catastrophe of having been born into the fearsome, loathesome packaging of an 'other' body."[52] Since slavery, African Americans have not controlled their own bodies. The body of the male slave was the laboring body of his master, the body of the female slave was to reproduce the same master's labor and to serve as his sexual territory. Police batons, drugs and AIDS descend upon the Black body (in both its individual and social forms) from outside, they weaken it, wrest it from the control of those who live within it and thus render it easier to subjugate. Batons and boots, legal and illegal drugs, pollution and AIDS—the assault upon the Black body is strategic, multifrontal and omnipresent.

NOTES

1. Naming is again a problem. I have followed the practice of much African American discourse by using "Black" and "African American" almost interchangeably. African American discourse also uses titles such as "Dr" or "Professor" when white discourse would not: I have adopted this practice as well.
2. Cited in Alexander Cockburn, "Beat the Devil," *The Nation*, 15 April 1991, pp. 474–5.
3. Ibid.
4. Two years later his family was awarded $1.1 million in damages. The jury found that the police had used excessive force and were guilty of negligence in the beating and hogtying. The award, however, was halved because the jury considered Mayberry to have contributed to his own death by confronting the police. *Wisconsin State Journal*, 21 October 1992, p. A6.
5. Cockburn, "Beat the Devil."
6. Ibid.
7. Cited by Jack Miles, "Black vs. Brown," *The Atlantic Monthly*, October 1992, p. 44.
8. Black Liberation Radio started life as WTRA (Tenants Rights Association). Its founder, then called Dewayne Readus, has now taken the name Mbanna Kantako. Accounts of "Rebel Radio" such as Black Liberation Radio (or WTRA) can be found in Richard Shereikis, "Making Radio Waves", *Chronicle*, July/August 1990, and *Columbia Journalism Review*, July/August 1990, p. 12; Bruce Girard and Ron Sakolsky, *Cultural Democracy*, no. 39, Spring 1990; Luis J. Rodriguez, "Rebel Radio, Rappin' in the 'Hood'," *The Nation*, 12/19 August 1991, and the Transcript of "Liberation Radio," *Radio Free Detroit*, 28 June 1990; Manning Marable, "Liberation Radio Shutdown," *The Guardian*, August 1984, p. 2; Michael Townsend, "WTRA: One-Watt Radio," *ArtPaper*, 19 January 1990; Bruce Girard and Ron Sakolsky, "Radio Activity: Community Action you can dance to," *Cultural Democracy* 39, Spring 1990, p. 306; Richard Shereikis, "Radio Free America," *Mother Jones*, vol. 15, no. 4, June 1990, p. 16; Michael Townsend, "Mbanna Kantako and the Micro-radio Movement, *Big Red News*, vol. 16, no. 50, December 1991; Ron Sakolsky, "Anarchy on the Airwaves: A Brief History of the Micro-Radio Movement in the USA," *Social Anarchism*, no. 17, November 1992, pp. 5–14; Jacob Ross, "The Power of the Pirates: Black Radio," *Artrage*, Winter 90/91, pp. 21–15.
9. Rodriguez, "Rebel Radio."
10. Ibid.
11. *Black Liberation Radio Newsletter*, Winter 1992, p. 4.
12. *Radio Free Detroit*.
13. Ibid.
14. Rodriguez, "Rebel Radio."
15. Ibid.
16. *Gary Byrd Show*, 13 December 1991.
17. Patricia Williams, *The Alchemy of Race and Rights* (Cambridge, MA: Harvard

University Press, 1991), p. 136.
18. Mike Davis, *City of Quartz* (London: Verso, 1990), p. 8.
19. Williams, p. 142.
20. James Traub, "A Black Counter-Reality Grows in Harlem," *Harpers*, August 1991.
21. *Times*, 28 March 1988, cited in Davis, *City of Quartz*, p. 272.
22. *New York Amsterdam News*, 10 August 1991, p. 1.
23. Ibid., p. 31.
24. *Harpers*, October 1991.
25. *Harpers*, November 1991.
26. Jawanza Kunjufu, *Countering the Conspiracy to Destroy BlackBoys, Volumes I, II, and III* (Chicago: African American Images, Vol. I 1982, Vol. II 1986, Vol. III 1990).
27. Listed below is a study that was done by several doctors comparing African and European American children and their ability to recognize stimuli and respond to it.

   (1) Nine hours old, being drawn up into a sitting position, able to prevent the head from falling backwards (Euro: 6 wks).
   (2) Two days old, with head held firmly, looking at face of the examiner (Euro: 8 wks).
   (3) Seven weeks old, supporting herself in a sitting position and watching her reflection in the mirror (Euro: 20 wks).
   (4) Five months old, holding herself upright (Euro: 9 months). Taking the round block out of its hold in the form board (Euro: 11 months).
   (5) Five months old, standing against the mirror (Euro: 9 months).
   (6) Seven months old, walking to the Gesell Box to look inside (Euro: 15 months).
   (7) Eleven months old, climbing the steps alone (Euro: 15 months).

   Kunjufu, pp. 4–5.
28. Cited in Studs Terkel, *Race: How Black and Whites Think and Feel about the American Obsession* (New York, NY: New Press, 1992), p. v.
29. Ibid., p. 35.
30. Ibid., p. 35.
31. William H. Grier and Price M. Cobbs, *Black Rage*, 2nd edn (New York: Basic Books, 1980).
32. Barbara Ransby, "The Gang Rape of Anita Hill and the Assault upon all Women of African Descent," *The Black Scholar*, 1992, vol. 22, no. 1 & 2, p. 83.
33. Dr Frances Cress Welsing, *The Isis Papers*.
34. A letter by Omega Allah to the *New York Amsterdam News* (26 February 1991, p. 12) is an example of this conspiracy on a global level:

   I stand with Saddam! Why would I fight for America when I know that the US military's Germ Warfare Department intentionally created the AIDS virus by splicing a virus in sheep called "visua virus" and a retrovirus in cattle known as "bovine leukemia virus." Smallpox vaccinations which were bound for Africa were then intentionally spiked and millions of Africans infected with the deadly disease.

35. Welsing, p. xii.
36. Kunjufu, *Lessons from History.*
37. "African Americans in the 1990s," report by The Population Reference Bureau.
38. Andrew Hacker, *Two Nations: Black and White, Separate, Hostile, Unequal* (New York: Charles Scribner's Sons, 1992).
39. Derrick Baker, "Moral Covenants: Moving Ahead or Standing Still," *Dollars and Sense Magazine*, 1988, vol. 13, no. 5, p. 66.
40. *New York Amsterdam News*, 31 August 1991, p. 12.
41. *New York Amsterdam News*, 9 February 1991, p. 10.
42. Rosemary Coombe, "Postmodernity and the Rumor: Late Capitalism and the Fetishism of the Commodity/Sign," in W. Stearns and W. Chaloupha (eds), *Jean Baudrillard: The Disappearance of Art and Politics* (London: Macmillan, 1992), pp. 98–108.
43. "Klan Rumor Helped Ruin Sport Clothing Firm," *San Francisco Chronicle*, 22 July

1989, in Coombe, "Postmodernity and Rumor."

44. *Ebony*, "Are State Lotteries Stacked against Blacks?," June 1991, pp. 126–30.
45. Patricia Turner, "Church's Fried Chicken and the Klan," *Western Folklore* 46, 1987, pp. 294–306.
46. *Adbusters*, Fall/Winter 1991, vol. 2, no. 1, p. 42.
47. *What Counts: The Complete Harpers Index* (New York: Henry Holt, 1991).
48. The term was coined by the civil rights leader, Rev. Benjamin Charis Jr. An influential study has been that of Prof. Robert Bullard, *Dumping in Dixie: Race, Class, and Environmental Quality*. The growing awareness of this problem among minority Americans resulted in the first National Minority Leadership Summit, which was held in Washington DC, in 1991. See also Lester Sloan, "Dumping, A New Form of Genocide?," *Emerge*, February 1992, pp. 19–20. In 1992 the Environmental Protection Agency admitted its failure to protect minority communities from pollution, but could make few effective recommendations for change, *USA Today*, 25 February 1992, p. 3A.
49. Commission for Racial Justice, "Toxic Wastes and Race in the United States," 1987.
50. Cited in Sloan, p. 20.
51. The lapel button, "Cocaine *I*mport *A*gency" makes the belief wearable.
52. Williams, p. 4.

12

POWER WORKS

POWER STRUGGLES

In critical cultural theory, power has replaced ideology as the key to the door behind which lurks the explanation of why late capitalism works so well for those who do so well in it, and why those who do not have seemingly not done much to change it. Power works, as I have argued, through alliances of social interests forged around specific issues that arise in particular conditions. The strategic fluidity of these alliances may cut across social categories or classes, or it may conform fairly closely to them, but a social theory that is grounded upon categorical difference, as ideology theory was, will miss or marginalize the fluidity. Equally, however, a theory that is purely poststructuralist or postmodern may miss or marginalize the struggles within this fluidity, for social struggles are often engaged in from the basis of a social category which is the organizing point for an alliance of interest. In the last chapter I recorded some voices whose defining and linking feature was their Blackness, but their Blackness did not associate them with all Black voices, nor did it exclude them from an association with non-Black ones. Their Blackness defined their particular mobilization of interests against white power without recruiting all Black people to their cause.

Social categories such as race, age, gender and class still matter, but they matter because they work as guiding principles in the formation of alliances and the promotion of interests, not because they determine the structure of social experience. And here we ought to separate race and gender from the others, for these stay with us for life, whereas age does not and class need not; race and gender provide less flexible determinations, and thus the intersections between them as social categories and the alliances formed to promote their interests are more closely matched than in other cases. But still, social categories function to operationalize power rather than determine ideological relations.

The shifting identities and relations that characterize daily life are formed along multiple axes of power, and this fluid multiaxiality loosens up the relations between the categories whose names we typically use to identify each end of each axis: masculine ↔ feminine; blue collar ↔ white collar; African American ↔ European American; African American ↔ Jewish American; African American ↔ Korean American. These categories do exist materially, but the articulations[1] among them by which they are made to make sense and through which they are put in practice are not always as fixed as they appeared to be in a structural world to a structuralist theory. Their effectivity (and categories are only formed because they *do* something, not because of what they *are*), which is their power dimension, is in constant process, and the alliances that particularize their multiaxial potential in any one application are formed by an agency (strategic or tactical, of the power-bloc or the people) that is able to see the relations between its interests and its immediate conditions.

An African American, for instance, can never escape the social category of Blackness, but the way that s/he or others put that category into practice is not a determined effect of the category alone, but a way of making it operational in social experience. The category has no essence that produces predetermined effects in identity or social relations, but it has a strong history of operations that shape those which can be set into motion in current conditions. The flip side of the coin, however, is that top-down racism often does conflate strategy with category, and will treat all African Americans as categorically and simply black. Crude power can always essentialize and operationalize a category when doing so will serve its interests. Such racist categorization is only one of the many forms that the relations between African American formations and ones of the power-bloc can take, as can those between African American and other racially or ethnically based social formations, and the differences between these relations both determine and are determined by the ways that "Blackness" is put into practice and its interests mobilized. These ways of knowing and practicing are the means by which a social category is turned into a social force. Racism can no longer be understood as the ideological structure of race relations which naturalizes one race's superiority, but must be seen as the struggle over the power to promote social interests that are always racial but never purely so and that function by putting racial difference into practice.

Blauner suggests that this "new racism" is more clearly understood by Blacks than by whites:

> Whites tend to accept older definitions of racism, common until the 1960s, that interpret it as an ideology of white superiority. ... Black respondents, however, tend to embrace newer definitions of "structural racism" that focus on the way discrimination is built into systems of power and institutions in the United States.[2]

This new racism crosses class differences between African Americans, for all feel it equally: professional, successful African Americans report no reduction in their encounters with discrimination in everyday activities such as working, shopping or banking.[3] This point was well made on CNN's *Moneyline* just after the LA uprisings. Stuart Varney introduced Robert Johnson as "the President of Black Entertainment Television, the first Black controlled company to be listed on the New York Stock Exchange ... [and] the founder and principal shareholder of the Black Entertainment Network." Addressing Robert Johnson directly, he asked:

> Sir, to be personal for a moment, you are clearly at the pinnacle of economic power and personal status in America, do you personally, today, encounter overt racism?
>
> JOHNSON   Absolutely. There's not a Black man or a Black woman alive that could not just as easily have been in the same situation as Rodney King.[4]

He went on to give a number of examples, including when standing by a parking lot being asked to fetch a white man's car. Having servant status taken for granted and being beaten by cops are very different, but the same power is at work in each. White power is applied by whites treating Blacks differently, and that treatment reduces the control Blacks have over their daily living: it simply makes life harder and its restrictions explicit. The waiter who, when two customers sit at his table, greets the white but not the Black, or the cashier who requires more forms of ID for a Black customer paying by check than for a white one, are both points of application of white supremacy.

The white power that bears down upon Black people in all the details of their lives spans the continuum from constant irritants, through major denials such as refusal of a mortgage or a loan to start a business, up to a systematic and merciless war such as that waged by the paramilitary LA Police Department upon African Americans and Latinos.[5] bell hooks finds the term "white supremacy" better than "racism" to explain her experience.[6] She quotes with approval John Hodge's remark that "the problem of racism is not prejudice but domination"[7] as a way of understanding how liberal whites welcome Blacks into their workplaces and their homes, but, when there "what we saw was that they wished to exercise control over our bodies and thoughts as their racist ancestors had—that this need to exercise power over us expressed how much they had internalized the values and attitudes of white supremacy."[8] She points out, sadly I feel, that while many of the changes in social policy and social attitudes produced by the Civil Rights Movement, particularly those encouraging racial integration, may have reduced the old racism, they have also served to reinforce and perpetuate white supremacy. Racial power operates effectively enough without an ideology of racial superiority and inferiority to underwrite it; indeed, the benign rejection of such an ideology may actually increase its efficiency.

This new racism is one of power rather than ideology, and Madonna, at least, would recognize its equivalent in gender politics. In explaining how she believes her work advances women's interests, she emphasizes her power to control her image, to control her behavior and to control the production and distribution of her work. The ability of a woman to control her femininity and be in charge of its social circulation is more important to her than the ideological meanings of femininity. Madonna does not reject all patriarchal meanings of the feminine; what she rejects is the patriarchal power to control them and to use them for patriarchal interests alone.

But if race, gender and other social relations no longer function within solely ideological structures, their field of operation is far from structureless. They operate always within a field of power, and their particularities typically take the form of hegemonic struggles. Hegemony theory accommodates the fluidity of alliances that characterizes poststructural conditions in a way that ideology theory cannot. Gramsci saw the signs of this fluidity developing as capitalism became more highly elaborated, and predicted that, as a result, wars of position (multifrontal, protracted, of varying intensity) would replace wars of maneuver (monofrontal, of crisis proportions, and focussed on a decisive breakthrough).

But though hegemony theory is adaptable to poststructural conditions, it differs from a Foucauldian theory of power in that its struggles are ones between identifiable social interests and not ones against a power system that is detached from them. Foucault's accounts of power at work do sometimes allow us to ignore the fact that some interests benefit more than others from its operations. The absence of a concept equivalent to that of the power-bloc debilitates Foucault's theory and may well account for his lack of analyses of resistance. Resistance against an "it" (a system) is harder to mobilize than resistance against a "them" (an identifiable social alliance), and thus most instances of resistance have been more readily understood by hegemonic analysis than by poststructural power analysis. My account of the equivalence of the oppositionalities between imperializing and localizing powers and those between the power-bloc and the people is an attempt to Gramscianize Foucault while Foucauldianizing Gramsci.

Foucault can show Gramsci that a vital battlefront is the body, for it is the focal point upon which multiaxial forces are brought to bear. Part of the intensity of bodily experience (which Grossberg has convincingly theorized as "affect")[9] is the arousal of the body's sensations produced as these focussed powers are momentarily evaded. The "hysteria" of the Elvis fan, the baseball fan taken out of her "self" by the excitement of the game, and the homeless men cheering and whistling at a movie all know their bodies as sites of pleasure where top-down power is experienced as its grip is shattered: the intensity of the pleasure involves both the grip and the release. Affect is not in itself either hegemonic or counter-hegemonic, it is neither power-bearing nor resistant, but it intersects with hegemony and power in ways that may on occasions resist, or in others exert, them. With the homeless men the intersection was resistant, and their pleasure lay in taking a trick in that endless game in which the deck is always stacked against them. The arousal of their physical sensations, which could emerge only in cheers and whistles not words, was not in itself resistant but it occurred in resistant relations to a field of power. The stationing power of the text of *Die Hard* to situate its characters, events and viewers in particular relations to the interests of the power-bloc, and to work hegemonically to promote them, was reproduced in the shelter's physical layout, its regulations and its function in applying the discourse of charity. This bimodal stationing (discursive and physical) saturated the men's environment, and the intense pleasure and arousal evidenced by their cheers can be understood only as a bodily escape from the grip of the station.

The affective moment of evasion does open up spaces where localized power and knowledge can operate. These spaces are not inevitably filled, but in this case they were. The bodies of the cheering homeless men became localized sites of experience where capitalism was known by ways other than hegemonic ones. Affect lies outside hegemonic power, but is always articulated to it, and can occur only in conditions produced by it.

"Hysteria" is the affect of the Elvis fan, and can be experienced only in a body situated where the axes of gender, age, race and class intersect in a power-saturated complex working to station her as "suburban." This affect is produced at the point of contestation between imperializing and localizing powers, between "their" station and her locale. Her locale is constituted in part by affect, for affect brings together the physicality of the fan's body and the social axes along which power flows and on which she must resist it. Her "hysteria," then, is an unstable mix of physical, hegemonic, power-bearing and affective forces. Her body is where they all come together: its physical adrenalin and hormonal surges; the hegemonic complex of the different sexisms of rock-'n'-roll and of the suburb—of race, age and class; the stationing power of the suburb to hold her body and behavior within its norms; and the affective intensity of her experience in breaking them. The body-locale of the fan is where her rearticulation of gender, class, race and age enables her to turn the oppressive sexism of the suburb into a rock-'n'-roll sexism which can work for rather than against her. ("Turning" is a common "trick" of localizing power—as Bill, the homeless man, exemplified when he turned the word "decent" to work in his interests.) Affect can be emancipatory only in its relation with this repressive complex of hegemony and imperializing power: peeing in the pants is not in itself liberatory, but in certain social relations it can be. The body (or, in this case, bladder) outside of a field structured by hegemony and power could never behave in this way.

Like his fans, Elvis's body, too, was a site where the normally disempowering ends of the axes (race, class, age and gender) could be rearticulated and turned into localizing power. The teenage locale so constructed was thoroughly articulate in both senses of the word: it spoke, or rather shouted, with its own voice of its own position in the social structure. Sports fandom appears to involve friendlier negotiations between affect, hegemony and power. The power-turning involved in male fan spectating and knowing complements hegemony and fills a lack in the experience it normally offers. In conditions like these, affect can work to secure hegemony and ally it with localizing as well as imperializing power. Blue-collar and/or young male sports fans gain power by allying themselves with operations that, in the normality of school or the workplace, work to disempower them.

The interests of the people take a wide variety of relations to those of the power-bloc. These are not always oppositional or evasive, but may involve accommodation or the seeking of a better fit between these interests. Daily life cannot be lived in conditions of continuous antagonism, the comfort of accommodating one's interests with those of the power-bloc is necessary, if only for periods of respite. What matters is that the movement in and out of those relations is controlled by the people and not by the power-bloc. Because "the people" is a shifting set of alliances that transsects social categories (including that of the individual) the same person may at different times ally her- or himself with formations of oppositional, evasive, accommodatory or any type of relationship with the power-bloc. Many of those rising up on the streets of Los Angeles may also have been, at other times and in other formations, sports fans, Elvis fans, churchgoers and disciplined members of the workforce.

While hegemony theory has much to offer, its limitations are reached sooner or later, and at this point, only a theory of power is adequate. The theory of power I have attempted to explore in this book is one which dissociates power from a categorically identifiable ruling class, but which grants the power-bloc privileged access to use its mechanisms to promote its interests, and it is one in which consent is nice but not necessary. Ted Stevens was not concerned to reach an agreement with the Smithsonian or with Carlos Fuentes: he wanted to use his power to silence them when they told "untruths" (his definition, his power). More importantly, in race relations, there is no sign of any consent on the part of African Americans to the new racism, nor that the Los Angeles Police Department, for instance, is working to achieve it. Cases like these lie far beyond the explanatory range of ideology theory, for in its account the disadvantaged acquiesce because they cannot know their disadvantage. In the US today, however, the disempowered know their disempowerment all too well, and if they are quiescent it is because they know equally well the power ranged against them. There is a despair among US underclasses for which ideology theory cannot account, but which overwhelmingly top-down power produces and only localizing powers can change.

RODNEY KING, ANITA HILL AND THE POLITICS OF POWER

Neither ideology nor hegemony played much of a role in the acquittal of the four police offices charged in the beating of Rodney King. Power won the day. Its key application was its success in moving the trial from South Central Los Angeles, where the incident occurred and where the population is largely African American and Latino, to nearby Simi Valley, a prosperous white neighborhood. But Simi Valley was not just any white neighborhood: 2,000 of the 8,300 officers of the LAPD lived there,[10] and as a result, all 300 of the prospective jurors had ties to the law-enforcement community—the twenty-seven who did not were excluded by the defence.[11] (It is also, maybe not coincidentally, the home of the Ronald Reagan Presidential Library.) This relocation had a significant effect upon the demographics of the jury pool, which resulted in a trial jury that included no African American.

This is an example of the "new racism," working through systematic power rather than a supremacist ideology. The defense arguments that won the day were based upon "objectivity": jurors who lived in the locality of the beating would have been too personally involved to be "objective." Because the instrumental effectiveness of objective knowledge has served the power-bloc well, it has institutionalized its exclusive claim to produce "truth." The "objectivity" of the inhabitants of Simi Valley, then, would guarantee the truth of the verdict they produced, and would exclude any possibility that such a "truth" had more to do with their social proximity to formations of the power-bloc than their objectifying distance from the incident. Moving the trial and knowing how to produce "truth" are techniques of power. The result was that a white defense was given a white context (discursive and social) to work in, and a Black prosecution was taken out of a Black one. The power to do this was equally discursive and physical: it was the power firstly to put the issue into the discourse of "objective truth" and thus to locate "justice" in the discursive field of the power-bloc; equally it was the power to ensure that this discourse would circulate in its home territory: a physical place and a social space that nourished power-bloc alliances. The defense won because it could put the power machine to work in a multimodal field (discursive, social, physical) that facilitated strategic alliances between it, a largely white middle-class jury, a white police force and a white judicial system.

The new rarely replaces the old, but usually overlies it. There were traces of the old racism in the naturalized assumption that a non-pigmented jury would be fair whereas a pigmented one would not. But ideological racism only exists when it works, and in the ideological realm the verdict failed: it was widely seen by Americans of all races and classes (even by President Bush) as unfair; it did not naturalize the ideas of the ruling class into the ideas of the nation. But power worked: the police were acquitted on all but one charge.[12]

In the Rodney King trial there was a worthwhile objective for power to achieve. In the case of the Black endzone dance, however, the value of the objective was less obvious, and it seemed that power was exercised simply to maintain its strength—it was lifting weights in the gym rather than lifting a block to build a pyramid. Muscles built in the gym may appear to be excessive and to perform no function other than that of impressing the weak, but, once built, they may always be put to physical use. To be able to do its work when it is necessary, power must exercise even when it is not.

The new racism of power can also be seen at work when African Americans who are comparatively successful in white America come up against what feminism has called "the glass ceiling"—an invisible barrier or force field which they cannot penetrate and which confines them where the power-bloc wishes. Vernon Andrews, a self-identified Buppie (Black urban professional) with "the condo, the BMW, tailored shirts, European vacation and designer ice cream,"[13] tells how he constantly banged his head against this "ceiling" in a large Silicon Valley computer firm, and how these experiences made him recall what

[B]lack radicals and my family, all of them well intentioned, had drummed into my head. "The white man will never let you get ahead. He'll always let you get just so far—then he'll either make you stay put or slap you down. He can take everything you have in a minute. Oh, he'll say he's your friend and he'll smile in your face, but never trust him. He's only using you."

I felt powerless in the matter. No matter how far I succeeded in this world, if eventually I was fired or otherwise failed, my family would chime, "See, I told you the white man would only let you get so far." If I continued to succeed indefinitely, some blacks would warn "Watch out, he'll only let you get so far."

Andrews knows that this knowledge, which is his Black knowledge, is also white power, for not only does it hold him back, it deprives him of the ability to control his own destiny. This "new racism" resembles the work of hegemony in that it appears to give the subordinate enough to win their consent to the system that subordinates them, but the resemblance only goes so far. The "glass ceiling," whether racial or gendered, is not a "point of consent" arrived at by struggle or negotiation, but a barrier erected by the power-bloc to safeguard its own position. When many Black men supported Clarence Thomas in the televised hearings for his appointment to the Supreme Court, it was not because they were sexist and either thought Anita Hill was lying or that his sexual harassment of her was unimportant; it was because what they saw was a Black man about to break through the glass ceiling, and in this light they knew that the white (male Democrat) Senators who were opposing his nomination were using Anita Hill not to advance the cause of women, nor to keep the court progressive rather than conservative, but to reinforce a racist barrier to power. Clarence Thomas may well have been conscious of this when he strategically "turned" the politics of the hearings from gender to race by referring to them as "a high-tech lynching of an uppity Black man."[14]

The hearings were such a significant and controversial event in 1991 partly because their politics were so complex and so contradictory. They could be understood in a number of different ways according to how the multiple social axes involved were articulated: party political thought articulated them around the axes of Democrat vs. Republican, progressive vs. Conservative, left vs. right; in gender politics they showed a lone woman up against ranks of men wielding immense institutional power; in racial politics they showed white against Black, and also what sort of Black a given formation of whites would support or oppose; in more populist politics they showed one of "us" against "them," the ordinary person against "Washington" (a distant echo, perhaps, of Elvis against the "upper echelons").

These hearings provide a clear example of the problems facing the analyst in poststructural politics when the social categories have lost the fixity of their relations to each other. In them, progressive women who supported Anita Hill formed a tactical alliance with Senator Edward Kennedy, whose personal sexual politics, like those of most of the Kennedy men, are ones they would vehemently oppose. But the intersection here of the gender politics of the workplace (sexual harassment) with the gender politics of the law (Thomas was believed to want to overturn Roe v. Wade) and with progressive social policies in general not only allied them *on this issue* with a male chauvinist, but against a Black who was about to maintain the only non-white presence on the Supreme Court (an objective they would normally applaud). For them, Thomas's conservatism and maleness were articulated more emphatically than his Blackness; on other issues the articulations may have been reversed. Equally contradictorily, this alliance was formed around a woman who was widely perceived as conservative and who, in a previous hearing for an appointment to the Supreme Court, had supported "that man with the notoriously racist and sexist reputation, Judge Robert Bork, in his unsuccessful campaign for a seat on the Supreme Court,"[15] and had taught in the right-wing Christian fundamentalist Oral Roberts University. (Anita Hill claims to have been misunderstood on her support for Bork.[16]) Similarly, racist Republican supporters would have had to ally themselves with Democrats, feminists and a Black woman to maintain the glass ceiling and "keep Blacks in their place." So it is not surprising if, on this issue, some progressive non-sexist Black men gave highest priority to the racial axis and allied themselves with white Republicans whom normally they would oppose. Robert Staples gives his account of the tactical and strategic fluidity and the consequent apparent contradictions of the alliances involved:

> And old alliances meant nothing. The former segregationists, the current perpetuators of racial buzzwords (e.g., quotas, welfare, crime) found themselves supporting a black man, with a white wife. Anita Hill's most visible supporters were middle-class white women, who identified with her issue—if not with her. Most non-southern white Democratic males sided with Hill and Republican white males overwhelmingly supported Thomas. Since people claimed that it was impossible to tell who was telling the truth, they came down on the side of their racial, gender or political preferences and interest— at least the whites did. Blacks were almost divided down the middle over Thomas (about 60% supported him after the hearings).[17]

Politics that are fought on a multiaxial terrain; politics that are fought around perceived social interests in which gains often have to be paid for with losses; politics that involve strategic and tactical alliances formed for occasions and issues; these politics of fluidity, contradiction and uncertainty are the politics with which we have to cope in late capitalism, and while they pose problems for analysis, those involved in them are able to pick their positions with reasonable surefootedness.

Apparent victories are no more stable than the struggles that precede, and often succeed, them. In this case the power-bloc won and Clarence Thomas was admitted to the Supreme Court. But nine months later, the *New York Times* ran a front page story that began:

> Sexual harassment complaints to the Equal Employment Opportunities Commission are up sharply [by over 50 per cent], Congress and the White House have responded to complaints of sexual abuse in the military in ways that would have been unimaginable nine months ago. Employers are scurrying to hire sensitivity trainers to teach men how to treat women. And men are wondering how they failed to notice the anger of their female colleagues. This change in American attitudes, experts of both sexes and all political persuasions agree, is a direct result of last fall's nationally televised colloquium on sexual harassment, the Anita Hill–Clarence Thomas hearings.[18]

The article could have added that donations to the Women's Campaign Fund have run at double their pre-hearings rate, that more women than ever before have stood for election in 1992, that enrollments in women's studies courses in universities surged, and that for months after the hearings women were wearing lapel buttons proclaiming "I believe Anita Hill." *60 Minutes* ran a sympathetic portrait of Anita Hill's life after the hearings, and the sitcom *Designing Women* delayed its prepared episode and, the week after the hearings, aired one in which its characters watched them on TV, argued about them, and gave a national voice to women's pride in Anita Hill's courage, to their anger at her treatment, to their dismay at the verdict and to their determination not to take it lying down. The episode climaxes with a passionate outcry by Mary Jo:

> I'm sorry! Your time is up. Listen, I don't mean to be strident and over-bearing, I used to be nice, but quite frankly, nice doesn't cut it. We want to be treated equally and with respect. Is that too much to ask? Like a lot of women around this country tonight I'm mad! I'm mad because we're 51 per cent of the population and only two percent of the United States Senate. I'm mad because 527 men in the House of Representatives have a pool, a sauna, a gym and we have six hair dryers and a ping pong table. I'm mad because in spite of the fact that we scrub America's floors, wash her dishes, commit very little of the crime, and have all of the babies, we still make 58 cents on the dollar. As a matter of fact, I don't know about the rest of the women out there, but I don't give a damn anymore if you call me a feminist or a fruitcake—I just know I am so mad I am going to get in my car and drive to the centermost point of the United States of America and climb to the top of a tower and shout "Don't get us wrong, we love you, BUT . . . who the hell do you men think you are?"

The episode ends with a series of shots from the hearings, and then one of President Bush in the White House rose garden, flanked by Clarence Thomas, proclaiming to the crowd and the cameras: "America is the first nation in history founded on the idea, on the unshakable certainty, that all men are created equal." As he speaks the word "men", the screen shows us a close-up of Anita Hill's weary and (momentarily) defeated face.

If, on the gender front, the victory was uncertain, on a more populist one, Washington lost. There was a widespread belief that regardless of the outcome, the hearings gave the US public a clear view of how badly politicians could behave. On the front of "Them" vs. "us," of "Washington" vs. "everyday America," television inflicted grievous damage upon the credibility of "the system." Not only fictional programs refused to let the verdict be the last word: typical of many responses was that of WXYZ TV in Detroit. Bill Bonds, a news anchor on the station, interviewed Orrin Hatch, one of the Republican senators who had attacked Anita Hill so unscrupulously:

BILL BONDS I have to say to you, sir, as an American from the Midwest, that, frankly, that was kind of an embarrassing spectacle. Do you regret that that went on?

ORRIN HATCH It was a tense, difficult process, as it should be. And it was made worse because of one dishonest senator who leaked raw FBI data...

BONDS Senator, you guys leak all the time.

HATCH No, that's not true.

BONDS Who are you trying to kid? You guys leak stuff all the time.

HATCH Let me just say something, that's not true.

BONDS Yes, it is.

HATCH No, not FBI reports from the Judiciary Committee. I've been here fifteen years. I have not seen leaks of FBI reports, because they contain raw data...

BONDS Okay, your conduct was great. You guys all looked terrific; 250 million Americans are really proud of Senator Orrin Hatch and all the rest of you guys.

HATCH I'm not, I'm not...

BONDS You did a marvelous job. You never made the country look better. Let me ask you something: what are you going to do if you find out six months from now that Clarence Thomas—who you've just about made into a saint—is a porno freak?

HATCH Don't worry, we won't. But I'll tell you this: if you're going to interview us in the future, you ought to be at least courteous. You're about as discourteous a person as I've ever interviewed with. I don't like it, and I don't like what you're doing. I go through enough crap back here, I don't have to go through it with you. Let me tell you something...

BONDS No, let me tell you something...

HATCH   No, you tell yourself something. I'm tired of talking to you. [Removes microphone and steps off-camera.]
BONDS   Okay, fine. I'm tired of talking to you. See you later.[19]

The anger between Bonds and Hatch is symptomatic of the antagonism between the people and Washington, and the abrupt termination of the interview is a sign of the broken trust of which the antagonism is only one consequence.

But these are white turnings of the Senate vote: their positioned victories were won by different alliances within the white population. In African America, the hearings were seen very differently. One widespread view was that whites won and Blacks lost. Trellie Jeffers felt that "black women were raped on national television, and black men were doused with gasoline in front of one million viewers."[20] Charles Lawrence saw the hearings as a continuation of "a history of black men lynched and castrated, of black women raped—with no fear of consequences."[21] US Representative Charlie Hayes considered that both Thomas and Hill were lynched by the hearings, and that "if one or both parties were Caucasian the scenario would have been drastically different, Americans would not have been privy to such a spectacle." [22] Two Blacks fighting in front of a white audience is a recurrent event in US history, and one whose only beneficiary is white power.

Other African Americans saw that the hearings represented "our total subordination in the political machinations of a tiny calculating elite."[23] Many shared the view that Anita Hill was used by white Democrats and white feminists to advance their own agendas, but not that of Black people in the same way as Clarence Thomas was used by white Republicans to advance theirs. It was tragically easy to see the Hearings as a contest between a Black man and white feminists,[24] and even moderate Black women were critical of the feminist performance:

> Content to rest their case on a raceless tale of gender subordination, white feminists missed an opportunity to span the chasm between feminism and anti-racism. Indeed, feminists actually helped maintain the chasm by endorsing the framing of the event as a race versus a gender issue.[25]

For other Black women, however, the erasure of gender rather than race advanced Black patriarchy, for it defined the race as implicitly masculine and thus continued the double oppression of Black women: "The Hill-Thomas confrontation reinforced the perception that any Black woman who raises the issue of sexual oppression in the African American community is somehow a traitor to the race, which translates into being a traitor to Black men."[26] Calvin Hernton makes the point forcefully when he writes:

> The ideology of race first and sex second fosters both white supremacy and male supremacy, and it underpins the racial oppression of black women and men. At the same time it underpins the sexual oppression of both black and white women...
>
> Because it is impossible to separate their sex from their race, and since they are at once sexually and racially oppressed, the primary target of the ideology of race first and sex second are black women ... the ideology of race first and sex second verifies and denies that sexual oppression exists, and it prohibits and penalizes anyone who says that sexism and racism are intertwined and that they should be fought as one.[27]

In this light, Anita Hill's decision to break the silence imposed by the ideology of "race first" could be seen as a victory. The Hearings allowed a Black woman and her oppression to be heard by millions across the nation:

> But here is the bottom line. Supreme Court Justice Clarence Thomas was confirmed because he invoked the image of a black man hanging. They don't make ropes for black women's lynchings or destroy us with high drama. Instead, it is the grind of daily life that wears us slowly down, the struggle for a dignified survival. Black women work the same endless day white women do, but when we juggle work and family, we also bear the burden of the racism that shapes the composition of our households. We are not lynched, just chipped at by the indignity swallowed, the harassment ignored, the gossamer thread of job security frayed by last hired, first fired. We have been taught silence, and Anita Hill's lifted voice is evidence that she finally found the Sojourner within her.[28]

On television, Anita Hill showed Americans "the place where African-American women live, a political vacuum of erasure and contradiction... existing within the overlapping margins of race and gender discourse and in the empty spaces between, it is a location whose very nature resists telling."[29] But Anita Hill told it, and her story was the spur for Black women to form a grass-roots organization called *African American Women in Defense of Ourselves*. Their manifesto, signed by over 1,600, was published in a full-page advertisement in the *New York Times*[30] and reprinted widely. They continued the public speech that Anita Hill began. Barbara Smith calls this a "watershed in black feminist organizing." "Never before," she writes, "have so many black women publicly stated their refusal to pit racial oppression against sexual oppression," and she goes on to record the continued outpouring of support and the organizers' intention to create a mechanism for organizing and speaking out.

This intersection between the race and gender axes is complicated still further when class enters the scene. Nellie McKay has pointed to class differences among Black women:[31] for instance, the agony of trying to reconcile the damage to African Americans in general caused by the hearings with the empowerment of Black women by Anita Hill was a middle-class agony; among working-class Black women there was a feeling that Anita Hill was a middle-class wimp, and that a working-class woman would have dealt firmly with his harassment at the time—if necessary with an appropriately aimed shoe. Nancy Fraser, too, suggests that there was a counter-discourse of class resentment that was mobilized against Anita Hill: it worked to bourgeoisify her as well as whiten her.[32] George Bush's claim that only the elites and leaders (both Black and feminist) opposed Clarence Thomas, whereas ordinary Americans supported him, was a strategic use of this discourse. Orlando Patterson, on the *New York Times* Op Ed page, showed how another conservative Black man in alliance with the power-bloc could use the discourse of class to trivialize Thomas's sexual harassment: he argued that it was only Anita Hill's elitism that made the remarks offensive, and that either a working-class or a (truly) Black person would have taken them as lightly as they were intended in Thomas's "down-home style of courting."[33] In these arguments there is a hint that class is an important factor in attributing priority to race or gender. There may be a general agreement among African Americans that racism overrides classism; but overriding is not erasing.

Twelve months later *Ebony* dubbed 1992 "The Year of the Black Woman": "For this year . . . the power and presence of Black women is being felt in politics, literature, sports, entertainment, science, education and religion."[34] The magazine leads its account of Black women's achievements with that of Carol Moseley Braun, the Illinois Democrat Senate nominee who became the first Black woman to be elected to the Senate. She won the primary election over two well-financed white men, one of whom, the incumbent Alan Dixon, voted for Clarence Thomas and lost the primary because he did so. Her success was attributed to the alliance that she forged between inner-city Blacks, women and others disillusioned with Washington politics; the most influential factor in making this alliance possible was Anita Hill. Braun is not alone. Black women challenged for seats in either the House of Representatives or Congress in at least ten states.[35] Johnetta B. Cole, the first Black woman president of Spelman College, summarizes "The Year of The Black Woman":

What dynamics have come into play to make this possible? Surely it is a complex of factors, but among them must be: The role of law professor Anita

Hill in bringing the issue of sexual harassment before the eyes of millions of Americans; the fact that large numbers of Americans are tired of the antics of so many politicians and are interested in seeing if women can do any better; and the coming of age of Black feminism as a connector between the modern Black Liberation and Women's movements.[36]

If the Anita Hill case can indeed be made to forge alliances between the Black Liberation and the women's movements and to bridge the gaps that have sometimes separated them, then this may prove in the long term to be the most politically significant victory of all. Nellie McKay believes that it can; she is confident in her belief that Anita Hill is the best thing that has happened to the feminist movement for the past twenty-five years. The success of Carol Moseley Braun is a welcome indicator that the possibility can be realized.

The struggles to reclaim the verdict of the hearings were as contradictory and multiaxial as the alliances formed around them. But we must recognize that this analysis of their multiaxiality comes with the benefit of hindsight and from outside the battleground: those who engaged in the struggle at the time did not fight on all axes but tended to give high priority to one or two, and to ignore or minimize others. It would appear that effective engagement requires a focus of energy that reduces the fronts on which one fights and therefore the alliances one forms, whereas long-term coalition-building requires a much broader grasp of the contradictions that often work against effective action. Politics in a poststructural world are far from easy.

Mbanna Kantako, who speaks for a community with relatively homogeneous social conditions, can work along more generally agreed and more singular axes. In his locale, the alliances that matter are first those between the Black spokespeople and his community and white fellow travellers, and second those between the white "cave-boys" and black "Afro-Saxons," or "house niggers," who oppose them. In local struggles alliances can be simplified and thus made more operationalizable, and the more local the locale, the clearer the battle lines. The Black community of *WLIB* is set in more diverse social relations than is *Black Liberation Radio*, so that *WLIB* has to face problems of alliance forming between African Americans and Latinos that are not an issue in Springfield.

On its home turf in Washington, the power-bloc may have won the Hearings, on other fronts it did not. In wars of position, a victory on one front can always be countered by defeats on others: in this case history has yet to tell us which victories and which defeats are the more significant.

In the Rodney King trial, too, the power-bloc on its own turf won and the police were acquitted: but when that verdict sparked the worst urban uprising in US history it is hard to see it as a clear cut victory.[37] The smaller but no less significant uprisings in Black communities across the nation were more than just explosions of pent-up anger. They contradicted emphatically and publicly the official view that it was individual police officers who were on trial. The uprisings argued forcefully that what was on trial, and wrongly acquitted, was the system of policing and the white supremacist power that directed it. The not-guilty verdict of the Simi Valley jury was contradicted by numerous guilty verdicts across the nation.

Wars of position are popular wars because in them defeats (and the people suffer many) are never final, and victories (and the people win few) are never secure. Popular fighters need tactical mobility, and cannot allow themselves to be stationed fixedly in a social category or a set articulation of forces. Mobile ways of framing social conflict are of greater use for them than social categories; the framing devices of "the haves vs. the have-nots" or "issues where I can or cannot make some difference" (see Chapter 2) are used opportunistically and tactically both to select the fronts on which to fight and the alliances by which to organize one's forces.

WEAK RACISM

In these poststructural politics, fought by alliances around issues, we need to recognize a clear distinction between imperializing or "strong" racism, and localizing or "weak" racism. Strong racism is where the strategic interests of the power-bloc are operationalized, but weak racism is that of the racially oppressed seeking to defend their own interests. Its defensiveness does not mean, however, that it never uses aggressive tactics: in times of crisis, or when defenders feel that their boundaries have been compressed too far, then defensive interests may well result in aggressive behavior. When the enemy is an alliance rather than a social group then this aggression may, at times, be misplaced onto a social group (or a race) that appears to embody that alliance, for a social group has a material presence against which anger can be physically, often violently, directed in the way that an alliance does not.

"The haves" is an alliance that is perceived from below rather than one forged from above. Its fluidity enables race, class, gender and age to be mixed within it according to the conditions of its use. In commenting on the LA uprisings, both Wesley Snipes (a Black actor) and Charlie Sheen (a white one) used it:[38] Wesley Snipes argued to Jim Morelli the need

to confront on a daily basis issues of race relations, exploitation and oppression—and the *despair* that's in this country—especially by those

267

amongst the haves, and *we* are in the haves, the upper echelons who will never experience what people are acting out, *crying* out against...

He sets "the haves," "the upper echelons" (and later "the powers that be") against the "people," or the have-nots, and goes on to argue, echoing Black feminists in the Anita Hill case, that the have-nots are deprived not only of material goods but of voices:

I've seen women with children out there protesting, and doing other things, these are the people who don't usually have a voice, and usually feel that the powers that be are so great that they'd never win anyway so why open my mouth about it, but ... this situation affords them the opportunity to lash out and cry out and basically to take what they feel they deserve.

What "the haves" call "looting" is also speaking, asserting a presence, and the stores of South Central, many of which were Korean, became opportunistic sites for reversing both material and semiotic deprivation. In the LA uprisings, the Korean store counter became one of physical boundaries between "the haves" and the "have-nots," for through Black eyes the Korean store owner looked like one of "the haves": they had the power to locate their stores in Black neighborhoods and thus to continue the white strategy of taking Black dollars out of the Black community, they employed Koreans, not Blacks, as part of this strategy, and in one notorious case one had the power to shoot a Black teenage girl for appearing to steal a bottle of orange juice—15-year-old Latasha Harlins was shot in the back of the head by Korean grocer Soon Ja Du and died with the money for her purchase in her hand. Mike Davis was told repeatedly on the streets of South Central "This is for our baby sister. This is for Latasha."[39] A white judge sentenced Du to a $500 fine and community service. This verdict, the incident and the store video camera's recording of it were well known among the LA African community; the connections between this verdict (almost an acquittal) and the Rodney King one were clear and were used to situate Korean Americans alongside whites in the alliance of "the haves" that allows white cops and Korean grocers to kill Blacks with impunity.

The boundary between the categories of "the haves" and "the have-nots" (which often identifies a material point of difference between the power-bloc and the people) moves according to who is constructing the category. For these Blacks, the Korean store owners fell into the same category as whites; for the Koreans, however, this would certainly not have been the case; and whites would have included Koreans in their social category only when it suited them to do so. One of these relatively rare occasions was when Pat Buchanan in his speech to the 1992 Republican Convention called the Korean store owners "the heroes of LA."

In the uprisings, Korean stores were one of the targets of Black and Latino rage: "Koreatown" is part of South Central Los Angeles, and thus Korean store owners were seen as that fraction of "the haves" upon which the anger of "the have-nots" could be most effectively directed. For some African and Latino Americans the Korean store was the best immediate object of racial anger because it was in their locality, because it was one of the weakest targets in "the haves," and because, therefore, it was the point where the weak could best gain a tactical and visible "victory." Of course, the white power-bloc interests are well served when racial antagonism flares between two minorities, and the white media gave us many images of the conflict between Koreans and Black and Latino youths. (Spike Lee's movie *Do the Right Thing* had shown us similar tensions in New York some three years earlier, but he had shown them more from the viewpoints of those involved than from those of the white power-bloc.) But the point to make is that the category of "Korean American" is not structurally fixed, it may be articulated with that of the white power-bloc ("the haves") or with that of a racial minority ("the have-nots"). It is the second of these articulations that locates "Koreatown" in Black neighborhoods and that generally situates racial "minorities" in economically deprived inner-city areas.

It is this articulation, too, which limits the advantages that Korean Americans are able to win for themselves, while maximizing those of the white power-bloc. So, while Asian Americans are accorded the status of a model minority and their successful assimilation of "American" (read power-bloc) values is applauded, they are confined to the "working class" levels of white-collar industry and are kept below the same "glass ceiling" as women and African Americans. More importantly, their "success" is used to prove that the comparative "failure" of Black Americans and Latinos to assimilate and prosper in the same way is, therefore, their own fault. Korean Americans may be strategically useful to "the haves" but they are kept safely on the margins of that elite group.

From the point of view of the "have-nots," however, these distinctions are either invisible or unimportant. The Korean store in a Black or Latino neighborhood may be a concrete and glass sign of an alliance between Asian and European American interests that, in other forms, is used by some whites to argue against affirmative action programs, to harden social policies and, once again, to blame the victim. From this point of view, Korean Americans are articulated with whites and are heard speaking in their accents. It is this articulation that makes them local targets of Black and Latino anger.

Both articulations promote white interests, but only one of them can be made to serve even short-term Black ones. The problem with issue-specific articulations is that general structural articulations still exist and a focus on the one may keep the other off the agenda. In Crown Heights, New York, tensions between Jewish and African Americans may have focussed on the local issue at the expense of the wider structure; the LA uprisings, however, were of such magnitude that their effects reverberated at all levels.

Interracial antagonisms take many forms which pervade our current global and national relations. They constitute one of the most urgent problematics facing us. There is no utopian solution in sight, and probably none exists, but the absence of a solution should not discourage us from taking small steps along the path of amelioration. It may be impossible to conceive of a social order that is completely fair to all, but it is very easy to imagine one that is more fair than the one we currently live in. We can identify the direction in which we need to turn our steps, without necessarily having our ultimate destination in sight. Because interracial tensions take many different forms, many different steps will have to be taken to ameliorate them and to move towards a social order where racial differences can intersect at points of consent rather than points of antagonism.

Any movement towards such a social order will depend upon the power-bloc reining back its imperializing power and allowing subordinated social formations greater localizing powers to extend their terrain of control. If they do not, then what might have been points of consent will become points of antagonism, and what might have been peaceful will become violent. Violence is nourished by the lack of self-determined space, both physical and social, by sensing that the boundaries of the space one controls are always closing in, and knowing the pressure of power behind those enclosing walls. Eleanor Bumpurs saw the police coming at her through the door and Ronald Reagan through the walls, and she struck at them with her knife. And they killed her.

Imperializing power which, through desperation or greed, extends its reach further than it needs to simply because it can, prevents the subaltern from exerting what seems quite reasonable control over their immediate conditions. When the walls have closed in too far, the normally defensive stance of localizing power can become aggressive and antagonistic. In many instances this antagonism is misdirected away from the imperializing power whose operations occasioned it and towards the localizing power of other subordinated social formations. A localizing power is always weaker than imperializing power, and is all the better for being so, but when the squeeze of imperialism makes its inherent tolerance untenable it often tries to increase its control at the expense of a neighboring locale both because, being weaker, it offers less opposition, and because, being local, it offers an immediate target.

Violence necessarily operates within the physical dimensions of the locale, whereas the closing of the walls that is one of its causes operates as much in the dimension of social relations, identities and ways of knowing. The white power-bloc is strategically adept at keeping its bodies, houses and neighborhoods physically distant from those it represses, and thus the violence which its strategy often occasions is typically misdirected to targets selected for their availability rather than their tactical advantage.

In reporting the LA uprisings, television constantly replayed helicopter footage of Black youths dragging Reginald Denny, a white truck driver, from his cab and beating him as he lay on the ground. The video of the incident was presented—and, I suspect, received by many whites—as a reverse replay of that of the Rodney King beating. As such, it was a discursive strategy whose objective was to apportion blame equally between Black and white America and thus served to promote the interests of the power-bloc by erasing racial difference.

In California's Democratic primary elections for the Senate, which took place soon after the uprisings, Gray Davis ran a campaign ad using this footage, with a voice over saying "It's not white people's fault there were riots in LA. It's not black people's fault there were riots in LA. A few thousand thugs—black, brown and white—terrorized all law-abiding citizens." Putting the uprisings into the discourse of law and order ("riots," "thugs," "law-abiding citizens") rather than of social or racial justice is a power-bloc strategy that is part of the problem, not of the solution. The equalizing of "no blame" serves white interests more than Black, and is subtly contradicted by the discursive patterning of the voice-over—when discussing who is *not* at fault, "white" precedes "black," but when it comes to who *is* at fault, "white" comes after "black" and "brown." The same contradiction was activated by the visuals which showed black "thugs" and a white "law-abiding citizen." This apparent erasure of racial difference actually erased not the difference but the white responsibility, and the white power to produce the discourse of explanation. The whiteness of this power is foregrounded by the fact that this was an ad for a Democrat: when race enters the political arena, white party differences are often elided and support is given to the popular perception of both Republicans and Democrats as "them-not-us."

This power to erase racial difference depended upon the power to erase the discursive differences between this video and that of the Rodney King beating. These were as stark as the racial differences, and it is frightening to think that the power to deny them may well have been widely effective in white knowledge. Let me just list some of the most obvious: the second beating would not have happened if the first had not; Black youths do not wield the same power as white cops, nor do they wield it in the same way (the grim efficiency of the police beating differed sharply from the opportunistic, intermittent, though still horrific, violence of the second); an isolated incident in a crisis situation is not equivalent to a routine incident in an everyday one; Black people rescued Reginald Denny and took him to hospital, nobody rescued Rodney King. And the power to represent differed on the plane of the signifier: the Rodney King incident was videoed by an amateur, fixed in a poor viewpoint, at night, with cheap equipment, so the images were blurred and weak: the second incident was videoed from a TV station's helicopter, which could move to the panoptically most efficient viewpoint; its camera gave clear, close-up, powerful images.

This list of differences between the two incidents is intended to criticize the white discourse that equalized them, and to illuminate but not condone the violence of the second. While this violence may be understandable, it was completely misdirected. The whiteness of the truck driver and his presence in a Black neighborhood at a time of racial crisis did not make his body into a materialization of the power-bloc, and the blows upon it finally did more damage to Black interests than white, for they reproduced far too precisely the stereotypes of white racism. The violence was cruel, unnecessary and tactically inept.

The violence against Korean stores was also misdirected, but not so totally. As argued earlier, the stores could be seen as sites for the application of power-bloc strategy. Relations between racial minorities are a delicate and dangerous terrain for a white to enter, particularly as antagonism between them always serves the interests of white power. But white power is deeply involved in those relations, and white voices as well as rainbow ones need to criticize it. Negotiations to make the points of interface between racial minorities ones of consent rather than conflict (such as those between Koreans and Blacks in LA after the uprisings) must be conducted between those most immediately involved, but they must also be conducted in social conditions structured by white power. As the excessiveness of this power was formative in the conditions which nourished the violence, so a withdrawal of its repressive operations and an application of its more benign ones will be formative in the conditions within which the negotiations may succeed. As a white, I wish to direct my criticism to the formative operations of white power rather than to the behaviors of those subjected within it.

When in the eyes of one racial formation another appears to be forming alliances with the power-bloc in conditions which deny both of them the power to control adequate social terrain, imperializing power is operating in those relations as well as in their surrounding conditions. When the space available for control is squeezed, enlarging one's own may seem more achievable by squeezing further that of another subordinated formation. In Miami, African Americans and Latinos may struggle with each other for social space that the power-bloc denies both or either: in Brooklyn, Jewish and African Americans may contest equally constrained space. Though horizontal in their general direction, these conflicts are not precisely so: in each case one party is perceived as allying itself with the power-bloc against the other.

The antagonism between some African and Jewish Americans is one of the most distressing and stressful examples of inter-subaltern racial tension, particularly as it cannot be separated from a much broader history of anti-Semitism. But separate it we must, if only partially and temporarily, if we are to understand its particularity within the contemporary US. An example, a painful one, will serve to raise some of the issues we have to face. Talking on *Black Liberation Radio*, a historian (whose name I could not decipher) told of his research into a business spin-off from the slave trade. Entrepreneurs from the North East would take large ships to slave auctions in the South and buy cheaply those slaves whose injuries on the Middle Passage had rendered them worthless to plantation owners. (A fit slave may have sold for up to $40, but $1 was the going price for an injured one.) These injured slaves were kept alive until they could be sold as cadavers to North Eastern hospitals and medical schools for research. These businessmen were then identified as Jewish. Although the slave holocaust and much subsequent history is shown to be a white perpetration, the Jewish role within it was constantly remembered on *Black Liberation Radio*, and was argued to be part of a worldwide Jewish conspiracy to exploit whatever and whomever they can for their own interests. This knowledge appeared to exceed the needs of defensiveness: it could, therefore, be seen as racist and, by Jews, with some justification. But when whites call such weak racism "racist" they often do so to avoid acknowledging their own responsibility for the conditions within which it flourishes. The people are social agents, they do make their own history and they are responsible in part for the history that they make. But, as Marx reminded us, the conditions within which they have to work are not of their making: the formative effects of these conditions are not their responsibility nor are they responsible. These formative conditions are the responsibility of power-bloc alliances, for they are the product of that power's operations. As a white, I wish to focus my critique upon the conditioning effects of white, strong racism rather than on the tactical uses of defensive, weak racism within them. Changing those conditions is crucial for encouraging more consensual tactics.

It is difficult for a white to assess whether or not *Black Liberation Radio*'s discussion of the Jewish involvement in slavery exceeded defensiveness, but its weak anti-Semitism did not divert its account of white power as the major driving force of the slave business. Despite this, however, there was a tendency to explain the involvement of some Jews in the slave trade by their Jewishness, which is not unique to *Black Liberation Radio* but is typical of the tension between African and Jewish America. On other occasions Kantako's anger is explicitly directed at elite Jews and their alliances with white power, not against Jews in general. (A regular broadcaster, Ron Sakolsky, is in fact Jewish.) Here Black anger is well aimed. It is only when it is directed against an ethnic group in general, rather than at alliances between certain interests of that group and power-bloc interests, that it is misdirected.

Leonard Jefferies' account of the role played by Jewish moguls in Hollywood in deforming the representation of African and Native Americans is open to the same charge of misdirection, in that it explains the racism of the practice by the Jewishness of the moguls rather than by power-bloc alliances in the film industry in which the role of Jewishness may have been played by a non-speaking player hardly glimpsed on the edge of the screen.

Black Liberation Radio is not monoglossic and is often explicit that racial interests rather than biological racial categories are what matter. African Americans who ally themselves with the white power-bloc to advance their own interests but not those of other Blacks ("Afro-Saxons" or "House niggers" per Kantako) are criticized as whites, and, similarly, "fellow travelling" whites (whom Kantako distinguishes from the "cave-boys") are welcomed onto his airwaves. Indeed he has a regular two-hour slot called "Good White Sources" in which he plays tapes by progressive or radical whites such as Noam Chomsky, Sidney Willhelm or Barbara Honneger, and other whites, such as Michael Townsend, are among the station's longest and most deeply committed supporters.

Most of the time the station's anger, like that of most African Americans, is properly directed against power-bloc alliances rather than racial groups, whether Jewish or white, but there are times when it is misdirected and takes on some of the flavor of racism. But our under-standing of these occasions must be based on a clear distinction between a top-down, imperializing racism and a bottom-up, more defensive form that is directed against an ethnic group perceived to have exploited the subordinate race. While such localizing, weak racism shares some features with imperializing, strong racism, its locale-building, defensive aspects are not open to the same criticism, and consequently our evaluation of it has to be more finely nuanced to take account of the tactics and local conditions of its operation. A Black anti-Semitism in the contemporary US is not the same as the European anti-Semitism with its long history culminating in the Jewish holocaust. African Americans have never had the access to the power to institutionalize and operationalize anti-Semitism through power-bloc alliances. Because the power available to them is limited to their locales, any anti-Semitism is limited to verbal expression and, more regrettably, to occasional bodily violence. In these conditions, its defensive, pro-Black functions need to be evaluated differently from its aggressive anti-Jewish ones. But as African Americans gain better access to social power, as they inevitably will, then any anti-Semitism that remains will change as the conditions in which it is exercised change: it will then resemble more and more the strong European version from which currently it needs to be distinguished. A defensive racism (which is not racist in the normal use of the term) can have a locale-strengthening use that is socially progressive in conditions of severe repression. When those conditions change, however, so too must this defensive racism; if it does not, our evaluation of its politics will have to.

But this defensive, Black anti-Semitism is often countered by other Black voices which stress the similarities between Black and Jewish histories, pointing out that both races have suffered diasporas, both have suffered holocausts and both share a common African ancestry. Even the anti-Jewish attitudes that surface occasionally on *Black Liberation Radio* are contradicted when Kantako points out that Adam, Abraham and Moses were African, and that, despite the Old Testament's whitening of them, they form ancestral links between African Americans and Jews. Cress Welsing uses the word "Semite" to remind her readers that Jews are only semi-white and thus semi-black: she explicitly dissociates Jews from the whiteness she analyzes so critically in the Cress Theory. Jesse Jackson, too, is vehement in his opposition to anti-Semitism whether by Blacks or whites.

One hopes that as Black access to power increases, its tactical use of defensive anti-Semitism will decrease, and that the Black voices speaking of similarities between African and Jewish Americans will play greater roles in negotiating the points of interface between them. One hopes, too, that Jewish ears will listen to those voices and temper the equally defensive Jewish exclusivity of a history that is claimed to be shared. While *WLIB* in Harlem does express anti-Jewish, anti-Latino and anti-Korean sentiments, it is more multivocal than *Black Liberation Radio*, for these sentiments are regularly countered by others arguing that the Black cause is served better by building interracial alliances than by promoting conflicts. The mutuality of interests between African and Native Americans is taken as a given (as it is on *Black Liberation Radio*), but relations with other racial or ethnic groups are much more in question. In general, however, it seems to be that *WLIB*'s panelists, who have privileged speech, are more in favor of interethnic alliances, while interethnic problems are often raised from the floor.

If we are in the process of changing our social order into one where social differences are respected and power differences reduced, and in which the points of interface are negotiated into points of consent rather than conflict, that is, into a society of multiple points of consent rather than one of a singular consensus, then it seems paradoxical that one step along this path may involve a form of what appears to be racism. But negotiators of consent can only talk and listen open-mindedly if they have a secure base from which to operate; and the prime aim of weak racism is to secure its base. Lacking this, negotiators are more likely to attempt to extend and secure their locale at the expense of others, rather than to discuss boundary lines that can be mutually agreed upon. A defensive form of separatism, even if it looks like bottom-up apartheid, may be a progressive step, not just for those who practice it, but for the social order in general. But those who practice it progressively in current conditions must be responsible for recognizing when those conditions change and therefore when that practice, if unchanged, becomes repressive and socially reactionary.

NOTES

1. Articulation is a concept derived from Stuart Hall (e.g., 'On Postmodernism and Articulation, An Interview," *Journal of Communication Inquiry*, 10, 1986, pp. 56–9) and elaborated by Grossberg, *We Gotta Get Out of This Place* (New York: Routledge, 1992). Hall stresses both meanings of the word: connecting and speaking. To articulate is, in its first sense, to link flexibly the different domains of social experience or axes of power as by a hinge; the social position of this hinge point of articulation is one from which one may speak (the second meaning). Grossberg develops a more comprehensive theory of the first meaning than the second. Articulation is a key operation of social agency, for though one cannot escape axes of power, the social agent can negotiate to an extent their intersections in particular social conditions. The ability to produce the point from which one speaks is a crucial part in gaining control over what one speaks.
2. Cited in Karen Winkler, "While Concern over Race Relation Has Lessened Among Whites, Sociologists Say Racism is Taking New Forms, not Disappearing," *The Chronicle of Higher Education*, 11 September 1991, pp. A10–A11.
3. See, for instance, Joe Feagin, "The Continuing Significance of Race: Antiblack Discrimination in Public Places," *American Sociological Review* vol. 56, 1991, p. 101–16.
4. CNN, *Moneyline*, 1 May 1992.
5. Mike Davis in Chapter 5 of *City of Quartz* (London: Verso, 1990) gives a detailed and passionate account of this war and the alliances betwen the police, the courts and the city council that direct its strategy.
6. bell hooks, *Talking Back: Thinking Feminist, Thinking Black* (Boston: South End Press, 1989).
7. John Hodge (ed.), *Cultural Bases of Racism and Group Oppression* (Berkeley: Two Readers Press, 1975).
8. bell hooks, *Talking Back*, pp. 112–13.
9. Grossberg, *We Gotta Get Out*.

10. Marc Cooper and Greg Goldin, "Some People Don't Count," in Institute for Alternative Journalism (ed.), *Inside the LA Riots: What Really Happened and Why It Will Happen Again* (New York: Institute for Alternative Journalism, 1992), p. 46.
11. Kevin Uhrich, "Policeville: Why People Who Know West Ventura County Weren't Surprised by the Verdict," in Institute for Alternative Journalism, *Inside the LA Riots*, p. 58.
12. There may well, however, be evidence of ideology's refusal to lie down and play dead in the fact that, since I wrote this paragraph, the police officers have been indicted on federal charges of violating Rodney King's civil rights. An acquittal in the second trial may be seen as power dealing with the contradiction between its operation and that of ideology by demonstrating that ideology was either wrong or unimportant or both: a guilty verdict, on the other hand, might be evidence that power is weakened if it cannot underwrite its operation ideologically.
13. Vernon Andrews, "'White Like Me': From Black at Chico State to Black in Corporate America," *CN and R*, 11 February 1988, pp. 15–17, p. 15. Black accounts of the new racism abound with similar accounts, see Feagin, "The Continuing Significance," and Gloria Abernathy-Lear, "African Americans' Relationship with Day Time Serials," Dissertation, University of Wisconsin-Madison, 1992.
14. Statement to the Senate Judiciary Committee, 11 October 1991.
15. Sarah E. Wright, "The Anti-Black Agenda," *The Black Scholar*, 1992, vol. 22, no. 1 & 2, p. 109.
16. "Anita Hill: No Regrets," an interview with Jill Nelson, *Essence*, March 1992, p. 116.
17. Robert Staples, "Hand Me the Rope—I Will Hang Myself: Observations on the Clarence Thomas Hearings," *The Black Scholar*, 1992, vol. 22, no. 1 & 2, p. 96.
18. Jane Gross, "Suffering in Silence No More: Fighting Sexual Harassment," *New York Times*, 13 July 1992, pp. A1, D10.
19. Interview transcript in *Washington Journalism Review*, December 1991, and reprinted in *Harper's*, February 1992, p. 18.
20. Trellie L. Jeffers, "We have heard, we have seen, do we believe? The Clarence Thomas–Anita Hill Hearing," *The Black Scholar*, 1992, vol. 22, no. 1 & 2, p. 56.
21. Charles R. Lawrence III, "Cringing at Myths of Black Sexuality," in ibid., p. 65.
22. *Chicago Defender*, 19 October 1991, p. 16.
23. David Lionel Smith, "The Thomas Spectacle: Power, Impotence and Melodrama," *The Black Scholar*, 1992, vol. 22, nos. 1 & 2, p. 95.
24. Margaret A. Burnham, "The Supreme Court Appointment Process and the Politics of Race and Sex," in Toni Morrison (ed.), *Race-ing Justice, En-gendering Power* (New York: Pantheon, 1992), p. 311.
25. Kimberle Crenshaw, "Whose Story Is It, Anyway: Feminist and Anti-racist Appropriations of Anita Hill," in Morrison (ed.) *Race-ing*, p. 415.
26. Barbara Smith, "Ain't Gonna Let Nobody Turn Me Around," *The Black Scholar*, 1992, vol. 22, nos. 1 & 2, p. 91.
27. Calvin Hernton, "Breaking Silences," in ibid., p. 42.
28. Kimberle Crenshaw "Whose Story," p. 403.
30. *New York Times*, 17 November 1991.
31. Nellie McKay, untitled talk at Borders Bookstore, Madison, WI, 1 December 1992.
32. Nancy Fraser, "Sex, Lies and the Public Sphere: Some reflections on the confirmation of Clarence Thomas," *Cultural Inquiry* 18, (Spring) 1992, pp. 589–613. She gives more evidence of the role of classes in the hearings than I can summarize here, and is one of the few commentators to do so.
33. Orlando Patterson, "Race, Gender and Liberal Fallacies," *New York Times*, 20 October 1991, p. E15, reprinted in Black Scholar (ed.), *Court of Appeal*, pp. 160–164.
34. *Ebony*, October 1992, p. 112.
35. Other achievements in the political sphere include the emergence from the LA uprisings of "a new political star, Rep. Maxine Waters, who has emerged as *the* central advocate for urban renewal," and numerous candidates for office at state and local levels. In the arts, three Black women had their novels simultaneously on the *New York Times* Best

Seller Lists, and others won major awards in music, cinema and television. In sport, Black women won thirty-two medals, including eight gold, in the Olympics, and, professionally they were "presiding in corporate board rooms, leading national professional organizations and leading major colleges and universities more than ever before."

36. *Ebony*, October 1992, p. 118.
37. The uprisings caused $800 million in property damage, nearly seventy deaths, over two thousand injuries and required ten thousand troops to put them down. (The London *Observer* headlined its account of them, "Superpower retakes gutted second city.")
38. CNN, *Showbiz*, 1 May 1992.
39. Mike Davis, "Burning All Illusions in LA," in IAJ, *Inside the LA Riots*, p. 99.

13

COUNTER POWER WORKS

COUNTER CENTER

The model of historical change which underlies poststructural politics is that of a change from one regime of power to another. Because power is as diverse as its technologies and sites of application, this type of change occurs at different speeds and different times in different domains of power. Unlike revolutionary change, it does not provide the historian with pivotal points where the new may be said to succeed the old. It is a much messier business, more drawn out, more contradictory, more a mixture of advances and retreats, movements and counter movements. But within it, there are traceable regularities, one of which is the movement between the margins and the center. What was marginalized or repressed in one regime of power may become more central in the succeeding, and vice versa. But the new regime of power does not necessarily replace the configuration of the old while merely changing the position of players in the game: it may produce a new configuration. A homogenized strong-power regime with stark contrasts between the center and the margins may be replaced by a more diversified one, where the strength at the center is spread more equally among a number of weaker, though not necessarily equal, power centers. I hope the US and the world are moving in this direction.

But whatever configuration a new regime of power may take the change always involves a decentering process. This decentering takes place in all domains, the political, the industrial, the educational and the cultural. In poststructuralism, cultural and particularly literary decentering is often called deconstruction. By decentering a text, deconstruction works to weaken its power to make monovocal sense by restoring to full audibility those voices which it had reduced to a whisper, and whose silencing was necessary for its coherence. The deconstructed text is made to listen to voices which it dislikes, fears, denigrates and attempts to repress. Such a deconstructive spin tells us that the crucial work of the text is performed at its margins: the traces of excluded meanings, the echoes of silenced voices, and the glimpses of other realities have to be recovered from their marginalization if we are to understand what the text is doing. But what needs deconstructing more urgently than any text is the imagination of the power-bloc.

The margins matter, for the margins are the future. A change from one regime of power to another reconfigures the relations between the margins and the center, it decenters the one and recenters (some of) the other. History offers us no guarantees of the direction of its changes, so there is no inevitability about what will be recovered from the margins and what will remain on them, there is no inevitability about the form of the new regime. The politics of deconstruction lie in large part in its choice of what to recenter or demarginalize: Decentering is only a start, but it is an important one, for when a regime of power is reaching the end of its period of efficiency its power-bloc responds to the crisis by centering its interests with even greater urgency and desperation. Its repression of the margins becomes more overt and harsh and thus their recovery becomes even more important if the change is to be peaceful.

The imagination of the power-bloc and of the nation can only be decentered if it learns to listen, really listen, to voices from the margins. George Bush needs to hear what Bill and Paradise, the homeless men, have to say, Ted Stevens needs to listen to Carlos Fuentes (and Jesse Helms to Robert Mapplethorpe); the varied formations of the power-bloc need to know what they and the world look like from the locales of Elvis fans, and they need to learn about the different social relations and identities that are kept alive there; they need to realize why it is that so many other ways of living can maintain themselves only by evading their power, by hiding from their monitoring gaze, and why their power debilitates and limits other "weak" powers even when it is not directly threatened by them.

Monovocality, monoculturalism, and the singularity of truth are the hallmarks of strong power whose effectiveness depends upon its ability to exclude and enclose. The power of TWA's computers lies in its enclosed reservation center: it is the power of the panopticon to enclose all that it deems necessary to see and to see that totally. It is a power that excludes other powers, that excludes locales, that excludes diversity. It excludes because it has to, it excludes because it can. While it may extend its enclosure as far as it imperialistically is able to, what goes on within it is limited, for the most powerfully effective knowledge is, paradoxically, limited by its own exclusivity. The unblinking focus of its gaze is what makes its power effective, but it also makes it narrow-minded.

Multiculturalism matters because of its potential to extend the imagination of the formations of the power-bloc beyond the blinkers of the gaze of power: it may be able to enhance the peripheral vision of their mind's eye. An expanded vision is ethically and politically preferable to a focussed one. Power becomes less greedy, less repressive, and more humane when it admits what it excludes, when it centers what it marginalizes, not in order to incorporate and enclose it, but to enter relations with it that are, to a degree at least, two-way. Power must allow itself to be monitored from below, to be known by knowledges other than its own.

An expanded, less focussed imagination may enable the power-bloc to recognize, for example, that the ways of knowing–doing–living by which Elvis fans construct their *communitas* is not only validly different from its own, but that the difference carries a critique which it would do well to listen to. Like the Elvis fans, it needs to open its circle to include shy fourteen-year-old girls in its dance. The *as if* world within which this *communitas* really exists is a world whose conditionality critiques the limitations of the world that *is*; and the world that *is* has established its "realness," has staked out its claim to truth, by power—epistemological, technological, political. The marginality of the *as if* exposes the strategic repressiveness of the centered reality, and its knowledge of what might be recovers some of that which is repressed as unreal. Listening to this conditional world can nudge us to reformulate the relations between the margins and the center and thus decenter the power to marginalize. At the margins the world that might be can be put into practice, can be embodied and lived, albeit unknown and disregarded by the power system. The Elvis fans may have little to gain by using their way of knowing to challenge and disrupt the official one; for them, their localized control is best exerted unseen. The interests of the power-bloc, too, have nothing to gain from admitting this way of knowing/living. But the social order in general *has*: We have much to gain from recognizing other ways of knowing, where identities can be constructed from the bottom up, and individuals, who are not individuated, can form social relationships that are under their own control. The *communitas* of Elvis fans is an incisive critique of panoptic individuating discipline; its incisiveness is sharpened because it is lived as practice but blunted because its practice is unseen.

The decentering of racial power is one of the most urgent tasks in our immediate future: the problematic of making imperializing power step aside and make room for localizing powers to move inwards is a multifrontal one that cannot be addressed at the center alone; it will not be solved by a key victory in a war of maneuver but requires a constant war of position, a contestation of the points of interface between imperializing and localizing powers as they arise. But one component common to each interface is the white imagination, the white way of knowing. If white power is to be decentered and its relations with other rainbow powers to be reconfigured, we whites have to learn to listen to rainbow voices telling us how we look to them. We cannot continue the historical practice of the masters and mistresses of slaves and servants who forbade their blacks to look at them. The power not to be seen, or to repress what is seen, is one of the first we must weaken.

It is not comfortable for us to learn that whites appear as terrorists to Blacks, but bell hooks tells us how the terrifying and terrorizing power that white Americans have historically exerted upon Blacks can emerge at any time in the Black perception of any white person or behavior. She tells of the terror experienced by Black children when a white man enters their neighborhood or home. Usually he is selling something (such as insurance or Bibles) but his economic exploitation does not provide a full explanation of his terrorization. His very presence embodies whiteness and the whole Black history of white power, and it is this, rather than his salesmanship, that renders Black children silent in his presence. Identifying her place on the margin, bell hooks writes:

> Returning to memories of growing up in the social circumstances created by racial apartheid, to all black spaces on the edges of town, I re-inhabit a location where black folks associated whiteness with the terrible, the terrifying. White people were regarded as terrorists.[1]

As a white professor in a major university, I participated unknowingly in a power-bloc that terrorized. It was at a conference which bell hooks also attended. She describes her experience of it:

> I went there because I was confident that I would be in the company of likeminded, progressive, "aware" intellectuals; instead, I was disturbed when the usual arrangements of white supremacist hierarchy were mirrored both in terms of what was speaking, of how bodies were arranged on the stage, of who was in the audience, of what voices were deemed worthy to speak and to be heard. As the conference progressed I began to feel afraid. If progressive people, most of whom were white, could so blindly reproduce a version of the status quo and not "see" it, the thought of how racial politics would be played out "outside" this arena was horrifying. That feeling of terror that I had known so intimately in my childhood surfaced.[2]

I was on the stage (centered) at that conference when she broke its smooth progress by speaking from the floor (the margin) of her terror, of her being terrorized. Her charges were linked to her critical response to the paper I had just delivered, and I remember vividly the severity of the deconstructive jolt she gave me. I took her charge personally and reacted defensively: in my own eyes I am anti-racist and progressive—precisely one of those "aware" intellectuals she had expected to meet. But these eyes of mine did not "see" the racial politics of the conference as did hers, they did not "see" my role, my alliances, my political effectivity that ran counter to both intention and self-perception. But the pain of the jolt (and it did hurt) lasted longer than my defensive innocence (me a terrorist? inconceivable!), and it allowed me no escape from the discomfort of having to face the difference between a Black view of me and my own.

The Cress Theory can deliver similar deconstructive jolts. I was introduced to it by a Black student who told me how frequently she had seen it referenced in her reading of Black people's struggles to gain control over their own history and identity. She told me too of a Black woman saying how profoundly useful it was to her in her job as a New York cop: its insights made her experiences understandable and therefore bearable. But some whites react to it very differently: one publisher's reader of this manuscript called it racist and warned me that in not criticizing it as I summarized it I ran the risk of endorsing it. Other whites have patholo-gized it as paranoid or have denigrated Cress Welsing's book as poorly argued, lacking in evidence, or as just naive. But there are other whites who have received its jolt and have allowed it to deconstruct, even if only by a little, the knowledge structure by which they know themselves as white.

If the Cress Theory is racist, and to some eyes it will inevitably appear so, it is "weak" racism, for it is defensive and not imperialist.[3] It has none of strong racism's strategic instrumentality by which the power of the dominant race is exerted directly upon the bodies, societies, identities and histories of the subjected one. The Cress Theory's assertion of Black "superiority" is used not to justify a future Black domination of whites, but to empower the Black refusal of white domination and to counter the white, truly racist, grounding of domination upon assumptions of racial superiority.

To African Americans it is literally inconceivable that human beings could behave towards others in the way that whites did in slavery. Yet Blacks did experience such behavior and continue to experience variants of it today. For them, therefore, the behavior and those who practice it have to be excluded from the category of the human. So on *Black Liberation Radio*, Mbanna Kantako likens white power to bestiality and often refers to it as "The Beast" that African Americans confront every day. He calls the anti-Black moves of this Beast "anti-human," and extends the context of the confrontation beyond the US to the world. Globally, the 7 per cent of its population that is white has acted against the normal, and therefore humane, majority. For Malcolm X, the inhuman white was the devil. The correlative of this, as Gloria Abernathy-Lear points out, is a deep conviction among African Americans of their ethical superiority to whites.[4] The beast (Kantako), the overcompensating weakling bully (Cress), the terrorist (hooks), and the devil (Malcolm X) are particular versions of the widespread knowledge that whites are not to be trusted and that Blacks must never let their guard down. In his history textbook, Jawanza Kunjufu tells of ways in which Black people have been taken advantage of by being too trusting, and concludes with the general lesson:

> Look for the good in everyone, but never turn your back. Never trust people outside your race and be careful of those within. There are three criteria of Blackness: color, consciousness, and culture. To be Black or African means to look Black, to think Black, and act Black.[5]

The primary function of these Black insights into whiteness is to strengthen African Americans in their daily lives by obeying the old advice to know thine enemy; but when glimpsed or overheard by whites they are equally useful in disturbing white knowledge of itself.

I do then endorse the Cress theory and equivalent Black knowledges, not for any essential "truth," but for their deconstructive counter to white ways of knowing whiteness. Not only are we (the social order in general) kept alert, if a little edgy, by such counter-knowledges, but we (whites in particular) need to develop the ability to listen to them if we are to mitigate the divisiveness of our current society and to avoid the antagonism which it produces.

People become violent when they are not heard. Racial violence has a whole complexity of causes, but a structuring component of the conditions which nourish it is the Black knowledge that the white power-bloc does not listen to Black people, that it has neither the ability nor the desire to learn something of Black views of Black experiences, nor to recognize that Black experiences of our society are as valid as white ones; in particular it refuses to allow Black views of itself to enter its own self-perception.

COUNTER HISTORY

Any deconstruction of the present without an equivalent deconstruction of the past is insecure and tactically weakened. The decentering of history can take a number of forms. One is the production of a counter-history which recovers from the margins what official history has strategically white-washed into invisibility. Dr Cress Welsing scrubs the whitewash off Cleopatra and restores her to her Africanness, arguing that her whitening was a strategy to repress racial domination from the stories of her love affairs with Octavius Caesar and Mark Antony. This deracialization meant that her death could be comfortably represented by and for whites as a result of tragic passion rather than of racism. White Christianity allies its effort with those of Hollywood and the school system by whitening Jesus and the Virgin Mary. The tribes of Israel had migrated from Africa, she argues, and Mary and Jesus were Black and of African descent; indeed, many of their earliest visual representations were black (and the few "black virgins" that remain are typically granted special significance by formations of the people, if not by the official church). But as the Christian Church allied itself with the emerging political, economic, and military power-blocs of Renaissance Europe, it whitened its key figures and robbed them of their Africanness, so that now it is almost impossible to understand the crucifixion as a racist act of whites upon a Black man. Yet, she argues, the white supremacy in the act can never be totally repressed, and it resurfaces in the burning crosses of the Ku Klux Klan.

This white robbery of Black history is widely recognized and focusses particularly on knowing Egypt as a Mediterranean (that is, white) country rather than an African (Black) one. The great civilizing inventions of writing, medicine, mathematics and religion were all African, the world's first university and first great library were African, but white history has stolen them, and called them Greek, "just as the Greeks stole the books from the library of Alexander."[6] Dr Leonard Jeffries argues that the moguls of Hollywood have worked, like the white school-history curriculum, to denigrate both African and Native Americans and to "strip Africa of its significance and its place in the world." "This was by design," he concludes, "by people who knew what they were doing."[7] To give one more example: Ralph Wiley argues that the Sphinx and other great Egyptian sculptures have had their noses defaced by whites to remove the most visible signs of their Africanness.[8] The Sphinx's nose was blown off by Napoleon's artillery: the only one of Napoleon's generals to dissent from his invasion of Egypt was Thomas Dumas, who was of African descent. Wiley writes: "Napoleon and some of his generals just couldn't handle these great works of immense size and antiquity looking more like Thomas Dumas than Napoleon Bonaparte. Of course, Dumas was accused of mutiny ... [and] was refused honorable retirement, back pay and pension by Napoleon."[9] Thomas Dumas was the father of the novelist Alexandre Dumas whose Africanness, like that of the Russian novelist Pushkin, has been written out of white literary history. Beethoven's African ancestry has been similarly repressed from music history, Spinoza's from philosophy, and Aesop's from his tales.

By robbing Black history, the white power-bloc advances its interests by disempowering contemporary Black consciousness, and by promoting within Blacks the white knowledge that they are historically, as well as contemporarily, inferior to whites. Slavery stole Africans not only from their lands, but also from their histories and their social identities. Our current de-Africanization of their history is seen by many African Americans as a direct continuation of the slave system; its reclamation is, therefore, a necessary part of their struggle to free themselves. "We built the pyramids!" proclaimed a panelist on *WLIB*, "Don't tell me what we can and cannot do."

Such counter-histories deconstruct the power to produce historical truth at a relatively general level: they become powerful in locales when they are connected to counter-memory. For George Lipsitz, counter-memory works with the local, the immediate and the personal. It recovers the particularities of experience and the hidden histories that are excluded from official history.[10] For Foucault, too, counter-memory's particularities and trivialities deconstruct official history and its claim to produce a singular coherent truth.[11] These particularities carry the experiences of history's victims, they are the way history is experienced from below rather than the way it is written from above. The grand narrative by which power writes its own history and justifies its own present sweeps micro-physical experiences under the carpet of its generality, so to recover these micro-truths challenges not only the grand truth but also the power that produces it. Memory is the presence, and therefore a politicization, of history, and a counter-history is a narrative aggregation of counter-memories that exceeds the limitations of the particular without erasing its truth.

Counter-memories can be understood better within a theory of power than within a theory of ideology, for they depend upon the particularities of experience which ideology theory reduces to insignificance. A discussion on *Black Liberation Radio* may serve as an example of a Black counter-memory undressing white power. If slavery is "capitalism with its clothes off" the resulting nakedness is that of both power and of the body upon which it is applied.

The historian gave many micro-physical instances of counter-memory, of which two will suffice here. The first was of an incident in 1857 after slavery had been declared illegal. A slave ship, under the command of Captain Holman, had been spotted in mid-Atlantic by four British patrol boats:

HISTORIAN They chased him until night fell. Under the cover of darkness he brought all the slaves up, lined them around the railing of the ship, all of them already handcuffed with manacles, then he took a rope and tied each brother to the next brother to the next brother, and he did just the same way with the sister women and the children, all six hundred of them, then he tied the first brother to the anchor, cut the anchor loose, and he let it drag all six hundred slaves all around the railing of the ship until all six hundred were in the water drowning. And by this time the British had boarded the ship ... you could see the water coming up, the turbulence in the water, but by that time there was nothing they could do because the slaves weren't aboard the ship. And the white boy, after they exited, turned it around and sailed right back to Africa and got him a new cargo. And these are the types of people...

KANTAKO Oh man, oh man...

HISTORIAN And the sharks, the sharks are still travelling those slave routes looking for the bones of thousands of dead Afr...

KANTAKO I heard, man, I heard that there was no sharks running these particular routes until the slave t—, I don't want to call it a "trade," brother, you know what I mean?...

HISTORIAN Trade? It was a holocaust...

KANTAKO It wasn't that civilized.

HISTORIAN White man calls it "a trade"...

KANTAKO That's just to put a civilized look to it, you know, the slave holocaust I mean, I heard that the sharks didn't even hang out on the East coast of this country until after that.

HISTORIAN I think you're probably correct, I heard that also, that the shark routes were established eating the left-overs and the throwaway Blacks that were tossed overboard.

KANTAKO And of course, even though they were aware that this cracker had just dumped, you know, X amount of Black folks in the water, because of their law, and you know we see them follow their laws to the letter, they...

HISTORIAN They didn't do anything.

KANTAKO They didn't do anything. You know, the cracker went right back to Africa and stole him some more.

HISTORIAN Exactly, and you know this is how we lost so many people. White people want to count the small numbers, you know, they say there weren't enough ships, there weren't enough this...

The white power over Black bodies is the same as the power to put slavery into discourse as "trade," and not "holocaust," to frame laws that may be fair in their wording but not in their execution, and to write a history that minimizes both the atrocities and the numbers.

The second instance concerned the use of the Caribbean islands as "breaking grounds" where Africans would be "seasoned" and made into slaves before being brought over to the mainland for sale. The object was "to break our spirits, to break our will, and make us into people that could be enslaved—and we're still the people that they made us into." But while the object may have been the African will, the means to it was the African body:

The islands were where most of the atrocities were committed, women were ripped apart, pregnant women had babies snatched out of them and stomped on the ground, women were tied—that were pregnant—tied to the ground and then had a leg tied to two trees that were pulled down, tie each leg to a tree, then cut the trees loose and rip the lady apart catapulting the baby into the air... These were the types of atrocities...

He continues his harrowing account with details of the instruments of torture by which power was applied on the body and by techniques of whipping and bodily degradation. The story he tells gives gut-churning evidence to support Foucault's belief that the key to control over social identities, social relations and thus the social order is the body.

In slavery, the technologies of this power were applied to the physical body; in the "new racism" their application is as much upon the social body. Environmental and economic racism work on the black social body as did the whips upon the physical body. Retelling the atrocious narratives of slavery, such as those on *Black Liberation Radio*, evokes shudders in the bodies of those who hear them. These shudders are experiences of affective intensity of the body's recognition that what touches it *matters*, and they are theoretically comparable to the homeless men's cheers at *Die Hard* or the Elvis fans' ecstasy, even though their intensity is of horror rather than pleasure. This bodily affect enables the power that oppressed the bodies in the narrative to be taken into the bodies of the listeners and turned against its origin.

Such counter-memories of slavery are relatively readily available, because many of them have been written in white "anti-histories" which have facilitated their excorporation into Black counter-history. An anti-history of slavery contests the history of slavery in order to oppose it, but not necessarily to empower its victims. The contest between "history" and anti-history is between factions of white interests, and while the objective of anti-history is to change white knowledge of history and thus white behavior towards its victims, it does not seek, as do counter-history and counter-memory, to empower the victims in their own terms. It is a rewriting of history *for* African Americans rather than *by* African Americans and it typically stops short of explicitly merging the past into the present. There is no counter-memory in anti-history, but there is in counter-history, and it is counter-memory that both accents history in the voices of its victims and carries that history into the contemporary consciousness of its current victims.

The Smithsonian exhibit *The West as America* produced an anti-history rather than a counter-history, for it contained no American Indian accounts of the invasion of their lands, and although American Indian interests would be served better by this anti-history than the one it opposed, it was not their own history, told in their accents, of their experiences which still live in their counter-memories. The argument between the paintings and the wall texts was between different factions of the white power-bloc.

The historian on *Black Liberation Radio*, however, was producing a counter-history, and in the discussion he and Kantako constantly showed how a living counter-memory located this counter-history firmly in the consciousness of the present. The memories of the Black head-whippers of the plantation who controlled slaves for their masters in return for access to a tiny piece of white power and privilege are organically part of understanding "nigger cops" today. So, too, today's "Afro-Saxons" such as Clarence Thomas are yesterday's "house niggers."

These continuities between past and present contradict Foucault's claim that counter-memory is fragmented. He mounts this argument as a criticism of the way that official history's grand narrative overlooks the particularities of experience by which history is lived rather than narrated. His insistence on the ability of these particularities to disrupt the power to narrate smoothly in the interests of the narrator is confirmed by these Black counter-memories, but, because he lacks a notion equivalent to that of localizing power, he underestimates the power to reorder these fragments into a counter-history and thus a counter-knowledge of the present. Disrupting the centeredness of the grand narrative is a useful deconstructive move, but it is not, in itself, enough: it may dislodge some of the certainties of the current regime of power, but it does little to promote the next unless some further steps are taken.

COUNTER CULTURE

Culture is a weapon, and our enemy's first attack upon us was to take our jobs, to take our language, to take our religion; taking our identity through our culture.[12]

This caller to the *Gary Byrd Show* did not include history in his list of what whites have stolen from African Americans, but he might well have. Robbing a people of their history is a way of disempowering them in the present. Equally, control over history, as Ted Stevens knows well, extends itself into control over the social identities of today. A counter-history, then, helps produce a counter-identity, and therefore, even more importantly, a counter-future. Ted Stevens and his allies felt so threatened by the Smithsonian's anti-history and Carlos Fuentes's proposed counter-history because they knew that history secures the future, and what they wanted was a white history for a white future.

A counter-history is always set against a dominant one. It is a form of localizing knowledge in opposition to imperializing knowledge and it works through a counter-knowledge to produce a counter-reality. Scientific rationalism, that way of knowing which imperializing power has developed so successfully, works through separation and categorization; indeed, its motto, both politically and epistemologically, is "divide and rule." The more that subordinate social formations can be separated from each other, and the more that people can be individuated into disciplined, monitored bodies and identities, the better they can be controlled. The breaking up of the Black family and, emblematically, the separation of the Black male from his family, wife and children is understood as a deliberately hostile act aimed at weakening Black society and thus rendering it more controllable. Epistemologically, too, scientific rationalism exerts its control over the world by dividing it into ever smaller categories, by drawing ever finer lines of distinction into nature.[13] Imperialism and scientific rationalism both exert their power through division and separation. In this power pattern lines which connect and maintain similarity are horizontal; vertical relationships are ones of difference and separation.

A localizing knowledge, on the other hand, will typically, though not essentially, see the continuities between actions of imperializing power which that power separates from each other. The CEO of Nike, for example, would deny that his policy is part of the same power operation as the whitening of Cleopatra in school history books: industry and the curriculum are relatively autonomous domains and each is able to function as powerfully as it does because its autonomy is stressed and its overdetermined connections masked. But a Black knowledge sees the continuity clearly. So, too, a Black counter-history is continuous with the Black counter-memories that constitute the present and the future. One characteristic of this Black counter-knowledge and counter-reality is its diametric difference from the imperializing power to which it is opposed. At its core is a principle of unity and wholeness that informs both a way of knowing the world and a way of practicing social relations within that world. As Dr Leonard Jeffries puts it: "the African value system is built on the three C's—communal, co-operative and collective."[14]

This African value system was articulated to African Americans by Dr Maulana Karenga, one of the leaders of the Black Liberation Movement in the 1960s. He argued that

[T]he key crisis in Black life is the crisis of ideology and culture, i.e., the critical lack of a coherent system of views and values that would give them a moral, material, and meaningful interpretation of life as well as demand an allegiance and practice which would insure their liberation and a higher level of human life ... furthermore progress in struggle is directly linked to progress in thought and that until the oppressor's monopoly on our minds is broken and we acquire new values and views of self, society, and the world, liberation is impossible and by definition, unthinkable.[15]

As a base for this cultural movement he proposed the *Nguzo Saba* or Seven Principles:

UMOJA (Unity)—To strive for and maintain unity in the family, community, nation and race.

KUJICHAGULIA (Self-determination)—To define ourselves, create for ourselves and speak for ourselves, instead of being defined, named, created for, and spoken for by others.

UJIMA (Collective Work and Responsibility)—To build and maintain our community together and to make our sisters' and brothers' problems our problems and to solve them together.

UJAMAA (Co-operative Economics)—To build and maintain our own stores, shops, and other business and to profit from them together.

NIA (Purpose)—To make as our collective vocation the building and developing of our community in order to restore our people to their traditional greatness.

KUUMBA (Creativity)—To do always as much as we can, in the way we can in order to leave our community more beautiful and beneficial than when we inherited it.

IMANI (Faith)—To believe with all our hearts in our people, our parents, our teachers, our leaders and the righteousness and victory of our struggle.

Kwanzaa was the festival which he originated to embody these principles and to provide a time and place for African Americans to come together to reaffirm and enact them. Kwanzaa was to be, in Dr Karenga's words,

[A]n earth-rooted, social holiday, a holiday of definite people, with definite needs, history and social purpose. It is not a time for star-reading, spreading guba dust, or praying to invisible beings or forces ... moreover it is not a Black Christmas or Black Chanukkah or anything similar. These holidays already exist and duplications of them with only the word Black to distinguish the difference is an apish imitation in which no self-respecting, self-defining, and self-determining people should be involved.[16]

The politics of Kwanzaa lie in its concrete social practices materially situated in current social conditions:

Kwanzaa is not an imitation, but an alternative, in fact, an *oppositional alternative* to the spookism, mysticism, and non-earth practices which plague us as a people and encourage our withdrawal from social life rather than our bold confrontation with it.[17]

Of the seven principles the one to which I heard most frequent references was that of *Umoja* (Unity) which is the first and the organizing principle. The white habit of thinking about economics, culture and social relations separately is contradicted by it; it is characteristic of an African American way of knowing and living in which the economic is unified with the cultural domain, and the social relations it promotes are, unlike the divisive ones of capitalism, ones of mutuality. So Kwanzaa is a festival in which culture, food and goods are shared: meanings, money and the means of subsistence are circulated within the African American community more for the good of all, rather than for the profit of some. The market place of Kwanzaa is where goods and food (often home-produced) are consumed within the same social formation that produced them; the hierarchy in the distinction between producers and consumers is denied.

A communal economic system (*ujamaa*) established within a competitive one is clearly at constant risk, and many African Americans are on the alert to defend Kwanzaa against a profit-driven economics (which is white even if practiced by Blacks) and the social divisiveness and, ultimately, elitism which it is designed to produce. Many voices on the *Gary Byrd Show* expressed concern that one function (a $100-a-head dinner) in the 1991 Kwanzaa was starting to slide down this slippery slope. The more unified view was expressed by a caller who made the two points, or rather two sides of one point, that he gained enormous pleasure from the cultural events of Kwanzaa and that he spent his money there: in his experience the cultural circulation of meanings and pleasures and the economic circulation of money were not separated into different domains but were part of a communal circulation.

The sense that "our people are buying and dealing with each other, supporting our own businesses," is extended beyond Kwanzaa into the economics of every day. In Harlem, for example, there is a "Family Card" which encourages Blacks to spend their money in Black businesses. Unlike white schemes such as the frequent-flyer or regular-customer cards this one "sells" itself by offering its advantages not to the individual customer but to the community that encompasses both buyers and sellers. The aim of the Family Card Economic Awareness Program is to keep Black money in the Black Family not just for the good of Black businesses, but for the good of all. *Ebony*, a magazine aimed at upscale, successful African Americans, concludes too that the only way to survive the "new racism" is economic self-sufficiency.[18] Arguing that the "new racism" is "furtive but virulent" and that today's whites are more anti-Black than ever, the article concludes that social acceptance can no longer be the goal, and that the way forward must involve building a separate Black nation based upon economic self-sufficiency. It quotes Arthur Fletcher, the chairperson of the Commission on Civil Rights: "If we're smart enough and bold enough to use [the gains we've already made], we'll have the control of the wealth in our communities and we won't have to worry about racism." In this he was echoing Malcolm X who, thirty years earlier, had argued that Black people should "trade with each other—exclusively where possible—and hire each other, and in so doing, keep black money within the black community."[19] On the rebellious streets of LA in 1992, the most influential Black leader was Louis Farrakhan, who continues much of Malcolm X's politics, and his goal of Black economic self-determination was broadly embraced. In this light, the burning of Korean grocery stores was not mere destruction. According to Mike Davis, the Englewood gang summit on 5 May referred repeatedly to developing a Black economy out of the ashes of Korean businesses: "After all," an ex-Crip member told him, "we didn't burn our community, just their stores."[20]

The ability of white supremacy to change its form but not its substance over the centuries has convinced a significant social formation within Black America that its best survival strategy is the construction of a self-determined community that is as separate and as different from the white as possible. The dynamics of this community are to be recovered from the Africa that preceded white exploitation and at the heart of them all is *umoja*. Without *umoja* neither the collective economics of *ujamaa*, nor the self-determination or *kujichagulia* that it promotes, will be achievable.

Umoja is not just a concept of unity, but is a knowledge system that emphasizes the interconnectedness of everything and of all experience. It is thus quite different from scientific rationalism, which exerts its power over its object by dividing and categorizing it. The power of *umoja* is the power to link and connect, it offers a holistic way of knowing, not a taxonomic one. This unifying principle operates across both what white knowledges typically characterize as different social domains and across different levels of social relations. In a society practicing *umoja*, buying and selling are not separate spheres in the economic domain and the economic domain is not separated from the cultural, but all are unified so that the circulation of money and of meanings are part of the same social process.

Just one broadcast of the *Gary Byrd Show* illustrates how *umoja* operates across all levels of social relations and social experience. A panelist defined *umoja* as the striving to maintain unity in identity, family, community, nation and race. A caller agreed with him, and told how she tried to establish *umoja* within her family by teaching her children to support, respect and protect each other. The basis for this, she argued, was another of the seven principles, *kujichagulia* (self-determination). We must know ourselves, she argued, know who we are in order to find that respect that we must give to others. Not surprisingly in a knowledge system that emphasizes interconnectedness, each of the seven principles leaks into and supports the others when it is put into practice. So *umoja* and *kujichagulia* work simultaneously and inextricably to connect identity, family, community, nation and race into a continuum of experience. The reclamation of African history works as both *umoja* and *kujichagulia* on all of these levels, so too does the use of African words: many African Americans are changing their American names into African ones and are using African words of greeting such as "Hotep" (peace). For Molefi Asante, changing "slave names" into African names is practical politics because of the "identification of names with people."[21]

Mbanna Kantako jettisoned his original "slave name" for his current African one as a sign of reclaiming an identity from the individuated one that existed in white knowledge and white systems of record, and resituating it in relation to Black *communitas*. His name identifies him in communal relations with African Americans but does not individuate him in the white sense. When I asked if he wished to comment on a draft of this chapter, he pointed out that I had individualized him (as did other white accounts of his work). I had failed to understand not just the support of his family and his community, but the fact that he is only able to speak as he does because his voice, like that of his family, is of the community and not of an articulate individual. Indeed, his family is centrally involved. His wife, Dia, and his young sons, Kanodi and Mbanna Jr., each have their own daily hour of airtime, during which they read from Afro-centered books and mix in appropriate music, and Dia joins in his discussions with guests. He is Mbanna Kantako, a communal voice, and not, as he used to be, Dewayne Readus, and I had not adequately recognized the difference.

Gramsci would, I think, recognize Mbanna Kantako as an "organic intellectual," that is, one who analyzes and theorizes the experience of a social formation as a member of it, and whose analysis is therefore part of the experience that is its object. The organic intellectual does not strive for an objectivizing distance but speaks within and for the community whose experiences her or his theorizing explains. Such analysis makes this local experience understandable and accessible to those in other social formations and thus enables alliances to be formed. The organic intellectual provides the mortar with which to build a popular bloc.

Mbanna Kantako and those like him on *WLIB* are not individuated and separated by vertical power from horizontal relations, but have maintained control of their own individuality and have constructed it within a *communitas.* The African name is a sign of the individual speaking communally, whereas white "naming" words are seen as individuating and hierarchical. There is a strong movement to expunge white patriarchal terms for women from the Black vocabulary and, if English words are to be used, to select only those that express community, particularly "Brother" and "Sister." Sexism is a problem in Black communities as in most others, but those working to establish *umoja* recognize its divisiveness and combat it wherever possible: both *WLIB* and *Black Liberation Radio,* for example, are explicitly committed to promoting gender equality, for *umoja* is an anti-sexist principle. The usage of "Sister woman" or "Brother man," therefore, is not linguistically redundant but promotes non-sexist gender relations and connects the consciousness of the immediate relationships within the family to those larger ones of humanity in general. Determining one's own history, language and identity is a unified and unifying process.

This reclaimed African identity extends into the reclaimed African family. The divisiveness by which white power is exercised has been most effectively applied in the weakening of the Black family: "We invented the extended family," said a panelist on this *Gary Byrd Show.* "We must re-establish it within our community." The social debilitation of Blacks through a continual assault upon the structure of the Black family is not to be regained by rebuilding a white, nuclear family, but through the recovery of a communal, extended family that is part of *umoja*'s continuum from identity through to community. The Black use of the word "family" to encompass immediate blood relations, through relations of local community up to the relations of the Black Family on the global level, is an example of this principle put into discursive and therefore social practice. The Family Card Economic Awareness Program works to unify "Family" across all these levels of social experience and also to merge economic relations into communal and race relations. *Umoja, ujamaa* and *kujichagulia* are interdependent and mutually supportive principles.

Umoja extends through the family community level into that of nation. The *Gary Byrd Show* contained a detailed discussion of how American Blacks and Latinos could ally their interests and also of the problems encountered in doing so. The *New York Amsterdam News* routinely reports on Native American matters as though there were an inevitable alliance of interests between Native and African Americans. And *Black Liberation Radio* plays music by African Americans, African Caribbeans, Latinos and Native Americans along with its monitoring of local police activities. As an instance of this *umoja* given form in a textual flow, Ron Sakolsky played a sequence of musical numbers by a Caribbean band, a band of Ojibwe Native Americans from Canada, an African American rap group, and an African American soul singer. Before the last number, over a slow rhythmic backing, in a quiet, unemphatic voice, he said:

> Well, we might wonder what all this fuss is about—Christopher Columbus, that great hero, well, I'd like to read from his ship's log, these are the man's own words, and you judge for yourself. He said on seeing the Arawak Indians when he arrived in the New World, and notice that the New World and the New World Order have a lot in common. These are his words: "They would make fine servants and they are intelligent, for I saw that they repeated everything said to them. I believe they could easily be made Christians for they appear to have no idols. Should your Majesties command it all the inhabitants could be taken away to Castille or made slaves on the island. With fifty men we could subjugate them all and make them do whatever we want. ... Christopher Columbus."[22]

Some fifteen minutes earlier, Sakolsky had played "Columbus Lied" by Shadow, which, to a soca beat, argued that the discovery of the New World was a lie, for a populated land could neither be "new" nor "discovered." The recovery of a native history requires the expulsion of the colonizing truth which has occupied it for so long. By revealing the motivations shared by Columbus's voyages and the slave trade, Sakolsky points to the ways in which African Americans, African Caribbeans, Latinos and Native Americans have all had their racial identities constructed as appropriate terrains for white power, just as happened to India at the hands of E.M. Forster and to California-Alaska at those of Grayson and Stevens. Each is a historical product of the white imperialism of which Columbus's voyage is a particularly effective instance; and while their own histories and identities may be as different as their musics, they have been given a historical commonality by the effect of white power upon them. *Umoja* is the attempt to redefine this commonality and to turn it against the interests of those who originally imposed it.

Umoja denies any arbitrary distinction between nation and race. The *Gary Byrd Show* appeals to African Americans to support their brothers and sisters who are refugees from Haiti in the US air base on Cuba. The appeal is for money, clothes, sports equipment and for pressure on the White House and the (equally white) Pentagon to reverse their unexplained decision not to airlift these humanitarian supplies.

Though *umoja* emphasizes commonality and unity, it reveres leaders and spokespeople, but only that form of leadership which is based upon wisdom and the ability to provide insight as opposed to that which is based upon power: it is leadership whose power is *for* others rather than *over* others. The ability to articulate common concerns and to work to put them into practice is deeply respected, and those who possess it are typically referred to by titles which signal this respect for wisdom—particularly "Professor" and "Doctor," both of which are accented in Black discourse to promote quite different social relations from the hierarchical ones they do when spoken in white accents (which is why I have used them in this section of the book but not in others).

The spokespeople on the *Gary Byrd Show* attempt to contain a wide diversity of opinion within an overall unity of purpose, to "disagree without being disagreeable." Not surprisingly, most of these disagreements focus on issues that arise on the boundaries between white and Black societies, where the power relations are embodied in material points of control and contestation. Whether Blacks should participate in a white police force is a recurrent issue on the *Gary Byrd Show*: the relationship between Blacks and the white military is another. An equally significant issue was locating Kwanzaa, a Black festival, within the Museum of Natural History, a white institution. On the one side were voices arguing that the Museum contained artifacts from African societies and histories, albeit in a white institution, and that African Americans needed to reclaim them: there could be Black uses of a white institution, and by them Blacks could Africanize it. Equally without these Black uses, the institution would remain irredeemably white and would serve white interests only. "The Museum of Natural History is cold, we need to take it back: when we are there we warm it up with our truth, our culture."

Against this was the opinion that "the Museum of Natural History is a robber of African peoples' cultures, artifacts and history. For us now to take Kwanzaa to the Museum of Natural History is an abomination: we should find an African arena, the Museum of Natural History is not African and never can be." The mounting passion in the speaker's voice as he reiterated the words "Museum of Natural History" cannot be reproduced in print but it is important to hear imaginatively. There was also an economic dimension to the discussion, which debated whether locating the festival in the Museum was once again putting Black money into white pockets or whether it was getting some Black return for the tax dollars they contribute to the white economy.

This section of the book has tried to encourage white people to listen to what some Black voices are saying. Among African Americans there are obviously many different social positions and many different opinions on the best way to cope with race relations in our current social conditions. These run the gamut from strategies of assimilation at one extreme to revolution on the other. I have not felt it appropriate for a white to listen to these debates within African American cultures, but have focussed rather upon a selected set of knowledges and strategies formed around the points of contact between Black and white.

Centuries of white supremacy have convinced many African Americans that some form of separatism is their only hope of survival. Such a separation, of course, can never be absolute, for the African American nation that may develop will be one in constant geographical, political, economic and cultural contact with those of European, Asian, Native and other Americans. But these points of contact will surround a large area of *kujichagulia* where, for the first time since slavery, African Americans will have greater power than European Americans over their own social conditions. The self-determined separatism that leads in this direction is simultaneously defensive, productive and reclamatory. African Americans have first to defend their locale against white imperializing power. This localizing power is mobilized on all fronts, defending Black bodies against white assaults, defending Black consciousness and Black history against semiotic slavery, defending the Black family against white sabotage. This defensiveness is not just reactive, it is also proactive. The localizing powers which it mobilizes are not defined by, nor contained within, the power system that they contest—there is a Black core to these powers which lies beyond the reach of white imperialization, and which, however con-strained and oppressed, has proven over history to be undefeatable. The productive, creative process is the restoration of this Black core within the boundaries secured by the defensive power.

The principles of *umoja*, *ujamaa* and *kujichagulia* may appear to have features in common with a *communitas* (horizontality, communality, and so forth), but any similarity should not blind us to a major difference which makes this community of *umoja* potentially stronger than any of the examples of *communitas* described earlier in this book. A *communitas* has to develop its new social relations from the resources of the social order which has been dominated by interests that it opposes. The resources upon which it draws are only partially its own, and even these may have been made into its own by "turning" what the dominant has provided. Such "turned" cultural resources always bear the traces of their origin. The community built around *umoja*, however, can draw upon a powerful African history which long preceded white supremacy. Consequently *umoja* does not bear the traces of white supremacy, it is a concept with no equivalent in white consciousness. Superficially similar notions such as solidarity or collectivity are often limited to, or too centrally focussed upon, the conditions of production and thus of class; they also contain echoes of the imperialization they contest—the aim of solidarity is to gain power not just over one's own social conditions but finally over the class that currently dominates. In listening to Black people talk about *umoja* I hear no hint of that form of imperialization. *Umoja* is a localizing power, even though its locale may be global; it is a power content to work within its own terrain, to defend that terrain fiercely and to expel hostile invaders from it. But it shows no desire to turn the tables and imperialize whites (or others): it is a peaceful power that does not wage war to exert its control. It is also a tolerant power which will give other localizing powers the space in which to exist around its borders, and it expects them to return the favor. But if imperializing forces do not respect its right to establish and defend its boundaries, do not allow *kujichagulia* within them, then the localizing power of its separatism may well become antagonistic and aggressive, at least around specific issues and possibly more generally. History may have shown that whites tend to win physical conflict, for we are the most efficient war-makers the world has ever known, but in war, even the victors suffer, and aggression from below is a tactic that may, under certain conditions, seem the best available. When the oppressed suffer so much that yet another defeat appears trivial, they may feel that the gains of an uprising are worth suffering its (almost) inevitable suppression.

The implications of this separatism are profound and, under the right conditions, need not be negative. They require us to think of a social order of largely self-determined locales or territories whose interrelations are formed not around a top-down consensus organized around the interests of a dominant power-bloc but by a continual process of negotiating consent (or dissent) at their points of intersection. A Black locale, however extensive and however complete its internal *kujichagulia*, must have many points of contact with neighboring locales. (This model may seem utopian in that it rests upon the possibility of a white locale built from a similar localizing, defensive power rather than an imperializing, aggressive one: while history provides no evidence of its possibility, our current and coming social conditions offer overwhelming evidence of its necessity.)

One such point of contact was the interface between Kwanzaa and the Museum of Natural History. The question debated on the *Gary Byrd Show* concerned the possibility or not of Africanizing the institution to the extent that it could become a point of contact between Black and white histories, Black and white consciousness. Could it be turned into a site where consent might be negotiated, or was it inescapably one where imperialization was continued and needed to be resisted? The school system and its curriculum is another such site. The attempt to diversify the historically white curriculum and to insert Black culture (amongst others) into it necessarily involves dislodging white culture from its position of dominance, but it does not involve removing it from the curriculum altogether. One study showed that 89 per cent of African Americans and 88 per cent of Hispanics in New York wanted to learn about "the common heritage and the values we share as Americans."[23] As what is shared in America is its white-dominated history and social order, these values are white. The mono-cultural curriculum has, historically, worked as an agent of imperialization, but when diversification is achieved it may well be rearticulated with other cultures and thus serve to produce multiple points of consent between communities rather than a monoglossic superiority over them.

Consent, whether in the streets, the schools or the law courts, requires give and take, and as the power-bloc currently occupies most of the territory it must give more than it takes. Willingly yielding control does not come easily to it, and many African Americans feel that the points where consent should be negotiated are currently points where imperializing power is most instrumentally exerted. Under these conditions, there are clear advantages in minimizing the points of contact and becoming as separate as possible. The degree of separatism and the likelihood of antagonistic social relations are determined primarily by the reach of imperializing power. If this power withdraws somewhat and allows the colonized a larger and more secure territory in the political, economic and cultural domains in which to develop *kujichagulia*, the points of contact between Black and white societies may become more rather than fewer and consensual rather than antagonistic. *But*, and this is the problem, not only is there no sign of the white power-bloc withdrawing its forces, there is not even a sign that it is aware of arguments that it should. If US race relations become more antagonistic in the future, the responsibility will rest upon the shoulders of the power-bloc.

It is difficult to be optimistic about a peaceful outcome. Signs of a way forward towards a diverse social order built around multiple points of consent exist within certain formations of African Americans (and elsewhere in our society), but they are far less visible in the formations of the power-bloc. Far from minimizing the power inequalities between white and non-white Americans, the power-bloc appears to be maximizing them, and thus, instead of moving towards a social order which facilitates the negotiation of points of consent, it is developing one in which the chance of such negotiations succeeding is so minimal that even engaging in them may seem pointless. Under these conditions, some Black opinion may well consider that only a severe jolt will motivate the power-bloc to enter negotiations and, when in them, to conduct itself with a negotiating rather than an imperializing attitude. The Black voices recirculated by this chapter are not ones advocating violence or aggression, and they will spread more widely within the Black community if they are listened to before rather than after a social uprising.

The problem is that imperializing power is not good at listening. Its instrumental effectiveness is a function of its control over the vertical flow of knowledge. The power of the panopticon rests upon its ability to see and document all that it is necessary to know to individuate and control those whom it monitors. Knowledge about the controlled that it does not deem necessary for its own purposes is excluded from the flows of knowledge upon which its power depends. Knowledge that originates among and serves the interests of the monitored is repressed by silencing it, by pathologizing it, by trivializing it—the control strategies are numerous and flexible—but the outcome of them all is that power has developed a finely tuned capacity for looking, but is retarded in its ability to listen. It wears earplugs with its eyeglasses. The voices of the colonized, the monitored, and the controlled thus fall on deaf ears, for deafness enables the power-bloc alliances to focus undistractedly upon their objectives. In particular, these alliances are self-interestedly deaf to voices telling them how they appear from below. Repressing the knowledge by which the oppressed know the operation of power is crucial to the operation of that power: power must be known by its own knowledge only. The power-bloc's repression of a knowledge which it neither requires nor desires does not work merely to make life more comfortable for those living within its alliances, it is a necessary condition for the efficiency of its power. The airwaves, the Smithsonian, the workplace, the curriculum and the streets are sites for the control and contestation of knowledge. On the one hand, the power-bloc is never totally victorious in these contests: because repressed knowledges are so securely grounded in material social conditions and in the historical experiences of those living within them they can never be eliminated. On the other hand, however, the partial defeats or setbacks of the current power-bloc provoke it to regroup its forces, and not, as would be far more progressive, to reconsider its motivation and mode of operation. It still wishes to maintain a social order built upon an imposed consensus that is organized around its own interests rather than develop one around points of consent negotiated among diverse interests.

The negotiation of consent requires both a readiness to withdraw and the ability to listen to repressed ways of knowing; the imposition of a consensus requires neither. In this section I have not attempted to give a comprehensive nor even adequate account of the ways in which African Americans know white power. Instead, I have tried to give enough examples of them to provoke whites and our power-interests into realizing the value and necessity of listening to what these voices have to say about us. A white imagination which extends beyond the limits of mono-culturalism, and which can produce for whites some sense of a non-white experience, is an urgent social necessity.

NOTES

1. bell hooks, "Representing Whiteness," in Lawrence Grossberg, Cary Nelson, and Paula Treichler (eds) *Cultural Studies* (New York: Routledge, 1991), p. 341. Also in bell hooks, *Black Looks, Race and Representation* (Boston: South End Press, 1992), pp. 165–78.
2. hooks, "Representing Whiteness," p. 345.
3. Paul Gilroy, in *There Ain't No Black in the Union Jack* (London: Pluto 1987) gives a good account in the British context of a similar Black defensiveness.
4. Gloria Abernathy-Lear, "African Americans' Relationship with Day Time Serials," Dissertation, University of Wisconsin-Madison, 1992.
5. Jawanza Kunjufu, *Lessons from History. A Celebration in Blackness*, Jr.-Sr. High Edition (Chicago: African American Images, 1987).
6. See, for instance, Jawanza Kunjufu, *Lessons from History, a Celebration of Blackness*, Jr-Sr High Edition (Chicago: African American Images, 1988).
7. *New York Amsterdam News*, 10 August 1991.
8. Ralph Wiley, *Why Black People Tend to Shout* (New York: Penguin, 1992).
9. Wiley, *Why Black People*, p. 44.
10. George Lipsitz, *Time Passages* (Minneapolis: University of Minnesota Press, 1990), p. 213.
11. Michel Foucault, *Language, Counter-Memory, Practice* (Ithaca: Cornell University Press, 1980).
12. Caller to the *Gary Byrd Show*, 23 December 1991.
13. Claude Lévi-Strauss, *Myth and Meaning* (New York: Schocken, 1979).
14. *New York Amsterdam News*, 31 August 1991, p. 28.
15. Cited in Haki R. Madhubuti, *Kwanzaa: A Progressive and Uplifting African American Holiday* (Chicago, IL: Third World Press, 1972), p. 4.
16. Ibid., p. 6.
17. Ibid.
18. Charles Whittaker, "How to Survive the New Racism," *Ebony*, October 1991, pp. 106–10.
19. *The Autobiography of Malcolm X* as told to Alex Haley (New York: Ballantine Books, 1973), p. 263.
20. Mike Davis, "Burning all Illusions in LA," in IAJ (ed.), *Inside the LA Riots: What Really Happened and Why It Will Happen Again* (New York: Institute for Alternative Journalism, 1992), p. 99.
21. Molefi Kete Asante, *Afrocentricity* (Trenton, NJ: Africa World Press), 2nd edn, 1988, p. 27.
22. *BLR*, November 1991 (day not recorded).
23. The *New York Times*, 12 December 1991.

CODA

THE SLAVE SHIP

Locale builders inevitably face the problems of where to draw their boundaries (and thus of which alliances to include or exclude) and of how to choose the best tools and materials with which to build inside them. To conclude this book I wish to accept an invitation by Paul Gilroy to consider "the slave ship" as a semiotic tool, and the Atlantic African as the key alliance around which to build Black consciousness.[1]

There are finely tuned differences between African American voices arguing for the particularity of the African American experience and thus the tactical value of stressing American alliances over African ones, and those who would prefer to reverse the emphasis. In their quite different accents, Cornell West and *Black Liberation Radio* give voice to the American experience of Africanness whereas, equally differently, Molefi Asante, Cress Welsing and *WLIB* put Africanness ahead of its American inflexions. Paul Gilroy contributes to the discussion by arguing for the tactical value of an Atlantic Africanness whose alliances are formed along all three passages of the triangle, not just the middle one. For him the history of the slave trade has produced a core experience that is common to US and Caribbean Africans, European Africans and African Africans. He argues that Black interests can best be promoted through alliances organized around the Black Atlantic diaspora rather than by stressing national differences within it. (This argument may be inflected by his Britishness, for most British Blacks re-enacted the third passage in the last two or three generations.) Indeed, he considers either national or ethnic absolutism to be anti-progressive, and argues that the historicity of the Atlantic diaspora can guard against the risks of absolutism or essentialism.

A diaspora involves movement, and what moved Africans around the

Atlantic was the slave ship. Diasporic relations are different from those of a settled community, for they are ones built around and against dispersal. In them, the machine of dispersal, the slave ship, may also paradoxically serve to build the community of the dispersed: One instance, at the level of relationships rather than relations, is provided by Bryan Edwards, one of the first historians of the slave trade. He writes in 1793:

> We find that negroes in general are strongly attached to their countrymen, but above all to such of their countrymen as came in the same ship with them from Africa. This is a striking circumstance: the term *shipmate* is understood among them as signifying a relationship of the most enduring nature.[2]

Diasporic Africans are all, in one sense, shipmates, and Gilroy goes on to point to the neglected role of ships and the sea in Black history and concludes with the provocative idea of Peter Linebaugh that "the ship remained perhaps the most important conduit of Pan-African communication before the appearance of the long playing record." [3] The slave ship, having broken one set of social relations, may be reclaimed and reused to form others.

I offer, then, some representations of "the slave ship" as a technology of power, both physical and discursive. The slave ship was a machine that transported and transformed; in transporting the bodies of Africans across the Atlantic, it transformed them into slaves. As slaves they were transformed into commodities (sugar, tobacco, cotton) which the ship again transported across the Atlantic to be transformed into profit and capital. In the ship's hold, the slave and the commodity were identical, the value of each a product of the other.

Gilroy points to one famous representation of the slave ship that serves well to locate the concept as a site of the struggle for meaning: it is Turner's 1840 painting *Slavers Throwing Overboard the Dead and Dying: Typhon Coming on* (also known, more succinctly, as *The Slave Ship*) (see Plate 11).[4] He writes:

> Turner's extraordinary painting of the slave ship throwing overboard the dead and the dying is a useful image not only for its self-conscious moral power and the striking way that it aims directly for the sublime in its invocation of racial terror, commerce, and England's ethico-political degeneration. It bears repetition that ships were the living means by which the points within that Atlantic world were joined. Accordingly they need to be thought of as complex cultural and political units rather than abstract embodiments of the triangular trade. Of course they are machines, but the writings and experiences of black intellectuals suggests that they are something more—a means to conduct political dissent and, possibly, a distinct mode of cultural production.[5]

John Ruskin, the art critic, owned the painting for twenty-eight years before its subject matter became too painful for him to live with. He tried and failed to sell it at auction at Christies in 1869, but in 1872 found an American buyer. In his *Modern Painters*[6] Ruskin claims the painting as Turner's greatest but confines his account of it to Ruskin's sublime rendition of the sea and the sky. The subject matter is relegated to a terse footnote, "She is a slaver, throwing her slaves overboard. The near sea is encumbered with corpses."

The painting, and much of Ruskin's commentary were reproduced by Du Bois in *The Crisis* in 1918:

> I think the noblest sea that Turner has ever painted, and, if so, the noblest ever painted by man, is that of "The Slave Ship," ... Purple and blue, the lurid shadows of the hollow breakers are cast upon the mist of night, which gathers cold and low, advancing like the shadow of death upon the guilty ship as it labours amidst the lightning of the sea, its thin masts written upon the sky in lines of blood, girded with condemnation in that fearful hue which signs the sky with horror, and mixes its flaming flood with the sunlight, and, cast far along the desolate heave of the sepulchral waves, incarnadines the multitudinous sea.[7]

Ruskin's use of the thesaurus is as overblown as Turner's use of the palette (at least, for today's taste) and readers of *The Crisis* may well have been grateful that Du Bois spared them more. Besides cutting out more adjectivally saturated descriptions of the sea and the sky Du Bois also omitted both the footnote and the final paragraph in which the critic gives the painting his highest possible evaluation:

> I believe, if I were reduced to rest Turner's immortality upon any single work, I should choose this. Its daring conception, ideal in the highest sense of the word, is based on the purest truth, and wrought out with the concentrated knowledge of a life; its colour is absolutely perfect, not one false or morbid hue in any part or line, and so modulated that every square inch of canvas is a perfect composition; its drawing as accurate as fearless; the ship buoyant, bending, and full of motion; its tones as true as they are wonderful; and the whole picture dedicated to the most sublime of subjects and impressions (completing thus the perfect system of all truth, which we have shown to be formed by Turner's works)—the power, majesty, and deathfulness of the open, deep, illimitable sea.[8]

Ruskin's repression of any mention of the slaves is remarkable and Gilroy, charitably, suggests that this may be a sign of his inability to face directly the source of the pain that the painting gave him. Less charitably, we might see it as a use of the discourse of aesthetics to silence or marginalize politically oppositional voices in much the same way as Jewett's aesthetic erased the American Indians from the landscape surveyed so proprietorially by the Grayson family. Another characteristic of the power-bloc in Ruskin's use of the discourse of aesthetics is its claim to a truth which is final because it is based upon the twin poles of a knowledge of life and the artistic imagination. But the struggle to repress other truths shows itself in the contradiction between the title of the painting and Ruskin's assertion that its subject was "The power, majesty and deathfulness of the open, deep, illimitable sea." The straining of the word "deathfulness" to limit death's origin to the sea and not the slavers invites deconstruction. Aesthetics is a discourse of white power-bloc alliances, and Du Bois was presumably quite confident of his Black readers' ability to deconstruct it, and recover the Black meanings that Ruskin repressed. Henry Gates would share that confidence: he writes "we have been deconstructing white peoples' languages and discourse since that dreadful day in 1619 when we were marched off the boat in Virginia. Derrida did not invent deconstruction, *we* did!"[9]

Ruskin has given the deconstructionist plenty to work on—his choice of the words "guilty," "blood," "sepulchral," "incarnadine" can indicate, however obliquely, where he and Turner stood in the abolitionist debate of the day. More direct was the timing of the picture's exhibition at the Royal Academy: it preceded by less than a month the opening of the Anti-Slavery League's World Conference in London. The conference was opened by Prince Albert who, in his first public address, lamented the League's failure, so far, "to abolish that atrocious traffic in human beings." Butler and Joll,[10] in their definitive edition of Turner's paintings, suggest that he may have been currying royal favor in the hope of patronage, but, whatever his motives, Turner clearly meant the picture to contribute to the Abolitionist side of the debate. For the exhibition he affixed to the painting some manuscript lines from his poem, *The Fallacies of Hope*:

> Aloft all hands, strike the topmast and belay;
> Yon angry setting sun, and fierce-edged clouds
> Declare the Typhon's coming.
> Before it sweep your decks, throw overboard
> The dead and dying—never heed their chains.
> Hope, hope—fallacious hope!
> Where is thy market now?

If Ruskin and Turner were on one side of the abolitionist debate, the journalist critics of the day were on the other. The painting was widely ridiculed, and *Blackwoods* reviewer went only a little further than most:

Whether the MS. was made for the picture, or the picture for the MS., they are very much alike, out of all rule and measure. The lines are, however, absolutely necessary to explain the piece—without them, past the imagination of man to find out. There is evidently a vessel riding in a chaos of red and yellow stuff, supposed to be meant for water, but that it quits the horizontal line and runs uphill. Of all the birds in the air, and all the fishes in the sea, what have we in the foreground? It is a black leg thrown overboard, and round it run fish great and small. There is a whale-like fish booming large in obscurity, which Mr Turner may mean to represent "Typhon's coming." Is it allegory? Between the vessel and the fish there is an odd object that long puzzled us. We may be wrong; but we have conjectured it to be a Catholic bishop in canonicals gallantly gone overboard, to give benediction to the crew, or the fish, or Typhon. Is it "Bishop Blaze," amid a dreadful conflict between sulphur and carmine? The fish claiming their leg-acy is very funny. What could have given rise to the dream of the colour pots?[11]

Even *The Times* mocked "the leg of a negro, which is about to afford a nibble to a John Dory, a pair of soles, and a shoal of whitebait,"[12] and *The Athenaeum*, that forum of high culture and classicism, described the painting, as "a passionate extravaganza of marigold sky, and pomegranate-coloured sea, and fish dressed as gay as garden flowers in pink and green, with one shapeless dusky brown leg thrown up from this particoloured chaos to keep the promise of the title."[13] Nearly forty years later, the US critic Thomas Woolver wrote "I can't congratulate your wife's cousin's purchase of The Slave Ship, for I think it one of Turner's failures, tho' containing workmanship of the highest order."[14]

The predatory intentions of Turner's fish are unmistakable, but he was no biological illustrator and the fish themselves do not much resemble sharks. Granted this, however, it is still difficult to see the critics' mockery of the Black dismembered, fettered leg surrounded by scavengers as anything but a refusal to align themselves or their readers with the painting's attack on the slave trade. In particular, Blackwood's pun on the "leg-acy" can only be smiled at after a herculean labor of repressing both the humanity of the leg and the inhumanity of the slave ship. But presumably many readers succeeded in doing so.

Butler and Joll suggest that Turner may well have read the story of the slave ship *Zong*. When disease ran through its cargo the captain ordered the slaves to be thrown overboard, for he could claim insurance on those drowned at sea but not on those who died from disease. The sharks in the sea, the sharks on board the vessel, and the sharks in the slave trade and the insurance business are either the subject of Turner's painting or are excluded from it altogether. The meanings are worth fighting over—for both sides.

The shark endlessly circles the figure of the slave ship. Sharks would follow the ships for the whole of their three or four month voyage, feeding on the bodies tossed overboard. But the feeding was not confined to that of sharks on slaves, as an anonymous crewman wrote to his sister in 1723:

> We caught a great many fish in the passage especially sharks. Our way to entice them was by towing overboard a dead negro which they would follow till they had eaten him up. They are good victuals if well dressed. The negroes fed very heartily upon them, which made us salt up several of them to save the ship's provision.[15]

The feeding circle of body upon body is closed and direct. The slave routes were shark routes, and sharks of every persuasion grew fat on them.

The slave overboard (to lighten the ship, to claim insurance, to avoid arrest, to catch a shark, or, conversely to escape) represents the unfigurable, the conditions inside the hull. Turner's metaphoric displacement of these conditions into the elements outside may be deconstructed as an equivalent admission of their unfigurability, at least aesthetically.

Technical illustrators, however, had no such problems. A number of diagrams of how slaves were fitted into the ships were produced in the eighteenth and nineteenth centuries. These engineering drawings made the slave ship look a model of efficiency and order with each individuated body neatly stored in its allotted space. The neat arrangement of these dehumanized, degendered figures made the situation appear reassuringly under control (see Plate 12). Another image, with a similar calmness, was provided by John Newton, a slave-ship captain: "The slaves lie in two rows, one above the other, on each side of the ship, close to each other, like books on a shelf."[16]

This image and the engineering diagrams put the slave ship into a white discourse whose calm sense of order and control contrasts vividly with the elemental chaos of Turner's painting. The diagrams disguise atrocity as geometry. They are a scientific discourse making its normal claim to truth and mobilizing that truth in the interests of the power-bloc. These slave-ship diagrams look similar to Bentham's designs for the Panopticon: both show the efficient application of order and power upon the disposition of bodies. But the materiality of the overcrowded and inhumane conditions of the slave ship give another truth that these discourses of order can never repress entirely, and that makes them readily vulnerable to deconstructive readings that unmask their power upon both the Black body and the white imagination.

Changing the viewpoint from that of panoptic exteriority to that of the insider changes the way the body of the slave is known. Inside the hold there is no order and neat patterning, but only a body of disorder, a body so out of control that the only thing it could not do was change its position. Its blood, its urine, its excrement, its vomit escaped all attempts to control them. Olaudah Equiano was a slave who published his autobiography in 1789, and although his discourse is clearly that of the white other which he has learned, traces of the Black experience remain within it.

> I was soon put down under the decks, and there I received such a salutation in my nostrils as I had never experienced in my life: so that with the loathsomeness of the stench, and crying together, I became so sick and low that I was not able to eat. ... At last, when the ship ... had got in all her cargo, they made ready with many fearful noises, and we were all put under deck, so that we could not see how they managed the vessel. ... The stench of the hold while we were on the coast was so intolerably loathsome that it was dangerous to remain there for any time ... but now that the whole ship's cargo were confined together, it became absolutely pestilential. The closeness of the place, and the heat of the climate, added to the number in the ship, which was so crowded that each had scarcely room to turn himself, almost suffocated us. This produced copious perspirations, so that the air soon became unfit for respiration ... and brought on a sickness among the slaves, of which many died. ... This wretched situation was again aggravated by the galling of the chains, now become insupportable; and the filth of the necessary tubs, into which the children often fell. ... The shrieks of the women, and the groans of the dying, rendered the whole a scene of horror almost inconceivable.[17]

Alexander Falconbridge, a white surgeon, gives a similar view from the inside.

> The deck, that is the floor of their rooms, was so covered with the blood and mucous which had proceeded from them in consequence of the flux, that it resembled a slaughter-house. It is not in the power of the human imagination to picture to itself a situation more dreadful or disgusting. Numbers of the slaves, having fainted, they were carried up on deck, where several of them died and the rest were, with great difficulty, restored. It had nearly proved fatal to me also.[18]

After citing this passage in his history of the slave trade, James Pope Hennessey comments straightfacedly, "and Falconbridge was serving on the better class of English slaver."[19]

The historian on *Black Liberation Radio* adds a more general account of the slave ship to his particular narrative of Captain Holman (see pages 286–7):

HISTORIAN What I also do is deal with the voyage that the brothers had to make over here, in the holocaust, because they were packed on the ship just like you would pack animals today, and when you see these trucks come by on the freeway with the hogs and pigs and even cows and the animals are packed so tight their heads are sticking through the railings, that's the way they were packed on board these ships...

KANTAKO   Sometimes with the animals...

HISTORIAN   ...had to sit in one another's laps, you know when one brother would throw up or urinate or defecate he would do it in a person's lap in front of you or the brother's lap behind you, or the sister's lap, in front or behind...[see Plate 12]

KANTAKO   You can see then the beginning of the sowing of the seeds of self-hate, just in the way we were brung over here.

HISTORIAN   That's right, it was such a demoralizing tragedy, human tragedy, that people's spirit was really broken, the weaker of us would give up just through the hardships of the middle passage, in fact thousands of Africans jumped overboard, committed suicide, threw their children overboard, to escape the horrors aboard ship. ...The average slave ship would be destroyed after four journeys from the filth and disease and the rats and so forth, and this is the condition that our people travelled in...

KANTAKO   Four trips is all a ship could last?

HISTORIAN   All ... a ship would be destroyed by a good slave trader after four journeys because a ship would be unsafe for the crew. Average crew, only half the crew would make it back on an average journey from America to Africa and back to get slaves...

KANTAKO   Hey, whoa, wait, wait, wait, whoa now...

HISTORIAN   Yes sir.

KANTAKO   Wait now, only half the white boys who would go over to get slaves would ever make it back?

HISTORIAN   Would ever make it back. Generally the average ship went through two captains or more on one voyage.

KANTAKO   Mmm.

HISTORIAN   It was a rough experience.

KANTAKO   So it was never really like they depicted it, it was something they could easily do ... it ...

HISTORIAN   Never.

KANTAKO   I mean, it was something, you know, *low down* to do it, you know what I mean, look at the losses you're putting upon your side.

HISTORIAN   Yes sir.

According to Oliver Ransford the mortality rate was often higher for the crew than the cargo because a crewman was worth less than a slave, and so the captains cared less about keeping them alive. The expendability of the crew was compounded by the fact that fewer of them were needed for the third leg of the triangle: commodities required less overseeing than slaves. The alliances of power-bloc interests were not formed around racial axes alone, but by articulations of class or economic ones with race.[20]

  Black Liberation Radio's narrative of the middle passage tells also of the additional axis of white power upon the body of the African woman:

> All of the women generally were raped, we're talking about all of the women, all of the young girls. The young girls and boys were kept naked, everyone was naked, and they were also branded when they boarded the ship, then they were stripped naked, and that's the way they were packed. Now generally the children, the children would be kept above deck, they would cover them with canvas at night, but the grown ups would be down in the lower decks and they would load the women last so that they would be accessible to the men without going through the holds and horrors of the slave ship.

For African men the slave ship may have been hell on water; for the women it was both Bethel and brothel. This double disempowerment of the Black woman, through the intersection of race with gender, may have begun on the slave ship, but it continued through the whole experience of slavery and remains inerasable in the collective memory. Ironically, this double disempowerment has been one of the forces behind "the strong Black woman" who has played such an important role within the family against the whole range of disabling forces that surround it.

The slave ship is such a productive figure not only because of its central role in the African Atlantic diaspora, but also because it has always been a site of contestation, both physical and discursive. Although one of the most powerful agents of capitalism and of white supremacy, it is also the ugliest, and not even the most powerful of discourse can repress that ugliness. The ship, in general, has been crucial to imperialization—in exploration, conquest and trade—and the glorious navies of the West resonate powerfully in the white imagination, but the slave ship is the ugliest vessel in the merchant navy (other ships would have to keep up to two miles away from it to avoid its stench) and as such its resonance in the white imagination is ready made for deconstruction. If the word "Nigger" can be reclaimed and turned against those who used it, if "black" can be similarly turned into "Black," then the slave ship too can be turned to serve the interests of those whom once were its victims.

For those victims who endured it physically, the slave ship was a place defined by the bodies in it, probably the most degrading ever produced by a top-down, greedy power. But even in this extremity, localizing powers could be mobilized to contest imperializing power. Occasionally there were collective mutinies when the body of slaves rose up, but more typically the individuated body was the site of this power struggle. When the weak are reduced to nothing but their bodies and have apparently lost control even of them, then suicide (by jumping overboard, by refusing to eat, or by simply giving up the attempt to stay alive) becomes an obvious way of controlling one's own body, and thousands of Africans took it, and in taking it stopped being slaves and became Africans once again. Alternatively, when one's body appears to be totally in the power of another, one can escape that power only by escaping the body, and thousands of Africans took that route too ("madness" or "hysteria" as whites called it) by leaving their physical reality to enter a fantasy one that, however "unreal," was at least theirs.

If localizing powers can hold off imperializing ones and gain tiny spaces against them even in the hold of a slave ship, they can do it anywhere. They have demonstrated their ultimate undefeatability. If weak power is properly called "weak," then its weakness is such only in its immediate relations to strong power in immediate conditions. Over the long haul, weak powers prove stronger than strong ones, their strength lies in their endurance.

NOTES

1. Paul Gilroy, "Ethnic Absolutism," in Grossberg et al. (eds), *Cultural Studies*, pp. 187–98.
2. Bryan Edwards, *The History, Civil and Commercial, of the British Colonies in the West Indies* (London, 1793).
3. Gilroy, "Ethnic Absolutism," p. 191.
4. The Museum of Fine Arts, Boston.
5. Gilroy, "Ethnic Absolutism," p. 193.
6. John Ruskin, *Modern Painters*, Volume 1, Sec. 5, Ch. III, sec. 39.
7. *The Crisis*, vol. 15, 1918, p. 239. *The Crisis* was the journal of the National Association for Advancement of Colored People.
8. John Ruskin, *Modern Painters*, Volume 1, sec. 5, Ch. III, sec. 39.
9. Henry Gates, Jr., "Authority, (White) Power and the (Black) Critic: It's All Greek to Me," *Cultural Critique*, vol. 7, 1987, p. 38.
10. Martin Butler and Evelyn Joll, *The Paintings of J.M.W. Turner* (12 vols) (New Haven and London: Yale University Press, 1984).
11. *Blackwoods Edinburgh Magazine*, September 1840, p. 380.
12. *The Times*, 6 May 1840.
13. *The Athenaeum*, 16 May 1840.
14. Letter to Henry Adams, 4 March 1877, cited in Butler and Joll, p. 237.
15. Quoted in Peter Hogg, *Slavery: The Afro-American Experience* (London: The British Library, 1979), p. 22.
16. In Hogg, *Slavery*, p. 23.
17. Olaudah Equiano, *The Interesting Narrative of the Life of Olaudah Equiano, or Gustavus Vassa, The African* (London, 1789).
18. Alexander Falconbridge, *An Account of the Slave Trade on the Coast of Africa* (London: 1788).
19. James Pope Hennessey, *Sins of the Fathers*, p. 102.
20. Oliver Ransford, *The Slave Trade* (London: John Murray, 1971).

INDEX

ABC News 30
Abernathy-Lear, Gloria 176, 180, 277, 283, 302
aboriginals 128
accent 31–2, 62, 110, 174, 177, 185, 288
    see also multiaccentuality; uniaccentuality
Adams, Robert 167, 170, 175
Aesop 285
aesthetics 59, 77, 87, 153–4, 168–9, 171–3, 188, 305
AFDC 27, 239
affect 91, 255–6, 288
African Americans 12, 27, 37, 38, 39, 42, 43, 45, 53, 61, 63, 78, 128, 176–7, 212, 227–312
Afro-Saxons 266, 274, 289
AIDS 238, 247–8
agency 21–3, 32, 42, 57, 62, 78, 120, 252
    of the people 21–3, 32, 41–3, 66, 82
    of the power-bloc 21–3, 25, 79
agents 64, 78, 273
    socially interested 21–3, 25, 79
Ali, Mohammed 105, 197
allegiance 5, 106
    social 11
    power-bloc 23
alliance 45, 99, 104, 107, 168, 171, 251–2, 260, 266–7, 274, 283

economic 51, 96, 99
interracial 275
popular 99, 110, 173–4
of the power-bloc 10, 15, 30, 96, 99, 110, 168–71, 173–5, 258, 272–4, 310
of social interests 10
Althusser, Louis 38, 64
Anderson, Benedict 172
Anderson, Elizabeth 143
Andrews, Vernon 61–3, 79, 258–9, 277
anti-history 288–9
anti-Semitism 173–5
apartheid 143, 276
Archer, Marjorie 34
Asian Americans 39, 43, 53, 177, 257
"as if" 117, 119, 126–7, 129, 131, 138–9, 184–5, 191, 194, 281
Asante, Molefi 294, 302–3
astrology 188, 191–5
Atlantic Africans 303

Baker, Holly 223–4
Bakhtin, Mikhail 33, 42, 53, 59, 69, 76–8, 80, 98, 118, 123, 188, 231
Barry, Marion 240
Baudrillard, Jean 35
Bauman, Zygmunt 34
Beatles 101–3
belief 108, 116–17, 184, 193, 199

Cold War 5, 7, 47, 177
Cole, Johnetta 265–6
colonization 38, 51, 153, 161, 162, 203, 241, 296–301
Columbus, Christopher 296
commodity 21, 35, 70, 103, 149, 159, 207–11, 218–20, 272, 304
communitas 68–9, 79, 80, 85, 88, 91, 96, 110, 117–18, 186, 210, 221, 233, 292–4, 298
community 19, 40, 48, 85
computers 67, 71, 73–5, 83
consciousness 7, 9, 12, 13, 20, 21, 23, 24, 30, 31, 35, 36, 39, 42, 43, 58, 66, 141, 243
    Black 62, 243, 284–5, 298
consensus 21, 39, 40, 41, 43–5, 46–7, 51, 276, 299, 301
consent 41–2, 44–5, 50, 170, 223, 257, 259, 272, 299, 301
    points of 44, 46, 47, 270, 276, 300
conspiracy 234, 238–9
contestation 21, 23, 26, 39, 41, 44, 174, 301
control 13, 17, 18, 19, 20, 21, 22, 24, 25, 30, 31, 36, 38, 58, 60, 62, 67, 71, 88–9, 94–5, 156, 216, 218, 223, 231, 239, 254, 290
Coombe, Rosemary 249
Cooper, James 168–9, 172, 179
Corbin, Alain 224
counter-center 279–84
counterculture 289–301
counter-history 210, 284–9, 290
counter-knowledge 284–9, 289–90
counter-memory 286, 288–90
counter-reality 230, 238–9
creativity 42, 70, 220–21
Crenshaw, Kimberle 277
Cress Theory 242–3, 275, 283–4
Crigler, Ann 33
Crisis, The 305, 312
culture 13, 14, 20, 25, 36, 40, 51, 58, 61, 62, 147–8, 156, 162, 168, 172, 175, 218, 289–90

Black/African American 104–5, 176–7, 212, 214–221, 243, 284, 297–99
    commercial 174–8
    folk 220
    popular 71, 97, 212, 220
curriculum 51, 65, 66, 171–2, 285, 290, 299, 301
    see also canon

Dahmer, Jeffrey 237
Dances with Wolves 174–5
Dannon, Sharon 71, 80
Davis, Mike 36, 38, 50–53, 234, 268, 277–8, 293, 302
Dawson, Robert 33, 140
Dean, James 95, 104
De Certeau, Michel 33, 42, 53, 69, 70, 76–8, 80, 122, 199, 212, 220, 223–4
decentering 52, 279–81, 284
    see also central, the; counter-centre
deconstruction 48, 279–80, 282–4, 286, 289, 306, 308
defensive action 13, 215–16, 223, 230, 233, 246, 267, 270, 275, 298
Democrats 6, 260, 271
Denny, Reginald 271–2
deprivation 22, 23, 25, 28, 38, 121, 124, 127, 189, 218, 220, 268
Designing Women 161–2
determination 8, 35, 62, 192, 251–2
diaspora 275, 303–4, 311
Die Hard 3–5, 8, 12, 15–16, 18, 20, 23, 29, 70, 124–9, 255
difference 77, 98, 149
    gender 40
    power 160, 276
    racial 40, 149, 173, 270–71
    social 7, 21, 28, 32, 34, 41, 42, 173, 276
discipline 13, 17, 18, 21, 25, 42, 49, 58–66, 69, 71, 74–6, 88, 96–7, 99–103, 118–19, 137, 191, 217